The Fifth New York
Cavalry in the Civil War

The Fifth New York Cavalry in the Civil War

Vincent L. Burns

McFarland & Company, Inc., Publishers
Jefferson, North Carolina

LIBRARY OF CONGRESS CATALOGUING-IN-PUBLICATION DATA

Burns, Vincent L., 1945–
　The Fifth New York Cavalry in the Civil War / Vincent L. Burns.
　　p.　cm.
　Includes bibliographical references and index.

　ISBN 978-0-7864-7690-9
　softcover : acid free paper ∞

　1. United States. Army. New York Cavalry Regiment, 5th (1861–1865) 2. New York (State)—History—Civil War, 1861–1865—Regimental histories. 3. United States—History—Civil War, 1861–1865—Regimental histories. 4. United States—History—Civil War, 1861–1865—Campaigns. I. Title.
　E523.65th .B87 2014
　973.7'447—dc23　　　　　　　　　　2013045126

BRITISH LIBRARY CATALOGUING DATA ARE AVAILABLE

© 2014 Vincent L. Burns. All rights reserved

No part of this book may be reproduced or transmitted in any form or by any means, electronic or mechanical, including photocopying or recording, or by any information storage and retrieval system, without permission in writing from the publisher.

Cover photograph: Silver Union cavalryman's identification badge worn by Lt. C.M. Pease of Company H, 5th New York Volunteer Cavalry (www.historicalimagebank.com)

Manufactured in the United States of America

McFarland & Company, Inc., Publishers
Box 611, Jefferson, North Carolina 28640
www.mcfarlandpub.com

For
Virginia Lorraine Burns,
a descendant, Fifth New York Cavalry

Table of Contents

Preface	1
1. And the War Came—1861	7
2. Spring in the Shenandoah—1862	27
3. In the Defenses of Washington—1863	45
4. Advance and Pursuit—1863	57
5. Three Days in July—1863	84
6. Retreat and Pursuit—1863	107
7. Virginia in Summer, Fall and Winter—1863–1864	128
8. Across the River—1864	168
9. Wilson's Raid—1864	193
10. Autumn in the Shenandoah—1864	219
11. Cedar Creek—1864	242
12. The Final Months—1865	252
Epilogue	263
Chapter Notes	275
Bibliography	285
Index	289

Preface

> Head Quarters, Fifth New York Cav., Purcelville [sic],
> Va., July 18, 1863
>
> My dear children
> As we are resting our weary selves and horses today, and having just been looking at your mother's miniature and yours, I thought I would write you as a source of pleasure to myself and you. Imagine in your mind yourself sitting under a tree to shield me from the rays of the sun; bivouacked about me a whole corps of cavalry, not less than ten thousand men and horses. The men are this morning all firing off their pistols and cleaning them, as the weather has been very wet, and many of their pistols are in bad condition. The men are, in addition, also resting themselves as best they can; some are washing their shirts, some caring for their poor jaded horses. We have had a great many horses killed, but more have given out by forced marches and want of food.[1]

With these words Major John Hammond, in command of the Fifth New York Volunteer Cavalry Regiment, ended the Gettysburg Campaign. In July of 1863, a point in time midway through its existence, Hammond and the men of the Fifth New York had been chasing and fighting Robert E. Lee's retreating Army of Northern Virginia for thirteen days. Immediately previous to this the regiment had spent nine days riding and fighting both in the movements prior to Gettysburg and in the battle itself.

That which follows is the history of the Fifth New York Cavalry, the men, volunteers, and their service during the Civil War. This project began as an inquiry into the Civil War career of one individual who had been interned at Andersonville Prison Camp during the last ten months of the war. Corporal George Lamb of the Fifth New York was one of many from the regiment captured during what was called Wilson's Raid on the Southside and Weldon Railroads at the start of Grant's siege of Petersburg in June 1864. The various documents were gathered from the National Archives, and the *Official Record* was thoroughly mined for all the relevant facts relating to the raid, the unit's movements and everything else that could embellish the little portrait of George Lamb and his service in the regiment. For the family whose ancestor he was, a paper was written containing all the facts accumulated. It was only after this that I thought there might be a wider story to tell, that of the regiment itself, one of hundreds of volunteer units that did the fighting and dying in that long American tragedy.

Now a century and a half removed from the events, there remains little, if any, Civil War subject matter of significance that hasn't previously been researched and written of, usually more than once. The possible exception is in the area of regimental histories that lean on the scholarship of previous historians of the conflict as well as contemporary sources left to us regarding a particular unit. What follows is the history of the Fifth New York, within context of the war, its degree of detail limited only by the vagaries of the original sources, the absence of others or by the inherent lack of depth in some.

Louis N. Boudrye became chaplain of the Fifth New York in February 1863, and except for a forced excursion to Libby Prison in Richmond in the aftermath of Gettysburg, remained with the regiment until it was disbanded at war's end. He experienced almost everything the troopers did, including some of the actual fighting. His observations, recorded in a journal, are centered generally on himself, but occasionally he paints a small picture of regimental life that gives us insight into what was happening to these men. In addition, scattered through its pages the reader occasionally comes upon an insight that might be taken to represent what these men thought at certain points in time during the final two years of the war. In the closing months of the war, with the regiment still in the field, Boudrye began gathering documentary material for a regimental history. He published his history in the fall of 1865. These two contemporary volumes, the *War Journal* and the *Historic Records of the 5th N.Y. Cavalry*, will be a principal source for color and texture in what follows. Unfortunately for us, in many cases these two sources are the only record of events in which the Fifth New York took part.

The Fifth New York was involved in a number of significant cavalry actions during the war in the Eastern theater and brushed up against glory on a few occasions. On occasion it had been lucky for not being involved in actions where other mounted units suffered significant losses. After nearly four years of mounted warfare, what emerges from the record is a somewhat fuzzy portrait of one Union volunteer cavalry regiment. Words such as typical, average, or above average, for that matter, are adjectives I hesitate to use because after doing the digging into their lives and times, I cannot think of the men of the Fifth New York in terms implied by those words. From a standing start in 1861, they approached a level of professionalism by 1863 equal to any regular army cavalry regiment that had been in existence for years. In the documentary sources coming down to us there are numerous comments by contemporaries asserting that the Fifth New York was considered one of the best cavalry formations to take the field.

Overall, the regiment was ably led throughout its four years on horseback, particularly by John Hammond in 1863 and 1864. However, as for the brigade and/or division to which it was attached, there are times where this cannot be said. But these men did what was required of them by their times, they did it as volunteers, and they deserve that something be said in their regard.

Rendered for all time, the judgment of history can be harsh. Obviously, it is better that the judgment be favorable. The good will stand, even if some historian ages in the future might be bothered by some small negative. But if the contemporary evidence is bad, God help you. Eventual historical rehabilitation, although not an impossibility, will always contain many "ifs," qualifiers, standing beside the body of fact. Between the positive and negative judgments lie the vast middle latitudes of history. The men incased within this region are, for the most part, our past's silent majority. These people and organizations were there, the men did their jobs and then faded in history's haze, leaving little, if any, record of their treading the pages of the books some of us actually read, those that speak of their era and, generally, of them. Only a precious few get mentioned. The majority are but a blur to us, as if they had moved while the plate was exposed in a period photograph. Only the record proves they were there. The Fifth New York Cavalry is one of these.

The Fifth New York Cavalry in the Civil War, according to the sources available to us in our age, was a well-managed citizen-soldier military unit, one that occasionally distinguished itself in battle. This is not a difficult conclusion to reach and not one that would be out of favor with those men. Reflecting upon their service, these men had to have been proud of their record and what they accomplished. Be that as it may, the regiment suffered hardships none of us today can imagine and while doing so helped save the Union we have inherited. They fought with extraordinary heroism, died on battlefields, in hospitals and in prisons long forgotten, but the majority knew why they were there and the importance of it all. When conflict ended they quickly returned to their homes and went about living their lives, some perhaps thinking that the world would little note nor long remember what they had done. They had, however, their memories of riding with men on a mission and the knowledge they had accomplished something that to them — as well as us — was of lasting value. Certainly they had one or more veterans' fraternal organizations in which to associate and reminisce with others who had fought. And there were reunions, but in the remaining decades of their century, the men of the Fifth New York were what they had been before the war: ordinary citizens contributing in their way to a growing, expanding United States.

Although several men from the regiment were awarded the Medal of Honor, only one of their number became prominent after the war. In the contemporary record there is no end to the complimentary adjectives used in describing John Hammond, who commanded the regiment for a full fifteen months. He was with the Fifth New York from the first day, a volunteer, an extraordinary citizen-soldier and a natural leader. A colonel when he left the regiment, he was elected to Congress from New York in 1879, serving until 1883. With the exception of the regiment's chaplain, Louis Boudrye, the remaining men of the Fifth New York are names out of regimental reports, rosters and pension rolls.

Almost every regiment in the years following the war had a history of sorts inscribed in what are now old and musty volumes, generally forgotten. This history is offered with hopes to update one of those volumes.

A Note on Sources

Writing after the Civil War, an obscure Union general, John Beatty, penned a telling comment about the after-action reports written by unit commanders during the war. It is a cautionary note that all historians of the conflict should keep in mind as they dig through the *Official Record*. The general wrote that to him it was clear "absolutely that many of the reports [of Civil War actions were] base exaggerations — romances, founded upon the smallest conceivable amount of fact. They are simply elaborate essays, which seek to show that the author was a little braver, a little more skillful in the management of his men, and a little worthier, than anybody else."[2] To a greater or lesser degree, this is probably true of all such reports from any war.

In considering the history of the Fifth New York Cavalry, the principal primary source material consists of what is in the *Official Record*. In addition, there is the *War Journal* maintained by the regiment's chaplain, Louis N. Boudrye, and any other contemporary writings by individuals either in the regiment, those in command of brigades or divisions to which the unit was attached, or those coming in close contact with it. As for the small number of reports from the Fifth New York residing in the *Official Record*, General Beatty's caution need not apply when considering those forwarded from the desk of John Hammond, commanding the regiment in 1863 and 1864. The after-action reports written by the regiment's longest-serving commander are models of how to comply with orders to pen a report while providing little or nothing of the concrete, verifiable information and the descriptions that a historian desires most. Hammond had no underlying motives, no agenda and, apparently, no real interest in the reports other than writing in compliance with orders. Therefore, as far as they go, these reports can be trusted for what Hammond and his command saw and did at a particular point, provided he thought it was significant enough to write down.

The *War Journal* faithfully maintained by Chaplain Boudrye while with the Fifth New York can be looked upon as several things at the same time. It is a primary source for some elementary color relating to life within the regiment at a given moment and a somewhat accurate record of places where events occurred, where the command was, at a particular time. Also, it is a view of what concerned Boudrye at a given moment as it relates to the unit. Acknowledging that the chaplain was maintaining the journal for himself and not us, the volume remains superficial when it could have been a detailed account of important occurrences and is thoroughly colored by its author's obvious religious outlook. But in it we find the chaplain to be a good man, dedicated and honest, doing a job he believed in and leaving us with what we can only wish were more. Despite this, the *War Journal* remains one of the few records that has come to light in our age that covers, however incompletely, some events occurring within the unit. In the closing months of the conflict, Boudrye gathered material for a regimental history. The *Historic Records of the 5th N.Y. Cavalry* was completed and published within months of the war's end. A reading of the journal makes it obvious that Boudrye used it as a basis for the chronology presented in his history, adding tables of fact and a few contemporary accounts written by other individuals serving in the unit, while he polished the language to strict nineteenth century standards. By digging into it, considerable factual material can be mined, but like the journal, it is essentially superficial.

What remains regarding the regiment appears in the letters written by the Fifth's troopers at the time, what they say of things, people and events. These are by far the most truthful, being generally private communications between individuals never intended for other eyes. But they are accurate as to events only so far as an individual trooper could see from where he stood. Individual memoirs published after the fact, as well as histories of regiments operating in unison with the Fifth New York, are helpful and can be relied upon after careful evaluation of their tone and any underlying bias of the author.

Nevertheless, the historian attempting to relate to a reader the story of a particular group of men separated from us by many decades is forced to rely heavily on these sources. The historian is forced, somewhat against his nature, to extrapolate from what he is reading, to infer, so that he can relate to the reader what he believes to be the truth of what happened, why and what it means.

Given the above, heavy reliance in this work had been placed on the research done by historian Stephen Z. Starr. His three-volume history, *The Union Cavalry in the Civil War*, is the preeminent work on the subject and has proven invaluable in fashioning this rendering of one unit. Indeed, without it this could not be.

It is sincerely hoped that by using these sources, however inadequate some might prove to be, the reader might acquire at least a semblance of the environment in which the men of the Fifth New York Cavalry lived, fought and died.

Brigadier General James H. Wilson was for six months in 1864 in command of the cavalry division of which the Fifth New York was part. Like most commanders from this era he had his positives and negatives. His reports from the field are generally straightforward affairs, although he could occasionally neglect mentioning a fact or two. However, he did commit to paper one thing — a memory — that to this writer at least rings true. Decades later, writing of the moment when he left command of the division, he said, "Its two best regiments were the Fifth New York and the First Vermont from opposite sides of the Champlain Valley. They were ... steady, amenable to discipline, natural cavalrymen, devoted to the Union and without hatred or passion, they were ever ready for the fray."[3] Based on the research presented below, this quotation can be considered valid.

1
And the War Came — 1861

[A]nd in less than twenty minutes, from right to centre, and from centre to left, the clear notes of the bugles rang out the welcome charge; and with one long, wild shout those glorious squadrons of Buford and Kilpatrick, from right to left, as far as the eye could see, in one unbroken line, charged the foe. The shock was irresistible; the rebel line broke — the routed enemy confessed the superiority of our men, as they fled from the wellfought field, leaving their dead and dying behind them.[1]

What is missing from this contemporary description of a cavalry charge is the incandescence of sunlight flashing on steel sabers held aloft by the blue-clad troopers and the rolling thunder as thousands of mighty horse hoofs hit the ground as the great tidal wave surged forward. To be sure, there were many cavalry charges in the Civil War and if there had been motion pictures or video we wouldn't need this kind of language. Nevertheless, a charge was usually made by elements much smaller than in this description and it was an exception rather than a rule. Usually they were ordered by a commander, a prudent one, as a quick way to overpower the enemy of equal or lesser numbers or as an act of desperation and escape. The real role of cavalry in this war was of a much less spectacular, but vital, nature. And it would evolve during the four years after 1861 to a degree not foreseen at the opening of the conflict.

At the beginning of the Civil War a cavalry formation operating with an army, in theory, had a number of tasks assigned to it. Primarily the cavalry, either in brigade or regimental strength, was to locate the enemy either in a fixed position or as they moved. Also, if its own army was moving, the cavalry was expected to screen that movement from the enemy's eyes (enemy cavalry). Cavalry was needed to scout ahead of an army as it moved and, occasionally, cover its withdrawal. It was expected to move with supply trains, guarding them from enemy marauders. Generals, more often than not, needed a number of mounted men to serve as escorts and couriers. There was little, if any, thought given as to how to use cavalry in combination with an army as an offensive force as that army did battle with the enemy or how to use it to penetrate enemy country to cut supply and communication lines. By 1864, in the last full year of war, the Union Army had developed to an advanced level all the methods and uses to which cavalry formations could be used in war. But it hadn't been easy. The learning through experience had been expensive, most particularly in lives lost. During the initial two years of the Civil War, thousands of men and boys enlisted as citizen-soldiers in cavalry regiments organized within Northern states. These volunteers, and the men who would lead them, had a lot to learn and their learning would be done under the duress of combat with a Rebel mounted force that initially was far superior to them in aggressiveness, tactics and leadership.

Prior to the year 1833, those few cavalry regiments employed by the United States in war had been quickly disbanded once the crisis was past. Cavalry formations had been used in both the Revolutionary War and the War of 1812, but between the end of the latter war and 1833, the U.S. Army had none. In peacetime, regiments of cavalry were simply too expensive to maintain in garrison for a young and frugal national government. The change in thinking came with territorial growth, particularly beyond the Mississippi River, where settlers and traders were ever encroaching on the domain of the plains Indians and, later, when wagon trains of immigrants were striking out for the promised lands of the Oregon Territory. It became clear to the national government that mounted troops were needed to provide protection for people on the frontier. In the 1820s traders from Missouri were traveling overland on the Santa Fe Trail seeking the benefits of commerce with northern Mexico. Frequently attacked en route by hostile Indians, the traders began clamoring for protection of their caravans by the army. Little was done, however, until 1831, when two traders were killed and a report was sent to President Andrew Jackson. He in turn asked the Congress to establish a unit of mounted troops. On October 15, 1832, the Congress passed a funding measure establishing what was to become the U.S. Cavalry. The next year portions of that first mounted regiment were escorting trading caravans along the Santa Fe Trail. This first mounted regiment posted in the west — initially called dragoons and based loosely on a European model — was primarily to serve only as mounted riflemen, in essence infantrymen on horses for greater mobility.[2] In the years prior to the war with Mexico in 1846, other mounted commands were organized and scattered to frontier outposts. When war with Mexico came, some of these cavalry units were called upon to join the invasion force below the Rio Grande, while others marched into and fought in the land that would become part of the United States at war's end. During the 1850s more regiments were added. In 1861, at the outbreak of Civil War, the U.S. Army had five cavalry regiments distributed across the west. The bulk of these were quickly called back to Washington to help deal with the secession crisis.

As Rebel cannons attempted to blast Fort Sumter to rubble in Charleston Harbor, General Winfield Scott was at his desk in Washington, in command of the entire — and meager — U.S. Army. Scott was a veteran of both the War of 1812 and the Mexican War. He was one of only two officers in the army at that moment that had ever handled in the field a formation larger than an infantry brigade. Both of these officers were now past the age of seventy. There was to be war and it would be led in the field by officers from the standing U.S. Army and Cavalry using primarily 75,000 volunteers organized within the loyal states into the basic building block of the Civil War army, the regiment, and forwarded by the governors to Washington. In addition, the War Department under Secretary Simon Cameron asked the Congress for funds to form eight more regular army infantry regiments and one more of cavalry.[3]

In addition to infantry, loyal state governors had been offering to form volunteer cavalry regiments for use by President Lincoln in the war effort. These offers were initially declined by both Secretary of War Simon Cameron and General Scott. To some who carefully considered the situation, it did appear obvious that more mounted units would be needed. In the spring of 1861, some observers thought that the war might have to be fought over the entire eastern seaboard and even in the Mississippi Valley. But to General Scott, it would be a short war with massed troops located primarily in Virginia, and these would defeat the Rebels. To his thinking, by the time state volunteer cavalry regiments were equipped, trained and deployed, there would be no significant role for them to play. Besides, the geography of Virginia, where it was thought the main effort would take place, Scott considered unsuitable for cavalry operations. Finally, regiments of cavalry were simply too expensive. The initial cost to equip a cavalry regiment with horses, saddles, weapons, uniforms and the ancillary equipment required to maintain field operations was simply too much, upwards of $500,000 each. The annual maintenance cost was estimated at $90,000.[4]

From today's perspective, Washington's initial rejection of volunteer cavalry units and the plan to fight a land war with just five regular regiments of cavalry seems ill-advised at best; at worst, stupidity fossilized by years of conventional military thinking. After considering all the elements comprising the War Department's position, one cavalry historian says:

If the secretary of war and the commanding general of the Army truly believed that the regular service would carry the Cavalry's burden in the coming war, they were either ignorant or deluded. In fact, the five mounted units available to the nation in April 1861, the youngest of which had been in existence for only six years, were too few to meet the needs of a single army in wartime, let alone the several field commands the Union would establish before year's end in various theaters of operations. Moreover, years of lax recruiting, heavy detachments of officers to staff duty and the resignations of dozens of officers and men of Southern birth or inclination, a trend that increased as more states joined the Confederacy, had depleted the strength and compromised the readiness of every [regular cavalry] regiment.[5]

To move the point further along, when volunteer cavalry was finally accepted for use, "for all practical purposes the Union had to start from scratch to build whatever it wanted in the way of Cavalry."[6]

Essentially, this was the situation during the initial months of hostilities, from April to July of 1861. The volunteer infantry regiments from the loyal states were sent to Washington and organized into what was thought to be an army, and that army, along with regular troops, would restore the seceded states to the Union. It would be short effort, a short war, and all would be set right. In July this new army of mostly volunteers marched from the immediate area of Washington, headed in the direction of Manassas, Virginia.

What neither General Scott nor Secretary Cameron foresaw or took into account was the extreme difference of the Rebels' views about cavalry's cost, inhibiting geography, or anything else. By the evening of July 21, 1861, federal illusions of a short war and a quick reunification were as dead as the hundreds of ill-trained Union volunteers lying in the fields near a Virginia stream called Bull Run. As the beaten army trudged over the Potomac bridges and into Washington, it had to be clear to all that an initial 75,000 volunteers and a small standing army with just five cavalry regiments wasn't going to be enough. In addition to a call for more troops on July 2, the administration asked for another 300,000 volunteers on August 4, in the immediate aftermath of Bull Run. This time volunteer cavalry formations would be accepted and mustered into Federal service.

Within a few weeks of this call, what would become the Fifth New York Cavalry began forming. On July 26, 1861, the secretary of war authorized Othneil De Forest of New York City to recruit and organize a cavalry regiment. Although absent from the regiment's records, De Forest must have been a man with at least a modicum of political influence, and as a patriot rushed to the assistance of his country in time of crisis. As a result of his efforts, De Forest would become the first colonel leading the new regiment. Largely for political reasons and to maintain home-front morale, volunteer regiments in

1. And the War Came—1861

the Civil War were identified by the state where they were organized, and were numbered consecutively as they were mustered into Federal service. For the Fifth New York, actively recruited during August and in camp on Staten Island by the end of September and being the fifth such, five would remain its designation during the coming four years.[7] In addition to its assigned designation as Fifth New York Volunteer Cavalry Regiment, the command took unto itself the name Ira Harris Guard, in honor of one of the New York's U.S. Senators.

Today it is nearly impossible to identify the precise reason why a particular individual volunteered in the Union cause unless he has told us in some document written at the time that has come down to us in the present. For the thousands upon thousands who joined, only a small percentage spoke of their motives. For the majority, the historian is forced to use a broad brush and extrapolate. Why the cavalry? Some no doubt thought of it as an elite force, imbued with romantic legend derived from contemporary novels. Besides, surely riding was preferred to marching. Friends had volunteered. To some it just didn't look or seem right to stay behind as one's friends went off to war. Was it simply Lincoln's call for additional troops in the summer of 1861 and news of the disaster at Bull Run that pushed them to volunteer? One Pennsylvania volunteer, writing after the war, thought so. "Hardly had the echoes of the contest [at Bull Run] died away, ere we crowded to the recruiting office and camps."[8] Almost certainly in that summer there was resident in each native-born cavalry volunteer some degree of patriotism, of preserving though his efforts the government under which he had been raised. Some probably considered it their duty, both to those who had established the Union as well as to future generations. But in all likelihood there were as many personal reasons for joining as there were men in the group that would become the Fifth New York Cavalry: a job he disliked, a family situation of one kind or another, or any of a hundred reasons. It is as likely that at least some of these men were not thinking simply in terms of a cherished constitutional principle, or that any at all were motivated by a deep antagonism toward the institution of slavery. Indeed, if they had been told in 1861 that they were joining a war to free slaves, most probably would not have come to the regiment. Freedom for slaves was not in the least a pervasive motivation for volunteering in the testimony that has come down to us. And that the war was to be fought so that democratic institutions would survive in a nineteenth century world nearly devoid of such was a concept that would only later filter into the consciousness of the more reflective of these nascent cavalrymen. However, the preservation of the Union was a motivation, and a significant one. What moved these men that has come down to us in their words is most

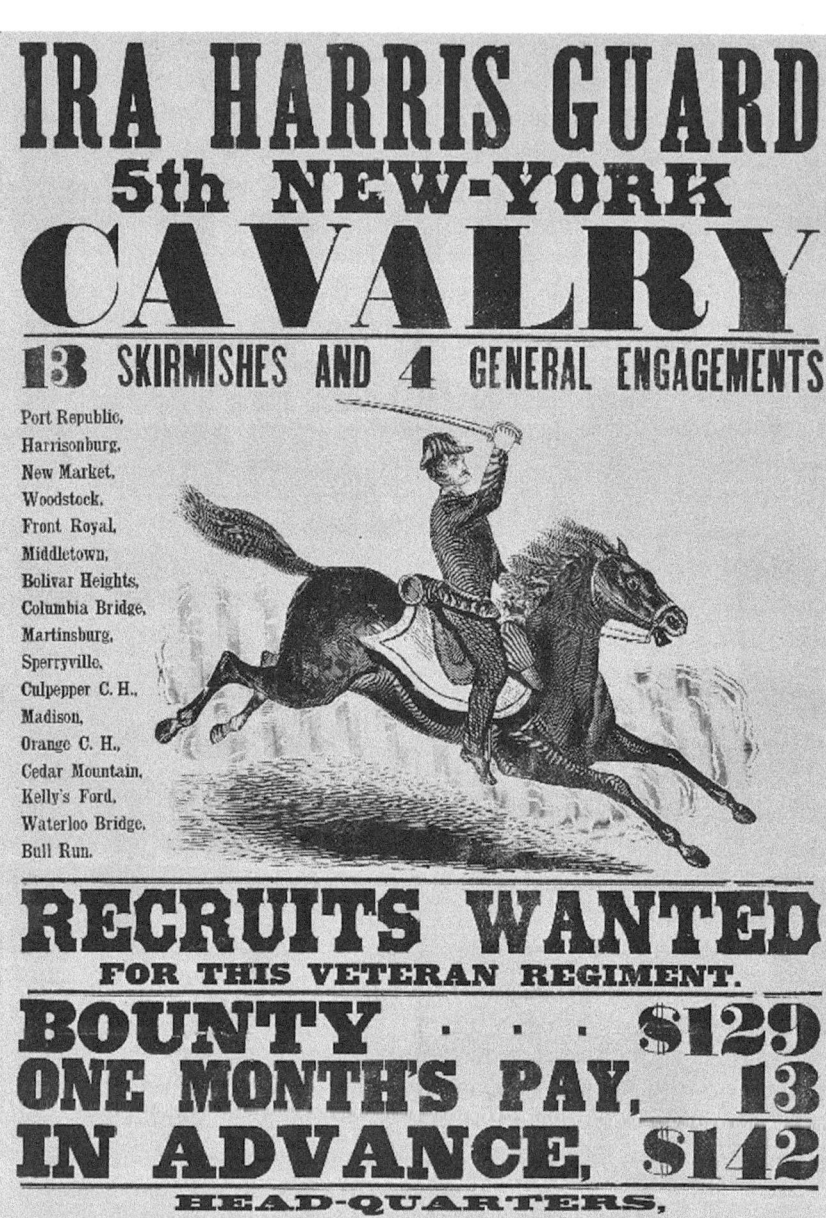

Fifth New York Recruiting Poster, circa 1862 (Library of Congress).

1. And the War Came—1861

often framed in terms of preservation of the American Union. A typical quote, cited by historian James M. McPherson, comes from a New Jersey recruit, who says he is fighting a "grate [*sic*] struggle for the Union, Constitution, and law.... We will be held responsible before God if we don't do our part in helping to transmit this boon of civil & religious liberty down to succeeding generations." A West Point graduate wrote later of the early months of the war, saying that it was his impression that the Northern soldier "felt that slavery was wrong and altogether out of harmony with civilization and the spirit of a free government, yet in the beginning of the war they had no desire or intent to interfere with it in the states."[9]

The sectional conflict rooted in slavery, decades old in 1860, had finally come to a head with Lincoln's election and in the emotion-charged months immediately after the nation's political institutions, for myriad reasons not germane to the discussion here, had failed. The accommodations and compromises over slavery and the institution's extension into the territories had run their course. The election of the Republican Party's Abraham Lincoln—considered in the South as the embodiment anti-slavery politics in all its forms—quickly pushed the lower South to exit the Union even before the new president took the oath. President Lincoln, after four years of war, arrived at an understanding of what had happened in 1861. In his second inaugural address, he summarized his thinking and, probably, the embryonic thinking of the men who had volunteered for the Fifth New York Cavalry in 1861. That slavery had caused the conflict was clear, but beyond that, "Both parties [North and South] deprecated war; but one of them would *make* war rather than let the nation survive; and the other would *accept* war rather than let it perish. And the war came."[10]

This is the typical explanation, painted with the broad brush, given in histories of this time, and there is undeniably a significant degree of truth to it. Although there was a significant migration from the farm to urban centers in the thirty years prior to 1860, nevertheless, for the majority life in the nineteenth century, particularly rural life, was insular, confining, with men rarely leaving the communities into which they were born. And if a man did leave, either to go west or to seek employment in some city, it was usually a one-way move for economic betterment. It was so vastly different that we today have trouble imagining it; we who, with the twist of a key in a car, can go anywhere at any time, hundreds of miles from home on a moment's notice.

What we know for certain about these volunteer cavalrymen is that they were generally young. And as with all who are young, the potential for adventure, excitement, the chance to see something different and the opportunity to ride in the company of men with a purpose must have played some part, large or small, in their volunteering. Patriotism and a healthy dash of youthful eagerness — along with any number of intangibles — moved the men who would fill out the Fifth New York Cavalry to sign up.

A volunteer unit of this era was usually raised or organized by a prominent citizen of a particular community who, more often than not, became its commander, regardless of prior military experience. Beginning in August 1861, the Fifth New York Cavalry started organization at Camp Scott on Staten Island, New York. Charles T.S. Pierce enlisted as a private, and years later wrote brief summary or sketch of the regiment:

> On the 26th of July, the Secretary of War authorized Col. Othneil De Forest, of New York City, to raise a regiment of cavalry. By the last of the following September there had been gathered on Staten Island, New York Harbor, the nucleus of a fine cavalry brigade. From this assemblage of recruits was organized the Fifth New York Cavalry, known as the "First Ira Harris Guard," in honor of Senator Ira Harris of Albany. New York City had contributed liberally of men, though whole companies and parts of companies were raised in Essex, Wyoming, Allegany and Tioga Counties. A few men were also obtained from the States of Massachusetts, Connecticut, and New Jersey. No bounties were paid to recruits; but a bounty of $100 was promised to be paid by the United States, at the expiration of [a three year] term of service.[11]

A portion of the Fifth New York appears to have been grafted onto it from another attempt at the formation of a cavalry regiment. One Colonel W.S. Bliss had tried recruiting a command — to be called Bliss's Cavalry — but it seems the recruitment numbers were not to be had and the companies it did have were joined to the Fifth New York, designated as companies A, B, I, K and M. Companies A, B and K were recruited in New York City. Company I received men from the city as well as Orange County, New York, and Plainfield, New Jersey. Company M had men from Green and Columbia Counties as well as from New York City. The remainder of the companies in the regiment came exclusively from counties in western and/or upstate, the exception being Company D, which was composed of men left over from cavalry regiments formed in Massachusetts and Connecticut.

In the late summer of 1861, John Hammond of Crown Point, Essex County, New York, recruited a cavalry company consisting of 127 men from the immediate area. The early regimental history has it that Hammond received assistance in the recruitment from one C.F. Hammond, Esq., his father. It was the latter Hammond "who furnished all the original horses for the company to the number of one hundred and eight." John Hammond had earlier "assisted" in raising Company H of the Thirty-fourth New York Volunteer Infantry, and "after the battle of Bull Run, [he] determined to raise a company of cavalry and to go to the assistance of the Government himself."

The men who enlisted, mostly farmers and mechanics between ages twenty and thirty, did so as privates, but having been the inspiration behind the recruitment, John Hammond, listed as joining Company H on September 5, 1861, was elected captain of the company on September 14. They arrived on Staten Island already mounted on Vermont Morgan horses, one of the very few volunteer cavalry outfits to do so. "The horses were inspected and accepted for government service. Charles F. Hammond was reimbursed at this time up to $125 for each mount, even though he had paid as much as $200 for some of the horses."[12]

An exemplary citizen-soldier, Colonel John Hammond, longest-serving commander of the Fifth New York Cavalry (Massachusetts Commandery, Military Orders of the Loyal Legion, U.S. Army Military History Institute).

Training and equipping the regiment consumed the weeks between Company A's being mustered into service on August 15 and October 31, when companies I, K, L and M formally joined federal service. When the regiment left Camp Scott on November 18, Colonel Othneil De Forest led 1,064 men. The heavy recruitment in New York City—the recruiting office was at 4 Pine Street—seems to have given the Fifth New York a unique blend of men from various occupations and backgrounds. There are 126 different previous occupations and trades listed in the regiment's records, including, blacksmiths, stage drivers, showmen, hatters, artists, sail makers, and at least one actor, one minstrel and a "hotel keeper." However, the majority of the recruits were listed as farmers prior to joining, reflecting the large rural contingent within the unit. And the regiment was not a homogenous collection of native-born Americans. The Fifth New York, according to the record, had recruits from nineteen foreign countries, of which 221 listed Ireland as their place of birth.[13] This is a result of the heavy recruitment in the immigrant-rich city that was New York.

One typical record for someone volunteering for the Fifth New York is that of George H. Lamb, who came to the regiment as a volunteer in February 1863. There is some vague reference that Lamb had previously enlisted in a New York infantry regiment, been discharged and re-enlisted in the cavalry. His reasons for volunteering both for the cavalry and the Fifth New York are unrecorded. He left us nothing of his motives. Although not absolutely clear on this point, the record indicates that Lamb, a native of Orange County, joined in "New York" (presumably the city) for three years on February 17, 1863, and arrived at the regiment as a recruit on the February 22. The Fifth was then posted at Germantown, Virginia, in the defenses of Washington. In April 1863, Lamb received a $25 advance authorized by the War Department on the $100 enlistment bounty. Mostly likely this advance was sent home to his family, as it was with most recruits. Assigned to Company L, we can catch a quick glimpse of the new volunteer. The Company L Descriptive Book says that he was eighteen at the time and born in New York, New York. Actually, Lamb was from Cornwall, New York, then a small community on the west bank of the Hudson River, about halfway between West Point and the larger town of Newburgh to the north. At five feet eight inches tall he can be considered slightly above average height. His complexion was "light," his eyes blue and hair brown. "Clerk" was listed as his previous occupation and at the time could mean anything other than his being a tradesman or farmer. His basic cavalry training was in the field with the regiment, given the five days from enlistment until arriving in Virginia. He must have absorbed the training well because the following year, on March 1, 1864, Lamb was promoted to corporal. George Lamb would ride with the Fifth New York until he was captured on June 28, 1864, and sent to Andersonville Prison Camp.[14]

Although George Lamb told us nothing of his reasons for joining the Fifth New York, Francis Conroy of Portland, Maine, did. At the age of nineteen in 1861, he had traveled to New York City looking for work but could find none. On September 15, 1861, he wrote to his mother in Maine:

> I now write to you to let you know that I am in good health at present.... I have looked for something to do. I could not get anything to do so I have enlisted in the horse regiment call the Ira Harris Cavalry or Guard. I get 14 dollars a month. I am sorry mother but I could not help it. My Uncle Michael lost one of his fingers. He was in the hospital for 6 weeks. I did not like to stay with him because he had plenty of his own to take care of. So did George have enough to do to take care of his family? There is nothing at all a doing anywhere.... Mother I don't want you to feel bad for me to enlist. I could not help it. I want you to pray for me mother. I will go to my duty regular. Fear not mother I will return with the help of god and then I can come and stay with you. Mother it was a good day to me when I left this place. If you seen me to day you would not

1. And the War Came—1861

know me. I am bigger and stronger today than a man of 30 years. I am 5 foot and 10 inches. I want you to write to me as soon as you get this letter and let me know how you all are getting along.

Francis Conroy was in the hospital in Washington in January 1862 with what appears to be a respiratory problem when he was discharged from the army. He returned home to Portland and died there on February 15, 1863. Later, a nurse responded to an inquiry from Francis's father: "Frank was so gentle and patient it was a pleasure to do any thing for him. He often spoke of his mother and with a longing to get home among you all [if] it was only for a short time.... I am sorry I can't tell you more of his illness here, but that he had kind care I'm sure. It is some time since he left and I regret I cant remember more, but I'm only visiting in Washington & have worked most of my time among several hospitals and find it impossible to remember each individual case."[15]

Twelve cavalry companies made up the regiment, and prior to their receiving their full complement of horses, the men were drilled and trained in dismounted tactics. Then, in November, the regiment was ordered to Annapolis, Maryland. Just before it left, Senator Ira Harris, the command's adopted mentor of sorts, attended the formal presentation of the colors to the regiment at Camp Scott. He was quoted in the newspaper as providing these words of encouragement, interrupted by cheers from the novice cavalrymen: "I shall watch your movements with the intensest interest.... But the life of a soldier is no holiday life. I know you will endure hardships as good soldiers, that you will brave even death itself in a cause so glorious. Some of you will fall in battle. Oh! it is a glorious death thus to die. Some of you — most of you, I hope — will live to return. But come not back, I charge you, until you come covered all over with glory to receive the plaudits of a grateful country." The newspaper reported that after his farewell speech the officers of the Fifth New York, thus encouraged, hosted a catered dinner for Senator Harris.[16]

In October, two-thirds of the horses needed for the regiment were delivered and training with them started. Given the heavy recruitment within New York City, it can be assumed that many men had, as the first order of business, to become familiar with handling a horse and learning how to ride. Also, the care and feeding of the animal on which the cavalryman relied had to be learned and practiced. The following remarks, quoted by Stephen Z. Starr, historian of the Union cavalry, can be considered typical of what the Fifth New York was up against when they received their horses. The would-be cavalrymen "had not been astride a horse until they were mustered into the United States service.... Many of them showed much more fear of their horses than they ever did afterward of the enemy. The wild fumbling after mane or saddle strap, the terror depicted on some faces when the commands 'trot' or 'gallop' were given, are a lasting source of amusement." This source goes on, "It seems that the qualifications of a recruit for the cavalry might be summed up in this: he neither knows how to groom, feed, water or ride his horse, and is afraid of him." Although the record of the Fifth New York says that the original horses supplied to the company raised at Crown Point were of the finest quality, this was not usually the case in all regiments. A cavalryman from Pennsylvania during the first months of the war addressed the issue. The horseflesh "furnished were in most cases very poor animals, due to fraud on the part of Government contractors, and the overtaxed resources of the Quartermaster Department." Indeed, negligence and lax procurement practices, as well as outright fraud, were serious issues as the War Department attempted to cope with a serious buildup of its volunteer cavalry.[17] There was constant drilling of the men in the regiment who had been issued horses up until the time they boarded the train for Baltimore. Those who didn't have horses would get them in Maryland and would have to catch up to the others with regard to horsemanship.

In that Othneil De Forest was charged with raising the regiment, he became its colonel. Generally speaking, officers during this period were assigned ranks commensurate with the number of men they had recruited. There was little or no consideration given to the potential leadership qualities or prior military knowledge of the volunteers assigned as officers. In some regiments, officers were elected, but while it is not specifically mentioned anywhere, it appears that the Fifth New York had most of its officers assigned at the company level by the numbers recruited. As mentioned, since John Hammond had been instrumental in raising Company H, this group of men "elected" him captain. Time and trial in the field would prove these selections one way or the other.

The volunteers were supposed to get a physical examination prior to being officially mustered into service, according to an order issued by the Army in 1861. This doesn't appear to have been done, whether because of the large numbers passing through the recruiting stations and camps or because of simple neglect. When the Fifth New York was getting ready to leave Camp Scott, it was found that eighty men were unfit and should not have been accepted into the cavalry. A report written by a medical director of the army shortly afterwards said, "There were eighty men with hernia and epilepsy in the Fifth New York Cavalry." Camp Scott, as well as all other training camps at this time, was a place where germs of all types were rampant. Before any volunteer outfit boarded a train south, many were either too sick to go or were already dead, victims of ignorance about proper sanitation and rudimentary medical care. The same report of the medical director that named Camp Scott went on to say it "found that conditions were so unsanitary that more than a hundred members" of another volunteer regiment, the Sixth New York, "had come down with fever and measles." The victims included the regiment's assistant surgeon and its hospital steward. Curiously, contemporaries found that recruits from the city fared better in resisting disease than those from the farm.[18] The struggle against sickness was a never-ending one in all regiments, and officers had to keep reminding their men of even elementary disease preventatives. That it was a continual problem is evidenced by the lieutenant colonel of the Fifth New York in an order issued nearly a year after the unit had gone into the field. On March 9, 1863, in Virginia, he issued an order. "The condition of the company tents is like a whited sepulchre, clean without and foul within.... Sickness seems to run in tents. The cause is obvious. When a soldier is sick the door of the tent he is in is strapped shut, the cap of the tent is fastened down, and all the air being excluded, his comrades breathe a foul atmosphere. Officers commanding Companies will see at once that there is free ventilation.... Such a day as this all blankets and bedding should be aired, and tents kept open and the cap of tents removed." Despite the colonel's orders, four officers and ninety enlisted men died of disease in the four years of the Fifth New York's existence. When the regiment left Camp Scott, health conditions did not seem to improve, and of course there were accidents. Captain Hammond wrote home on December 15, "I cannot write you with regard to Lieut. Benedict's death, as it is too unpleasant to again go over. Lieut. Penfield, who has gone home with the widow and remains, will give you the particulars.... Wednesday we sent two wagon loads of sick from Company H to the hospital at Annapolis." Lieutenant Benedict, according to the record, died as a result of the amputation of his right arm after having been bitten on the thumb by "a man."[19]

Through all the winters of the Civil War, winter camps were mostly hardships to be endured, but none more so than the winter of 1861–62. While the Army of the Potomac and the various units in the defenses of Washington were organized and trained in the wake of that summer's debacle at Bull Run, the Fifth New York had to live essentially in the open. As summarized by a historian of northern cavalry, the New Yorkers "were condemned to spend the winter in squalid, unhealthy camps deep in mud, drilling when the weather and the footing allowed, doing bootless errands around Washington, going on picket and on an occasional scout, and having the fine edge of their eagerness and enthusiasm blunted by the evident lack of progress in putting down the rebellion." There were inspections, reviews and regimental-size snowball fights, but the men really wanted only "to get at the job, win the war, and go home." As for the food the men of the Fifth New York were given in these camps, there is little recorded. Ralph Tolles from western New York wrote a friend from Camp Scott, "The grub is not quite as good as it was at home[.] Did not expect it would be[.] There is enough but the less said about the quality the better[.]" Extrapolating from this trooper's comment and applying some imagination, the camp's cuisine probably had many remembering the food at home in favorable terms. However, there is a record of a rebellion by the Sixth New York Cavalry while at Camp Scott. It started over a breakfast prepared by contractors working at the camp. On a morning in December 1861, breakfast included just too much rotten fish for their liking. The men began tearing down the cookhouse and only stopped when their colonel, pistol in hand, "reasoned" with them.[20]

Leaving Camp Scott on November 18, the Fifth New York arrived in Baltimore the next day and started for Annapolis on November 25. By November 28, the regiment was camped outside Annapolis at a place they called Camp Harris. It was there, through the winter, that regular army officers provided further training. All Union cavalry regiments contained twelve companies, referred to as troops. Two companies made a squadron and two squadrons equaled a battalion and, therefore, a regiment contained three battalions.[21]

As the training continued at Camp Harris, the regiment was brought up to strength in horses and the necessary equipment was issued to the men. In all likelihood the troopers didn't receive every item required for the fully equipped cavalryman, but they had enough to strike camp at the end of March 1862, heading for the Shenandoah Valley.

Ideally, a cavalry trooper had a saddle, saddle blanket, saddlebags and haversack, to accompany the halter and bridle, curry comb and brush, all equipment associated with the horse he was to ride and care for. Attached to his belt was a holster for a pistol and a box for cartridges and another and smaller box for percussion caps for his firearms. There was another belt for his 40-inch saber. On his saddle was rolled his blanket and poncho. He also carried a tin cup and a small skillet for cooking. For clothing, there was the basic Union cavalry uniform that included a cap modeled on the French kepi. On it was a brass badge, crossed sabers with a letter above indicating his company and a numeral below, the number of his regiment. The uniform was typically wool. The trousers were light blue and reinforced in the seat and with the cavalry's traditional yellow strip down each leg. There was a short-waisted jacket of dark blue and knee-high boots. Also, there was an overcoat. When the carbine and pistol were added, there was approximately fifty pounds of equipment sitting on the horse's back, to which the rider's weight would be added. But everything didn't get supplied, as it should have been. John

Hammond, commanding Company H, did something about it outside Army procedure. He wrote home, "The government only gave us shoes entirely unfit for service in the saddle. I just received an invoice for cavalry boots through George Royce, who, in a kindly way, got them for us at about half price; the men will pay me for them when they are paid. It was a sight to see how happy the men were, and the men of other companies all flocked around looking regretful at not having the same. One or two companies have asked me to do for them as I have done for Company H. I shall write at once for them."[22]

The most important accoutrements, of course, were the cavalryman's weapons. These included a saber with a saber belt, a revolver with a holster, and a carbine hung from the saddle by a ring. At this time in the war, if he was lucky, the trooper received a Sharps carbine. But only a minority had them at the start of campaigning in 1862. The Ordnance Bureau in Washington had been aware of General Scott's not wanting to enlist volunteer cavalry and had placed few orders for carbines. The most common American manufactured carbine, early in the war, was the single-shot Sharps breechloader. Accurate up to 400 yards, this carbine fired a paper and linen cartridge that was consumed in the firing and had a spring-loaded wafer primer fed from a magazine, thus eliminating the need for a percussion cap. Later in the war the seven-shot Spencer carbine appeared in large numbers. A tubular magazine inserted in the stock of the Spencer fed self-contained rounds into the chamber when the trigger guard was levered forward by the shooter. The Spencer carbine was the best single technological enhancement made during the war, increasing the firepower of the cavalry exponentially. Trooper John Morse of the Fifth New York wrote to his father about the Spencer carbine in 1863 when larger numbers were becoming available and the Fifth New York acquired them. Morse wrote the regiments "all have the Spencer rifle and can make the rebes [sic] get right up and get with them. They [the Rebels] cant [sic] think what kind of a gun have got. We can shoot twice to thare [sic] one and that makes a great difference when they stand they have to load up and then we can give them one before they can get loaded."[23]

The trooper's pistol in all likelihood was the Model 1860 Colt .44 revolver. Each of the six cylinders contained a cartridge with powder and ball and fired via a percussion cap on each cylinder. Once all six shots were expended, it was difficult and time-consuming to reload, especially when in or near action and on horseback. As a result, many troopers, by one means or another, acquired two .44s. In the early months of 1862, the cavalrymen of the Fifth New York were probably carrying carbines of European manufacture, weapons quickly purchased by the government and as quickly shipped into the country. These were eventually exchanged for the Sharps as soon as they became available. It would take all 1862 for the Union cavalry's demand for the latest weapons to be filled. It wasn't until 1864 that the entire cavalry force of the army was fully equipped with the latest model, the seven-shot Spencer repeater.[24]

The training regime during the winter of 1861–62 at Camp Harris began before sunrise and continued, on a typical day, until after dark. The horses were fed and cared for starting at about 6:30 A.M., followed by breakfast for the men an hour later. Although the daily routine varied between regiments, usually there were two training sessions in the morning, lunch, and another session in the afternoon. Then the horses were again cared for by the men while the officers received tactical instruction until dinner was called around 5:00 P.M. After dinner there usually was a dress parade before lights-out was sounded at 9:00 P.M. With days packed with such activity it is a wonder there was time for any diversion for the volunteer trooper. But even in this era the innate ingenuity of the American citizen-soldier would not be denied. The men and their officers got their liquor, sometimes in packages relatives sent from home or, on or about paydays, from sutlers who intalled themselves near every army camp and sold cheap whiskey at exorbitant prices. On December 21, 1861, Sergeant Charles H. Greenleaf of Company D wrote from Camp Harris to his parents that his company commander had died. Greenleaf wrote, "The doctor said [he died] of brain fever but others say of delirium tremens." By 1863, some units had become wise in the matter of liquor coming into camp. A trooper from the Fifteenth New York Cavalry recalled that officers sometimes inspected the packages arriving from home before giving them to the

A Union cavalryman with one more pistol than was regular issue in the Union cavalry (Library of Congress).

men. But sometimes the liquor was still not discovered, in that bottles were hidden inside loaves of bread or in other ways camouflaged so as not to be recognizable.[25]

Along with packages from home came letters. Those letters available to us from troopers to relatives invariably ask for news from home and of friends. Francis Conroy tells his mother, "Write to me as soon as you get this. Don't forget to write news. I have no pen or ink so I must write with pencil." Daniel Wright reminded his brother to "tell the girls that they must write." Farquin Chapman of Company D admonishes his parents, " I would like to have you write and should like to hear from the boys and I cant see anny [sic] good reason why some of you cant send me a letter as often as once a month it had been a most 2 since I have had one." Troopers were also curious about the larger picture, their view of the war limited to just the regiment. Seldon Wales told his sister, "You must send the New York Herald for I want to hear how the war is getting along. You must answer me soon as you get this letter." Halstead Hickson Fowler wrote his mother in December of 1861, "We do not get any news about the war at all nor do not know anything about what Congress is trying to do about the war and I wish you would write the news."

Remembering the importance of mail from home, a trooper in another regiment wrote after the war, "Men who never wrote a letter in their lives before, are at it now; those who cannot write at all, are either learning, or engage their comrades to write for them.... Some men carry pocket-inkstands and write with pens, but the majority use pencils.... I suppose in this way we are not only making, but writing history."[26]

Although the regiment's training was under the supervision of regular army officers, it cannot be considered what we of a later age would call either complete or comprehensive. As a historian of Union cavalry says, "It is a fact that hardly any regiment of volunteer cavalry, whenever or wherever it was raised, had had adequate training, either of its men or horses, when it was called upon to face the enemy." This led inevitably to losses in the actions that were to come in the spring of 1862. The officers and men would learn primarily by doing, gaining experience day by day. Those who learned quickly, men like John Hammond, rose in the ranks. This evaluation is set against another. Improvements were noticed as 1861 gave way to 1862 and the beginning of a full campaigning season. Incompetent officers, says one cavalry historian, "who held back their regiments' progress were gone, having been persuaded to resign, dismissed from the service, or weeded out by the officers' examining boards that sprang up throughout the army in late 1861 and early 1862. The result was a cavalry force increasingly confident of its abilities and ready — even eager — to meet in battle the vaunted cavaliers of J.E.B. Stuart."

Within the Fifth New York, officer attrition in its first year of existence appears from the record to have been quite high and must certainly have been related to a process, in one way or another, of weeding out the incompetent. As early as November 9, while camped on Staten Island, Ralph Tolles of Co. F was wondering: "I have some confidence in our officers but they are not as capable as I wish they were but they will have some chance to improve yet and I hope they will see it but whatever is to be will be[.] If it should be [my] lot to fall I know I have friends away up in Western New York who will say he tried to do his duty." Although there might be more than one factor contributing to this high attrition rate of officers, of the twelve company commanders in the regiment when it was initially formed, eight (two-thirds) were out of the service by the following December, and a ninth, Captain Thomas Coyle, "died of disease." Coyle, commanding Company D, is obviously the commander referred to by Charles Greenleaf in his letter home dated December 1861. Indeed, only two initial company commanders, Abram H. Krom and John Hammond, served until the expiration of their enlistment. Overall during its existence, thirty-six of seventy-seven men listed as officers in the regiment resigned during the war (forty-seven percent). Of these, twenty-three resigned during 1862. One can only conclude that having gone through training and seeing combat at close range, these men left a situation they were not prepared to confront, or else they were, in one way or another, convinced their services were no longer needed. However, it must be said that by the closing year of the Civil War the volunteer regiments of cavalry raised in 1861, and particularly the Fifth New York, officered overwhelmingly by competent volunteers, were considered by some in authority to be as good as any in the world. A factor in this can be illustrated by looking at the twelve company commanders, captains of the Fifth New York, when the regiment was disbanded in 1865. Of the twelve, eight had enlisted as privates in the Fifth New York in 1861 and had risen to command not merely as a result of attrition but by competence.

As the Fifth New York's unit efficiency must have improved in these initial months, there was the matter of discipline. Private William Comer of Company L was caught stealing a watch and chain from another trooper in December 1861. His sentence was the loss of one month's pay and "to be confined in the Guard Tent one month during the nights, for fourteen days of the said month to be fed on bread and water, and during all the month to report each morning to the Surgeon, for police and fatigue duty at the hospital."[27] Gradually most of these men acquired the form and look of soldiers despite their backgrounds. A trooper from another New York cavalry regiment commented on this transformation during the initial period of organization. Speaking of the Second New York Cavalry, he wrote:

We are now fairly out upon the ocean of our new life, and are beginning to feel its influence.... The very lowest stratum of life among us, such as represents the loungers in the streets and lanes of our cities,— those who have neither occupation nor culture, is amazingly influenced for the better by military discipline. These men now find themselves with something to do, and with somebody to make them do it. The progress is very slow ... but this is evidently the general tendency.... On the other hand ... our regiment is made up principally of young men from highly respectable families ... who find that the highest standard of morality presented here is much lower than they were wont to have at home, and they soon begin to waiver [*sic*].[28]

Discipline within a given volunteer regiment varied, due in part to the nature of the duties assigned to it. But primarily the degree of discipline within a given regiment, either in camp or in the field, was due in great measure to the junior officers, the lieutenants and captains, and their commitment to it. Good officers made for well-behaved commands in terms of unit discipline. Nevertheless, "cavalry units as a rule were not so well disciplined as those of other branches, owing largely to the relative independence with which they operated and a certain jaunty, devil-may-care attitude which, while possibly adding to their effectiveness in combat, had the opposite tendency in other aspects of soldiering."[29] From the record compiled over four years, it appears that the Fifth New York struck a middle ground. There were problems recorded in the documentation coming down to us, but not so many as to say the regiment suffered at all from any overall lack of discipline.

Louis Napoleon Boudrye was commissioned as chaplain of the Fifth New York and reported for duty in February 1863. Except for several months spent as a Confederate prisoner in the summer and fall of 1863, he served with the regiment through the remainder of the war. During his service he kept a war journal and, as mentioned, during the closing weeks of the war he began gathering regimental records that he would use in writing a history of the Fifth New York as soon as he got home. His work, *Historic Records of the 5th N.Y. Cavalry*, was published in the fall of 1865. Two other editions were brought out in subsequent years and these, along with his journal, are two contemporary sources of events within the regiment during its existence.

Chaplain Boudrye was born in Highgate, Vermont, in 1833, and from the age of fifteen until his twenty-first year he worked as a farm laborer, in the process migrating to Albany, New York. During these years, the French-speaking Boudrye largely educated himself and took to studying the bible. Born a Catholic, he converted to Protestantism in 1854 and became a Methodist minister. To support his wife and himself, Boudrye worked in Albany teaching French until he obtained a chaplain's commission from New York State. He traveled south to join the Fifth New York where his brother,

Charles Boudrye, was already serving as a private in Company H. On February 21, 1863, Boudrye arrived in the camp of the Fifth New York, at that time located about five miles from Fairfax, Virginia, at a place described by him as the "destroyed settlement" of Germantown.[30] In his journal, Boudrye writes primarily of himself and the daily life he lived. After this, usually, his attention in his daily writing concerns his ministering to the regiment's men and then his other duties. There is little spoken of about operations in the field, except on a few occasions. What observations he includes are clothed in the complex sentence structure of the day and colored by his deeply religious outlook. For his *Historic Records of the 5th N.Y. Cavalry*, Boudrye obviously used his wartime journal to chronicle the regiment's movements and operations, and there is slightly more detail regarding engagements. This detail, in all likelihood, came from notes of conversations he may have had with surviving participants at war's end or were written into his history as he remembered them being told to him at the time. Other than the after-action reports written by the regiment's commander, in themselves models of brevity, there is little else in which the men of the Fifth New York speak to us directly. Given this, and employing these documents along with later histories, we can follow the Fifth New York beginning when it finished its training at Camp Harris in Maryland and moved into the field in the spring of 1862.

2

Spring in the Shenandoah — 1862

> But although nearly overwhelmed with grief we do not regret his going to the defense of his country.... I have no more Sons for my country, but my nephew Edward is still with you.... We beg you to convey to Captain Wheeler and each member of his company for the special regard to our son while living and your more than generous munificence in sending home the remains without expense to us, our most heartfelt gratitude.
> — James S. Tolles to Lt. Levi Curtis, Company F, May 29, 1862, after the death of Ralph Tolles near New Market, Virginia[1]

In the wake of the defeat at Bull Run in July of 1861, President Lincoln called to Washington General George B. McClellan. Thus far in the war nothing significant had been accomplished in putting down the rebellion. The lone small exception was the limited success McClellan had had over Rebel forces in western Virginia. Lincoln was worried, apprehensive, if not desperate. Something had to be accomplished. McClellan got his mission from Lincoln. He was to train the masses of men camped around Washington and the others that would be arriving, turning them into an army, and then use that army to defeat the Confederates.

George McClellan was a complex figure who became a controversial one, one with an ego as large as the army was to command. A West Point graduate, he had left the army to become a railroad executive before returning to the colors quickly once the conflict began. McClellan carried out the training aspect of his mission through the remaining months of the year and into 1862, instilling in the army a new confidence in itself and, as a by-product, its commander. As the spring of 1862 approached, McClellan, prodded by Lincoln, settled on a plan to defeat the Confederates. The Army of the Potomac, as this force was now called, would move by water to the Virginia peninsula

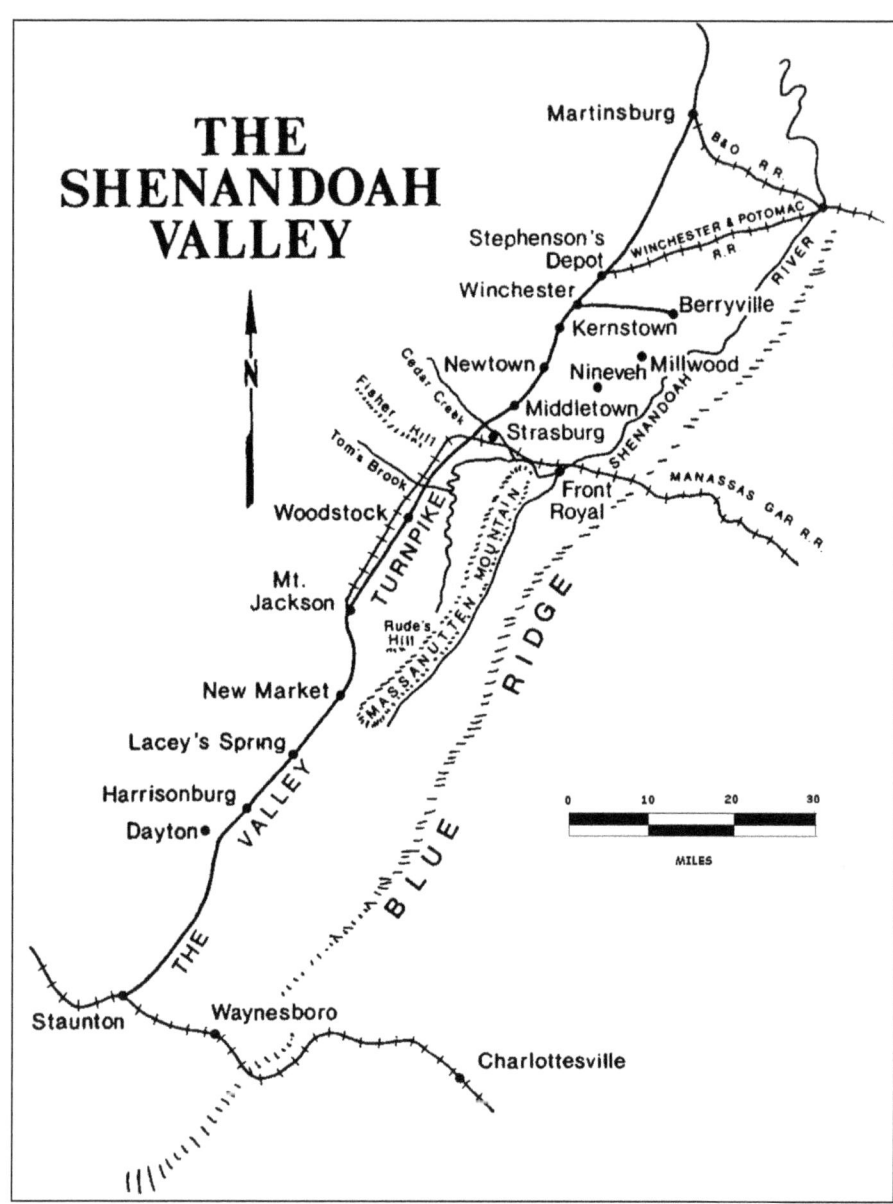

between the James and York Rivers. From there it would march on the Rebel capital, Richmond. Thus moved, McClellan's army would have about fifty miles of territory to cross before it reached and captured the Rebel capital, its flanks secured by the rivers on its right and left. From where the army stood about Washington at that time, McClellan and his men would have to advance over one hundred miles of Virginia before Richmond came into view. This territory was filled by what McClellan's intelligence sources considered a huge Rebel army and was traversed by many rivers running eastward from the Blue Ridge Mountains. In such an advance, the Rebel army would contest each river crossing, a series of fights not to McClellan's liking. Therefore, the flanking movement, the general thought, was the best way to win at least Richmond, if not the war. Whatever reservations he might have had, Lincoln approved the plan. However, always fearful of a move by the Rebels on an under-defended Washington, the president ordered that enough troops be retained in the defenses of the capital to defend the city from any Rebel thrust.

Part of the defensive force McClellan left behind near Washington was an army corps under the command of General Nathaniel Banks. Banks was a "political general," a Democrat and former speaker of the House of Representatives whose support the Republican president needed, thus his appointment by Lincoln as major general. A trooper in the Fifth New York spoke of the general when he first saw him: "I can't say as much of Banks as he looks more like some old merchant than anything else I can think of." However, beyond being a force that could ultimately join the defense of the capital, Banks was to block any threat coming from the northern exit of the Shenandoah Valley that threatened Maryland and the major supply and communication link with the west, the Baltimore and Ohio Railroad. Also, if possible, he could advance in the Shenandoah Valley and defeat General Thomas "Stonewall" Jackson, who was then leading Rebel forces in that area. This was an ambitious project for a politician turned general, but Banks did advance into the Valley and forced Jackson to abandon Winchester, the largest town in the northern Shenandoah. Troops assigned to Banks advanced and fought an engagement near Kernstown on March 23, forcing Jackson to withdraw further south. Banks followed slowly, using the macadamized road called the Valley Pike, the primary north-south artery in the Shenandoah. It was to this sub-theater of the war that the Fifth New York was assigned. The New Yorkers were ordered out of Camp Harris in Maryland on March 31, prepared for operations in the field.

In early April 1862, the Fifth New York performed various escort duties in the vicinity of Washington and between the capital and Harpers Ferry. "Until the ninth [of] April the battalions were separated from each other, and sent from one post to the other as though the authorities did not know where they were really needed." By April 16, 1862, the Fifth New York was in camp near Harpers Ferry. Captain Hammond of Company H wrote to his wife, "I think there will not be a cavalry regiment in the field so well armed as we shall be. Our regiment is now supplied entirely with McClellan saddles, Colt's pistols, Ames' sabres and the cavalry rifle. The poor horses have all been culled out, so that now all horses are A no. 1." Then on April 20, the regiment moved west and into the Shennandoah, entering Winchester, Virginia. "This was then a beautiful town. 'Grim visaged war,' with her fire and sword, had not yet desolated the fine public buildings, nor destroyed the beautiful shrubbery and foliage of the streets. But Winchester was then as rebellious and aristocratic as it was beautiful."[2] There would be three more Aprils in three more years before the troopers of the Fifth New York would finally leave Winchester for home and peace. In the Shenandoah that spring the Fifth New York joined with the First Vermont Cavalry, a unit with which it was to share many actions in the coming years. "The two regiments," wrote the historian of the First Vermont, "were after side by side ... and formed a fast friendship which outlasted the war." Also joining this new mounted command was an assortment of companies from Michigan and Maryland regiments, all under the command of General John P. Hatch.

Washington Wheeler had raised a company of volunteer cavalrymen in Wyoming County, New York, in 1861 and became its captain. The company became part of the Fifth New York the previous September while the regiment was training at Camp Scott. Captain Wheeler became an occasional correspondent to the *Western New Yorker*, and this publication printed his description of the Shenandoah dated June 14, 1862:

> This valley is without doubt the most fertile, and producing in large amount the material for the support of an army than any other section of the same area, south of Mason & Dixon line. It has a limestone base, and produces wheat of the finest quality, as well as enormous crops of clover; and, in fact, I can scarcely conceive of a country better adapted, naturally and geographically, to the successful growing of bread and wheat, than in the Valley of the Shenandoah.... The lands are owned and farmed in large tracts, as is usual in all slave holding countries, ranging from five hundred to one thousand acres, with occasional larger and smaller farms. The cultivation has hitherto been with slave labor. As near as I can estimate, 50 per cent of the slaves of those living within five miles of the main road traveled by the armies, have escaped....[3]

By this time, Banks and his command had advanced south into the area surrounding Strasburg. From Winchester on April 22, the Fifth New York marched south to Strasburg, then on to Woodstock. On April 29, the regiment was ordered on a scout and in the process captured its first prisoners. This was described in the regiment's history as "a big thing." Over the next few days, scouts were made; one, by Company A, went from Harrisonburg to Port Republic. There the company stumbled upon Rebels, part of Jackson's force, and shot it out with them before retiring. In this action, the Fifth lost its first man, Pvt. John Beaumont, captured by the Rebels.[4]

2. Spring in the Shenandoah—1862

On May 3, the regiment was ordered to Harrisonburg, where it reported to General Hatch. The town of Harrisonburg is about 30 miles south of Strasburg on the Valley Pike. By operating in this area, it is clear that Banks was actively patrolling and seeking engagement with the enemy, proactively keeping Jackson as far as possible from the extreme northern end of the valley. During this period, General Banks frequently telegraphed Washington reporting on his situation. On May 6, he reported the activities of the Fifth New York. The regiment "had a sharp skirmish with Ashby's cavalry ... near Harrisonburg. They made a succession of the most spirited charges against superior numbers, killing 10, wounding many, and capturing 6 rebels. Their conduct gave the highest satisfaction. Their chief weapon was the saber." Chaplain Boudrye gives us an account of this incident, slightly at variance with the casualties reported to Washington by Banks. On the morning May 6, the regiment was at New Market when it learned that Confederate cavalry under Colonel Turner Ashby was moving north along the pike from Harrisonburg. A detachment of the Fifth New York was ordered to respond:

> Within five miles of Harrisonburg, they encountered the redoubtable Ashby. Our men all eager for a fight, fell like a whirlwind upon the enemy, and using their sabers with terrible effect, soon scattered and turned them back in confusion. And now commenced a scrambling race. Clouds of dust arose from the road, which almost entirely enveloped both the pursued and the pursuers. Occasionally the Rebels rallied, but were swept away again, and finally chased into the suburbs of the town, badly defeated. The conflict cost them 8 men killed, 5 wounded and 7 prisoners, besides several good horses. On our side we lost Asabel A. Spencer, Co. E, killed, who was the first victim of the regiment, offered to the God of battles. William Mills, Co. I, was wounded. Sergeant Wm. H. Whitcomb, Co. M, was captured, but escaped through dint of Yankee ingenuity. "The Rebels had stripped off his arms and were using the indecorous language with which the Yankee prisoner is usually saluted," when he informed them that they had been pursued by only a dozen Yankees whom they might all capture by dashing back upon them. They charged back, were scattered, and some of them captured by our boys, and Whitcomb escaped.

This was the largest action the regiment had yet seen. The chaplain credited it as the first saber charge of the war, while the *New York Times* called it "a very gallant affair."[5]

Among those troopers in this action was Ralph Tolles. He and his cousin Edward Tolles had enlisted when Company F was formed in Wyoming County in western New York in 1861. A few days after the action with Ashby's cavalry, Ralph was accidentally shot by an unnamed trooper while the regiment was in camp. The doctors attempted treatment, but to no avail. Edward Tolles wrote to Ralph's father, "The Surgeon has just been here. He is still undecided where the ball is. Some of his symptoms are better and some war worse. Indeed

Uncle in my opinion you must be prepared for the worst." At some point later, it isn't recorded when Ralph died. Among his belongings inventoried and sent to his father was $15 in gold U.S. Treasury notes, fifteen three-cent stamps, three one-cent stamps, one pocketknife, one tobacco box and one gold pen.[6]

By May 12, Banks had been ordered to send one of his infantry divisions east of the Blue Ridge, where it was needed as part of McClellan's movement on Richmond. This reduction in combat power forced Banks to reposition his command and would eventually tilt the odds in favor of Stonewall Jackson as he contemplated regaining control of the valley.

Unknown to Banks, Stonewall Jackson was moving, planning to clear the entire valley of Yankees. He led his force, numbering about 17,000, north from near Port Republic, up the Luray Valley (a subsidiary to the Shenandoah to the east, separated from it by Massanutten Mountain). On May 15, Banks had sent from Strasburg to Front Royal an infantry regiment with two artillery pieces under a Colonel Kenly. This was to the east of Strasburg, a place from which to watch for movement in the Luray Valley and to guard against guerrilla activity in the rear of the force. When Jackson came north through the Luray Valley he could easily sweep this command aside. And this is what happened early on the morning of May 23, when Stonewall suddenly appeared near Front Royal in overwhelming numbers. By coincidence, that same day Banks had ordered forward Companies B and D of the Fifth New York to reinforce Kenly's detachment at Front Royal. Colonel De Forest designated Major Philip Vought to lead this detachment that numbered about one hundred men while the remainder of the regiment stayed in the Strasburg vicinity. Major Vought later reported, "When about 3 miles this side of the town I received a message from the colonel to hurry on with my cavalry; that he had been fighting the enemy since sunrise; that they were in large force.... I immediately ordered my baggage to the rear about a mile and put my column under a fast trot, and in less than fifteen minutes we were at the colonel's headquarters."

When Major Vought rode up he found "the colonel with his small command, less than 500 infantry, with only two pieces of artillery, on high ground about 1 mile north of the town, and being in much danger, the enemy having from 5,000 to 6,000 infantry and three pieces of artillery." The two Fifth New York companies joined with the already imperiled Union detachment in the fight. They advanced,

> but finding such a large force of the enemy behind a stone wall on my left and in a small wood on my right, I withdrew my men under the cover of a hill.... We held our position for some two hours, sent out skirmishers and checking the

2. Spring in the Shenandoah—1862

enemy on every side, when we saw a large body of cavalry, from 1,000 to 1,500, deploying out of a wood some 3 miles on the opposite side of town. We then commenced our retreat, and drew off our forces in good order across both branches of the Shenandoah, my cavalry covering the rear and setting fire to the bridges, the enemy following close on us, and wading the river — both cavalry and infantry — with perfect ease.

On the other side of the river, Vought led a fighting withdrawal but was eventually caught in a general melee with the Rebels coming at him from all sides. He ordered the mounted troopers to cut their way out and head north in the direction of Winchester. Vought's two companies were scattered with no hope of rallying. Waiting until dark hidden in some woods, he and most of his men then rode on to Winchester. Companies B and D, along with the infantry defenders of Front Royal, were for the time being lost as a cohesive fighting unit.[7]

From his written report and the testimony of Charles Greenleaf, Vought and his small command seemed to have given as good an accounting of themselves as was possible in such a situation. However, inexplicably, Major Vought resigned his commission on July 1.[8]

As for Companies B and D, they were scattered along with the others they had sought to reinforce. In a later report, Banks told the authorities in Washington that in reality the portion of the Fifth New York that was scattered at Front Royal was expected to eventually report back to him in some number once they found their way through Rebel lines. Vought reported twenty-seven troopers as casualties in this action.[9]

Meanwhile, General Banks, at Strasburg, had been alerted about the fight at Front Royal by Charles Greenleaf of Company D. Greenleaf wrote home of his exploits on May 23:

> Williamsport, Md., May 26, 1862
>
> Dear Father and Mother: You have probably heard by this time of the three days' fighting from Strasburg and Front Royal to Martinsburg. Our company and company B were ordered to Front Royal in the mountains, twelve miles from Strasburg, last Friday, and when we got within two miles of our destination we heard cannonading. The major [P.G. Vought] ordered the baggage to stop, and our two companies dashed on, and found several companies of our infantry and two pieces of artillery engaged with several thousands of the enemy. Just as we arrived on the field, Col. Kenly, who had command of our forces, rode up to me, and ordered me to take one man and the two best horses in our company, and ride for dear life to Gen. Banks' headquarters in Strasburg for reeforcement. The direct road to Strasburg was occupied by the enemy, so I was obliged to ride around by another, seventeen miles. I rode the seventeen miles in fifty-five minutes. Gen. Banks did not seem to think it was very serious, but ordered one regiment of infantry and two pieces of artillery off. I asked Gen. Banks for a fresh

horse to rejoin my company, and he gave me the best horse I ever rode, and I started back. I came out on the Front Royal turnpike, about two miles this side of where I left our men. Saw two men standing in the road, and their horses standing by the fence. I supposed they were our pickets.

They did not halt me, so I asked them if they were pickets. They said no. Says I, "Who are you?" "We are part of Gen. Jackson's staff." I supposed they were only joking. I laughed, and asked them where Jackson was. They said he was in the advance. I left them and rode toward Front Royal, till I overtook a soldier, and asked him what regiment he belonged to. He said he belonged to the Eighth Louisiana. I asked how large a force they had, and the reply was "twenty thousand." I turned back and drew my revolver, expecting either a desperate fight or a southern jail; but the officers in the road did not stop me, and I was lucky enough not to meet any of their pickets. But if it was not a narrow escape, then I don't know what is. When I got out of the enemy's lines, I rode as fast as the horse could carry me to Gen. Banks, and reported what I had seen and heard. He said I saved the army.

In less than an hour the whole army was in motion toward Winchester. After I left Front Royal to take the dispatch to Strasburg, our two companies of cavalry, who were covering the retreat of infantry and baggage, were attacked on three sides by about three thousand of the enemy's cavalry. Our boys fought like devils, till nearly half of them were killed or wounded, and then retreated to Winchester. Capt. White, William Watson, Henry Appleby, and nine or ten men of my company are killed or taken. William Marshall is all right, except a slight sabre cut in the shoulder.

We had a fight at Winchester, got licked and retreated.... We rode all the way from Winchester to Martinsburg, with cannon shot and shell flying around us faster than it did at Bull Run. We crossed the Potomac last night [May 25]. It was so dark that we could not find the ford, and had to swim our horses across....

The regiment's history says that when the retreat finally ended on the north bank of the Potomac River, many of the men of the Fifth were "discouraged" and took "*French* furloughs." Some of these men probably never returned to the regiment.[10]

Having been warned for a second time, Banks now could see what Jackson was attempting. By moving on Winchester from the Luray Valley, Stonewall could now cut the Valley Pike, which was Banks's supply line as well as his line of retreat. The Union forces would therefore be isolated from any support and defeated in detail. Immediately after hearing from Charles Greenleaf a second time, Banks ordered his outnumbered force onto the road, headed north. It was to be a race to Winchester.

Colonel De Forest, with the remainder of the Fifth New York and other cavalry detachments in and around Strasburg, was ordered to cover the rear of Banks's retreating force and escort those wagons that were loaded and could move. Colonel De Forest reported that the next day, May 24, on orders from

Banks, he had all the Federal supplies that could not be moved from Strasburg burned. Moving north out of town with a wagon train of supplies, De Forest soon found that the Rebels were already between his command and Banks's retreating force, with stragglers retreating toward Strasburg. "After a hasty consultation," De Forest wrote, it was decided "to try and rejoin the main body by a mountain road on the west of the pike." With the regiment, and elements of several others, De Forest headed generally for Winchester. The movement had to have been slow with thirty-five wagons of supplies rescued from Strasburg. The next day and the next, De Forest moved west and north. Finally, as they were approaching Winchester from the western side of town, John Hammond, sending out scouts, reported the enemy in force on the Valley Pike. De Forest bypassed Winchester and set out in the direction of Martinsburg. Getting there, he found that town surrounded by Rebels. Moving further west still, the regiment and accompanying wagons searched for a ford on the Potomac. One was eventually found for the mounted troops, and although it was shoulder-deep, the command crossed to the Maryland side. The wagon train had to drive further west to Hancock and was there ferried across the Potomac. Once over the river and safe from the enemy, the regiment moved to Williamsport. There had been no casualties on the eighty-four mile retreat and only three wagons had to be abandoned. In his report to Banks, General Hatch, De Forest's superior, took note of the Fifth New York and its commander. "I cannot with justice close the report without mentioning with praise Colonel De Forest, of the Fifth New York Cavalry, who by his energy saved a large train."[11]

It was during this retreat, on May 24, that John Hammond, then captain of Company H, with eight or ten men, came upon a small group of Rebels. The New Yorkers gave chase and a running gunfight ensued. Hammond rode up behind one of the Rebels and tried to pull the man off his horse by his coat collar. Both horses became tangled and went down with Hammond and the Rebel struggling on the ground. When one of his men rode up, Hammond ordered the trooper to shoot the Rebel he was trying to subdue. The shot grazed the man's head but was enough to make him surrender.[12]

The race between Banks and Jackson to Winchester was a closely run affair, with the Union commander and his troops getting there just ahead of Jackson's "foot cavalry." Jackson hit Banks at Winchester on May 25 and what ensued was a rout. Scattered elements of Banks's command made for the Potomac. Jackson chased them but his men were exhausted from marching the length of the valley, and the Yankees were able to reach the Potomac and get across to Maryland at Williamsport. The Fifth New York, once across the river and discouraged at being thrown out of the Shenandoah, caught its breath while getting ready for the next move.[13]

Reunited on the Maryland side of the river, the Fifth New York didn't re-cross until May 31. Moving in two columns to the Virginia side, the regiment advanced to Martinsburg before encountering Rebels. That day the regiment captured a wagon, weapons and ammunition, and several prisoners. On June 4, advancing, the regiment again entered Winchester and Jackson marched his men south. For most of the remainder of June, the Fifth New York, along with the rest of the cavalry under General Hatch, cautiously probed south and occasionally encountered the Rebels. Generally, the Yankee cavalrymen retired when encountering Rebels in strength. By this time, Banks's army was part of the three-pronged effort to trap Stonewall and his men in the Valley. The plan had been concocted in Washington and might have worked if the three elements had moved quickly. But despite prodding telegrams from President Lincoln to the generals involved, none of the three thrusts could be brought to bear in unison and defeat Jackson's hard-fighting command. Soon Jackson and his Army of the Valley got itself over the Blue Ridge and rejoined the Confederate forces that were now struggling with McClellan's Army of the Potomac on the peninsula before Richmond.

Most of the stories and headlines in Northern papers during the summer months of 1862 were generally given over to the activities of McClellan and his army on the peninsula. For the Fifth New York these weeks in the summer and into the fall were mostly spent on the move, scouting and patrolling, fighting any number of spirited skirmishes with their counterparts on the Rebel side. Boudrye's history of this period is a chronicle of marches and fights at places with names, now mostly on the east side of the Blue Ridge, that are both familiar and unfamiliar to those acquainted with the war during this time. General Hatch had been ordered to move his cavalry over the Blue Ridge and south to Gordonsville. There he would attempt to cut the railroad coming east from the Shenandoah Valley that was a principal supply line to the Confederates about Richmond. Although no direct mention is made of this small campaign in Boudrye's history, he does give examples of what the Fifth New York was doing during this period. One of the chaplain's entries for July 1862, relates that the regiment was

> advancing on Culpepper [sic] Court House on the twelfth [July], where it had a skirmish with the enemy, drove them through the town and captured fifteen prisoners. The sixteenth the boys enjoyed an all-day march through an all-day rain, to Rapidan Ford. The next day they marched into Orange Court House, expelling, after a short skirmish, the enemy that was in town. Being the first Union troops that had ever visited this place, they were objects of excited obser-

2. Spring in the Shenandoah—1862

vation. But to the intense satisfaction of the people, they left on the eighteenth and returned to Rapidan Ford. While on Picket at Bernett's Ford, a large portion of Company A was captured."

Captain Wheeler of Company F wrote to the *Western New Yorker* his impressions of the area to the east of the Blue Ridge and of the area around Culpeper Court House on July 18, 1862:

> Culpepper [sic] Court House is the shire-town of Culpepper [sic] county, lying just east of the Blue Ridge contains probably 800 inhabitants, black and white. All of these villages in Virginia bear an entirely different appearance from towns of the same character in the loyal States. The buildings are mostly of stone or brick, and the lines between town and country clearly defined. The country through which we have passed, lying on the eastern slope of the mountains, is of the poorest land, and improvements not to be compared with those in the valley of the Shenandoah. There is one thing that strikes the observer, without exception and that is the entire absence of all able-bodied men. The whole day may be occupied with a march, and you will fail to see the first man capable of bearing arms.

Wheeler continues his letter for a few more sentences before saying, "But I must close, as I have just received an order, 'to horse' for a reconnaissance towards Gordonsville, and I have no time to spare."

With the First Michigan cavalry and two infantry regiments, General Hatch was now making an attempt to cut the rail line coming east from the Shenandoah. The Fifth New York was part of this effort, riding for several days in heavy rain, skirmishing with Rebel cavalry elements. In one incident, already noted by Chaplain Boudrye, twenty men from Company A were captured. The operation failed to accomplish its goal of cutting the railroad. When he returned, Captain Wheeler penned a summary for the *Western New Yorker* that was printed the following month: "We arrived safely in camp, the 1st Michigan having lost twenty men, and the 5th New York twenty-eight, taken prisoners, or missing. I lost no men, having pains to keep my men from straggling. At this time we first learned that our expedition was unsatisfactory 'to the man whose headquarters are in the saddle' and a new expedition ordered."[14]

In a long passage in his history, Boudrye chronicles the regiment's movements during these weeks:

> During the remainder of July no force of the enemy was encountered, but the regiment was almost constantly on the march, having passed and bivouacked by the following places:— Sperryville, Woodville, Culpepper [sic] Court House, James City, Wolftown, and into the Luray Valley, by way of Swift Run Gap, to Luray, Woodville again, and back to Culpepper [sic] Court House near which

they bivouacked until the 1st of August. On this day they marched to Raccoon Ford. At this place was encountered quite a force of cavalry, under Gen. Crawford, preparatory to an important movement. During the month Gen. Hatch was removed from the command of the cavalry in this department. Gen. John Buford succeeding him.[15]

Failure to cut the railroad coming east from the Blue Ridge to Gordonsville was one of the reasons given for relieving Hatch. Another explanation speaks of Hatch being ordered back into the Shenandoah with his brigade to rip up the railroad leaded west to Staunton. A trooper in the Second New York Cavalry recalled, "He [Hatch] commenced the movement; but after passing through the narrow defiles of the mountains at Swift Run Gap, he felt that there was no hope of accomplishing any thing, and returned. General Pope immediately relieved him from command, and appointed General John Buford ... in this place."[16] Now the Fifth New York would be part of John Buford's cavalry, a leader from this era who has come down to us in the record as one of the finest commanders, cavalry or infantry, in the Civil War.

There was an intense fight on August 2, when the regiment returned to Orange Court House. The brigade, including the Fifth New York, was in this action commanded by General Samuel W. Crawford, an infantry commander Boudrye's history of the regiment contains the following account, probably the recollection of one of the participants and reworked by the chaplain:

> Gen. Crawford with the 1st Vermont, 1st Michigan and the 5th New York advanced at an early hour to reconnoiter the force and position of the enemy about Orange Court House. Scarcely a Rebel appeared until the column approached the town. Without opposition the advance entered the town, whose streets they found deserted, while a stillness like that of death seemed to reign all around. But suddenly volley after volley broke the stillness, and proclaimed the presence of a heavy force of the enemy. On reaching the suburbs of the town, a strong flanking party, consisting of Cos. G and H, under command of Capt. Hammond, was ordered around to the left toward the Gordonsville road, whither they dashed off with spirit, under their gallant leader.
>
> The main column encountered a heavy charge of the enemy in the street, which, at first, drove our fellows back a little. Rallying from the first shock, they now dashed back upon the enemy, and a fierce conflict from pistols and carbines followed. Shots flew in every direction, killing horses and men alike. The fight was furious in the narrow streets; and just as the enemy's column began to waver, Capt. Hammond, who had fought the enemy at the depot, and was now partially surrounded, with drawn sabres charged upon the rebels in his front, crying as he flew forward, 'Give them your hardware, boys!' ... The enemy could not stand these 'hardware' dealers, and fled in the utmost confusion, leaving their dead and badly wounded in our hands.... Fifty prisoners were captured...."[17]

2. Spring in the Shenandoah—1862 39

The *New York Tribune* carried a report of this engagement two days later, headlining: "Our troops attacked and surrounded by rebel cavalry, routed of the latter with terrible slaughter." The story continued:

Two hundred of the 5th New York Cavalry and 300 of the 1st Vermont went on a reconnoisance from Culpepper [sic] Court Hours to Orange Court House, 17 miles. They left at 3 o'clock in the afternoon on Saturday last, encamped at night near Racoon [sic] Ford. Early the next morning the march was resumed, driving in the enemy's pickets. About 1 o'clock, while marching into the town they were attacked by the enemy, about 600 strong, surrounding our men on all sides. After two hours severe fighting our force drove them from the town, killing between 30 and 40 — 21 of their dead lying in one street — wounding between 50 and 60, and taking 43 prisoners, among them one major, two captains and two lieutenants.

The Union party were commanded by Brigadier-General Crawford in person. The enemy were Ashby's Cavalry. Col. Robinson, Co. G and Co. H of the 5th N.Y. Cavalry captured nearly the whole of them. Many of the prisoners were badly wounded by sabre cuts.

The Major would not surrender, when he was struck a terrible sabre blow on the top of his head. One of the captains had one of his ears cut off. The prisoners are now in Culpepper [sic] Court House. The enemy had every advantage over us in position. The following are the names of the killed and wounded of the 5th, Ira Harris:_____Cooley, chief bugler, killed; Lieut. Gear, shoulder; Sergeant Clough, stomach, mortal; Private Quinn, eye; Corporal A. Morris, Co. B; Archibald Frazer, Quartermaster's Sergeant. Three others were slightly wounded, but could not learn their names.

In the Vermont regiment five or six were wounded.

With each day spent in the field, the Fifth New York was gaining confidence in itself. The affair at Orange Court House had been the biggest action the regiment had been in to date. "This engagement clearly proved our superiority over the enemy's cavalry, which, in this instance, consisted of their best Virginia regiments lately under Col. Ashby." So Chaplain Boudrye wrote after hearing stories from veterans of the regiment. They were becoming a hardened, aggressive and confident outfit.[18] In particular Colonel De Forest and Captain Hammond had been singled out as competent combat leaders.

General McClellan and his Army of the Potomac had, by this time, been bottled up on the Virginia peninsula by Confederate forces. After his initial landing on the peninsula, McClellan had led his forces in a sluggish advance toward Richmond, giving the Rebel considerable time to plan defensively. The wounding of Confederate General Joseph E. Johnson in fighting before the capital in June brought General Robert E. Lee to command of the defense. General Lee was as aggressive in defense as McClellan was deliberate in offense. Not waiting for the blow to fall, in July Lee attacked. There followed a series of battles known as the Seven Days. Despite the severe bleeding inflicted on the Rebels after seven battles in seven days, Lee and his men had pushed the Army of the Potomac away from the immediate vicinity of the capital.

At the end of the Seven Days, McClellan had become so impotent his army was now huddled in an enclave on the James River under the protection of the Navy's guns. He had all but ceased to be an offensive threat. And this timidity was seen in both Washington and at Lee's headquarters. McClellan's army, as it stood, was doing nothing and was ordered to abandon the peninsula and return to Northern Virginia. McClellan proved as slow in re-deploying his force as he had been in moving on Richmond. The aggressive General Lee moved first. Lee would move against the army that General John Pope had deployed to advance in what was supposed to have been the second crushing force — along with McClellan's — descending on Richmond from the north. The plan concocted by Pope was for him to move on Richmond from northern Virginia while McClellan advanced up the peninsula. In theory, Lee would have to fight on two fronts to save the city. But with McClellan bottled up and showing no sign of offensive movement, Lee had latitude to maneuver against Pope. The army under Pope was mainly composed of the troops left to defend Washington and the Shenandoah and the Fifth New York Cavalry, in July and August, was now part of the forces under General Pope.

General Lee, now in overall command, sent Stonewall Jackson and his corps toward Pope. The result would be a battle at Cedar Mountain that would force a Union retreat back to the vicinity of Manassas.

The regiment continued its movements, scouting and reconnaissance, but in the process was slowly falling back to the Rapidan in the face of Jackson's advance against Pope. "From Wolftown to Stannards on the [August] 7th we formed a line of pickets; and on the 9th was fought the memorable battle of Cedar or Slaughter Mountain. Only a few of the regiment were engaged in this battle, one of those being killed."[19] As Jackson maneuvered against Pope after Cedar Mountain, the regiment's history sees the command at nearly a different place with each entry. For August 23, the regiment was at Warrenton and on the next day, August 24, was at Waterloo Bridge. There was a "severe engagement. Our men suffered from the Rebel batteries which were brought to bear upon them. During the fight a shell took effect in our ranks killing instantly three horses belonging to the three officers of Co. I...." So noted Chaplain Boudrye in his regimental history. Quartermaster Sergeant of Company G, John Tribe, was awarded the Medal of Honor for his actions at Waterloo Bridge that day. The citation merely stated that Tribe, from Oswego in Tioga County, "voluntarily assisted in the burning and destruction of the bridge under heavy fire of the enemy."

The Fifth New York continued scouting and picketing when not chasing or skirmishing with various Rebel cavalry commands. On August 27, something new was ordered. Three companies were detailed as orderlies and escort for General Samuel P. Heintzelman, one of McClellan's subordinates, whose command had been ordered up from the James River to reinforce Pope. One company escorted General Banks and the remainder of the regiment became the escort for Pope as he moved his headquarters back to the north, a movement designed to counter Jackson's maneuvering.[20]

Two days after the Fifth New York became escorts and orderlies, there was another clash on a familiar field. "To-day commenced what has generally been known as the second Battle of Bull Run, better named Groverton. The Rebels were in overwhelming force, driving Gen. Pope before them. Our lines fell back, and on the 30th the conflict was renewed on the field of the first Bull Run. The field though hotly contested, was again won by the enemy, and though not panic-stricken we were compelled to retreat. Gradually on the 31st our forces fell back toward Washington." The Fifth New York during the battle had heard the guns but played no role other than acting as messenger and rounding up stragglers. Captain Wheeler wrote home of the only action the Fifth saw in the battle:

> I was near the rear of the column and approaching the head, when the whizzing of another round shot made me duck my head involuntarily, and I cast my eyes towards the company, having a presentiment of evil. A cloud of dust and a riderless horse told the tale. I gave an order to move the company close under the brow of a hill near by, and dismounted 4 men with orders to go and ascertain the amount of injury. They returned with the body of John H. Claus, of Hume, both arms having been cut off by the ball above the elbow. Life was almost extinct. He was leaning forward with both hands on the pommel of the saddle, when the ball struck him. We left the body on the field, after a fruitless attempt at burial, and the march was resumed.

By September 5, the regiment was camped at Arlington House, within sight of the Capitol. Wheeler of Company F had a lot to say about the Second Battle of Bull Run and none of it would concede defeat. But of more interest is his impression of the enemy that had just driven Pope back to the Potomac. Under a flag of truce to tend to the wounded and dead on the Bull Run battlefield, Wheeler had an opportunity for observation:

> Troops [of the Army of Northern Virginia] were constantly passing us in the road and I had a good opportunity to judge their condition. They fight exceedingly well and though they are not well dressed, yet there is an air of cheerfulness and determination in their appearance, that will naturally excite surprise. Many were barefooted and ragged, yet they were active in their movements and all apparently governed by one idea, and that of securing their independence. The

troops from the extreme south are the most vindictive and have the most of the braggart about them.

And then, in an effort perhaps to encourage the folks at home, Wheeler goes on, "Our troops fought bravely, and it was truly inspiring to see with what energy and determination they met the enemy pressing upon them in overwhelming numbers.... Our army is composed of brave men, willing to brave anything and dare all, but we must have a leader, a head in which we have confidence." Washington Wheeler had been promoted to major on July 1, but inexplicably, he resigned his commission on September 26, nineteen days after his last communication with the *Western New Yorker*.[21]

Boudrye says nothing in his history about the Antietam Campaign other than that a "memorable battle" was fought there. It is to be assumed that the Fifth New York remained within the defenses of Washington during most of September while the action and the armies shifted north and west into Maryland. For the period from September 1 through the first week of October the regiment's history has nothing to say. For October 8, it records only that "Lt. Col. Johnstone with one hundred and ten men went out with the brigade on a reconnoissance [sic] to the Rappahanock [sic], returning, without meeting the enemy on the 11th."[22]

By early September, McClellan's entire army had been transported up from the peninsula, and he relieved Pope after the defeat at the Second Bull Run. General Lee was advancing on Maryland, and McClellan began moving, cautiously, in reaction, with his and what had been Pope's army. The maneuvering would culminate in the Battle of Antietam, the bloodiest single-day engagement of the entire Civil War, and one during which there was no significant cavalry action. From the sketchy record for this period it appears the Fifth New York was part of the defensive force shielding the capital, doing its duty of picketing and scouting. Historian Stephen Z. Starr has provided a summation of the situation the Fifth New York found itself in at this moment: "At the beginning of September 1862, the exhausted and nearly unhorsed Federal cavalry was back in the defenses of Washington, which it had left with high ambitions and high hopes in March and April, but it was not the same cavalry it had been. A little of the amateurishness, a little of the ineptness, had worn off, and a modest degree of professional skill was beginning to show itself."[23]

Even before the summer's campaigning was over, some cavalrymen were beginning to wonder where all the riding, the fighting and the movement of so many men might lead. The Fifth New York had seen its first action and had taken its first casualties, and it seemed longer than a mere few months since it had come to the seat of war. By July of 1862, and for a multitude of reasons, the strength of the regiment had been reduced to a critical point, in John Hammond's estimation. Also, an element of frustration related to what had been happening around the command began to creep into his thoughts. It was a year since the defeat at the Battle of Bull Run, a large and trained Union army was now in the field, and as yet nothing seemed to have been accomplished — other than the creation of a long casualty list — in putting down the rebellion. Hammond wrote home on July 22, 1862:

> We must have more men; our regiment had not been recruited at all. The force of our cavalry companies is very much reduced in numbers. They certainly have not more than one-half what they had when they crossed the Potomac.... It looks bad for our cause, and a bold policy and vigorous effort must be made at once or the rebels will never be brought back to their allegiance. My hope now is, since Congress has adjourned, that Old Abe will push matters to extremity. We must have more men and more heart in the matter. There are many good and true men in the field, men who feel that they have a duty to perform for their government and for the cause of freedom, but even they are getting almost disgusted with the apathy of our people.

Some days later Hammond's frustrations surface again in another letter: "Will not our people come forward and fill up out regiment? We are weak in numbers. No praise of human tongue can do justice to the rank and file of those men now left to stem the current of almost constant defeats. These are unworthy leaders, but the men are ever ready and eager to renew the conflict." By December of 1862 there had been a Second Battle of Bull Run, a Union defeat, and the Battle of Antietam in Maryland, a drawn contest that had at least compelled Robert E. Lee to retire back into Virginia. John Hammond's darkened spirits, his frustration, still made their way into his letters, but appeared abbreviated possibly because he didn't want his feelings to depress those at home. On December 7, he included in a letter to the family: "As a rule I am the one sent to face the enemy and do all the detail work.... I came here, or into the service, for a purpose, and want to do all I can to accomplish it, and return to my own matters." A month later, on January 4, Hammond adds this to another letter: "When will we ever get at the rebels and crush them, as we ought to have done before this."[24]

The Fifth New York spent the remainder of 1862 as they had since they had crossed the Potomac in April in scouting and reconnaissance and picket duty. Indeed, picket duty could be an element feeding John Hammond's frustration during the latter half of the year; it simply didn't seem rewarding to stand guard out in the countryside when the force should "get at the rebels and crush them." During the final three months of the year, the Fifth New York visited practically every place name on the map of northern Virginia. There was even a brief excursion back into the Shenandoah Valley and an action there on November 29 that captured several Rebel officers, thirty-two men and some supply wagons. In this action, the regiment captured its first battle flag from the enemy. Typical of this period is the comment from trooper Hiram H. Earl, writing from Chantilly, Virginia: "I was in a charge the 21 [of December] on the Plains of Manasas [sic]. We gained the day and did not lose a man. I like it well it was the first that I had been in and I hope that we will have a chance at them once more. We expect to be sent back to Washington this week and if we are we will be in the City this winter. It is nice wether hear [sic] now and if we stay hear I hope it will be so this winter."

But it would not be so. It was winter, cold, wet and snowy. The enemy now wasn't the Army of Northern Virginia that General Lee had taken back behind the Rappahannock River, but guerrillas and the hazards of duty on the picket line, where it was cold and the cavalrymen struggled continually to keep warm. The regiment would establish its winter camp at a place called Germantown, a few miles west of Fairfax Court House.[25]

3

In the Defenses of Washington — 1863

> I take the liberty of recommending to your notice the officers and men who so gallantly repulsed and totally destroyed this rebel force, and in particular I would mention Colonel De Forest, Major Hammond, Captain Krom, Captain Penfield, Captain McMaster, and Lieutenants Munson and McBride, of the Fifth New York Cavalry.[1]
> — Report of Gen. Julius Stahl, May 5, 1863

The new year, 1863, saw the Army of the Potomac in winter quarters along the line of the Rappahannock River, facing the Rebels across the water. This army was now under the command of General Ambrose Burnside, who had been ordered into command after Lincoln dismissed McClellan in the wake of Antietam and his unambitious pursuit of Lee from Maryland, a pursuit Lincoln believed could have finished the Army of Northern Virginia. General Lee and his army had returned to positions behind the Rappahannock after the Antietam Campaign and General Burnside had followed, advancing to the north side of the river. From there the new army commander began planning an offensive. In December 1862, Burnside attacked Lee in his positions at Fredericksburg, Virginia. The Army of the Potomac was badly beaten in an ill-conceived frontal assault lacking even a semblance of stealth. The army under Burnside had to cross the Rappahannock under fire and then assail head-on the enemy in what was probably the strongest defensive position Lee's army ever held. The result was a blood bath rivaling Antietam. Once over the pontoon bridges engineers had put across the river, regiment after regiment had marched toward Lee's defensive line, uphill, against an unremitting hail of shells, canister and small arms fire. The utter futility of it all was clear to everyone, even Burnside. The Army of the Potomac retreated back over the river, its morale badly eroded, and sorely needing rest and refit. Rest and refit could be obtained by going into winter camp in the area surrounding Falmouth, Virginia.

Throughout the late fall and into the new year, the Fifth New York Cavalry was stationed in the defensive perimeter around Washington. Germantown, Virginia, would become their base, and they installed themselves there on January 10, along with the Eighteenth Pennsylvania and First West Virginia Cavalry. Quickly, the men started cutting pine trees and stacking logs to make crude shelters to keep out of the winter weather.

The Fifth New York was well settled into its winter routine when its new chaplain, Louis N. Boudrye, arrived for duty. He had left his home in Kinderhook, New York, on February 16, headed for Virginia and his volunteer assignment with the cavalry. With apparently no training whatsoever, but having previously known some of the volunteers in the regiment, Boudrye was to see to the spiritual needs of the Fifth's troopers and help in any other way the command saw fit. "I am going to do what I can for the interest of my bleeding country," was how he put it in the first entry in the journal he would keep through the war.[2] The chaplain had spent two days seeing the sights in Washington before taking a train to Fairfax Station, where he was met by his brother Charles Boudrye "with a horse for me to ride to camp, a distance of about 5 miles."[3]

"Mud, mud, mud! Over hills, through valleys, by abandoned and occupied encampments, we came to a region every inch of which is sacred with the blood of our countrymen, and rendered historical by many a battle.... At about 4½ we reached camp, situated not for from a destroyed settlement called 'Germantown,' on a pine-covered knoll. I was greeted very cordially by the boys I knew and very courteously by Major Hammond, Commanding Officer and other officers." Besides learning his duties and visiting with the sick and those in the guardhouse, one of Boudrye's first recorded impressions is of the food available to the Fifth New York at this time: "Our food consists of salt pork, hard tack, soft bread and coffee. Now and then we get molasses. We can buy butter at 40 cts. per lb. Occasionally fresh beef and potatoes are furnished the soldiers." And improving his quarters was a priority for which he had to ride into the countryside "to find lumber for the flooring of my tent and other arrangements. This was found by tearing down a deserted negro house in the rear of Chantilly mansion."[4] The chaplain, like all the Fifth's troopers, would quickly become a veteran at making as comfortable as possible "arrangements" for himself.

The principal activity for the regiment this winter was picket duty that was rotated through each regiment usually on twenty-four hours shifts. Out in the countryside, a line of picket posts, or videttes, would be established, each within mutually supporting distance of the other. Usually these posts were hidden from the view of any prying enemy eyes, but located so as to observe any enemy movement on roads or across open country. Behind this line a general reserve was stationed, usually about a mile to the rear and ready to come to the support of any post coming under attack. The troopers at the videttes would be rotated at two-hour intervals back to the reserve area, where they could enjoy the warmth of a fire and some hot coffee. Like life in camp, it was wet and cold duty.

The primary concern while on vidette in northern Virginia was to guard against guerrilla raids by the notorious partisan leader Captain John Mosby, whose men were mostly natives of the state's northern counties

Louis N. Boudrye, chaplain of the Fifth New York from 1863 until the regiment was disbanded in July 1865 (Massachusetts Commandery, Military Order of the Loyal Legion, U.S. Army Military History Institute).

and quite familiar with the countryside and its obscure paths and byways. Mosby was charged with causing general confusion in the Union rear, raiding to capture horses, killing Yankees and disrupting the supply lines supporting the Army of the Potomac further to the south along the Rappahannock. During this winter every trooper in the defenses of the capital knew the name Mosby. And it was practically certain a promotion, furlough or both awaited the man who eventually killed him. On March 9, 1863, Mosby launched the boldest raid of that winter. Boudrye recorded it in his journal:

This morning about 4½, our camp was aroused by a messenger from Fairfax C.H. who announced that shortly before, a force of Rebels under Capt. Moseby [*sic*], numbering about 50 men, made an attack upon our Brigade Hdq'trs there; took Brig. Gen. Stoughton and staff prisoners, the Post Master and ransacked the mail, also Capt. Barker of our Regt. and others to the number of about 30. After destroying some military stores, and stealing about 50 of the best horses they could find, they made their escape, but the direction they took was not fully known. A large scouting party of our Regt., commanded by Maj. Hammond was immediately prepared and ere the sun shone upon us, they gave pursuit to the enemy.... Finally about 4 P.M., the return of our scouts without having accomplished the object of their search. This is one of the most disgraceful incidents for us, which had occurred for a long time.[5]

Colonel John Mosby, Rebel raider, partisan and the man most wanted by the Fifth New York (Library of Congress).

3. In the Defenses of Washington—1863

It was more disgraceful than Boudrye knew at the time. Only later, in the regimental history, did he provide the answer as to how Mosby could penetrate the brigade picket line and raid its headquarters:

> About three o'clock A.M., Mosby and his gang, led by Sergeant J.F. Ames, formerly of company L, of this regiment, having safely passed by the pickets, entered Fairfax Court House. Without scarcely firing a shot, they captured fifty fine horses and about thirty prisoners, including Brig. Gen. Stoughton, and Capt. Barker, Fifth New York Cavalry.... Such a raid, five or six miles within our lines, resulting in such heavy loss to us, reflects very uncreditably upon some of our military leaders, while it shows how wily a foe we have to contend with. It is thought that not a few of the inhabitants of the region are more or less engaged in the business of giving Mosby important information, which lays the foundation for his success.

In a footnote in the text, Boudrye comments about Sergeant Ames: "Ames, after deserting to Mosby, was called Big Yankee. He became efficient for the Rebels and was finally killed." The regimental roster has James F. Ames as enlisting as a corporal in Company M on October 29, 1861, in New York City. He deserted on February 10, 1863.[6]

Mosby liked the bold, spectacular move, and for the rest of the war he was successful in diverting cavalry units from combat against conventional Rebel forces. Instead, they were detailed to chase his band of guerrillas about northern Virginia. For most of February 1863, the Fifth New York had moved about northern Virginia scouting, doing picket duty and, although not specifically mentioned in the record, looking for Mosby. On February 25, the Eighteenth Pennsylvania was on picket when Mosby attacked them. The command's picket reserve was captured, about twenty troopers and thirty horses. The next day one hundred and fifty men from the Fifth New York were sent scouting, no doubt trying to find where the guerrillas had gone. In the following days excursions to Bealeton Station and Falmouth, and one to Aldie, failed to find anything. It seems that the guerrilla leader was lying low after his expedition against the Eighteenth Pennsylvania.

But he resumed his offensive on the fateful night of March 9, certainly the most publicized exploit of his career. As Mosby relates the episode in his *Memoirs*, he obtained the help in the expedition from James F. Ames of the Fifth New York, the Big Yankee referred to in Boudrye's history. As Mosby relates, "After a few weeks of partisan life, I meditated a more daring enterprise than any I had attempted and fortunately received aid from an unexpected quarter. A deserter from the Fifth New York Cavalry, named Ames, came to me. He was a sergeant in his regiment and came in full uniform. I never cared to inquire what his grievance was. The account he gave me of the distribution of troops and the gaps in the picket lines coincided with what I knew and tended to prepossess me in his favor."[7] Mosby and his men were suspicious that Sergeant Ames was sent among them to lure raiders into some kind of trap. To test his sincerity, Mosby decided to send Ames back to the Fifth New York to obtain a horse. Mosby sent one of his dismounted men with Ames and a couple of days later they returned from the Fifth New York's camp on horses. While on this mission, Ames told the man he was with, James Williamson, he had deserted because of Lincoln's Emancipation Proclamation. He had joined the fight for the Union and had left the cause because he now saw the war as one fought for the Negro. As a result of this mission, Ames was conditionally accepted into the guerrilla band but remained unarmed.

The next raid was apparently the one against the Eighteenth Pennsylvania where many horses were captured. Mosby was pursued by Colonel Percy Wyndham, presumably with the brigade that he commanded and which, at this time, included the Fifth New York. This is probably the expedition that Boudrye says took the Fifth New York to Bealeton Station on February 27.[8] The next "daring enterprise" decided on by Mosby was the famous one involving the capture of General Edward H. Stoughton. In an article written years before he published his *Memoirs*, Mosby tells a tale that is slightly at variance with the with one related above as concerns Sergeant Ames of the Fifth New York. Mosby's object in this rendering is the capture of Colonel Percy Wyndham, the brigade commander, as well as horses. And Ames had already told Mosby that his reason for deserting to him was the Emancipation Proclamation. However, Mosby adds, "I always suspected that it was some personal wrong he had suffered. He seemed to be animated by the most vindictive hatred for his former comrades. I felt an instinctive confidence in his sincerity which he never betrayed."[9]

Near midnight on March 9, Mosby advanced in misty weather to within range of the pickets at Chantilly, five or six miles from Fairfax Court House. Sergeant Ames led Mosby unseen past the pickets and the cavalry camped in the Centerville area and on to Fairfax Court House, entering the town along the rail line. Luckily for Colonel Wyndham, he had gone to Washington earlier and was out of danger, but not General Stoughton, an infantry brigade commander headquartered in the town. Mosby's men quietly went through the town picking up sleeping soldiers and guards, plus all the horses they could find, and cutting the telegraph lines. Among those captured was a Captain Elmer J. Barker, temporarily assigned to Wyndham's brigade staff. Barker had been Ames's captain while in the Fifth New York and the deserter introduced him, no doubt smiling, to Mosby. Then it was on to the house where General Stoughton was sleeping. With a loud knock on the door, Mosby aroused the general's staff, and on being asked who was there, he replied, "Fifth New York Cavalry with a dispatch for General Stoughton." The door was open and the staff captured. Upstairs the general was rudely awakened with a slap on his posterior and told to dress. With about three times as many prisoners as he had men, Mosby rode quietly out of town. But this was not before an attempt was made to capture Lt. Colonel Robert Johnstone, temporarily in command of the brigade in Wyndham's absence, and the then current commander of the Fifth New York. According to Mosby, Johnstone, awakened by the noise in the street, called from an upstairs window of the house he was using, asking why there was so much cavalry moving about at that late hour. Mosby ordered some men into the house to take Johnstone. Inside, they encounter the lieutenant colonel's wife, who "met them in the hall and held her ground like a lioness to give her husband time to escape." Mosby's men retreated before the lioness as Johnstone escaped into the nearby countryside.[10]

When the raid became known, the entire brigade started in pursuit, but not knowing the direction Mosby went, the various regiments went in several different directions. John Hammond led the Fifth New York along the road to Herndon Station. No one found Mosby, and eventually General Stoughton was delivered to General Fitz Lee as a prisoner, his army career ruined. Needless to say, the pickets were doubled in the Fairfax-Centerville area as a result of Mosby's raid. And soon after, Mosby was promoted to major.[11] Chaplain Boudrye does not, in his history or journal, tell us anything more about the Sergeant Ames after it became known that he was riding with Mosby. Almost certainly there were men in the regiment who might have known something of the sergeant's real motives for deserting. But if the chaplain ever inquired among the men, anything he might have learned went unrecorded. This is an example of the lack of depth inherent in the Fifth's records. In fact, Ames rode with Mosby for eighteen months and was promoted to lieutenant. The history of the First Vermont Cavalry credits Ames with killing one of their own, a Lt. Woodbury, in an action against Mosby's command occurring near Dranesville, Virginia, on March 31, 1863.

During the Gettysburg campaign, Mosby and his raiders crossed the Potomac headed for Pennsylvania, hoping to join Lee's forces. At some point while this expedition was heading north in search of the Rebel army, Ames is quoted by Williamson as saying, "Well, I am going with you, but I will not fire a shot.... I will not fire a shot on Northern soil." Finally, on October 8, 1864, Ames met his end. He was killed in a fight with three companies of the Eighth Illinois Cavalry that Mosby attacked while the troopers were guarding a work gang engaged in reconstructing the Manassas Gap railroad. This action occurred near a place Williamson called Piedmont, Virginia. Ames was "buried close to the spot where he met his death."[12] Ames's "career" illustrates that at least one Union soldier, and probably more, at that period of the war were strongly in opposition to Lincoln's Proclamation nominally freeing the slaves, and, therefore failing to see its necessity as a military measure aimed at weakening the Confederacy.

Mosby and his guerrilla command were active throughout the winter and spring, and usually his raiding led directly to a chase and a running fight. Chaplain Boudrye reported such an incident when he was visiting the Fifth New York picket line on March 23, 1863:

> Went out on picket again. About 5 P.M. Mosby made an attack on the pike, introducing himself by shooting the first vidette he came to through the head. The main reserve being alarmed, formed and pursued this force about three miles. Here a barricade of trees is thrown across the road, back of which the guerrillas had formed themselves. Our column was stopped by a fire of carbines and pistols, and by a flank fire from the woods. At this inopportune moment the Rebels made a charge, which broke our column. Our boys were then driven back furiously. Some horses gave out, the hapless riders were captured. By the heroic exertions of Major White and the arrival of the reserves from Frying Pan, the boys were rallied and the Rebels again driven back, and pursued for eight miles. But they escaped after inflicting upon us very serious injury. For some reason the regiment never acted with so little concert, and was never so badly beaten by so small a force, supposed to be about eighty strong. Every one felt mortified at the result of this day's work, and resolved to retrieve our fortunes on some more fortunate occasion.[13]

An occasional scouting mission was a relief from picket duty. In these, a regiment or a component thereof went on a sweep of the neighboring countryside. The purpose was to stir up guerrillas and spoil any raids they were planning, or if Rebels were encountered, to capture or kill them. More typically the regiment rode in reaction to the initiative shown by Mosby. As an example the following account from Boudrye illustrates a typical action the Fifth engaged in during this period: "January 26th. Mosby made an attack on the 18th PA on picket duty near Chantilly Church, capturing 11. The Fifth N.Y. was sent in pursuit of the guerrillas. Having reached Middleburg, Maj. Hammond, in command, ordered a charge through the town ... resulting in the capture of 25 prisoners and scattering of Mosby's men. The entire party, save one man captured, returned safely to camp, after a journey of 34 miles."[14] James Penfield, in command of Company H, kept a cryptic diary at this time and entered the following about this incident:

> Rebs come in Take eleven Penn men on their post-about 4 o'clock Capt. Krom + Lt. Waugh pursue them to Aldie-Maj. H[ammond] ordered to start at Midnight

with 100 5th NY + 80 [West] Va. To go to Middleburgh [*sic*] — at 1 A.M. we start dark with appearance ~ of rain.... Reach Middleburgh just after daylight — Charge into town. Krom in advance-rebs gone with Prisoners.... In Hotel find 5 rebs in bed- + horses in barn — One chaplain + 13 others with several deserters-A Lady with streaming Hair mounted her pet horse- to prevent it being taken. Fed our Horses and Counter march'd just as our rear was leaving ... a squad charged in. The Maj. + Capt. Krom went in pursuit for about 3 miles. Captured 3 Men + Lost one Horse at Aldie.[15]

This dangerous but routine work has hardly ever made it into general histories of the conflict. Yet, if the casualty figures of the regiment could be broken out by the numbers of men lost or wounded in these activities and those lost in regular engagements against organized Rebel forces, the losses on picket and scouting duty would likely be higher.

While in camp on winter days the men of the regiment occupied themselves by writing letters and reading. There were, of course, card games and other forms of gambling. On days when the Virginia weather cooperated and the air grew warmer with the approach of spring, inter-regimental horse races were sometimes organized and the men played a rudimentary form of baseball that pitted various units against one another. And always, the horses had to be watered, fed and cared for. The officers ordered exercises and drills, and Chaplain Boudrye always held services on Sundays when the regiment was not in the field. And throughout this winter, the chaplain made serious efforts encouraging the men to temperance, speaking to whomever would listen about the evils of drink, and getting those who were receptive to sign a pledge renouncing spirits for life.

On March 25, 1863, Brigadier General Julius Stahl assumed the command of the cavalry forces deployed in the defenses of Washington. Stahl was also a volunteer. He had emigrated from Hungary, becoming a newspaperman in America. He had served until this point as an infantry officer, no doubt relying on training he had received earlier in Europe, where he had fought with Lajos Kossuth in the Hungarian revolution of 1848. "He was a 'dapper little Dutchman,' as everybody called him." For the next three months he would lead what was called Stahl's Cavalry Division in picketing and scouting from his headquarters at Fairfax Court House. But the pace quickened as spring, with its better weather, made its appearance.[16]

On May 3, the largest action of this period took place. Early in the morning the First West Virginia, which had been out scouting, was dismounted and the men tending to their horses when they were attacked by what was called a mixed force of Rebel cavalry and Mosby's raiders. The West Virginians, on foot, were scattered as the Rebs charged through them. A number scrambled into a nearby house for cover and a gun battle with pistols broke out. Mosby is reported to have yelled over the shooting that those inside the house should surrender before he set fire to the structure. Their answer appears to have been in the negative because Boudrye says that the house was set to the torch. "At this critical moment," writes Boudrye, "the Fifth New York, which had bivouacked in a grove at a short distance from the scene of action, with Maj. Hammond commanding in person, descended like an avalanche upon the guerrillas. Mosby is reported to have exclaimed, 'My God! It is the Fifth New York!'" In the wild melee that ensued, the regiment used its sabers and counted later twenty-three wounded Rebel prisoners. Hammond chased the remaining force as far as Warrenton Junction, where the Fifth New York again charged, scattering Mosby's force in every direction. The regiment lost one killed and fourteen wounded in this action. A New York newspaper reported on this action in a dispatch from Fairfax Court House dated May 3, 1863. The paper substantiates the regiment's history, adding that Hammond chased the Rebels to Warrenton and perhaps beyond it: "The Rebel loss is heavy, the dead being left upon the field. We have taken twenty-three prisoners, fifteen of whom are wounded. Among the prisoners is Dick Moras, the notorious bushwhacker, badly wounded. Templeton, Moseby's [sic] spy, was killed. Moseby [sic] is reported wounded…. Our men fought gallantly and the Rebels acknowledge that they got hold of the wrong party that time." When the reports were written, General Stahl included the following: "The major-general commanding congratulates Colonel De Forest of the Fifth New York Cavalry, his officers and men, for their gallant rescue of a detachment of the First [West] Virginia Cavalry, surprised and overpowered by rebel guerrillas under Major Mosby, and for the thorough manner in which they defeated them."[17]

This kind of action was repeated several more times that spring. Boudrye reported in his history another encounter with Mosby on May 30, 1863, this time near the town of Greenwich, Virginia. Mosby and his raiders had derailed a supply train heading south to the Army of the Potomac on the Rappahannock. John Hammond, in a letter written to an unnamed friend, relates the story:

> Gen. Stahel [sic] hearing of the affair ordered me to take what men there was in our Regt. & the 1st Vt and go to Kettle Run as twas supposed it must be Stuart as Moseby [sic] had never had artillery. It appears that Moseby [sic] had about 100 men and one piece of artillery, which had been sent him by Fitz Lee but four days before. He attacked the train about three miles from where we are posted…. Moseby [sic] planted his piece in the woods near the track loosened a rail attached a wire to the same and as the train came up pulled it off which brought matters to a stand at the same time opening upon the Locomotive with Grape &

Shell; the guard on the train all ran away (which is what we expect them to do being Vt 9 months men).

The Fifth New York with about sixty men, and the First Vermont with about one hundred, rode to the sound of the firing. Hammond continued, "Our men came up with them first about 6 or 7 miles from where they attacked the train and pitched into them at once. [Lt.] Elmer [Barker] found that our men were like to be repulsed and called for volunteers to charge on the gun."

With the approach of these troopers, Mosby fired a few shots at the New Yorkers and then retreated in the direction of Warrenton. Chaplain Boudrye reported that Lt. Barker of Company H, now paroled as a prisoner and back with the regiment, cried out to his men, "That gun must be silenced or captured, and who will volunteer to charge it with me?" About thirty men came forward and with Barker leading them, they charged the gun as it fired canister into them. Hammond, who was at the scene but does not mention his role in the fight, reported, "The road was narrow with high banks flanked by dense forests of pines which was excellent cover for the Rebs and from which they poured in a murderous fire. Elmer charged on the gun with about 20 men and when within 2 rods of the cannon the Rebs opened upon them with grape and canister killing or wounding all but one of the 7 that were in the advance with Lieut. Barker — this was about the last shot they had — the Vermonters coming up at this time the rebs deserted their piece and took to their heels." Three of the volunteers were killed and Barker wounded, but the remainder of the men, with their sabers, slashed at the Rebels and killed a few of them. The chaplain reported that Private George H. Jenkins of Company F, although wounded by the shotgun-like blast from the gun, was called upon by a Rebel captain to surrender. No doubt cleaning up the language, Boudrye says that the Rebel called out, "Surrender, you damned Yankee." In reply, Jenkins, apparently on the ground, said, "I will see you damned first." According to the chaplain, this "was Jenkins' characteristic reply." As he said it, the private pulled his Colt .44 and shot the Rebel captain in the neck, killing him.[18] John Jackson reported this incident slightly differently, and since he was there and Boudrye's account is secondhand, his account is quoted here:

> A white smoke curled up from the cannon as the gunner pulled the cord. Instinctively we hugged the steep banks on either side, as canister shot came down, scattering death and destruction. Five fell from the saddle, and only ten of us [were] left mounted and unhurt in the lane. The Lieutenant received two canister shot in the leg, and his horse was struck in several places, but did not fall. He wheeled his horse, and we fell back to the main column — repulsed, leaving our dead and wounded in the lane. But we were not disheartened. The 1st Vermont came up at this juncture, and falling in together we charged again, this time driving the Rebels from their gun, with the loss of the Lieutenant and

gunners in charge of the piece.... The road was strewn with fresh fish, oranges, &c., which they had taken from the cars. Our total loss was four killed and fourteen wounded.... Six fell into our hands.... Company F had three men wounded and four horses killed.[19]

"Mosby himself barely escaped being captured on this occasion," wrote a contemporary, "and he carried the mark of a sabre-cut on his arm. The fight was desperate on both sides, but the guerrillas were badly worsted, and driven away.... In their flight the spoils, which had been taken from the captured train, were left behind, strewn in every direction. This fight occurred near the little village of Greenwich, and gave Mosby a blow quite as severe as any he had ever received." In his letter of June 3, Hammond reported, "Elmer [Barker] had two grape shots through the left leg about half way between the knee and hip, no bones injured.... Elmer is seriously wounded but we have the best assurance that he will get along and not lose the leg — he had the best attendance by Doct's Wood and Gale & I am going to keep Maria here to nurse him until he is able to accompany [sic] him home." One of the troopers killed, Corporal Orlando Drake, was from Company H, part of the original company raised by Hammond in Crown Point. Hammond wrote, "The boys in Co H shed many tears over the death of Drake and have sent his remains home." Also, one of Mosby's casualties was Captain Bradford Hoskins. "[O]ne of Co F's boys killed Capt Haskins [sic] of the British service who has been with Moseby [sic]____ month — he had 6 medals on his body 2 Crimean, 2 Garibaldean & 2 Turkish."[20]

After the regiment had spent the majority of the winter and spring chasing Mosby and his men, the coming of summer was to signal a change in how the Fifth New York was employed, as well how it was led. Beginning in early June there grew among the New York troopers a sense that something significant was going to happen soon. This volunteer regiment had learned its job well in the year it had been actively in the field and was about to put that learning to use. The Fifth New York was about to ride in its first great campaign.

4
Advance and Pursuit — 1863

There was no more fruitful or comfortable regions in the North, or in the world, than they looked down upon on the morning of the 30th of June.
— Henry C. Parson, First Vermont Cavalry

Lee ... was somewhere in that region ... we knew. We were searching for him and the time was close at hand when the two armies must come into contact, and oceans of blood would flow, before the confederates could be driven from Northern soil.
— James H. Kidd, Michigan Brigade, Third Cavalry Division

June 30, 1863

The general commanding of this army has called the attention of all commanders, as well as the troops under them, to the immense issues involved in the result of the engagement that may soon be expected with the enemy.... Proud of his confidence in the brave soldiers under his command, every assurance exists that future actions will add luster to their honorable fame.

Corps and other commanders are authorized to order the instant death of any soldier who fails in his duty at this hour.
— Pleasonton, Major-General, Commanding[1]

John W. Jackson of Company F was in the habit of writing newsy letters from the Fifth New York to a newspaper back home, the *Wyoming County Mirror*. He was from Eagle in Wyoming County, New York, in the western part of the state about midway between Rochester and Buffalo. This county provided many recruits to the Fifth New York in 1861. "The report now current in these parts is that Lee contemplates a forward movement on our right. [O]ur Regiment has received a new lot of horses, and turned in some of the worn out specimens of horseflesh. They [*sic*] weather is warm, dry and pleasant, and the health of the troops excellent."[2] This was John Jackson's thinking on June 4, 1863, thinking the newspaper printed a few days later. These three

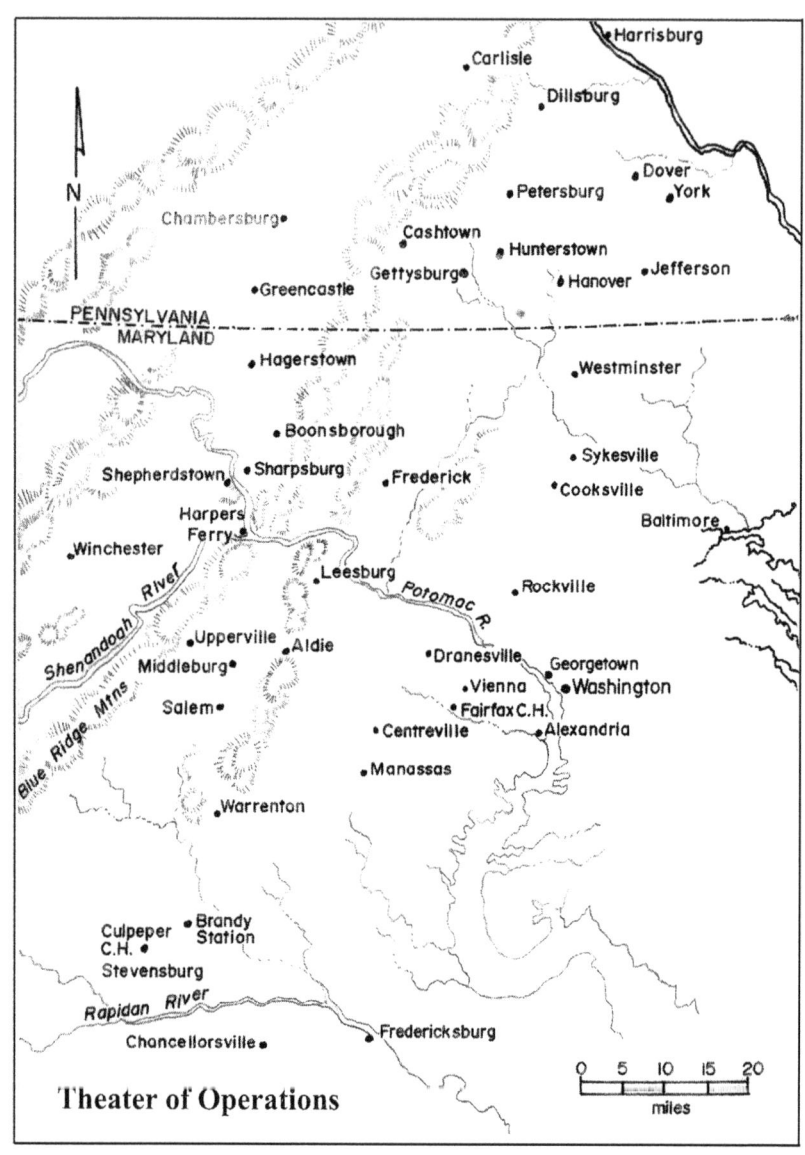

Theater of Operations

sentences are proof that not all army rumors are false. Robert E. Lee was on the move. Even in the Union army after two years of fighting, a supply of new horses would not normally show up if nothing out of the ordinary were planned.

Captain James Penfield was from Crown Point, New York, and a cousin of John Hammond. Penfield had been promoted to captain of Company H

4. Advance and Pursuit—1863

on September 26, 1862, when John Hammond was advanced to major. On May 25, Penfield's company had received thirty-one new horses from the regimental quartermaster, and on June 15, Penfield noted in his diary: "Drew 20 saddles-25 pistols-20 sabres- 25 pistol holsters."[3] Spring was quickly evolving into summer, the weather good. Dry roads and sunshine meant movement, and movement meant a campaign.

During the winter just past, there had been another change in command in the Army of the Potomac in the wake of the bloodbath that was the Battle of Fredericksburg in December. Now Major General Joseph Hooker led the Army of the Potomac. "Fighting Joe," as he was called, improved conditions for the men as they sat in winter camps around Falmouth, Virginia, and set about planning his offensive against Robert E. Lee below the Rappahannock. Hooker also consolidated all of the cavalry assigned to the army into a separate corps and placed it under a corps commander. "This consolidation of the cavalry was by far the most important step that had yet been taken to increase the efficiency, and enabled it to act in its true role," wrote a contemporary cavalryman who after the war attempted to detail the story of this army's mounted force.[4]

In early May, "Fighting Joe" moved against General Lee and his forces. On paper the plan looked like it could succeed, and if it did, the end of the Army of Northern Virginia might be the result. But there was one problem: a large wooded expanse, second growth timber and scrub brush called the Wilderness. Hooker led his army upstream, crossed the Rappahannock and turned east back toward Fredericksburg. As he did this, two of his infantry corps put pontoon bridges across the river downstream from Fredericksburg and began a demonstration against the Rebels, hoping to hold Lee's force in place as Hooker struck from the west. Hooker, once across the river, advanced to a place called Chancellorsville, an open area within the Wilderness. Informed of his enemy's movements from the west and recognizing that he was facing a demonstration below Fredericksburg, Lee divided his army and rushed the bulk of it to the Wilderness to stem the threat from Hooker. The fighting in the tangled undergrowth and wooded terrain became ferocious, yet Lee, outnumbered two to one, managed to stall the Federal advance.

In the darkness at the end of the first day of fighting, Lee and "Stonewall" Jackson contemplated a formal reaction to Hooker's plan of battle. In arguably one of the most daring and brilliant maneuvers in military history, Lee, consenting to Jackson's thinking, divided his already outnumbered force a second time. The next day Jackson led his corps on its own flanking maneuver. "Stonewall's" troops crashed into the unsuspecting right flank of the Army of the Potomac, drove it, and nearly routed it. Hooker fought on for a few days as Lee continued to press him from two sides. Finally, the Federal commander ordered the force below Fredericksburg to re-cross the river as he prepared to do the same. The Army of the Potomac disengaged, crossed the Rappahannock and marched back to the camps it had thought it had left for good a few days before. Lee and his army had won another victory, but it was in this battle that he lost his most aggressive corps commander, the leader who had brought him victory at Chancellorsville, Thomas "Stonewall" Jackson.

Some days after this Confederate victory, one celebrated throughout the South, General Lee rode the train to Richmond and presented to Confederate President Jefferson Davis his ideas for a campaign he proposed to lead during the coming summer months. Although he had been victorious at Chancellorsville, and despite the rejoicing of the Southern public, it was not the kind of victory Lee desired most, one that would annihilate the Army of the Potomac — a victory that would eliminate the Union force as a cohesive military threat to the Confederacy — and not merely push his enemy back across the river. More than anyone in the Confederacy, Lee knew he may have defeated "Fighting Joe" Hooker, but he had not defeated the Army of the Potomac. After some discussion, Davis reluctantly approved Lee's plans and the general returned to his army and made his preparations. In late May and early June 1863, there were stirrings below the Rappahannock. To Hooker and his commanders above the river it was only a question of where and when the next clash would come.

The Fifth New York had a relatively quiet two weeks in early June. Still camped in the defensive parameter of Washington and relatively close to the capital, the regiment was paid on time, June 1. Two days later the troopers, apparently sensing that a major fight was on the horizon, used some of their money to acquire whiskey. "There are more drunkards, drunken men, in camp tonight, than I have ever seen in a long time," Boudrye reported. "Fighting & quarrelling are the order of things. Obscene songs & language are common enough. Oh! to what depths of degradation will men permit themselves to fall! And, Oh! What powerful influences will be required to bring them back to decency and to God!"[5] Despite the drinking and revelry of the moment, of much more import for the Fifth New York during these opening days of June was the change in the regiment's command. Major John Hammond took over leadership of the Fifth from Lt. Colonel Robert Johnstone. As of June 1, Hammond would lead the Fifth New York and do so for the next fifteen months.

From all the evidence, Major John Hammond was clearly the best choice to lead the regiment, then on the cusp of the most active campaigning it had yet seen. As noted by Civil War historian James M. McPherson, an observation coming after decades of research, the majority of officers like Hammond who had come "from civilian life took seriously their new profession. Many of them burned the midnight oil studying manuals on drill and tactics. They avoided giving petty or unreasonable orders and compelled obedience to reasonable ones by dint of personality and intellect rather than by threats. They led by example, not prescript. And in combat they led from the front, not the rear."[6] In the nearly two years of the unit's existence, John Hammond had proven himself to be such an officer.

The new leader of the Fifth New York was from a prominent and well-to-do family in Essex County, New York, where they had mercantile and mining interests. Born in 1827, he was sent to the St. Albans Academy in Vermont and later graduated from Renseelaer Polytechnic Institute. As the young are wont to do, he went looking for adventure and, hopefully, his fortune. Hammond traveled to California in the wake of the 1849 gold rush and spent three years there. Of his California activities, fortune apparently was not the result. In 1852, Hammond returned to Crown Point and joined the family's enterprise. He married that same year — one Charlotte Maria Cross — and had two small children by the time the Civil War came. At age thirty-four, Hammond helped organize an infantry regiment early in the war, a regiment that fought at Bull Run in July 1861. By September, Hammond had been chosen to be captain of the company of volunteer cavalry composed of men he recruited in Essex County. In June of this eventful year, 1863, the new regimental commander was described as having a dark complexion and black hair, and standing five feet eleven and a half inches tall. One of the men serving under him later wrote, "I never knew an officer who commanded the respect and confidence of his men to a greater extent than he did." In one of his more perceptive observations, Chaplain Boudrye noted of Hammond at this time, "He is strong and cool. He is a great favorite with the men of this command. He *leads* the men, does not *send* them. This they admire."[7] During the seven weeks following his assumption of command, Hammond would lead the regiment in the most far-ranging and difficult operation it had yet encountered.

The activity below the Rappahannock, by now, was known in Washington. On June 4, Chaplain Boudrye tried to get a pass to Washington to mail home the pay for some of the men. It was denied, he says, because "the authorities are in a panic, fearing that Gen. Lee will make a dash or raid into the capital ere long."[8] Within the army rumors flew about: Lee was moving north, somewhere beyond the Blue Ridge Mountains, out of sight. After their payday, apparently the regiment, without the chaplain, moved in the direction of Middleburg, Virginia, to scout for signs of Lee's movement and to gather any other intelligence the country could provide, but they encountered only a band of Mosby's guerrillas and made a capture on June 10. At Kettle Run, Virginia, Major Hammond wrote a brief report to brigade commander Colonel De Forest dated June 13:

> Returned last night at 11 P.M., with 1 captain and 6 men of Mosby's command, and 10 horses.
> Mosby returned from raid in Maryland about 2 P.M. on the 11th. He brought 17 prisoners of the Sixth Michigan, and dispersed his men at Middleburg four hours before the telegram was written ordering us in pursuit. He reported to have had 110 men, but no artillery.
> The prisoners will be sent in by first train. J. Hammond, Major, Commanding Detachment.[9]

On June 14, the regiment, at Kettle Run, was told to stay in camp and await orders. The next week was quiet but hot, one with the temperature reaching ninety-eight degrees in the shade on June 17 and 18. In a letter written from Fairfax Court House dated June 17, John Hammond wrote to his young son, "The soldiers all seem to be in good spirits; they have been passing here since night before last. This morning, at about one o'clock, I was awakened by their passing in solid column, which continued until after sunrise. After there came a long train of artillery, and then the ambulances and wagons, stretching out for a distance of at least four or five miles; and yet this is but a small portion of the grand army."[10] In essence, the great Gettysburg campaign was beginning.

The knowledge that something was stirring below the Rappahannock led General Hooker to order the Cavalry Corps of the Army of the Potomac, under the command of General Alfred Pleasonton, across the river to stir things up. The result was the Battle of Brandy Station on June 9. This engagement has been described as either a reconnaissance in force to ascertain Lee's intentions or a spoiling attack on Jeb Stuart's cavalry command, one that would certainly be extremely active in the coming summer weather. Brandy Station was the largest all-cavalry action of the Civil War. After initially being surprised by Pleasonton's early morning attack on his camps around Brandy Station, Stuart rallied his troops and fought through the day. Both sides took heavy casualties in the mostly mounted action. Pleasonton withdrew across the river late in the day, unable to claim a decisive victory. However, if the Union cavalry had not already demonstrated its fighting capabilities, it did in this engagement. The historian of the Eighth New York Cavalry, a regiment fully engaged in the action, summarized what the troopers in blue had become by the spring of 1863: "From that day [June 9] the rebel cavalry could not stand in front of our cavalry for an hour." If somewhat overstated, nevertheless there was a certain degree of truth to the attitude held by these New Yorkers.

The volunteer cavalry of 1861 had learned a good deal. By this springtime, when massed in at least division strength, it became a force to be reckoned with.[11]

In the days immediately following Brandy Station, the Cavalry Corps was charged with getting accurate intelligence on Lee and his army's movement. The Battle of Brandy Station had not altered or materially delayed General Lee's plans. Hooker had to know where Lee's his forces were, where his men were headed and their strength. Beyond the Blue Ridge, Lee's men were marching and General Pleasonton was charged with getting and then giving the information to Hooker. There were large cavalry actions in and around the towns on roads leading to gaps in the Blue Ridge, at Middleburg, Upperville and Aldie. At these places Pleasonton's cavalry brigades attempted to peer through the mountain gaps into the Shenandoah Valley. In these actions, Jeb Stuart was aggressively screening Lee's movement by fighting each attempted probe by Pleasonton to see into the Valley. In this the Confederate cavalry leader was successful. It was obvious to both Pleasonton and General Hooker that behind this proactive screening of the Shenandoah, Lee was moving north toward the Potomac. But what was his plan, his intention? And where, exactly, was he headed? Was the objective somewhere in Maryland or further afield, a strike into Pennsylvania?

John Hammond wrote down his thoughts at this time in a letter home.

> Fairfax Court House, June 17, 1863
> I suppose you have heard ere this that the rebel army has crossed the Rapahannock [sic], and that their advance guard is in Maryland and Pennsylvania. Lee's main army, however, is lying between the Blue Ridge and the Bull Run hills, while Gen. Hooker's army is occupying a line parallel with it, his forces extended from Manassas Junction to the Potomac, between Drainsville and Leesburg. We here are not sorry that the enemy have penetrated Pennsylvania, and wish that they would carry the war into New York, that the cowards and copperheads might have a taste of war, and that the loyal men might be quicken to do their duty.... Any hour may bring forth a battle, perhaps one of the most terrible of the war.[12]

The normally laconic John Hammond is here not only somewhat prophetic, but is telling us something of what he thinks of those not so committed to the cause as he. With nearly two years of service to the cause behind him, Hammond has grown to detest anyone — Northern sympathizers of the Confederacy, known as Copperheads, in particular — who would settle the war short of full reunion.

On Friday, June 19, Stahl's Cavalry Division and the Fifth New York got the word. All unnecessary baggage was to be sent home or to storage in Alexandria, Virginia. The regiment was to be ready to move at a moment's notice, into the field, indefinitely. The men worked through the night getting ready. The next day, though they were expecting to move at daylight, nothing happened. The move came on Sunday, June 21. While hearing heavy cannon fire from the direction of Aldie to the west where Pleasonton's cavalry was confronting Stuart, the Fifth New York saddled up. Between noon and one o'clock the regiment mounted and rode to Centerville, Virginia, passing over the Bull Run battlefield. The chaplain noted, "A skull is kicked along by the horses as they move over the muddy way! No one seems to care much about it, for worse sights have so often been seen before." The regiment moved on to Gainesville and camped that night near Buckland Mills. On June 22, the regiment moved through New Baltimore and on to Warrenton. "No force of the enemy was here encountered, as had been expected. Small scouting parties were sent out in various directions, and the division bivouacked for the afternoon and night in the field adjacent to the town." On June 23 they moved back to Gainesville and then back to their original camp near Fairfax Court House. They had ridden a long way and had nothing to show for it, no real intelligence to report.

The next day, June 24, can be said to be the beginning of the Gettysburg Campaign for the Fifth New York. The regiment marched north, under orders from Hooker, headed in the general direction of Harpers Ferry. Boudrye was riding with the regiment's train and was under the impression the division was headed for Leesburg. A change of orders arrived on June 25 telling Stahl to report to General John Reynolds, commander of the leading wing of the army that was crossing the Potomac at Edwards Ferry. The Fifth New York arrived at the crossing and saw "miles and miles of train [are] waiting to cross the river." With two pontoon bridges in place over the Potomac by Friday, June 26, Hooker's army was fully in motion. The traffic congestion at Edwards forced the division to move some miles downstream to Youngs Island Ford, where they crossed, but the water was too deep for the wagons. The division's wagons had to wait their turn to cross on the pontoon bridges at Edwards Ferry. Now in Maryland, the regiment passed through Adamstown, Jefferson, Birkinsville and on to the vicinity of Rhoresville. The command got to Frederick, Maryland, on June 26, received its orders from General Reynolds, and headed toward the gaps in the mountains separating Frederick from Hagerstown, Maryland. By Saturday, June 27, the division's First Brigade was in position at Crampton's Gap, about five miles beyond Middleburg, Maryland. The Second Brigade was guarding Turner's Gap some miles to the north. Patrols were sent forward and preparations made to resist any Rebel probe through the gaps coming from the west.

4. Advance and Pursuit—1863   65

On June 28, Boudrye reported, "Gen. Pleasonton reviewed the division, and reorganized the entire force. We are now the Third Division of the Cavalry Corps, Army of the Potomac, with the gallant Kilpatrick in command. The first brigade consists of the 1st Vermont, 1st [West] Virginia, 18th Pennsylvania and the 5th New York, Brig. Gen. Farnsworth commanding. Brig. Gen. Custer commands the 2nd brigade, composed of Michigan regiments." Boudrye's journal recorded the following day, "Gen. Hooker is relieved of command. Had a good wash in the creek."[13]

Unknown to anyone in the regiment, things were taking place at the command level of the Army of the Potomac that would change the campaign and probably its outcome. In addition to being officially absorbed into the Army of the Potomac and the command changes of the division's two brigades, the Fifth New York had become one of the hundreds of volunteer regiments swallowed by the great Gettysburg campaign and battle. From now until July 18, almost three weeks, there would be nothing but hard riding and fighting for the regiment. All of it would be done under a new command structure composed of new personalities. By now it was known in the Army of the Potomac that not only were the Rebels fully across the Potomac, to the west of where the regiment now stood, but they were roaming deep within Pennsylvania, foraging as they moved. But what were Lee's intentions? Until this became clear, the Army of the Potomac kept moving also, keeping itself as best it could in position to block Lee if he moved to attack either Washington or Baltimore, while at the same time trying to learn his true intentions.

As for Lee and his army, in the quiet weeks prior to the Battle of Chancellorsville, the general had again turned his thoughts to the coming campaign season and what he believed needed to be accomplished. Lee and the Army of Northern Virginia had fought the entire year of 1862 in Virginia, the exception being the Antietam campaign in September. The general hoped with this summer's campaign to take the fight to the Yankees in their territory. This would get the enemy out from behind the Rappahannock River and spare his state another season of battles, allowing Virginia farmers in the affected region time to grow and harvest a crop unimpeded by troop movements. Hooker's attack and the Battle of Chancellorsville and his defeat had not materially altered this view. Also, the move north at this moment would spoil any plans the Army of the Potomac might be contemplating in the wake of Chancellorsville, clear the lower Shenandoah Valley of Union troops, and might pull Federal forces away from the western theater to reinforce the Army of the Potomac. Even a small redeployment of Union forces from the western theater would help Confederate commanders there, particularly General Pemberton in his struggle with Ulysses S. Grant around Vicksburg. And finally, while he was in Northern territory, Lee and his army would appropriate as much in the way of supplies and livestock as the rich, unmolested countryside could provide.

This was an ambitious plan, but Lee's opinion of the Army of the Potomac, since he had defeated it more than once, was so low that he concluded his goals were achievable. His opinion of General Hooker was nearly contemptuous, leading him to refer to the Union general as "Mr. F.J. Hooker." And most important, he believed in the near invincibility of the Army of Northern Virginia. Left unstated, but certainly discussed with President Davis by Lee, was his belief that if a decisive, annihilating battle could be fought and won by Confederate arms on Northern soil — on a battleground of Lee's choosing — such a victory might be enough to make the North finally acquiesce in Southern independence. This was the general scope of the campaign that Jefferson Davis had approved after Chancellorsville in May. By June 28, his intentions unchanged, General Lee himself was deep within Pennsylvania, his army cutting Northern rail communication from west to east and threatening to move on and destroy the railroad bridges over the Susquehanna River at Harrisburg.

And now Major General George Meade, like Hooker before him as commander of the Army of the Potomac, was charged with not only blocking any attack by Lee on Washington, but was expected to fight and defeat the Southern force wherever it was found. Meade, in command of the Fifth Corps until this moment, had succeeded to command of the Army of the Potomac early on the morning of June 28, when Hooker's rash request to be relieved had been consented to by President Lincoln. That General Henry W. Halleck, nominally the army's commander-in-chief, and General Hooker disliked each other was evident by Hooker's constant attempts at bypassing his immediate superior and dealing with Lincoln directly. Finally, in a dispute over control of a force stationed at Harpers Ferry that was denied him by Halleck, Hooker had asked to be relieved. After he had been replaced by Meade, most of the Harpers Ferry force was only then assigned, by Halleck, to the Army of the Potomac. And at nearly the same moment, Stahl's Cavalry Division, including the Fifth New York, was assigned officially to the army under Meade, as the Third Cavalry Division.

George Meade was a West Pointer and a Pennsylvanian. He accepted command of the Army of the Potomac more as an order than an opportunity. He had not delved in army politics to this point as other corps commanders and former army commanders had done. Meade, irascible and crusty, was competent. President Lincoln, after a series of command changes in the preceding two years, had now found *a* general. And despite an occasional detour along the way, it would be George Meade who would lead the Army of the Potomac to Appomattox.

On Monday, June 29, the Fifth New York, along with the rest of the Third Cavalry Division, started looking for the Rebels in Pennsylvania. No longer to operate in cooperation with General Reynolds's wing of the army — the First Cavalry Division under John Buford had been assigned this task — the division was to move in advance of the army's central wing.

During the period from June 14 through 18, as the Fifth New York was moving about northern Virginia, trying to gather intelligence on Lee's movements, what was Stahl's Cavalry Division had been on loan to Hooker from the defenses of Washington. But behind the scenes, Hooker had been lobbying the War Department to permanently assign Stahl's division to his army. He claimed that his other two divisions were becoming worn out having to fight engagements almost daily with Jeb Stuart's cavalry as the Rebels screened Lee's advance. Everything had come together on June 28, the same day Hooker's half-hearted request to be relieved of command had been formalized and General Meade had taken over. That day the War Department formally transferred Stahl's Cavalry Division to Meade and the Army of the Potomac. General Meade now had a cavalry corps consisting of three divisions which he immediately sent probing in advance of his army in an attempt to locate the enemy. With the transfer complete, Julius Stahl was immediately ordered to a position in Harrisburg, Pennsylvania, and replaced with Brigadier General Hugh Judson Kilpatrick, formerly a brigade commander and the man who would lead the Third Division until the following April. Cavalry Corps Commander General Alfred Pleasonton had seen Kilpatrick in action as a brigade commander in the fighting with Jeb Stuart's cavalry and thought the new young general would be a more energetic leader for his new cavalry division than the older "Dutchman" Stahl. In this, Pleasonton was correct.

Hugh Judson Kilpatrick is one of those individuals history has not treated well and, given the evidence, justifiably so. Of his courage on the battlefield, there is no doubt. Indeed, this trait is what brought him to Pleasonton's attention in the first place. However, other than courage in the face of the enemy, there is little to recommend Kilpatrick as a regular army officer. A fiction writer might be creative enough to draw a character like Kilpatrick as a counterbalance to his hero in a novel. But unfortunately, there is too much evidence coming down the years to recommend any judgment about Kilpatrick other than negative. One of the many "boy wonder" generals of the Civil War, Kilpatrick was the first Union officer wounded in the war and had fought at the Second Battle of Bull Run. He had ridden with the cavalry corps on an ineffective cavalry raid that had been part of Hooker's Chancellorsville Campaign and been heavily engaged with Stuart's forces just a week earlier near the gaps in the Blue Ridge. This record testified to his bravery. But Kilpatrick was "flamboyant in appearance, conniving in manner, and possessed of boundless ambition." A contemporary reported that Kilpatrick was a "brave, injudicious boy, much given to blowing."[14] It is not surprising then that the men under his command called him "Kill-cavalry." This West Pointer from the class of 1861 was "controversial in that he had more than once been involved in dealings of a suspected criminal nature." Although nothing was ever proven, he was imprisoned in 1862 on "suspicion of having confiscated Virginia livestock and government provisions and selling them for personal gain." Also, it was thought he was involved in a scheme to solicit bribes from contractors selling horses to his regiment. "In addition to lacking honesty and stability, he was a devotee of prostitutes," and at the same time a vocal temperance advocate despite having been jailed previously in Washington as a result of a drunken escapade in which certain government officials were the targets of his tongue. His "notorious immoralities and rapacity set so demoralizing an example to his troops that the best disciplinarians among his subordinates could only mitigate its influence." In action he was "a dare-devil, bordering on the reckless."[15] For the men serving under him, he had little or no regard, and the Kill-cavalry nickname — apparently already acquired before his coming to the Third Cavalry Division — tells all concerning how the troopers felt about him. As one officer under him noted of the nickname, "This was not because men were killed while under his command, for that was their business and every trooper knew that death was liable to be soon or late ... but

General Hugh Judson Kilpatrick, "Kill-cavalry," commander of the Third Cavalry Division at Gettysburg and through the winter of 1863–1864 (Library of Congress).

for the reason that so many lives were sacrificed by him for no good purpose whatever." After the war, his ambition to become president of the United States got him as far as minister to Chile, where he died in 1881.[16]

Things were happening fast in the Army of the Potomac during that last week of June 1863. After taking over from Hooker on June 28, and being briefed by him on what were thought to be Lee's intentions in the campaign that was then unfolding, General Meade, in one of his first administrative decisions, told Cavalry Corps commander Pleasonton that he was free to appoint to command those officers under him whom he believed would bring success. General Pleasonton, writing years later, remembered this episode differently. "I called his [Meade's] attention to a division of cavalry [Stahl's division] near Frederick City," Pleasonton recalled, "which he might place under my command, and I would like to have officers I would name specially assigned to it, as I expected to have some desperate work to do. The General assented ... [and] immediately telegraphed to have them appointed brigadier generals." In that Stahl's Division was already in the field operating with the Army of the Potomac, Pleasonton doesn't mention that the division had already been on "loan" to the army from Washington's Defenses for some days, and Hooker had already been pushing to have it incorporated permanently.[17]

Whatever Pleasonton thought of the replacement of the commanding general on the eve of what everyone thought would be a major engagement, he had to be appreciative that Meade was giving him reign to organize his corps as he saw fit. And Pleasonton wasted no time in putting new men in key positions. Everyone knew a major engagement was coming, yet Pleasonton injected into the Third Division an entirely new set of senior officers. This was a risk, but by Meade's immediate approval a feeling of urgency, if not desperation, can be sensed. Besides Kilpatrick, Wesley Merritt, George Armstrong Custer and Elon Farnsworth were immediately elevated by Pleasonton to brigade command and brigadier's stars fell on them at once. Custer and Farnsworth were assigned to the Third Cavalry Division under Kilpatrick, with the First Brigade going to Farnswoth — including the Fifth New York — and the Second Brigade to Custer, composed of Michigan regiments from his home state. Merritt took over a brigade of U.S. Regular Cavalry attached to the First Cavalry Division. During this reshuffling and to make room for Farnsworth, Colonel Othneil De Forest, former colonel of the Fifth New York who had been the First Brigade's commander under Stahl, was relieved. Whether De Forest was sent on leave or to Washington to wait for reassignment is unknown, but he would not long be in limbo. Of these command changes, an officer in the First Vermont later remembered, "The officers were unknown to us, except we had heard they were fighters, and we now expected with such leaders to carve with our sabers a gallant record."[18] All of these changes happened on June 28, with the Third Division actively in the field and two of its Michigan regiments, the Fifth and Sixth, already having scouted as far as Gettysburg itself. On that Sunday, the Third Division is reported to have had 3,902 men and was the smallest of the three divisions in the Cavalry Corps. The Fifth New York reported 420 men present and equipped.[19]

Newly minted Brigadier General Elon Farnsworth would lead the First Brigade for only a short time. But immediately he would show that despite being twenty-six years old, he would lead the command well and from the front. Farnsworth had originally worked for the army as a civilian after being expelled from the University of Michigan because of a prank that had left another student dead. With the coming of the war he joined an Illinois regiment as a lieutenant. Promoted to captain because of his ability in combat, he found his way onto Pleasonton's staff earlier in 1863. Farnsworth was the nephew of an Illinois congressman with whom Pleasonton had connections. And although there is no definitive proof of his uncle's intercession with Pleasonton, the young Farnsworth was jumped from captain to brigadier general literally overnight.[20]

On June 28, the Fifth New York, with the First Brigade, had been to the west of Frederick, Maryland, blocking a gap in the Cotoctan Mountains. Its mission on June 29 was to find the enemy, report such to the commanding general, and keep in contact with it, thus allowing Meade to bring his forces to battle. However, generally speaking, the division Kilpatrick had inherited was worn down from marching between twenty-five and fifty miles a day over the past week and it would only get worse from this point on.

Specifically, Kilpatrick's orders were to move out in front of the central wing of the army, looking for the advance of Lee's command, now believed to be in Pennsylvania in a quadrant immediately to the north. For June 29 he was to march and scout as far as Littlestown in Pennsylvania and to get there by that evening. General Richard Ewell's Corps of Lee's army was thought to be in the vicinity of Chambersburg, Pennsylvania, moving east, headed in the general direction of Harrisburg. From Littlestown on June 30, the Third Division would be in position that day to move on York, Pennsylvania, about twenty-five miles away, a place that would put the division, hopefully, on Ewell's right flank. This movement called for passing through the town of Hanover, Pennsylvania, about five miles northeast of Littlestown.[21]

On Monday, June 29, Boudrye reported:

> Left this bivouac at 10; went with the regiment, passed through the richest region I ever saw; beautiful land; came through Walkerville; Woodsboro; Ladiesville; Mechanicsville on Little Pifer [*sic*] Creek, Bruceville, on same creek

4. Advance and Pursuit—1863   71

Taneytown and finally Littletown [sic], Pa. We crossed the Pa. Line about 9¼. Great demonstrations of joy were made in this village [Littlestown]. Children sitting on a high balcony sang patriotic airs, while cheers from the men made the welkin ring. We bivouacked near the village on the northeast side. The inhabitants brought us grain about midnight for horses.

The chaplain added in the regiment's history, "How different was such reception from that we had been accustomed to have given us by the inhabitants of Virginia villages!" A Michigan officer in Custer's brigade also commented on what he was seeing now that he was out of Virginia: "During the day it was a constant succession of fertile fields and leafy woods. Commodious farmhouses on every hand and evidences of plenty everywhere, we reveled in the richness and overflowing abundance of the land." As for the food the troopers were offered along the road, "To be sure we had to pay for what we had. Especially after we crossed over into Pennyslvania among the frugal Dutch was this the case."[22]

Before moving toward Littlestown with the First Brigade on June 29, Kilpatrick sent Custer with two of his brigade's Michigan regiments scouting towards Emmitsburg, Maryland. Then Custer was to join him by that evening at Littlestown while seeing to it that the two other regiments, known to have moved further into Pennsylvania, returned to the division. Those other two regiments of Custer's brigade had already arrived in Gettysburg on June 28 looking for Lee's force. "Before we reached town it was apparent that something unusual was going on," wrote an officer with these Michigan troopers. "It was a gala day. These people were out in force.... They had seen enough gray to be anxious to welcome the blue." Custer's four regiments, on June 29 at Emmitsburg and Gettysburg, would converge at Littlestown early on the morning of June 30. The Fifth and Sixth Michigan cavalry regiments, while in Gettysburg, had heard reports from citizens that significant numbers of Rebels were moving in the surrounding area. Indeed, a Confederate force had already moved through the town a couple of days before, heading east. This information was reported up the army chain of command and it is almost certain that both Custer and Kilpatrick knew of it early on the morning of June 30, as the now reunited division prepared to move from Littlestown. Kilpatrick had the two regiments coming from Gettysburg remain in Littlestown with orders to scout the area and had Custer with his other two regiments lead the march to Hanover. There may have been some separation between Custer's and Farnsworth's commands that morning on the road to Hanover because there was a good deal of mud caused by several days of rain and Custer's horses had churned it up, thus making progress much slower for those following. Kilpatrick rode out of Littlestown, followed by Custer and his two Michigan regiments and the division's artillery component. The First Brigade, with Farnsworth leading, followed, the First West Virginia, First Vermont, Fifth New York and, lastly, the Eighteenth Pennsylvania, and then the division train. Kilpatrick rode into Hanover soon after 8 A.M. Once in the town, Kilpatrick obtained a map of the country from a citizen of Hanover and was informed by residents about the Rebels who had passed through their town a few days earlier.[23]

The violent and confused cavalry engagement at Hanover, Pennsylvania, on June 30 can be considered the overture to the Civil War's greatest battle. That Jeb Stuart's cavalry was moving on the same town at that particular moment and not already with Ewell or Lee's main body has remained one of the enduring historical controversies concerning Gettysburg that has come down the years. After Lee had successfully reached the Potomac, his orders for Stuart, generally, were discretionary. Stuart was to ride north from Virginia and cross the Potomac with three cavalry brigades, disrupting the Army of the Potomac's communication and supply lines as he went. Once through Maryland and into Pennsylvania, he was to move into a flanking position with Ewell's Corps as it moved toward the Susquehanna River and Harrisburg. Armed with these discretionary orders, Stuart chose a route north to find Ewell that was around and behind the Army of the Potomac. He then headed northward for York, Pennsylvania, where it was thought Ewell was most likely to be found. However, more important than the route he chose, Stuart, as he moved north, was to pinpoint the Union army's location and report it to the commanding general. No more than a few days were allocated for this maneuver. But by dawn on June 30, Stuart, by some estimates, was almost two days behind schedule. As the eyes of the Army of Northern Virginia and out of touch with its commander, Stuart's inability to report on Union troop movements to the army's commander essentially blinded Lee as to the location and intentions of his enemy. On at least one occasion Stuart had sent Lee a report, but the courier never reached the general. Moreover, Stuart's progress was slowed by his capture of a Union supply train outside Rockville, Maryland. As he moved north, his men were shepherding one hundred and twenty-five captured wagons loaded with the bounty of the Federal government, supplies needed by General Lee.

On June 29, knowing he was behind schedule and hoping to overtake Ewell quickly, Stuart pressed his men forward but encountered a Union cavalry detachment as they approached Westminster, Maryland. The Union cavalry were greatly outnumbered, but shot it out with Stuart's men nevertheless. Dispensing with the Union cavalry had cost Stuart more valuable time. On the night of June 29, the Rebel cavalry column stretched for miles from West-

4. Advance and Pursuit—1863 73

minster north along the road to the town of Union Mills, Maryland, and beyond. That night Stuart ordered his men and horses to rest where they stood. At daybreak on June 30, the column again started north, with Stuart himself getting to Union Mills as the residents were beginning a day among Rebel visitors clogging the main street. Stuart's scouts were out ahead of the column, searching for traces of Ewell's command. They discovered nothing. Nothing, that is, but the presence of another large cavalry formation to the northeast, near the Pennsylvania community of Littlestown. This information went back to Stuart, who certainly did not want another confrontation with Yankees. He needed a detour to avoid still another collision with Federal cavalry that would only cost him more precious time. It was at this moment, or soon thereafter, that General Stuart encountered one Herbert Shriver, a Union Mills resident and Confederate sympathizer. Shriver's young son could guide the general around the enemy cavalry in the area of Littlestown by way of Hanover, about eight miles to the northeast of where Stuart was now. Stuart took Shriver up on his offer and the Rebel column moved out with the young Shriver showing the way. Stuart crossed into Pennsylvania on a road leading north toward Hanover. As his point riders came over a rise that gave them a full view of Hanover, they were shocked to see a long column of blue cavalry and supply wagons marching into Hanover on a road coming from the southwest. What these Rebels were seeing was the Third Division's train and the Eighteenth Pennsylvania, the last regiment in Kilpatrick's column. The Yankees were on the road leading from Littlestown to Hanover, and if the Rebels stayed on the road they were traveling, it would collide with the Eighteenth Pennsylvania at an intersection a short distance from Hanover itself. This intersection, with a few farms bordering it, came to be called Mudtown or Buttstown in later years. If the Rebel column continued moving, there was certain to be another fight.[24] But it was already too late.

Whether the Rebels started the fight regardless of the delay it would cause, or whether it was merely two cavalry formations stumbling into each other and simply reacting out of instinct, remains one of the unknowns of this engagement. What is certain, however, is that it was not what Stuart had wanted.

Of that Tuesday morning, the chaplain has left us precious little in his account. The Fifth New York was the next to last regiment in the column and was at this time stopped on Main Street in Hanover. Boudrye says, "Left about 6 directly for Hanover. The day was beautiful as well as the country. At Hanover, the inhabitants came out in throngs to welcome us, freely giving us bread, meats, pie, cake, etc., etc. While we were thus feasting gayly [sic] and sumptuously, a charge of rebel cavalry was made upon us, mostly in the train, while a battery, before concealed, opened with shot and shell upon us.

Nothing could have been more surprising nor could take us at a more inopportune moment for us." Much later, an officer with the First Vermont recalled, "The town of Hanover, a quaint village with brick houses broad lawns and shades streets, welcomed them as deliverers. Flags waved everywhere. Bells were ringing." Corporal D.H. Robbins of Company H wrote years later that while he was in the town square, "A gun boomed in our rear, right where we had come from.... In about two minutes came another boom, and this time a shell came screeching up the street, and after a few minutes the pot and kettle brigade came dashing through our ranks, yelling that the whole rebel army was right after them."[25]

Earlier, when he had ridden through the town, Kilpatrick had been warned by citizens of Hanover that there were probably mounted Rebels in the area. He is said to have climbed the belfry of a local church and scanned the surrounding countryside looking for dust kicked up by either marching infantrymen or cavalry. He saw nothing. To the south, or in any direction, Rebel cavalry might be a threat but he had to push on and find the main body of Lee's army. By nine o'clock, Kilpatrick was down from the belfry and on the road leading north out of Hanover, heading for Abbottstown. He was riding to catch up with the leading Michigan regiment of Custer's brigade that had passed through the town earlier in the morning. Behind Kilpatrick came General Farnsworth with two of his regiments, the First West Virginia and the First Vermont. The Fifth New York, the next to last in the column, was still in Hanover when the attack started. The last element was the Eighteenth Pennsylvania followed by the division's train, and it was the train that had been struck while most of the men of the Fifth New York were milling about in Hanover's Centre Square, sampling the delicacies distributed by the town's citizens. Boudrye recorded in his history that it was about 10 A.M. when the action opened. Major Hammond wrote later that it was about noon when the Fifth New York got into the town. This confusion is one of many regarding the events of that day. Hammond reported, "While resting, an attack was made upon the ambulances and stragglers in rear of the Eighteenth Pennsylvania...."[26]

Besides the two Michigan regiments left in the Littlestown area, the only personnel from the division that were not within or coming into Hanover at this moment were two companies of the Eighteenth Pennsylvania that formed the rear guard for the division. They had been trailing the column at a distance of about a mile. The Rebels had spotted these Yankees. This Pennsylvania detachment, commanded by Lieutenant Henry C. Potter, marching on the road from Littlestown had seen the Rebels at almost the same time and quickened their pace. Whether Lt. Potter's encounter happened before, after or

4. Advance and Pursuit—1863

simultaneously with the artillery's shelling of the town cannot be precisely determined, but it all happened within minutes. Artillery attached to the lead brigade of Stuart's command, having advanced north from Westminster, had deployed on a hill south of Hanover. It is unknown who ordered it to begin firing.

Suddenly, as Potter and his men approached the intersection of the road coming from Union Mills at Buttstown, marching over a rise in the ground, they found their path blocked by about sixty mounted Rebels. This Rebel detachment was between the Pennsylvanians and Hanover. Lieutenant Potter quickly decided he had to fight his way through if he was to have any chance of getting into Hanover. He called to his men to draw their pistols and on his signal they would charge the

General George A. Custer, commander of the Third Cavalry Division from the autumn of 1864 through the end of the war (Library of Congress).

roadblock. As they approached the roadblock slowly, the Rebels in the road called out for the Pennsylvanians to surrender. Potter signaled and his two companies charged. The Rebels scattered in all directions as the Union troopers galloped down on them. Quickly, the Rebels regained unit cohesion and began chasing the Yankees down the road to Hanover. The main body of the Eighteenth Pennsylvania, now almost within the town, heard the pistol shots of their comrades in the rear and reacted. When the two companies of Potter's men came charging up the road, the rear of the Eighteenth dismounted and got ready to cover them with fire from their carbines. As the pursuing Rebels came into range, they were met with a hail of fire from the Pennsylvanians shooting from behind roadside rail fences and trees. Moments later, more Rebel cavalry were seen approaching directly from the south. They readily joined the fighting.[27]

A Confederate tide seemed to sweep up and wash into Hanover. The scene both in and out of the town was total confusion given the suddenness of the encounter. Recorded accounts of the action to follow testify to the confusion and cannot be totally synchronized with one another. "With his accustomed coolness and bravery," wrote Boudrye in his history, "Maj. Hammond, in command of the regiment, quickly withdrew from the street to the open field near the rail depot, ordered the boys into line and led the charge upon the Rebels, who then possessed the town. The charging columns met on Frederick street, where a hand to hand conflict ensued. For a few moments the enemy made heroic resistance, but finally broke and fled, closely pursued by our men. They rallied again and again but were met with irresistible onsets, which finally compelled them to retire behind the hills under cover of their guns." These guns now amounted to two batteries positioned in farm fields slightly south and east of town. There is little doubt that Boudrye was there at the moment the charge by Hammond was made because in his personal journal he recorded, "The rebels were within three (3) rods of me, while pistol balls, shot and shell flew in every direction. I turned out of the village with the 5th N.Y. in the rear of which I was marching, where they formed in line and charged the enemy."

John Hammond later reported that a portion of the Eighteenth Pennsylvania was driven up and into the rear of the Fifth New York by the rebel surge. At the same time he was trying to face about his command, he was "trying to clear the streets of the fugitives preparatory to making a charge upon the advancing column of the enemy. They finally succeeded; and, without waiting for orders, immediately charged upon the enemy, driving them to the outside of town, where we found a large force drawn up in the road as a reserve and received from them a severe fire, causing the men to halt for a moment." It was in this charge that the Fifth New York suffered some casualties. Later in the year, the regiment's adjutant, F.M. Sawyer, wrote to a relative of trooper Sergeant Selden Wales of Company A: "Selden was Killed at the head of his company in the first charge upon the rebels when the enemy were forced outside the town upon their reserve force. Our charging party, at the edge of the town, received a very sever[e] fire from the rebels which momentarily checked them and as Selden moved ahead calling upon his Company to follow he fell from his horse with a bullet through the heart."[28]

About a mile to the north on the road leading to Abbottstown, First Brigade Commander Farnsworth had heard the shooting in his rear. He immediately ordered the First Vermont and First West Virginia to face about and return to Hanover. He didn't wait for this to happen, but galloped off at once. In town some moments later, he found confusion, with the Eighteenth Pennsylvania scattered about and trying to reform. And as noted by the chaplain, "The dead and wounded of both parties, with many horses, lay scattered here and there along the street." And the Fifth New York, who had charged the Rebels, was now returning, having gotten too close to the Rebel guns. At this moment, also, more Rebel cavalry units were arriving, part of Stuart's lead brigade commanded by Colonel Robert Chambliss. It appears that at this time Farnsworth found Hammond and probably got a quick appraisal of the situation from him. And now, as elements of the First West Virginia and First Vermont were coming into town from the north, Farnsworth decided to lead another attack down the road toward Buttstown.[29]

Within moments, the Second North Carolina, commanded by Lt. Col. William Payne, hit the southern corner of the town from the roads leading from Buttstown and Union Mills, where disorganized elements of the Eighteenth Pennsylvania were lingering after riding into town. At the same time, Farnsworth, with Hammond and the Fifth New York, attacked. Another swirling combat bled into the side streets, allies and sidewalks of this section of Hanover. One of the Fifth's troopers involved in this melee, Pvt. Abram Folger of Company H, "performed an act of great coolness and daring. He got mixed up some way in the charge upon the Eighteenth Pennsylvania cavalry, [and] not having time to reload his carbine, he picket [sic] up a loaded one some person had dropped, shot a horse which the rebel Col. Payne was riding, the rider falling onto a tan-vat, and it was with difficulty Folger save[d] him from drowning." The colonel's orderly tried to get Folger to surrender while he was dealing with Payne and the vat of tanning liquid, but the trooper swung his carbine toward the Rebel saying that he would "blow his brains out" if he didn't surrender. The orderly gave up and Folger marched the two prisoners out of the action.[30] At about this same time the momentum of the Rebel attack ebbed, possibly as a result of the loss of Payne. And as Folger dealt with Col. Payne, the Fifth New York, with Farnsworth leading, pressed forward in its attack. Of the second charge, Hammond only says in his report, "The men were reformed, and made another charge, driving the rebels in confusion along the road and through the fields. Private [Thomas] Burke, of Company A, captured a battle-flag from the enemy in this charge."[31]

Boudrye says, "In less than fifteen minutes from the time the Rebels charged the town, they were all driven from it, and were skulking in the wheat fields and among the hills of the vicinity."[32] The chaplain's estimate of the elapsed time it took for all this action to take place is probably close to being accurate, as many of the actions described occurred simultaneously.

It was sometime after the initial pistol charge by the Eighteenth Pennsylvania rear guard, but before the arrival of Farnsworth, that J.E.B. Stuart arrived on the scene along the road from Union Mills. The fight he had not wanted was on. The evidence appears to indicate that given the force he had at his command, the lead brigade of his division, and his estimate of the force opposing him, Stuart calculated he could punch his way through the town and not lose precious time detouring around it. The order had then gone down to Lt. Col. William Payne's Second North Carolina to move forward and drive the Yankees out of his way. This unit, known as the Black Horse Cavalry, had moved on the town, the result being Payne's fall into a dye vat. The Rebel batteries of horse artillery were capable of firing both into the town and on to the road leading to it. It was at this moment that Farnsworth, with Hammond and the Fifth New York and other elements from the brigade, headed south out of town on the second charge. Then there was the collision with the Second North Carolina on the road leading back to Buttstown. The mayhem swirled and expanded and some of the confused fighting had reached back to the side streets and allies of Hanover. The report made by Hammond doesn't mention that Private Burke, in capturing the Rebel flag, shot and killed the flag bearer with his pistol in this action, or that it was the flag of the Thirteenth Virginia Cavalry. After shooting the flag bearer, Private Burke brought in two Rebel prisoners.[33] Stuart ordered in more Rebel cavalry while his horse artillery was firing for effect on the Union troopers. It wasn't long until the Fifth New York found itself, not only in the biggest fight it had ever had, but also back in Hanover proper. There they turned over wagons and threw up barricades in the streets as men from the First Vermont and First West Virginia formed a defensive line on the southern and eastern fringes of town. Now the Fifth New York troopers stood behind the hastily arranged cover with carbines ready. Nothing happened.

Two incidents, occurring in rapid succession, may have contributed to this stillness at Hanover. Just earlier, the capture of Lt. Col. Payne of the Second North Carolina might have contributed to stalling a renewal of the attack by this regiment. Also, to the north, elements of the Michigan regiments that had raced quickly back toward town following Kilpatrick were deploying in the field to the west of town. And at the same time, the division's horse artillery — referred to as Elder's and Pennington's batteries — were deploying on high ground slightly to the north of town at a place called Bunker Hill. The Rebels couldn't help but notice. One of the Michigan officers noted, "The confederate line of battle could be distinctly seen on the hills to the south of the town."[34]

Kilpatrick had dashed through fields to get back to Hanover and just as quickly got an assessment of the situation. His after action report on this engagement, and for Gettysburg campaign as a whole, is sprinkled with such

4. Advance and Pursuit—1863

flourishes of vocabulary that suspicions immediately surface in the reader's mind as to their worth as an eyewitness account. Indeed, the First Vermont's history called Kilpatrick's report "somewhat magniloquent." Speaking of the action at Hanover, the general says, "For a moment, and a moment only, victory hung uncertain. For the first time our troops had met the foe in close contact, but they were on their own free soil, fair hands, regardless of the dangerous strife, waved them on, and bright, tearful eyes looked pleadingly out of every window.... He [the enemy] had for the first time and last time polluted with his presence the loyal town of Hanover."[35]

Stephen Clark, a lieutenant in the First Vermont, had quickly returned to Hanover with the regiment. The Vermont troopers formed in an open area to the east of the town proper. When Kilpatrick charged up on his way back to town, he is reported by Clark as asking Lt. Col. Preston of the First Vermont, "What regiment?" Preston immediately answered, "The 1st Vt., General." "Kill-cavalry" then is remembered announcing to the Vermonters, "Men of Vermont, you don't know me. And I don't know you, but the time has come to try each other on the battlefield. Draw Sabers!" Clark then remembers that rather than charging the enemy, the First Vermont went to support the division's artillery that was then deploying on high ground to the north of Hanover.[36]

There isn't anything here that tells us what "Kill-cavalry" was doing to take control of the action. In contrast is Hammond's summation, quoted above, a report so sparse one wished he had just an ounce of Kilpatrick's flair.[37]

The Yankee battery under Lt. Elder opened on the Rebels positioned on the hills south of town and was soon joined by Pennington. This resulted in an artillery duel that by some estimates continued for the next two hours. This duel resulted in casualties to both sides and damage within the town. The First Vermont, Fifth New York and First West Virginia, on the eastern flank of the town and behind barricades thrown up in the streets, were positioned facing the southern end of Hanover to repel any further assault by Stuart.

Earlier, Confederate cavalry commander Jeb Stuart had a close call during the second charge by the Fifth New York. He and some of his staff had been chased from the fields to the south of Hanover by about twenty-five men of the regiment led by Lt. Krom of Company G. Stuart's escape was only accomplished by having his horse leap over a ditch that the record says was fifteen feet wide. Krom and his men were not able to follow and the general galloped off to the south. Stuart's capture by an element of the Fifth New York would have led to Medals of Honor and quite probably altered the course of the war in the east.

After Farnsworth posted the First West Virginia and First Vermont on the defensive at the southern end of town, he ordered the Fifth New York back to a supporting position for Elder's battery. But Kilpatrick quickly countermanded this. Hammond later wrote:

> On returning [from the second charge] ... where the rest of the brigade were drawn up in line, I was ordered to act as support to Elder's battery. Finding that our position endangered the town, we moved around to the eastern side, when, the Second Brigade having returned [from the road to Abbottsville] I was ordered by General Kilpatrick to flank the enemy's position, and capture the battery, if possible, and to order and advance of the skirmishers on the right, which was done. The enemy, finding what our intentions were, retreated, and we immediately started in pursuit, but failed to come up with him. We were then ordered back, and went into bivouac outside town.

Coming after their having made two charges on the enemy, this order could not have been appreciated by the men of the Fifth New York.[38]

It can be assumed that at this moment, Kilpatrick, back in Hanover, had scanned the defensive position established by Farnsworth and got a quick report on the situation. Apparently satisfied with what he saw, he went into Hanover's Central Hotel and began composing a message to General Pleasonton. The Cavalry Corps commander was at this time with General Meade at Army Headquarters now established at Tannytown, Maryland, about sixteen miles to the southeast. Given its wording, Kilpatrick's message was written at a time when the fierce hand-to-hand fighting had subsided, the barricades had been thrown up and, it can be assumed, the Rebel artillery had withdrawn:

> General, five minutes after your dispatch saying that Stuart was making for Littlestown, my rear was attacked in Hanover, driven in, and a vigorous charge was made on the rear and flanks of my command; at the same time the enemy opened with artillery from the hills at the right of the town. Brigadier-General Farnsworth quickly got his brigade into position, and, by quick and vigorous charges, checked their attacks and drove the enemy out of town. The enemy soon showed himself in force on the left of the center. One portion retreated toward York; the other passed to the right, toward Gettysburg. As the enemy is reported to be advancing from the direction of Berlin, I made no further attempt to intercept Stuart's command. I have taken one battle-flag, a lieutenant colonel, 1 captain, and 45 privates and upward of 15 of the enemy have been killed. My loss is trifling.[39]

Kilpatrick's later written report of the action at Hanover defines "trifling" more precisely, adding proof that this officer cared little for the men under his command. In his report, written after the close of the campaign, "Killcavalry" puts his losses on June 30 at two officers and seventeen enlisted men killed and 178 wounded or missing. It is true that he is speaking of the entire division, but "trifling" isn't a word a commander who respected those in his charge would use, even during the stress of combat. But these numbers do speak of the fierceness and violence of the engagement. Boudrye reported that he helped bury eighty soldiers, both Union and Confederate, in a common grave the next evening. "It was a solemn time under the moonlight. I made some remarks and prayed." Initially, the Fifth New York reported four killed that day, plus twenty-five wounded and thirteen missing.[40]

As the lull began after the second charge by the Fifth New York and as the artillery batteries deployed, Custer and his two Michigan regiments galloped into town. Custer, probably under orders from Kilpatrick, moved his men to the west side of town and dismounted about 600 troopers. "The confederate line of battle could be distinctly seen on the hills to the south of the town," noted an officer under Custer. The two horse artillery batteries, under lieutenants Pennington and Elder, with the guns on Bunker Hill began firing, trying to break up the Confederate formations that were still arriving from the direction of Union Mills. In turn, Stuart, with guns from Wade Hampton's brigade, started shelling the town. At some point while this was happening, probably in the early afternoon, the Fifth New York got its orders to try to flank the Rebel guns. As previously stated, Hammond had moved the regiment out from behind the barricades and back toward the artillery batteries. Then he was sent on his flanking movement but, says Hammond, "the enemy, finding out our intentions, retreated, and we, immediately started in pursuit, but failed to come up with them."[41]

Major Hammond mentions the time of day only once in his report, noting that it was about noon when the regiment was in the square at Hanover and attacked. Going into bivouac could have been at any time, but it seems probable that it was late in the afternoon when they returned to town from trying to flank the Rebels. The fighting, however, in the immediate vicinity of Hanover was probably over by 2 P.M. because Boudrye testifies that it was at about that time that he "went to our hospital in the village, where I saw several killed and wounded." He also states that he had visited a barn where the captured Rebels were being held and that he spoke with Lt. Col. Payne of the Second North Carolina. Of these prisoners, Boudrye says, "Some were badly wounded, I assisted in stopping the blood of one, who would have bled to death. He prayed earnestly. I was introduced to Lt. Col. Paine, (rebel) of Warrenton, captured by Lt. Krohn [sic] Co. G 5th N.Y.C., who came near capturing Gen. Stuart also."[42]

Back at the hotel, Kilpatrick was still dispatching messages to Pleasonton. Of course, the primary mission of his division on this day was to report the location of the enemy, be it Stuart's cavalry or Lee's entire force. But most likely he obtained some disinformation from Lt. Col. Payne, whom he had earlier questioned personally. Kilpatrick now told Pleasonton, "After their encounter with General Stuart's force, I have succeeded in cutting his column in two."[43] This wasn't exactly true, but an embellishment on what had become the tactical situation by evening. Stuart, ever trying to unite with Ewell, had now decided to detour around Hanover, moving his wagon train to the east and then north toward York while, after dark, the brigades under Hampton and Chambliss at the south end of town disengaged and moved away to the to the northeast. These also headed for York. Fitz Lee's brigade moved off to the west, in the general direction of Gettysburg, before turning northeast to York. It was this movement by Fitz Lee that Kilpatrick reported, in error, as a movement on Gettysburg by Rebel cavalry.

That evening at Hanover and on the road leading north to Abottsville, the troopers of the Third Division brewed their coffee, suspecting that the next day would bring renewed contact with General Stuart. Kilpatrick, if he was aware of Stuart's withdrawal, did not pursue. He sent word to Pleasonton that he expected another engagement with Stuart the next day.

The intelligence gathered from his prisoners he passed on to Pleasonton. It was not completely accurate, but it tells us what Kilpatrick thought he knew at the time and helps explain the movement of the division the next day. "A strong column of the enemy's forces left York at day break this morning," Kilpatrick reported, "to march to this place [presumably Hanover], from which circumstances and other information, I conclude that they are concentrating at Gettysburg. They have 15 wagons' also about 133 mules. They spoke in the camp today of burning these wagons as they could not carry them with them. I shall attack them if I can by any means find proper roads. My information is reliable." Further, he warned his headquarters, "The enemy [Stuart's command] is moving toward York, cutting his way through the field. I think there is a considerable force at Berlin [East Berlin, Pennsylvania]. I am now midway between Abottstown and Hanover. I cannot advance further and keep communications open with Littlestown. Scouting parties will be sent out in the direction of York, Dover, and Carisle. Stuart is moving toward York."[44] Kilpatrick seemed to know where and what General Stuart was doing, but as to exactly where Ewell and, for that matter, the rest of the Army of Northern Virginia was, he was guessing. His mention of Gettysburg is just a guess. After providing Pleasonton with his intelligence, Kilpatrick asked for reinforcements. By 6 P.M. Pleasonton is telling Meade that he "sent him every cavalryman that I could get hold of. I also informed him of the infantry at this place [Littlestown]. I think there is no doubt but there is a heavy infantry

4. Advance and Pursuit—1863

force at [East] Berlin and Gettysburg. Kilpatrick had information that Lee's headquarters are at [East] Berlin."[45] In fact, Kilpatrick's speculation as to Lee's location, and Pleasonton's reading of his subordinate's information, were off by miles. By June 30, Lee had moved his headquarters from Chambersburg to a small place called Greenwood at the western end of Cashtown Gap, some miles out on the road leading toward Gettysburg.

Trooper John W. Jackson of Company F wrote and sent to the *Wyoming County Mirror* a lengthy letter from Upperville, Virginia, on July 23, 1863. In it he gives us another view of the action at Hanover:

> Moving towards Hanover, Penn., we passed through several towns where we were warmly greeted by the local people,—especially the ladies, who waved the starry flags and sang patriotic songs besides distributing refreshments through the ranks. We found it quite different to the treatment we received from the fair sex in Virginia.
>
> At Hanover, the whole town turned out to welcome us. It was about 9 o'clock A.M. when we entered the place. Our brigade was drawn up in column of fours in the main street, and we were enjoying ourselves finely, when the report of a cannon and the bursting of a shell in our rear caused a great commotion. The rebels had attacked our rear. It was so unexpected as to almost create a panic. But our regiment, after forming in a line in an open lot, charged through the town driving the rebels back to their battery, capturing a Lt. Col., and fully fifty other prisoners, with the battle flag of the 2nd North Carolina Cavalry.
>
> Our loss was twelve killed and about forty wounded. Capt. Eldridge [Elder] of the 4th regular Artillery soon got his four pieces into operation and chose our regiment to support, which we did till the rebels withdrew leaving many of their dead on the field. A detachment from our regiment under Major Hammond followed them four miles, skirmishing with their rear guard.[46]

The engagement at Hanover on June 30 was an inconclusive affair with two cavalry formations meeting unexpectedly. Both mounted formations were trying to find the Confederate army. The Fifth New York was part of a division tasked with finding the main body of Lee's army and it was at least heading in the direction where Ewell's Corps of that army was moving on June 30. Stuart and his men were trying, almost with desperation, to find their own army known only to be in that quadrant of Pennsylvania while not allowing the Yankees to find them. After Stuart and Kilpatrick disengaged from the fight at Hanover, both continued their search completely unaware that the army they sought was at that moment groping toward the town of Gettysburg, not many miles to the west. The next morning, parts of Lee's and Meade's forces would stumble into each other outside that town and the great confrontation would begin. And the day following, Stuart and Kilpatrick would again do the same.

5
Three Days in July—1863

> Head Quarters 5th N.Y. Cavalry
> Hartwood Church, Va. Sept 4th 1863
>
> Mrs. Bowen
> Your letter to the Chaplain of this Regt. Dated Aug 3rd has been lying in my office since the time it was received. Had it been address to [t]he Commanding Officer it would have received prompt attention. Our Chaplain was captured July 4th and is still in Libby Prison. I thought from the manner of the address that it was from some one who desired information of some relative and I made bold to open it this eve. I wish that I had done so sooner.
> Your brother, Selden, is buried in Hanover, Pa. And every attention was paid to his remains by the citizens of the place. His grave is marked, so that there can be no trouble in finding it....
> Very Respectfully
> Your Obedient Servant
> F.M. Sawyer
> Adj 5th NY Cav[1]

"At 11 A.M. the 1st brigade moved to Abbotstown [sic], to [East] Berlin, and pursued Rebel cavalry from this place to Rosetown, capturing several prisoners, and returned to [East] Berlin at midnight and bivouacked." In his history of the Fifth New York, this is all the chaplain has to say of Wednesday, July 1, the first day of the battle at Gettysburg. On the maps of today, the town referred to as Berlin in the record is called East Berlin, just a few miles to the north of Abbottstown. Kilpatrick was still looking for General Lee and his army, unaware that the great clash of arms had already started earlier that morning at Gettysburg. There is slightly more in the chaplain's journal because Boudrye remained in Hanover after Kilpatrick moved out, looking after the wounded and burying the dead from the fight with General Stuart. "I have been in the hospital nearly all day. We can distinctly hear the fight in the direction of Gettysburg."[2]

5. Three Days in July—1863

There was considerable work for the chaplain to do. One of the wounded was his friend Emile Portier of Company F. "I wiped the sweat from his brow.... All his care was for his wife Louise, to whom he requested me to write and send his effects in case he dies." The chaplain remained in Hanover the next day, July 2. He commented on the condition of Henry W. Moore of Company E. Moore had been shot in the action at Hanover "so that the stones of the cherries he had eaten that morning passed through the wound. He got well." "This afternoon [July 2], we hear terrible fighting towards Gettysburg. We distinctly see smoke which arises from the field." And in a passage that was added to the journal for this day sometime in the fall of 1863, he remembered, "We could hear the cannonading distinctly, and see the smoke rising from the field of battle. During the day today, the firing was very brisk. We heard only contradictory rumors of the tide of battle."[3]

The regiment's early history says that Kilpatrick, on July 1, moved in pursuit of Stuart's cavalry, but actually "Kill-cavalry" was looking for Lee. If he happened to stumble upon Stuart, could not Lee be far away? It can only be said of Kilpatrick at this time that he sincerely believed he would find Lee somewhere in the general East Berlin area. There is evidence that those riding in the column heard the sound of battle coming from the west that day. But Kilpatrick did nothing to deviate from his course. "All that day as we marched," says the history of the Eighteenth Pennsylvania, "the distant boom of the cannon could be heard in the direction of Gettysburg...." There is little else recorded concerning what the Fifth New York was doing on this first day of July other than sending scouts out in all directions. It was only early in the morning of July 2, after Kilpatrick received orders to move on Gettysburg, that the division turned southwest. "On the 2nd of July, we turned back and moved rapidly toward Gettysburg. The sound of the conflict was sufficient guide." It was late in the afternoon when the two brigades converged on Hunterstown, a place about five miles northeast of Gettysburg.[4]

Having ridden northward from Maryland, Brigadier General John Buford's First Cavalry Division had arrived in Gettysburg on June 30 around midday. His mission was essentially the same as Kilpatrick's: scout ahead of the left wing of the army, and if Lee was found, report it General Meade. Once in Gettysburg, Buford heard all the stories told by the town's citizens about Rebels having passed through their community the week before. And clearly, Buford and his scouts could see indications of a continued Rebel presence in the surrounding area. Earlier in the day they had briefly skirmished with Rebels as they approached the town from Maryland. In the afternoon, Buford's scouts detected a Rebel infantry brigade marching east toward Gettysburg on the road coming from Chambersburg. The general immediately positioned his two brigades defensively, no doubt expecting this force not to stop until it got to town. For their part, these Rebels on the Chambersburg Road had heard rumors that a quantity of shoes, a commodity always in demand within the Army of Northern Virginia, might be found and appropriated in Gettysburg. The infantrymen were the lead element of one of the two corps marching with General Lee, and their officers were under strict orders not to precipitate an engagement if they were to encounter a Union force. When the lead elements of the Confederate force saw that Gettysburg contained blue-clad troops, it stopped and retired back down the road leading to Chambersburg.

General Buford deployed his division outside Gettysburg in an arc from west to northeast and sent more scouts out in all directions. The Rebel infantry could not determine what kind of troops were in town or how many. Given their orders, most were in camp some miles down the Chambersburg Road by sundown, no doubt sampling the acquired delicacies of the Pennsylvania countryside. Buford, as he positioned his force, also sent word back to General Reynolds, leading the left or western wing of the army up from Maryland, generally following the path the cavalry had taken. Before night fell on June 30, Buford knew that Reynolds would be marching into Gettysburg the next day and if there were any more Rebels than those already spotted, he would have support from at least that wing of the army. Instinctively, Buford knew something was going to happen tomorrow. But even this veteran cavalryman couldn't have imagined the size and scope of what would follow.

At daylight on July 1, the Rebels started down the road from Chambersburg on a reconnaissance in force to determine just what kind of Union presence was in Gettysburg and, if possible, get the rumored shoes. In doing so they tripped over Buford's pickets set at a distance from town. Almost immediately, shots were exchanged. The firing coming from Buford's men intensified as the Rebels advanced, and it wasn't long before the leading Rebel brigades deployed for battle in the fields on either side of the road from Chambersburg. They advanced as the Yankee pickets fired and fell back. The fighting withdrawal crossed Herr Ridge, over which the road from Chambersburg passed. Buford's cavalry then took position on McPherson's Ridge further to the east. John Burford was determined to hold even though the enemy wasn't stopping before his pickets and the fire from his horse artillery. There was only one ridge remaining for use as a defensive position, Seminary Ridge, just to the west of the town, and the last elevated position before this action might degenerate into street fighting in Gettysburg. General Reynolds arrived at about this time, closely followed by the lead elements of the First Division, and the engagement quickly spread outward from there. For the rest of the day the

Rebels would press the fight as more of their divisions than Union divisions appeared on the roads leading into Gettysburg. The Rebel pressure forced a Union retreat through the town and up and onto Cemetery Hill and Cemetery Ridge, elevations slightly east and south of Gettysburg. The shooting didn't stop until after dark as the Union infantry dug defensive positions on the hill and ridge. Clearly, the Union force had never had the initiative and had been pushed severely by Lee's troops, despite their orders that morning not to bring on a general engagement.

By moving all night after the action at Hanover, Jeb Stuart had gone north and then to the northwest, looking for Ewell. They missed each other. The part of Ewell's Corps — Early's division — that had been in the York area began its movement toward Gettysburg on June 30 while Stuart was still engaged at Hanover. Finding no sign of his comrades around York or Dover during the night of June 30, Stuart headed for Carlisle, further to the northwest. But earlier he had sent an aide with an escort off to the west looking for Ewell. The aide found Ewell — now engaged at Gettysburg — who passed him quickly along to General Lee, whom he reached late in the afternoon of July 1. By now the Battle of Gettysburg was some hours along and escalating as more units converged on the town. General Lee quickly told Stuart's aide the situation and ordered him to find his commander and have him report with his command to Gettysburg. It was 1 A.M., on July 2 when the aide found Stuart outside the Union-held town of Carlisle, Pennsylvania. By 2 A.M. Stuart's cavalry was in motion for Gettysburg.[5]

A Union courier during the day had also found the Third Division, still looking for Lee's army to the northeast of Gettysburg. The courier carried orders from General Pleasonton for Kilpatrick to quickly move on the town and go into position of the right flank of the army now in serious contact with the enemy at Gettysburg. Kilpatrick started there at once.

Stuart's cavalry, moving fast in response to Lee's order, passed through the small village of Hunterstown early on the afternoon of July 2. The rear brigade was that of Brigadier General Wade Hampton. General Hampton's rear guard was in Hunterstown when it made contact with an advanced element of Custer's brigade, approaching from roughly the southeast. A quick mounted skirmish ensued and drove the Rebel rear element from the town. This rear guard immediately sent word to Hampton that blue cavalry were moving on Hunterstown in force. Hampton in turn notified Stuart, who ordered him to hold. Hampton counter marched his brigade back along the road leading from Gettysburg to Hunterstown. Hampton came upon his rear guard being charged by a company of Michigan troopers of the Second Brigade with George Custer leading from the front. There was the inevitable crash of these two elements with sabers and pistols the primary weapons employed. Hampton's other troopers spread out on either side of the road and supported their comrades with carbine fire. Custer's horse was killed beneath him in this hand-to-hand clash and he had to be rescued by one of his troopers. The Rebels were able to bring greater numbers into the action against Custer and forced him to retreat back to Hunterstown. While this fighting had taken place, other Union regiments had deployed on both sides of the road outside Hunterstown in support of Custer's men. Pennington's battery began firing in support of the retreating Union troopers. Kilpatrick and Stuart had essentially stumbled into each other again. But this time, near the known battlefield at Gettysburg, both cavalry commands thought the other was trying to turn their army's flank and, therefore, a fight had to be made.

As the Michigan troopers galloped back to the position occupied by the Second brigade, the Rebels followed and were blasted by carbine and canister, enfilading them as they came down the road. This attack by Hampton's rear guard and assorted elements of other regiments did not last long or get close to the line held by the Second Brigade.

The Fifth New York, marching along with the rest of the First Brigade, arrived in Hunterstown as Custer's men were fighting beyond the town with Hampton's troopers. They were ordered to take up a position supporting Pennington's and Elder's batteries, to the right of the road leading to Gettysburg. The two artillery batteries continued to fire on the Rebels while the First Brigade stood ready with their carbines to repel another charge. As the summer twilight descended, Hampton was able to bring to his position a battery of Stuart's artillery. This battery began firing, trying to knock out Kilpatrick's guns. This action went on until after it grew dark. The Fifth New York had had another lucky day. If the regiment saw action at all, the Fifth New York merely fired its carbines from a defensive position as it supported the artillery batteries. The regiment suffered no casualties for July 2.[6]

One account of this action comes from John W. Jackson of the Fifth New York in his long letter to the *Wyoming Mirror*. It is Jackson's perspective and does not quite align with other accounts of the actions from other sources:

> On the 2nd we marched towards Gettysburg, where heavy cannonading was heard, and we could see the smoke of battle. Our division was ordered to the right wing of the army, and just at sundown encountered the enemy's cavalry, their battery opening on our advance. The 18th Penn. Cavalry made a charge driving the rebel out of Hunterstown. Our battery took position on an eminence, and did excellent work dismounting one of the guns in the rebel battery. Our advance was called in, and the 6th Mich. Cavalry, armed with the Spencer Rifle, (seven-shooters) were posted so as to command the ground in front. Soon, as we expected, the rebel cavalry came up on a charge, but being met with a

shower of canister shot and rifle balls, they went back faster than they came. Darkness now settled down upon us and thus ended the fight for that day.[7]

Kilpatrick, in response to orders received from Pleasonton, pulled the division out of Hunterstown starting about 11 P.M. that night. With Fransworth's First Brigade covering the rear, the division moved south, crossing behind the main Union line that had formed on Cemetery Ridge, slightly to the southeast of Gettysburg. The division stopped on the Baltimore Pike at a place called Two Taverns, about five miles southeast of Gettysburg. Getting there between three and four in the morning, the troopers slept by the side of the road, with the First Brigade on the road to the west of Two Taverns. And by 8 A.M., July 3, they had their orders. The division was to move to the southern end of the Union line and occupy the area between Round Top and Emmitsburg Road.[8] This mission, ordered by Pleasonton, as Kilpatrick understood it, was to "press the enemy, to threaten him at every point, and to strike at the first opportunity," at right flank and rear of Lee's army. As recalled much later by a junior officer in the First Vermont, Pleasonton's order was to merely "demonstrate against Lee's right flank." This difference in the intention or the true meaning of Kilpatrick's order for that day might significantly contribute to the controversy surrounding the conduct by "Kill-cavalry" later in the day.

As the men of the Fifth New York rode westward, the Second Brigade under Custer received an order by a circuitous route from Pleasonton. He was to move his brigade to a position vacated by a brigade of General David Gregg's Second Cavalry Division, then in position to the rear of the Union's main line of resistance on Cemetery Ridge. To replace Custer in the Third Division, Pleasonton had the Reserve Brigade, under Brigadier General Wesley Merritt, march from Emmitsburg north to Gettysburg and join Kilpatrick on his left.[9] As a result, the two brigades of the Third Division were separated on this day. Custer's Brigade took part in the day's major cavalry action against Jeb Stuart's full command to the east and rear of the main battle lines at Gettysburg.

The critical moment in the Gettysburg campaign came in the afternoon of July 3. Robert E. Lee had, on July 2, tried to defeat the Army of the Potomac by attacking the southern end of the Federal line. This echelon attack, it was hoped, would roll up the Yankees' left flank while Ewell's Corps attacked the right end of the Union line. A union corps isolated itself in advance of the Federal main line of resistance and was mauled in the Rebel attack. On the extreme left, Federal troops occupied the hill called Little Round Top mere minutes before the attack by the Rebels would have swept over the crest. In a heroic and bitter struggle, the Union force was able to hold and then secure this key position on the battlefield. The fighting on July 2 was intense, at times at close quarters and desperate. When the fighting sputtered out in the summer twilight, the day's results were essentially inconclusive. Now, on July 3, Lee would concentrate on the center of the Federal position atop Cemetery Ridge. He ordered a frontal assault by upwards of 12,500 troops that would carry the ridge while Stuart's cavalry swept in from the rear. In order to ensure the success of the infantry assault, practically all the guns Lee had were aimed at Cemetery Ridge. Preparatory to the assault, beginning at about 1 P.M., a massive artillery bombardment — possibly the greatest in history to that time and certainly the greatest ever on the North American continent — began and lasted about one hour. A resident of Gettysburg described the scene soon after the battle:

> From 11 A.M. to 1 P.M. there was a perfect lull, each party apparently waiting to see what the other was about to do, and to what point the attack was to be made.
> At seven minutes past 1 P.M., the awful and portentous silence was broken. [The artillery barrage produced] such a continuous succession of crashing sounds as to make us feel as if the very heavens had been rendered asunder — such as were never equaled by the most terrific thunder-storm ever witnessed by mortal man.[10]

The bombardment was designed to eliminate Federal artillery on the ridge. With this accomplished, the infantry assault would sweep the Yankees out of their position. No man alive that afternoon had ever witnessed anything like it. Indeed, the world would not see its likes again until the First World War, either the massed artillery or the massed infantry assault. Miles away in Hanover, Chaplain Boudrye clearly heard the rumble of the Rebel guns and the counterbattery fire from the Union lines. As this preliminary barrage ended, Confederate General George Pickett led approximately 12,500 men in the assault on Cemetery Ridge. The war and the Union could be said to have hung in the balance for those hours during which the bombardment and the attack by Pickett went forward. Long before 5 P.M. that afternoon, it was over. Reserve artillery had replaced the Union guns that were put out of action on Cemetery Ridge. Their firepower was brought to bear on the advancing Rebels. These Federal guns, as well as the rifle fire by Union troops in front and from both flanks, were the cause of massive casualties among the men under General Pickett.

After a brief penetration of the Union line that resulted in the capture of hundreds of Rebel prisoners, the lucky Rebel survivors retreated. Back within their lines along Seminary Ridge, they braced for an expected Union counterattack, one that did not materialize. Stuart's attempt to penetrate the

Union position from the rear had been defeated that afternoon by the combination of Gregg's Second Cavalry Division and Custer's brigade of the Third Division. It was now the late afternoon of a hot summer day, with a possible storm cloud building off to the west that could be rain later on. The survivors that lay on their rifles atop those two Pennsylvania ridges, Cemetery and Seminary, knew who had won the great battle. But as the summer twilight turned to darkness, the exhausted troops on both sides must have wondered whether their leaders would call for another day of bloodletting. General Robert E. Lee knew now, after three days, he could not get the victory he had planned for back in Virginia weeks before. He knew that George Meade and his Army of the Potomac had won the Battle of Gettysburg.

The Eighteenth Pennsylvania Cavalry by this time had been deployed by Kilpatrick closest to Emmitsburg Road to face generally north, waiting for further orders. An unidentified trooper remembered, "For two hours the most terrific cannonading I ever heard continued, which fairly shook the earth. All at once the noise ceased and every thing was perfectly still except as occasional shot from the skirmish line. But quiet did not last long.... Soon could be heard the rebel yell from Pickett's men as they went on their famous charge. The yell was soon mixed with volleys of musketry, little later with the booming of cannon and the yankey [sic] yell. We could hear all this noise, but could not see anything owing to the distance and the timber around and in front of us."[11] Certainly Kilpatrick heard it also. Some hours passed. Now, in the late afternoon and at the south end of the battlefield came, by all accounts, the general's worst moment as a commander, a moment when he was fully aware that Pickett's attack had been repulsed. With Custer's brigade on loan to General Gregg, "Kill-cavalry" had the First Brigade positioned in the area just south and the west of Round Top, facing roughly north with Emmitsburg Road on its left. He had been reinforced by the Reserve Brigade from the First Cavalry Division, and this command was set to advance north with Emmitsburg Road on its right. Kilpatrick still hungered for some glory before the lengthening shadows of afternoon became a midsummer's evening. For the Fifth New York Cavalry, July 3, 1863, was their luckiest day of the war. The regiment saw but brief action at this end of the field as Kilpatrick's futile and wasteful attempt to make a contribution to victory at Gettysburg played out. The regiment aligned itself in support of Elder's artillery battery that was positioned to support the advance of the division. Elder and his cannons had been dueling with Rebel batteries most of the afternoon, and except for some counterbattery fire from Rebel guns landing within the regiment's position, the lucky New York troopers were essentially out of the action.

Colonel Arthur Fremantle was a British observer with Lee's army. According to the colonel it was approximately 7 P.M. and the day's attack that he had witnessed from Seminary Ridge was long over. He recorded in his journal what he heard coming from south of his position on Seminary Ridge: "Firing entirely ceases in our front about this time, but we now heard some brisk musketry on our right, which I afterwards learned proceeded from Hood's Texans, who had managed to surround some enterprising Yankee cavalry, and were slaughtering them with great satisfaction. Only eighteen out of four hundred are said to have escaped."[12] Although Freemantle's estimate of casualties is far from accurate, it was a slaughter he heard. And his noting of the time of day coincides with the approximate time this action took place.

If a superior or more experienced officer had been there he might have altered, or even stopped, the events that now moved forward. The events in the late afternoon of July 3 clearly show us Kilpatrick's unreasonable recklessness and his lack of concern for the lives of his men. A Fifth New York trooper, writing home later, tells us what he saw that day:

> During the night [July 2–3] we moved along our lines and the next morning found ourselves on the extreme left flank of our line of battle. At daylight the ball opened all along the lines. At 10 o'clock Capt. Eldridge [Elder] had his guns at work. The rebels replied throwing shell into our ranks with great accuracy of range. Our regiment seemed to be favored with more than their proper share of bursting shells. Several exploded in our ranks; three horses were killed, but only two men were struck, one being killed instantly. We were obliged to change our position to get out of range. About 5 P.M., a charge was ordered, and Gen. Farnsworth led the 1st [West] Virginian cavalry, but on account of the nature of the ground it resulted disastrously. The column was repulsed by the storm of bullets and iron hail, but a squadron of the 1st Vermont was more successful in charging on the right, and brought in about thirty prisoners — all infantry of Longstreet's Corps. We found out what we were contending with. Fearing that Gen. Kilpatrick would turn his right, Lee had sent up a division of Infantry to support his cavalry force. By thus harassing his flank we drew forces from the center and did not allow him to concentrate all his strength at one point, as is the favorite plan in his tactics.[13]

This correspondent doesn't have all of the facts quite right, but it gives at least a partial view of the action of July 3. The single Fifth New York trooper who was killed by the Rebel shelling was Daniel Hurley, Company C, as the regiment stood in support of Elder's battery. Private John Buckley of Company C was wounded by the same Rebel shelling.[14]

Major John Hammond, during the Fifth's pursuit of Lee in the days following Gettysburg, somehow found the time to send off a note to his wife. This is his first written impression of what happened on July 3.

5. Three Days in July—1863

> Smithburg Md.
> July 5 1863
>
> My Dear wife,
> I improve a moment to write to you I am very well, but very tired after four day's bloody fighting at Gettysburg. The rebels are severely whipped and commenced retreating on the night of the 3rd. We fought them on their right flank; and on the 2nd, by making a night march, we passed clear around their left flank and fought a large division on them. The vigorous attack of our cavalry had a great effect in winning the day. Our division lost about two hundred men. Brig. Gen. Farnsworth was killed or missing.[15]

John Hammond was not a person ever to be extravagant with words. This isn't the whole story of July 3 and, admittedly, Hammond was probably in a rush writing this note. But it is clear that both of the above correspondents thought they had faced a Confederate infantry division. Curiously, both Hammond and the trooper were of the impression that Kilpatrick's attack contributed to the Union victory. Sadly, this was not the case. After the campaign had ended, Hammond submitted his actual after action report, but it is undated. Kilpatrick submitted his report on August 10, so it is reasonable to assume Hammond wrote his report sometime close to this date. As with the affair at Hanover, it is short and there is no color in it. It is quoted here to illustrate what he had seen and what the Fifth New York had done that, to him, was of importance.

> Battle of Gettysburg, PA., July 3
>
> At about 7 o'clock on the morning of July 3, the command was ordered to move, and march toward the left of our line of battle. On arriving on the field, we were ordered into position as supports for Elder's battery. Soon after taking position, in the edge of some timber, the enemy obtained the range so exactly as to throw their shells into our midst, doing considerable damage. General Farnsworth then ordered me to get under cover of a ridge a little more to the left, which was done. Shortly after, I was ordered to divide my command into two sections, and send Major Bacon with one on the right, while I took the other on the left, of the Eighteenth Pennsylvania, and, in connection with them, make a charge upon one of the enemy's guns, which was very troublesome. We moved forward some distance, when the enemy removed the piece, and we were ordered back, and took up a position in rear of our battery, and stood to horse during the remainder of the fight. At night we withdrew a short distance to the rear, and did picket duty upon the field.[16]

This brief thrust forward was the only aggressive movement by the Fifth New York on July 3. The rest of the day, until the division withdrew at dark, the regiment was in support of Elder's battery. Not in all the histories, general and specific, written in the years since the Battle of Gettysburg is there one in which the Third Cavalry Division is given credit for contributing to the "wining of the day," as Hammond announces in his letter home.

What really happened to the Third Division on July 3? The Fifth New York, with the First Brigade, had moved from the vicinity of Two Taverns that morning and reached the area southwest of Round Top — the larger of the two hills at the south end of the Union lines — between eleven o'clock and noon. Kilpatrick was soon supported by the Reserve Brigade under the command of Wesley Merritt that arrived from the south and went into position to the west of Emmitsburg Road. Kilpatrick's orders from Pleasonton, as he notes them in his after-action report written over a month later, were either to attempt to get in the rear of Lee's army by attacking from the southern end of the battlefield and to do as much damage as possible, or to demonstrate against the Rebel flank and, hopefully, pull enemy troops away from the expected main attack. Kilpatrick wrote his summary on August 10 and phrased it as follows: "At 8 A.M., received orders from headquarters Cavalry Corps to move to the left of our line and attack the enemy's right and rear with my whole command and the Regular Brigade." This order, if accurate, fitted nicely with his desire to acquire a little glory that had so far eluded him in this campaign. He sent Farnsworth with a small force into the area around Bushman Hill, to the west of Round Top to drive away Rebel pickets. This done, Elder's battery unlimbered and positioned its guns to support any advance by the brigade in a northerly direction. Slightly to the west, the First Vermont was sent probing north in the direction of the Bushman family farm, located slightly east of Emmitsburg Road. There was some sporadic shooting and the Rebel pickets in the area were driven back. The Rebels were now fully aware that there was a mounted force probing from the south and reacted accordingly, facing about infantry and guns to resist any further forward motion. The terrain in front of the brigade was broken and boulder-strewn, and fields were divided either with rail fences or stone walls. All the advantages of the ground lay with the Rebels, occupying terrain completely unsuited for cavalry operations. While this was happening, Merritt with the Reserve Brigade was probing northward, dismounted, along and to the west of Emmitsburg Road. This, too, was causing the Rebels to reorient their line to meet this threat. All the while, further to the north, Pickett's Charge was in preparation and, probably, the great preparatory barrage was underway.[17]

Now Kilpatrick sent the First West Virginia on probe forward. They moved against the enemy's position at the western base of Round Top, but were held up by fences that the cavalrymen had to try tearing down while under fire. The West Virginians withdrew. Apparently, there was now an artillery piece in position in this area and it had been firing at Elder's position. It was at this point that Farnsworth ordered Hammond to join with the Eighteenth Pennsylvania in a two-regiment thrust to do something about the gun. As Hammond reported, "We moved forward some distance ... and we were ordered back" once the gun was removed.[18]

Brigadier General Evander M. Law had taken over command of General John Bell Hood's infantry division after his wounding the previous day and was present when Kilpatrick and Farnsworth's brigade arrived to the south of his position. Later he recalled that it was at the time when the great preparatory bombardment was taking place but before Pickett's charge went forward. General Law wrote that Kilpatrick's command appeared and concentrated "in the body of timber which extended from the base of Round Top westward toward Kern's house, on the Emmitsburg road." Two of Law's batteries were turned about "and at once opened fire upon the cavalry, which retired beyond the woods and out of sight."[19]

With the Fifth New York now back supporting Elder's guns, Kilpatrick now turned to the First Vermont to renew the attempt to push the Rebels from the base of Round Top. Simultaneously, the Eighteenth Pennsylvania would attack further to the west, likewise pushing the enemy before it. At a point in time close to this, Farnsworth is reported to have asked for a survey of the terrain by some of his men in advance of any forward movement. What was reported to him was alarming; the ground was broken and unsuited for cavalry, and there was enemy infantry and artillery in position to rake the whole area with fire from three directions. The historian of the First Vermont confirms this with these words:

> Major Wells [First Vermont] had inspected the ground in front, and as he reported that it did not look promising, Farnsworth asked permission, before attacking, to send forward a party to reconnoiter. Kilpatrick granted the request with apparent reluctance. Captain Woodward with Company M of the First Vermont made the reconnaissance. It disclosed the presence of hostile infantry under Round Top, and of ample infantry supports for the two Confederate batteries in front. General Farnsworth reported the facts and expressed his opinion that it was a desperate thing to take mounted men into such a place.[20]

Nevertheless, Kilpatrick ordered the advance despite Farnsworth's reconnaissance.

Captain H.C. Parsons of the First Vermont wrote in later years his recollection of the scene, which, if accurate, gives us a glimpse of Kilpatrick at this moment. "I was near Kilpatrick when he impetuously gave the order to Farnsworth to make the last charge," Parsons recalled.

> Farnsworth with emotion: "General, do you mean it? Shall I throw my handful of men over rough ground, through timber, against a brigade of infantry? The 1st Vermont has already been fought half to pieces, these men are too good to kill." Kilpatrick answered, "Do you refuse to obey my order? If you are afraid to lead this charge, I will lead it." Farnsworth rose in his stirrups, "Take that back!" Kilpatrick returned his defiance, but soon repented. He said, "I did not mean it, forget it." I recall the two young officers at that moment in the shadow of the oaks and against the sunlight.

Parsons further recalls that this scene occurred at about 5 P.M. and "there was an oppressive stillness after the day's excitement." The "day's excitement" can be taken to mean that the day's great artillery barrage and Pickett's charge were long over.

Captain William Graham commanded the horse artillery of Merritt's Brigade and his later recollection supports Captain Parsons's rendering of this episode. He wrote in later years that he witnessed the exchange between Kilpatrick and Farnsworth, adding, "If Farnsworth had replied to Kilpatrick, 'I wish you would lead the charge General and I'll ride boot to boot with you, Sir,' the charge never would have been made, and all that knew Kilpatrick in Buford's Division agreed with me."[21]

Farnsworth had no choice; he had to attack. The young general then is reported, according to Parsons, as having one last exchange with Kilpatrick. "For a moment there was silence, when Farnsworth spoke calmly, 'General, if you order the charge, I will lead it, but you must take the responsibility.' I did not hear the low conversation that followed, but as Farnsworth turned away he said, 'I will obey your order.' Kilpatrick said earnestly, 'I take the responsibility.'" The general moved to prepare for the charge and no doubt encountered Lt. Col. A.W. Preston, in command of the First Vermont. If he spoke to him, it was not recorded. However, the words spoken by Farnsworth to John Hammond were remembered by Captain Parsons. "My God, Hammond," Farnsworth is reported to have exclaimed. "Kil is going to have a cavalry charge. It is too awful to think of...." Although Hammond made no mention of it in any report or letter, this recollection places him at the scene, even though the men of the regiment were in position near Elder's guns. Captain Parsons, either at that time or later, had no reason detectable in the sources to fabricate this exchange.[22] Years later, Hammond wrote what appears to be a statement of fact relating to the location of the Fifth New York's monument on the Gettysburg battlefield. In his statement, Hammond also gives credence to Parsons's account. Given the regard in which he was held by those who knew him, there can be little doubt as to its accuracy.

> As Major commanding the Fifth N.Y.C., I certify that on the morning of the 3d of July, 1863, the First Brigade of Gen. Kilpatrick's cavalry division, under the command of Gen. Farnsworth, reached the southwest base of Round Top.... The rebels had thrown up a stone wall from alongside Taneytown road, across the old road towards Devil's Den, as can be seen to-day. Farnsworth was ordered to send out scouting parties. One party of perhaps a company of, which regiment I cannot say, followed up Plum Run and ran against a force too strong for them, turned to the right and came in by the old road at a lively gait, with quite a number of rebels.... These prisoners were some of the ones who had put up the stone intrenchment [sic]. As for the location, I have in part described, Elder's Battery and my command were in the edge of an open oak forest, since cut down. Plum Run at the foot of the side of declivity. The J. Slyder house and Emmittsburg [sic] road in full view. Soon after his command was located, Farnsworth asked me to walk down with him and see what chance there was for the cavalry to charge. On our side of Plum Run was and is a stone fence, some of it having a few rails on top. On the opposite side was a swampy ground heavily timbered; on inner side of the run was a range of boulders and rocks that was appalling. Farnsworth said, "My God, Hammond, Kil is going to have a cavalry charge. Its too awful to think of,—will be but a slaughter for the boys,—they have no chance for themselves." I first visited Gettysburg with my brother, in the fall of 1872. At that time I had no trouble in going direct to our location on the 3ᵈ day of July.[23]

It was now after 5 P.M. and the great charge on the Union center had been repulsed. This fact was known to Kilpatrick and, presumably, to everyone else. Parsons reported later that it was near 5 P.M. when a messenger, headed somewhere other than to Kilpatrick, rode near the brigade and shouted out as he passed, "We turned the charge, nine acres of prisoners."[24] Although it is hindsight, it had to be clear to Kilpatrick that the battle was approaching its end, if not already there. Nothing in the charge he had ordered would have changed in any significant way — or contributed more — to that day's victory. But given his orders of that morning, or what he took to be his orders, Kilpatrick might have thought he was fulfilling those orders, even at this late hour. However, Kilpatrick should have relied on the reconnaissance information reported to him by Farnsworth or have gone and looked at the ground himself if he was not satisfied with what was reported. Beyond this it is apparent that he was trying to have something to report, something favorable as to his leadership of the Third Cavalry Division on that crucial day.

The charge Farnsworth led was composed of two battalions of the First Vermont and elements of the First West Virginia. A history of the First Vermont records what happened. "Farnsworth placed himself ... at the head of the column, and led it forward by a wood road through a piece of timber and through an opening in a stone fence into open ground, where it came under the fire of some infantry to the left. Passing on through a field and over a second stone fence," the charge encountered more infantry that they scattered. However, they in turn came under fire from artillery firing from the vicinity of Emmitsburg road, and this "emptied many saddles." The command then became divided, with one battalion fighting its way back in the direction it had come, while the other, with Farnsworth leading, pressed on. At this moment, Kilpatrick ordered Lt. Colonel Preston of the First Vermont to take the remainder of his regiment and go to the support of Farnsworth. As this was happening, more Rebel infantry joined the one-sided fight.[25]

Lt. Col. Preston details what happened in his later report:

> This charge [Farnsworth's] was made over severe obstacles, but succeeded in breaking the enemy's line. Many of our dead, together with the body of General Farnsworth, were found in the rear of the position held by the enemy's second line. I was immediately ordered by Brigadier-General Kilpatrick to support this charge with the balance of my regiment, which I did with the first battalion, under Captain Parsons.... In charging over the wall and hill carried by the first column, I encountered a very large force of the enemy, which had been sent in from their left to re-establish their line and cut off the retreat of the first column. The contest for the possession of this hill was most desperate. Being temporarily checked in a direct attack, I obliqued my force to the right, and succeeded in gaining the top of the hill by a flank movement. The opposing forces were now completely intermingled, and the contest became a hand-to-hand one, in which our sabers were effectually used. The enemy, being completely cut up, surrendered in squads, and were sent to the rear ... but being exposed to the fire of the enemy's batteries and sharpshooters, I was obliged to fall back.... Our loss on this occasion was 12 killed, 20 wounded (2 of whom have since died), and 25 missing.[26]

Farnsworth, with the initial charge, was killed while attempting to retreat. Between the Devil's Den and Bushman's farm, Farnsworth came upon a line of cannons supported by more Rebel infantry. As some of the men retreated south, Farnsworth was knocked from his horse by a shell. A nearby trooper offered the general his horse. Farnsworth took it and with a small group with which he was riding, turned and headed back the way they had come. It was during this retreat that the general was fatally shot. Captain Parsons lived to tell the tale although he was severely wounded in the action. It had been a large and unequal engagement. The better part of a cavalry regiment, more if Merritt's command are included, had charged the better part of a Rebel infantry brigade in positions it had occupied since the day before and supported by artillery. Elder's battery had fired in support of Farnsworth's charge as long as it could without causing friendly fire casualties. This supporting fire may have helped keep the casualties down to the level reported by Lt. Col. Preston.

5. Three Days in July—1863

The First Vermont's regimental history includes a statement made for it by a Confederate general who witnessed the action from a distance.

> Very soon the head of a line of cavalry in that road emerged from the wood, galloping, hurrahing and waving their swords as if frantic. Our artillery, which had been thrown forward across the road, opened on them. They rode on. An infantry fire from a wood on their left opened on them. They then turned to their right to escape.... Some of our men threw themselves behind the stone fence on the side of the lane and opened on them as they came down the lane. They then turned again to the right and entered a field and directed themselves back towards the point where they had first appeared to us. In doing so they had to pass a wood on their left. From this an infantry fire opened on them, and their direction was again changed to the right. The result was that they galloped round and round in the large field, finding fire at every outlet, until most of them were killed or captured. Every thing passed before our eyes on the mountain side as if in an amphitheater.

If nothing else, this observational statement, given by a Rebel who took no active part in the action, details the callousness, stupidity and the utter disregard for those under his command that Kilpatrick exhibited that day.

General Evander M. Law, after he had supervised the disposition of troops that were resisting the probing from the south by Merritt's brigade, had returned to a position where he could see the area where Farnsworth was to attack. Law later wrote, but gives no indication of the time, that "Farnsworth and the few of his men who remained in their saddles directed their course towards the point where they had originally broken in, having described by this time almost a complete circle. But the gap where they had entered was now closed, and receiving another fire from that part, they again turned to the left and took refuge in the woods near the base of Round top." It was here General Law says that Farnsworth was killed.

Recorded officially, the Vermont regiment lost that day fourteen killed, twenty wounded, and thirty-five captured.[27]

Later, in his report of August 10, "Kill-cavalry" explained things his way:

> At 1 P.M. General Farnsworth had reached the rear and right of the enemy's position and became engaged with his skirmishers.
>
> At 3 P.M. General Merritt came in on General Farnsworth's left and the enemy was driven over 1 mile.
>
> At 5:30 P.M. I ordered an attack with both brigades. The [Merritt's] Regulars, dismounted, were pushed in on the left, and Brigadier-General Farnsworth moved down with two regiments—First West Virginia and Eighteenth Pennsylvania—closely followed by the First Vermont and Fifth New York, through a piece of woods, and drove the enemy from one position to another until a heavy stone wall was reached, behind which the rebel infantry was gathered in great number. Our cavalry broke, rallied, and broke again before that formidable barrier, but the First Vermont and First West Virginia, led by the gallant

Farnsworth, cleared the fence, sabered the rebels in the rear, rushed on over a second line of infantry, and were only stopped by another fence and a third line of infantry and artillery. The artillery, under Elder and Graham [of Merritt's brigade], all this time was doing good execution.

The Fifth New York did not participate as Kilpatrick states in this report; instead it supported Elder's battery as it fired in support of Farnsworth's advance.

Kilpatrick continues: "Previous to this attack, the enemy had made a most fierce and determined attack on the left of our main line of battle, with the view to turn it. We hope we assisted in preventing this." This has to be a reference to Pickett's charge and illustrates what Kilpatrick might have been thinking, i.e., an attack by his command to foil the Confederate main advance. But it is clear the charge by Farnsworth was made long after Pickett's men had retreated back to Seminary Ridge. Nevertheless, the general continued: "I am of the opinion that, had our infantry on my right advanced at once when relieved from the enemy's attack in their front, the enemy could not have recovered from the confusion into which Generals Farnsworth and Merritt had thrown them, but would have been pushed back, one division on another, until, instead of defeat, a total rout would have ensued."[28] This is a reference to the counterattack Meade had not ordered after the repulse of Pickett, an attack fully expected by the Rebels on Seminary Ridge. It appears that "Kill-cavalry" in the above quotation is giving his opinion, written over a month after the fact, about what General Meade should have done late on the afternoon of July 3. A Federal counterattack, regardless of its results, if it had been executed, would have helped justify his recklessness in ordering Farnsworth's charge.

In the history of the First Vermont, its author accepts at face value Kilpatrick's reasoning and goes so far as to quote the Cavalry Corps commander, Alfred Pleasonton, who seems here to be at least supporting a subordinate if not actually covering for him. Pleasonton is quoted in the Vermont history, writing that Kilpatrick's attack "caused the enemy to detach largely from his main attack on the left of our line." This does not appear to be accurate. The "main attack" that day was the charge by Pickett earlier in the afternoon and the Rebel units confronting the cavalry under Kilpatrick were never included as part of that effort. However, H.C. Parsons of the First Vermont remembered that Pleasonton's order to Kilpatrick, arriving in the late afternoon, was to make "the most powerful diversion possible, preparatory to an infantry advance." As stated, Meade ordered no such advance, and Pleasonton, who was at Army Headquarters fully in communication with the commanding general, must have known that no infantry was going to move forward and most likely told Kilpatrick to "demonstrate." Instead, "Kill-cavalry" sent the bulk of his command into the teeth of Confederate infantry supported by artillery. Parsons recalled that the Vermonters at the time thought "the charge seemed ... unwarranted and fruitless." In an article written after the war and encompassing the entire campaign, Pleasonton mentions, only in passing, that on July 3, he had a cavalry division on Lee's right flank and nothing more; no elaboration and no details are given.[29]

There is absolutely no substantiation in the record that Kilpatrick was correct in issuing the orders he did that afternoon. Yet, as stated, all this action at the south end of the Gettysburg battlefield occurred some considerable time after Pickett and the main Confederate attack of July 3 had not only been defeated and thrown back, but the survivors were now well within their own lines. What the cavalry was charging were the established Confederate lines, lines that had been held by them for over twenty-four hours. Someplace deep within what little conscience he might have had, Kilpatrick must have suspected that what he wrote and reported about his handling of his command on July 3 was not the whole truth. He might have been worried that someone in authority would justifiably criticize his action. In all likelihood he would have been correct, but given the rush of events that July, no one ever did.

To rebut "Kill-cavalry's" written report one needs only to quote cavalry historian Stephen Z. Starr writing in his thoroughly documented history of Union cavalry: "Kilpatrick's report of the affair is a shabby, disingenuous fabrication from beginning to end. An account of far greater worth is that of Major Charles E. Capehart, commanding the First West Virginia." The use of the word "fabrication" in reference to Kilpatrick's report is charitable when any number of other words could have been employed. Included in Major Capehart's report is the following: "I cannot fail to refer you to the defensive position the enemy had availed themselves of, which is one that above all others is the worst for a cavalry charge — that is, behind stone fences so high as to preclude the possibility of gaining the opposite side without dismounting and throwing them down. The whole ground over which we charged was very adverse in every particular, being broken and uneven and covered with rock.... Any one not cognizant of the *minutiae* of this charge upon infantry, under cover of heavy timber and stone fences, will fail to form a just conception of its magnitude."[30]

In his testimony before the Joint Committee on the Conduct of the War about the Gettysburg campaign some months later, General Pleasonton briefly touched on the events of July 3, and the employment of his cavalry on the left flank of the Army of the Potomac. Without naming Kilpatrick as giving the order to Farnsworth to charge, the general speaks of the use of the brigades of Merritt and Farnsworth that afternoon:

> On the 3d of July Merritt's brigade was ordered up from Emmettsburg [*sic*] to take the enemy in rear at Gettysburg, and join Farnsworth's brigade in preventing the enemy turning our flank on the left. Both of these divisions [brigades] had very heavy fighting, and I have always been of the opinion that the demonstration of our cavalry on our left materially checked the attack of the enemy on the 3d of July, for General Hood, the rebel general, was attempting to turn our flank when he met these two brigades of cavalry, and the officers reported to me that at least two divisions of infantry and a number of batteries were held back, expecting an attack from us on that flank.[31]

This was then, and remains today, revisionist history of that epic July day that has never gained currency. The members of the committee listening to Pleasonton did not know enough of the details of the July 3 battle to question this self-serving and disjointed summary by the general. Was Pleasonton's force to attack and turn the Rebel flank or were the Rebels going to attack and turn the Union flank? Was Pleasonton's force demonstrating, defending or attacking? Were Hood's infantry and batteries that were supposedly "held back" by the cavalry a secondary attack on the Union flank as Pickett's charge went forward, or were they supposed to be part of the main thrust at and around the Union line? And how could two Rebel infantry divisions still be under the command of General John Bell Hood — only a division commander at this stage of the war — when he was wounded the day before and command of his division had devolved to Brigadier General Evander M. Law? If months later Pleasonton still didn't know of Hood's removal from the field on July 2, nevertheless, General John Beatty's expressed opinion remains correct. This was "romance," and of a high order, if not one general officer, Pleasonton, deliberately covering for another, Kilpatrick.

Second-guessing concerning Kilpatrick's ordering the charge and its failure began shortly after the end of hostilities and continued down the decades as memoirs and reminiscences were penned and printed by various participants on both sides. Merritt's brigade, positioned on the west side of Emmitsburg Road, had kept some Confederate units from moving to counter Farnsworth's charge, but there were already sufficient numbers oriented in his direction to adequately defend their ground. Indeed, the Confederate officers on the ground that afternoon realized that if Kilpatrick and Merritt had attacked in unison further to the west (both brigades on the western side of Emmitsburg Road) where the ground was more favorable to cavalry, the result of the encounter might have been disastrous to the Southern cause, possibly leading to the complete defeat of Lee's force if coordinated with a Union infantry

5. Three Days in July—1863

assault on the Rebels. A fast-moving strike by both "Kill-cavalry" and Merritt might have penetrated deep into Lee's rear, cut his line of retreat and destroyed supply trains and any ammunition that was left. Merritt did advance one regiment from his command in this manner, to Fairfield, but in its encounter with a much larger force of Rebel cavalry it was defeated. To cite just one mention of a lost opportunity, General James Longstreet, in whose Corps area all this occurred, commented in his memoirs that if the strike had been made to the west of Emmitsburg Road, "he [Farnsworth] would have had an open ride, and made more trouble than was ever made by a cavalry brigade."[32]

The actions by Kilpatrick and Merritt in the later afternoon of July 3 on the Confederate right were just that, actions, and not a preconceived counterattack planned and ordered by General Meade, the purpose of which would have been to clear the way for Union infantry to advance in a follow-up thrust to sweep the entire field of Lee and his army. It had not been planned and not ordered, although briefly considered by Meade. Therefore, the counterattack remains only aged speculation on what might have been. One or more of the generals on the field that afternoon might have considered it, might even have mentioned it to Meade — Pleasonton later said he did — in the moments after Pickett and his survivors had scrambled back to their lines, but it did not happen. As an example, while being carried wounded from the field, General Winfield Scott Hancock, commander of the Second Corps, in an oblique manner suggested to Meade that a counterattack should be considered. "[I]f the Sixth and Fifth Corps have pressed up, the enemy will be destroyed. The enemy must be short of ammunition," Hancock informed Meade. But except for a reconnaissance to the west of Little Round Top ordered by Meade, one that induced a brisk fire fight with Rebel troops at the south end of the battlefield — not those arrayed against Kilpatrick — the fighting was over. Farnsworth rode forward essentially alone and in the wrong place.

In his later testimony before the Joint Committee on the Conduct of the War, General Meade testified that he initially ordered a counterstrike at a point sometime after 5 P.M. but his order never really got beyond the discussion stage with the commanders in the area and upon his seeing the conditions on that flank. This led Meade to call it off. After Pickett's repulse, Meade said, "I went immediately to the extreme left of my line, with the determination of advancing the left and making an assault upon the enemy's lines." Preparations were being made, and then Meade reconsidered; the time it would take to form the units for an organized assault, and the reports verbally given him by unit commanders in the area about the afternoon's action, led him to stop. As the battle smoke cleared and he rode from his headquarters to the left of the line, Meade had to have seen the wounded, the prisoners and the general carnage resulting from the Confederate infantry assault. Meade says he concluded from reports provided him at this end of the line that "the condition of the forces in the front and left, caused it to be so late in the evening as to induce me to abandon the assault which I had contemplated." It is reasonable to assume that what Meade had seen and what he had heard reported by subordinates — if he hadn't already reached the conclusion — confirmed in his mind that he had won the day.[33]

To be kept in mind is the often-unrecognized state of mind of the senior commanders of the Army of the Potomac and what they knew at approximately 5 P.M. on July 3. They knew they had just been engaged in the most horrific bloodletting imaginable, possibly one unequaled in history to that time, its cost as yet incalculable. In their minds, and primarily in Meade's, attention to an unknown number of wounded and unknown numbers of prisoners, as well as the replenishment of badly needed ammunition, were real priorities. This would take time. In the span of a few hours, these Union generals had witnessed the most massive artillery bombardment and massed infantry assault ever seen on the North American continent. Even if they did not appreciate it at that moment, the psychological affect of it was already resident in their minds, and conceivably was still there some days later, near the Potomac River, when another assault was ordered up. Given the portrait that has emerged over the years from the record of the Civil War, General Pleasonton's urging Meade to counterattack late that afternoon, and his testimony before the Joint Committee on the Conduct of the War can be seen as imaginative, sounding more like self-promoting hindsight than history.

As for the charge by Farnsworth that may have coincided in time with Meade's riding to the left end of the battle line, cavalry historian Stephen Z. Starr has generously concluded:

> Just what was intended to be accomplished by attacking the Confederates at this point (from the southern end of the field and, presumably, at this late hour), over terrain totally unsuited for cavalry operation, where Law's scanty infantry had every advantage, is unclear. The attack might have had a chance of success if it had been coupled with a strong frontal attack on Law's division by the Federal infantry of the V Corps, which held the southern end of Meade's line, but no such attack was ordered. To order the cavalry to attack under such circumstances was an incomprehensible aberration.[34]

Further, Gettysburg was a meeting engagement that had quickly evolved into the war's battle of battles. There had been no advanced planning about how to fight such a battle; it had not been a planned operation to strike at Lee, as had been the Federal attacks at Fredericksburg and Chancellorsville. After three days of vicious combat, the physical and mental strain, and the exhaustion of the leading participants, must be given some, if marginal, consideration. A meeting engagement on a gigantic scale, no advance planning, little or no rest or nourishment, and casualties on an as-yet incalculable scale had had its effect on those left alive. In the late afternoon's heat and the lingering gunsmoke as he rode the Union line and saw the carnage, General Meade might have thought, even secondarily, he had accomplished enough, and he was probably right. He knew he had won.

In his after-action report, Kilpatrick lists four officers and thirty-four men killed, wounded 151 and missing 121. No doubt the action had been bloody, but in the Official Record the casualties for the action on July 3 are listed as two officers killed and four wounded and two missing. The enlisted men's total is seventeen killed, nineteen wounded and fifth-eight missing.[35] One is likely better served by relying on the figures not reported by Kilpatrick. In his report, Kilpatrick goes on to praise the now-dead Farnsworth, and in doing so provides us with linguistic flourishes for which he was noted, as well as a full measure of strained sincerity, knowing that he had sent the young general to his death: "In this battle the division lost many brave and gallant officers. Among the list will be found the name of Farnsworth, short but most glorious was his career — a general on June 29, on the 30th he baptized his star in blood, and on July 3, for the honor of his young brigade and the glory of the corps, he gave his life. At the head of his men, at the very muzzles of the enemy's guns, he fell, with many mortal wounds. We can say of him, in the language of another, 'Good soldier, faithful friend, great heart, hail and farewell.'"[36]

Except for the initial probe by the Fifth New York, the regiment had been extremely fortunate, taking little part in the day's events, and they were probably grateful when they saw what happened. The Third Division's surgeon, Henry Capehart, worked all that night and into the next morning "by the light of tallow-dips in the amputation of limbs and the various operations necessary under such circumstances."[37]

In none of the reports filed after the campaign does any officer speak of the massive Confederate bombardment and the sound it made that afternoon, or make any detailed reference to the tremendous attack upon the Union line atop Cemetery Ridge, the attack we today call Pickett's Charge. This is true also of surviving correspondence from Fifth New York troopers. The Third Division was too far away from Pickett's Charge to have seen it, but not so far as to not have heard it, as had a trooper in the Eighteenth Pennsylvania. However, the chaplain, miles away and en route from Hanover, clearly knew of it from the sound he was hearing. For this day, July 3, he reported "This

P.M., we left for Gettysburg. The weather was fine, but with an appearance of storm not far distant. The cannonading during some part of the day was perfectly terrific. There were times when the booming of cannon was continuous, with no intermission." Journals and diaries tell us the facts surrounding an event as its author knew them and sometimes the impression they made is recorded. They are used to corroborate if not enhance the story of an event. But sometimes they unwittingly tell us as much about the author, his insights, or lack thereof. Of all the things Chaplain Boudrye could have recorded about this day of days in Pennsylvania, he says:

> From Littlestown toward Gettysburg, the road was filled with carriages and wagons bringing the wounded to the rear and many wounded were on foot. It was a bad time. About 5 P.M., I came up near the field of action. The fight was over and the smoke was settling over the adjacent county. I saw before night about three thousand (3000) Rebel prisoners. They looked sorry. We came about 3 miles toward Littlestown and stayed near our train at a home. A heavy rain fell all night. This was in accordance to the theory that heavy cannonading always produces rain! This is a theory I have never heard before I came to the Army, or, at least I had never thought of. There is doubtless truth in it.

An opportunity was lost by Boudrye to record full details of the battle's aftermath, but, to be fair, he was probably not thinking of the desires of the historian. As a final point, however, Boudrye does note: "About 5 P.M. ... The fight was over."

It was *after* this hour that Farnsworth was charging forward with no chance of success or adding to the Union victory.

Boudrye caught up with the regiment the next morning, July 4, in time to join it in its pursuit of the retreating Confederate army.[38]

6

Retreat and Pursuit —1863

Smithburg, Md.
July 5, 1863

My Dear wife,
I improve a moment to write to you I am very well, but very tired after four day's bloody fighting at Gettysburg. The rebels are severely whipped and commenced retreating on the night of the 3rd. We fought them on their right flank; and on the 2nd, by making a night march, we passed clear around their left flank and fought a large division of them. The vigorous attack of our cavalry had a great effect in winning the day. Our division lost about two hundred men. Brig. Gen. Farnsworth was killed or missing. Last night we captured a part of their wagon train, which was in full retreat for Virginia. The rebels held the gap in the South Mountain, but we flogged them out of it, and captured a train about four miles long, And one thousand seven hundred prisoners.[1]

In this letter to his wife, previously quoted, the commander of the Fifth New York uses as few words as possible to tell us, his unintended readers, what the regiment did on July 4, 1863. In addition, Hammond, too, is under the impression that the division's attack on July 3 had helped settle the matter in the Union's favor. A trooper in the Fifth provided his hometown newspaper with a slightly different view:

> We slept near the battle field, and next morning, the 4th of July, we drew three days rations, and started on a raid to intercept a wagon train. The whole of us felt in excellent spirits when we heard what had been done the day previous, and that Lee's army was in full retreat to toward the Potomac. Even a heavy thundershower that came up soon after we got on the road did not dampen the ardor of any in the division. We marched steadily all day, passing through Emmittsburg [sic], Md., then we took a road leading through a Gap in the Blue Ridge. It was in this pass Gen. Kilpatrick proposed to celebrate [the] Anniversary of our Independence.[2]

It is interesting that this trooper wrote, "we heard what had been done." Clearly, he did not think what his regiment or the brigade had done on July 3 had contributed to winning the day.

July of 1863 was an unusually wet month in the eastern United States, particularly in the countryside the contending armies had to traverse. Rain and muddy roads would hamper movement as Robert E. Lee and his Army of Northern Virginia began a retreat back to its home state and George Meade began cautiously to follow, hoping to finish Lee and his command before it could cross the Potomac River. The rain had swollen the Potomac to a point that it could not be easily forded, and the pontoon bridge Lee had put across the river at Falling Waters on his way north had been burned by Union cavalry on July 4. The rain and the level of water in the Potomac might determine whether the Rebels would get back to Virginia without having to fight another major engagement. Whether in frustration or in an attempt at humor, even General Lee was driven to ask a subordinate familiar with the region, "You know this country well enough to tell me whether it ever quits raining about here? If so, I should like to see a clear day soon."[3]

The Army of Northern Virginia had held its position atop Seminary Ridge during the night of July 3, and through the daylight hours of July 4. General Lee expected — even hoped — a counterattack by the Army of the Potomac might come at them across the same ground they had traversed the day before. The repulse of a Union counterattack could turn what Lee knew was a bloody defeat into at least a draw. But the Yankees didn't advance. As Lee waited he also began organizing his withdrawal. Late in the evening of July 3, Lee ordered the collection of the wounded who were able to travel. They were soon started for the Potomac. By the afternoon of July 4, the long train of wounded was moving west along the road to Chambersburg in wagons and any other transport that could be pressed into service. On the morning of July 4, and reluctantly, Lee's orders were issued for withdrawal. Once darkness fell on July 4, the three corps making up the Army of Northern Virginia would move in the direction of Fairfield, to the south and west of Gettysburg and across South Mountain via Monterey Pass and Fairfield Pass. The supply trains of each corps were started first, with that of General Ewell's leaving in mid-afternoon of July 4, headed for Fairfield and Monterey Passes. Lee's objective was to get the army to the Potomac crossing in the vicinity of Williamsport, Maryland.

By the time this movement began, the Fifth New York, as part of the Third Division, had already started moving, headed for Emmitsburg. General Meade had ordered Pleasonton on the morning of July 4 to use his corps to harass and block any retreat by Lee back toward the Potomac crossing. Custer's

6. Retreat and Pursuit—1863

brigade had, by then, returned to the division, from its detached service with General Gregg the previous day, and it was dark when the Third Division arrived at the base of South Mountain and the road leading up and over Monterey Pass.

"Strange 4th of July for us," Boudrye recorded in his journal for this day:

> This morning was beautiful. Mud was deep. Early we set out toward Little Round Top where our Regiment was understood to be near the place where it had fought yesterday. It was soon found. We were glad to see the boys who had fought severely since Hanover.... At about Noon, we left for the direction of Emmitsburg. It was understood the Rebel Army was falling back. A very heavy rain fell about 2 P.M. Meanwhile in a large old barn near which the Division was drawn out in line, I wrote a letter to Mrs. Hammond, at his request, as he was very busy.... About 3½, we moved over the hills, through rain and mud, swinging around the Rebel line, through Emmitsburg and then toward Monterey Pass. It rained most of the night."

The text of the letter the chaplain wrote to Mrs. Hammond read in part:

> About two miles South of Gettysburg, Pa.
> July 4, 1863
>
> Mrs. John Hammond,
> Dear Madam and Friend,— By request of the Major, I write you a few lines, he is so very busy it is quite impossible for him to write at all. His health is excellent, and he is distinguishing himself by many deeds of valor. Yesterday this cavalry made some memorable and successful charges on the left [right] wing of the enemy. Gen. Kilpatrick spoke words of high commendation and lofty cheer to his command this morning. In yesterday's fight your friend, Capt. Harris, First [West] Virginia, was mortally wounded. The Major cautioned me particularly to mention this item. Yesterday was the grandest day for the army, in my opinion, during the war, between eight and fifteen thousand rebels were captured,— I saw myself about two thousand. The First Vermont Cavalry lost about one hundred men. The canonading was terrific, some say the most rapid, loud and destructive of the war. The enemy is said to be retreating, and this cavalry division is endeavoring to harass and cut them off. I am writing in a barn, while the rain is falling fast. It is a dreadful moment for the poor soldiers who are out. The wind blows furiously, which makes the rain doubly unpleasant. I never saw the Major looking better than now....
>
> Louis N. Boudrye
> Chaplain Fifth N.Y. V.C.[4]

At Emmitsburg, Kilpatrick was joined by a brigade led by Colonel Pennock Huey of General David Gregg's Second Cavalry Division. From there the column headed northwest toward a gap in the mountain called Monterey Pass. Beyond the pass was the valley through which Lee had advanced on his move north and he was thought, now, to be using it for his return. It was raining and in the darkness the march up the narrow road to the pass was slow and torturous and every trooper knew a Rebel could be within feet of the column aiming a gun. Boudrye, riding again with the regiment, says, "The night was pitchy dark, and the rain fell fast, before the train guards were met."

Earlier in the day, part of Ewell's train had entered the pass and was moving to clear it and get into the valley below. In his own words, Kilpatrick tells the story: "Without halting, passed out on the road to Monterey, intending to cross the mountain at that point.... The top of the mountain had nearly been gained when the enemy opened on the advance with artillery and infantry. At the same time, the rear of the column, under Colonel Huey, was fought off a probing attack by Stuart's cavalry. On my left was a deep ravine, on my right a steep, rugged mountain, and a road too narrow to reverse even a gun. To add to this unpleasant position, it was raining in torrents." A Michigan trooper named James Avery of Custer's brigade left his impression of a "wet column, as they wound their way beside the stream and across the bridge of a creek along the foot of the towering cliffs. Up. Up we went four abreast, the pitchy darkness, relieved only by flashes of lightening [sic] followed by rolling thunder. When a bright flash lit up the scene, we could see a deep abyss, so close to the path that a stumble would send one down hundreds of feet. On the other side, we could not see to the top of the overhanging cliffs."[5]

Kilpatrick reported what happened next:

> Never under such perilous circumstances had a command behaved better, not a word was spoken there was no confusion. From a farmer's boy I learned the nature of the road and country on the mountain, made my dispositions, and ordered a charge. In a moment the heights were gained and many prisoners taken. Now the rumble of the enemy's train could be heard rolling down the mountain. The enemy was in position half a mile further on, at the intersection of the road from Gettysburg to Hagerstown and the road upon which I was moving. The enemy's infantry and artillery were approaching rapidly on the Gettysburg road and he had already opened on my command. Pennington, always ready, always willing, quickly came into position, and returned the enemy's fire. General Custer's brigade was ordered to move forward, clear the road, and attack the train. The attack was successful.
>
> In the meantime, the First Vermont Cavalry (Lieutenant-Colonel Preston) had been sent along the mountain over a wood road to Smithsburg, and thence to Hagerstown, to intercept the train. A Strong force of dismounted men and two guns of Pennington's battery were now sent on the road in the direction of Gettysburg, to barricade the road and hold the enemy in check until the column

6. Retreat and Pursuit—1863 111

had passed. Many fierce but unsuccessful attacks were made on this position during the night.

At daylight [July 5] the whole command had safely passed, and Ewell's large train was entirely destroyed, save eight forges, thirty wagons, and a few ambulances loaded with wounded rebel officers (sent with the prisoners to Frederick City).

At 9 A.M. on the 5th, the command reached Smithstown with 1,360 prisoners, one battle-flag, and a large number of horses and mules, several hundred of the enemy's wounded being left upon the field. We lost 5 killed, including 1 commissioned officer, 10 wounded, and 28 missing, making an aggregate of 42 killed, wounded, and missing.[6]

There had been a small Rebel holding force near the top of the pass to discourage any cavalry from following the retreating train too closely. These Rebels had a cannon and used it and their rifles against Kilpatrick's approaching column. They in turn were charged and retreated. After a brief stop by Kilpatrick at the top of the pass, essentially the whole division lunged forward and down the western side on the mountain and into the wagon train. Henry Capehart recalled in later years, "The road down [the west side of Monterey Pass] was of the same dizzy character as that of the ascent, and for some eight miles was interspersed with teams, wagon, ambulances, forges, etc." Capehart goes on to say that many wagons were pushed over "the brink of the abyss." But many wagons were captured, the teamsters either throwing up the hands or jumping from their wagons and hiding the woods.

The Eighteenth Pennsylvania rode the length of the wagon column and set up a quick roadblock to prevent any troops on the road to Smithsburg from returning. And they had only been there a short time when they fired into an approaching column of Rebel cavalry coming back along the road to investigate the firing they had heard. Meanwhile, the rest of the command either disabled or set the wagons on fire. Of course, this was done only after the troopers liberated anything found in the wagons that might be of use. John A. Bigelow of the Fifth Michigan remembered that the "train [was] loaded with a promiscuous assortment of goods, as the rebs had gone into stores and dwellings and gathered up whatever was in sight.... Coffee, ladies' shoes, tea, calicos...." Bigelow states further that on "the train we destroyed that night not more than one half [the contraband] was legitimate army stores."[7]

Down the years Kilpatrick has been accused of greatly exaggerating the number of wagons and prisoners the division captured in this action, although with the exception of the numbers cited above, he did not give a total number of wagons destroyed in his after-action report. Because of the general's known loose regard for facts elsewhere in his reports, this is understandable. But the reports written by John Hammond are another matter. And this was the wagon train of a full infantry corps that had been liberally foraging in the Pennsylvania countryside for some time and had appropriated additional wagons for its use. The Fifth New York did not take an active part in clearing the pass of Rebels, but the regiment did ride the length of the wagons on a charge down the road leading to Smithsburg. Hammond's contemporaries held the commander of the Fifth New York in such high regard there simply cannot be a question about facts contained in his matter-of-fact reports. In his letter to his wife dated July 5 and quoted above, Hammond says, "We captured a train about four miles long, and one thousand seven hundred prisoners."[8] By "we" Hammond means the Third Division and a train "four miles" in length had to number hundreds of wagons.

Colonel Richmond of the First West Virginia had taken command of the First Brigade after the death of General Farnsworth. Leading the brigade, he reported that they weren't in the fight "until it reached the summit, after passing which we charged upon a long wagon train of the enemy, capturing nearly the entire train, together with a large number of prisoners." Trooper Avery, unknown to either Hammond or Richmond, recorded in his journal this about the capture: "Quickly, we came in contact with a heavy train of wagons with a strong guard, who held their own well for the darkness, but they were soon over powered.... When morning finally dawned, we found a curious sight, something that appeared like men covered with mud, surrounding a long train of wagons with nearly a brigade of prisoners, and a lot of horses. The train was burned, such of it was not needed for use."

The *New York Times* had a reporter traveling with the Third Division. The paper's correspondent, a man named Edward A. Paul, wrote of this wagon train that "hundreds were burnt in the road where captured. This burning took place only after the troopers helped themselves to whatever supplies of bacon, salt and sugar they could find." Still another witness gave numbers in his letter home: "At daybreak we ascertained that 200 wagons of all descriptions, with 1,870 prisoners, two pieces of cannon, caissons, &c , were the fruit our night's work." All of this destruction does not take into account the damage inflicted on the wagon train by civilians who were reported to have taken axes to the wagon that were unguarded after appropriating for themselves anything they wanted.[9] If the exact number of wagons in the train wasn't known precisely at the time, the number destroyed cannot be known. But the loss to the Confederates must have been significant.

Chaplain Boudrye in his journal makes little mention of the action at Monterey or about the capture of the retreating Rebel train on the night of July 4–5. He gives us no clue about where he was while this was going on, saying only that the column encountered the wagon train. In his history, however, the chaplain says, "A train of 200 wagons, mostly loaded with plunder from the stores and granaries of Pennsylvania, fell into our hand, and about 1,500 prisoners, among whom were several wounded. Most of the wagons were destroyed."[10]

Boudrye might be excused for not taking better notes on events occurring in the regiment at this time because at some point early on the morning of July 5, Stuart's cavalry found the chaplain: "About six o'clock this morning, in company with Chaplain O. Taylor, 5th Mich. Cav'y and a few other defenseless ones, I was surrounded unexpectedly by a detachment of Jenkin's [Jenkins's] Cavalry. It was hard to say 'I surrender.'" This cavalry brigade had been riding and scouting for Ewell's Corps as it moved toward Harrisburg before the battle and was now, in some manner, operating in the area traversed by the Corps' retreating wagon train.

The Rebel cavalry took Boudrye and the others to Mechanicstown, and then on to a place called Wolf's Tavern. There the chaplain provides us with a glimpse of General Jeb Stuart, with whom he spoke and who refused his request for parole: "He is a fine looking officer of florid complexion, sharp blue eyes, with features strongly marked. He was relentlessly on the lookout." The chaplain, in his history, left an impression he penned while on his way to Richmond, adding, "He wears a gray plush hat with a black feather; has plain uniform, and a short bowie knife by his side with ivory handle, attached to his person by a golden chain. He seems to trust no man to do what he can possibly do himself. But there is more chivalry in the exterior than in the interior, I fear." Boudrye was marched into Virginia and eventually sent to Libby Prison in Richmond.[11] He remained there until October 1863, when he was released with several other chaplains in a prisoner exchange.

Meanwhile, "the Fifth New York was pushed forward to Smithsburg early on Sunday morning July 5, but found only a small picket to interrupt their progress, and this ran away upon their approach. The town was held by the Fifth until the arrival of the main column, at a late hour in the day." As had happened along the route the Fifth New York marched the previous week, the town's population turned out. The sun had appeared after the storm of the previous night, and the residents came into the street offering the troopers "pyramids of white bread spread with jelly and butter, inviting all to partake." The men and horses were now able to rest for some hours after devouring whatever had been offered to them by the natives of Smithsburg. It was here that Major Hammond wrote his wife the letter dated July 5.

When main body of the Third Division and Kilpatrick arrived, he deployed his three brigades on hills near the town and facing South Mountain to the east, where he suspected Stuart and his force were moving. The Fifth New York and the rest of the First Brigade deployed on what was called Goat Hill, a location slightly south of Smithsburg and facing South Mountain. Here the division rested for most of the day. At about sundown, as the division got ready to move, the peaceful evening was shattered artillery fire. A Rebel battery from Stuart's command had gotten itself in position to the east on South Mountain overlooking the town and the cavalry division below. It opened up and did some damage to the town, but took no toll on the cavalrymen. Elder's battery quickly returned fire and an artillery duel continued for about an hour. Kilpatrick, for his part, did not want another fight, as his primary objective was to block the Rebel retreat and smash up their trains. So, after dark, he withdrew the division and headed southward for Boonsboro.

Major Hammond, in his report, gives us the meager facts as to what happened to the regiment that day at Smithsburg:

> As the command was in line awaiting the order to march, the artillery of the enemy opened to the right of the town, when I was ordered with Elder's battery to take position in the rear of the town. I posted the regiment in a corn-field on the left of the battery, and for a short time was exposed to the enemy's shells, which did no damage, however. After a time I was ordered to take position upon a high ridge to the left about half a mile, and the first squadron, under Captain McGuine, was sent forward to reconnoiter, as there were evidence of a flank movement by the enemy; but at dusk the reconnaissance, being completed, reported the enemy retreating. We then took up our line of march, and arrived at Boonsborough [sic] at 12 A.M., where we went into bivouac.[12]

Unknown to Hammond, Stuart continued on, hoping to occupy Hagerstown.

As an indication of the sparseness of Hammond's reporting, the *New York Times* reporter riding with the Third Division noted an incident that is nowhere else related in the documentation of this campaign. Also, even the number of words devoted to it by the newspaperman gives us an indication of the cruelty and the numbing effect that the mass violence of this conflict was having on those men. On the march to Boonsboro that night, "a private in the Fifth New York who was much intoxicated, deliberately and without cause killed Lieut. Williamson, of Elder's battery, by shooting him with a pistol. The men in the vicinity immediately killed the offending trooper."[13]

The town of Hagerstown, Maryland, was of considerable importance to General Stuart and the retreating army because it was there that roads from various points of the compass intersected and continued on to Williamsport. On Monday, July 6, both Stuart and the Third Division moved to secure the

6. Retreat and Pursuit—1863

town. The trooper-correspondent for the *Wyoming Mirror* told his readers what he saw. As the Fifth New York drew near Hagerstown,

> we found quite a force of the enemy. Their battery opened on us on entering the town, but did no damage. Our artillery soon replied, and the Carbineers were dismounted to skirmish with the rebel Sharpshooters. They were infantry armed with Minie rifles and it seemed impossible to dislodge them or drive them from the town. The 18th Penn. Cavalry charged through the town and took several prisoners from their line of skirmishers. They had, on first entering the town, captured Col. Davis who was commanding a brigade of cavalry, and was opposed to our division in the fight at Hunterstown, night of the 1 [actually the 2] of July.— He acknowledged they were badly handled at that point.
>
> We held one side of the town till nearly sundown, when Gen. K. withdrew the greater position of his command to reinforce Buford who had engaged Imboden's forces and was shelling a large train near Williamsport. Our brigade with two pieces of artillery were left to keep the forces at H[agerstown] in check; and at the same time fall back to the main body. "Johnny Reb" took advantage of this state of affairs, and followed us up closely. Our regiment supported the battery, and their cavalry charged with the intention of capturing the cannon. The cannon was loaded with double charges of canister and the rebel cavalry were repulsed with heavy loss. They fought with desperation, one of their number succeeding in reaching the gun, to get knocked from his horse by the swab in the hands of our cannonier. All this time their infantry were coming up in overwhelming numbers, on a double quick. For a short time the prospect was gloomy in the extreme. Their Infantry were posted behind trees and stone walls, the skirmishers being up with their cavalry. However, we succeeded in joining Buford about dusk. Our loss for the small number engaged were quite heavy— Capt. Lucas and six men from company F. are among the missing. Their names are, Thomas Donlon, George Wells, Nicholas Lzahter,— all Wyoming County boys. Brooks, Devanoe, and Lewis,— from New York city.[14]

This Fifth New York trooper here has summarized for his readers the entire day's fighting. That morning, there had been considerable street fighting inside of Hagerstown, both mounted and dismounted. This fighting was done primarily by the First Vermont and the 18th Pennsylvania. And unlike Hanover on June 30, some residents, of both Union and Confederate persuasion, reached for their guns and joined the fight. Hagerstown, when advanced on by the Third Cavalry Division, was held by advance elements of Stuart's cavalry. Later in the morning, Rebel infantry— the advance of Lee's retreating army— as well as Stuart and his main cavalry force arrived, converging on the town from the north and east. The Third Division was now outgunned and a withdrawal in the direction of Williamsport was ordered. It would be a fighting withdrawal, covering the miles to the vicinity of Williamsport.

Colonel Richmond and the First Brigade would fight the withdrawal while the Second Brigade, with Kilpatrick, was riding in the direction of

Williamsport at the request of General Burford. Two of Richmond's four regiments would retreat with a portion of Elder's battery while the other two regiments with another gun fired on the advancing Rebels. Once in position to defend their ground, the first element would open fire on the Rebels while the second element with their gun ran past them, taking a defensive position further to the rear. "The brigade thus fell back, fighting, and holding in check a greatly superior force. About two miles from the village, where the First Vermont and Fifth New York were facing the enemy, the latter got into the wood on both flanks, and gave them some sharp fighting." This leapfrog retreat went on until Colonel Richmond and his brigade reached the vicinity of Williamsport, where Kilpatrick and the rest of the division were attempting to help Buford in his attack on the Confederate wagon train there.[15]

Writing some days later, Major Hammond gives us a glimpse of what happened from his perspective:

> At 8 A.M. orders were received for the command to march, and we moved on toward Hagerstown. Arrived within a mile and a half of the town, and took position in rear of Elder's battery. A few rebel cavalry only being reported in town, we were again ordered on. Our advance having been repulsed by a force of concealed sharpshooters in the town, and the enemy's artillery opening to our right, skirmishers were thrown out in that direction. I was ordered to dismount my carbineers and send them forward into the town as a check upon the sharpshooters, and to take position with the rest of my command near the seminary, in support of the battery. After a while the enemy's sharpshooters became annoying to the artillerists, and a change of position was ordered, the First Vermont, First West Virginia, and Fifth New York alternately supported the battery during the change of position toward the left of the town. The enemy closely followed and kept up a sharp cannonade, which did no damage beyond wounding and killing a few horses.[16]

At the point in time Hammond was referring to Stuart's full command and an infantry force had arrived and joined the fighting.

Also, at about noon, Captain Ulrich Dahlgren's independent Union cavalry company arrived and immediately charged to the sound the guns. Dahlgren's men, with the captain in the lead, charged down Potomac Street and were shot at from every direction by Rebels and Rebel sympathizers. Dahlgren was wounded in this affair and had a leg amputated as a consequence.

It was now that the 18th Pennsylvania, on the outskirts of town, began its withdrawal. This movement had a cascading effect on the next unit, the First West Virginia. All this while — a period of about two hours — more Rebel cavalry were entering Hagerstown and then advancing on the position held by the Fifth New York and First Vermont in support of Elder's battery.

6. Retreat and Pursuit—1863

Now, as Kilpatrick and the Second Brigade rode to support Buford's efforts at Williamsport, the First Brigade began its fighting withdrawal, following the road "Kill-cavalry" had taken. The First Vermont and Fifth New York were covering Elder's battery in the retreat and were dodging bullets fired by the close-following Rebels. Colonel Richmond reported that he moved about two miles down the road, "fighting over every foot of ground, retiring two regiments and two batteries, and holding the enemy in check with two regiments and two batteries until those retiring again took position."[17] Richmond, in this report, confuses the issue concerning the guns used in the withdrawal. The division had only two horse artillery batteries, Elder's and Pennington's. Each battery was subdivided into two sections of two guns each. The colonel was fighting using a battery section to cover the withdrawal of the other section. No doubt, Kilpatrick took Pennington's artillery batteries with him when he rode to Buford's assistance.

John Hammond put more detail into his report of this action than any other during the campaign. Based on the number of words he employed, he must have considered this action to be the Fifth's toughest fight of the campaign:

> The enemy being superior in numbers, we were ordered to fall back, and I was ordered to bring up the rear with my regiment. Finally a stand was made about 2 miles from town, on the Williamsport road. One gun was placed in the road, with the First Vermont on the right and my regiment on the left in an open field. I was ordered to throw out one squadron as skirmishers, which was done under severe fire of the enemy, who followed us closely. They swarmed in the woods on both flanks, and poured in their fire, which was so sever[e] as to throw my men in some confusion. Hearing that the enemy were coming down a small by-road in our rear, I detached Lieutenant Dimmick with a small command to drive them back. In a few minutes they were driven back with loss, the lieutenant being severely wounded. I then sent Captain Penfield with more men to hold the way at all hazard, since which time I have not seen him. He and several others had their horses killed under them. And were probably captured. After being subjected to a very severe fire in an exposed position, and aiding in repelling several charges of the enemy, I received orders to fall back, which I did, though not without loss. The pursuit of the enemy being checked, we retired with the rest of the command, and went into bivouac. Next day reached Boonsborough [sic], and camped.
>
> Our loss was 5 officers and about 100 enlisted men wounded and missing. Of the number killed, nothing definite is known.[18]

The number of missing men may include those who lost horses during the fight and were scrambling over the countryside following the command while looking for a remount.

What Hammond doesn't mention was included in the report by Colonel

Richmond. One of Elder's guns was parked in the road and drew Rebel attention. Richmond reported, "Four different times did the enemy charge this piece, which was placed upon the pike, and as often were they repulsed with heavy slaughter, Lieutenant Elder pouring canister into their ranks with most deadly effect. So close was the conflict that No. 1 of the piece, turning his sponge-staff, knocked one of the enemy from his horse."[19] This is probably the same incident cited by the trooper-correspondent earlier.

The fighting at Hagerstown by only the First Brigade, while the Second Brigade moved on to Williamsport, made defeat that day inevitable. Even if the entire Third Division had been brought to bear, Stuart, with brigade-strength infantry support, still might have prevailed that day. In his report, Kilpatrick, referring to the fighting withdrawal from Hagerstown, said of the Fifth New York, "I am greatly indebted to the officers and men of the Harris Light Cavalry for the safe and successful retreat of the command."[20] High praise bestowed by the gallantåKill-cavalry."

Hammond, in a spare moment, wrote to his wife. His letter doesn't admit defeat, but the numbers speak for themselves:

> July 8, 1863
>
> We had a terrible fight yesterday with our division against one brigade of infantry and one of rebel cavalry. This morning I find I have but about one hundred and sixty men left. Captains Penfield and Lucas, Lieuts. Dimmick, Bryant and Merriman are missing. I think James [Penfield] is a prisoner or killed, as he had his horse shot out from under him. Lieut. Dimmick, when last seen, was wounded in the arm. Kilpatrick's division must have lost three hundred or four hundred men. Buford's division, which was fighting at Williamsport, lost eight officers and three hundred men. We have now had a fight every day for the last six.[21]

Major Hammond had on July 8, by the count reported to him that morning, one hundred and sixty-six troopers left. The casualties recorded officially for the day's fighting in and around Hagerstown were three killed, nine wounded and seventy-nine missing. This totals twenty-one percent of the regiment's strength for this single day of fighting, if the initial number of 420 men comprising the Fifth New York when it was absorbed into the Army of the Potomac is valid. By Hammond's own count a few days later, he had only one hundred and forty-four men present. This figure, however, probably included only those who still had horses to ride and were, therefore, combat effective. Those without horses had to follow along on foot until they could obtain a mount to ride. At the end of the campaign, Hammond had time to pen an explanation. "At least one third of the troopers are on foot. We take all the horses was can find belonging to the inhabitants, but there are but few, as the rebels have also helped themselves."²²

The casualty numbers reported in the *Official Record* for the Fifth New York for the entire Gettysburg campaign is 153 killed, wounded or missing, or 36 percent.²³ From its formation until the regiment joined the Army of the Potomac on June 28, 1863, the Fifth New York had experienced nothing like these casualties.

According to Boudrye, the First Brigade's fighting retreat from Hagerstown ended at Williamsport, where it met the rest of the Third Division and Kilpatrick, along with Buford's First Division. From there the Fifth New York marched to a place called Timball's Cross Roads. The next day the division moved to Boonsboro and bivouacked, remaining there, resting as best it could all that day.

Although he had been captured on July 5, Boudrye was near Hagerstown, but on the other side of the line, while the fighting went on. The group of prisoners with which he was marching was held outside of town until the fighting ended. Then they were again herded toward the Potomac. "At night, we passed through Hagerstown. Saw dead horses by the way. Bodies of men stripped of all their clothing, except their undergarments, lay along the road. Capt. Penfield of Co. H of my regt. was wounded by a saber cut on the head and captured. We spent part of the night about 3 miles from Williamsport. I took as much care of Capt. P as possible." The next day the chaplain reached the Potomac at about 11 A.M. "This morning Capt. Lucas of Co. F of my regiment was captured. He is a sorry looking man. Several privates were also captured; among them was Louis Labounty [Co. H].... Evidence of battle was all along the way — dead animals and men.... A terrible rain fell during the night...The Rebel Army was much demoralized and dispirited. Their ammunition was about expended." The chaplain, writing in his journal at a later date, comments that all the prisoners were hoping for an attack by Meade on the Rebel forces stacked up at this time in a defensive posture guarding the river crossing points at Williamsport and Falling Waters. They believed that if Meade attacked the Rebel army would have been crushed. But no such attack would be in the offing for a week.²⁴

The rain was also falling on the Fifth New York's bivouac at Boonsboro during the pre-dawn hours of July 8. The cavalrymen were maintaining a vigilant lookout in anticipation of a renewed attack by Stuart. "About noon the next day we were attacked by Stewart's [*sic*] Cavalry and a force of mounted infantry," a trooper wrote to his hometown paper. "Our artillery took position on a ridge half a mile from town, and for two hours the cannonading was brisk. All our Carbineers fought dismounted as skirmishers, and before sundown, your humble servant, with other skirmishers had the satisfaction of chasing them off the field. Some, in the haste, left their guns behind." Stuart was forcing the issue, launching a spoiling attack down the National Road from Hagerstown toward Boonsboro to keep the Union cavalry as far away from the road junction town for as long as possible while the rear of Lee's army marched through it on the way to the river crossing. "Kill-cavalry" and the division, supporting Buford's division, were engaged along Beaver Creek about two miles to the west of Boonsboro. Later in the day, Kilpatrick fought an essentially defensive action against an attempted flanking movement by one of Stuart's brigades. The action was mostly a dismounted fight that lasted into the late afternoon, with neither side obtaining an advantage. The firing was so intense and concentrated the troopers had to bring carbine ammunition forward to be distributed to their comrades. With darkness now coming on, Stuart's command was thrown back towards Hagerstown by Buford and Kilpatrick, uniting their divisions and charging the Rebels.[25]

Hammond's report of the events of this day includes the following:

> The enemy having advanced from Hagerstown and made an attack upon our forces, I received orders to move down to the field and support Captain Elder's battery. I put the column in motion, and moved over the hill, and took position on a ridge outside the town, on the left of the pike leading to Hagerstown. The battery opened upon the skirmishers of the enemy, and our skirmishers being ordered forward, drove those of the enemy. They, being re-enforced, in turn drove ours nearly back to the guns. I was ordered to send forward my carbineers to re-enforce them, which was done, and the enemy was gradually forced to retire. By sundown the enemy was in full retreat, and I was ordered to return to the camp I had left in the morning. Although the enemy's shells fell fast about us during the fight, I am happy to state we met with no loss in men and but a few horses.[26]

Hammond gave more detail to his wife the next day:

> Boonesboro [sic], July 9, 1863
> Our cavalry had another battle yesterday between the town and Hagerstown, which commenced at nine A.M., and continued until dark. We were attacked by nine thousand rebel cavalry. They drove us about half a mile and the fate of the day was quite uncertain until about five P.M. when we charged them the whole length of our line and drove them until after dark. Our line of battle was about two miles long. Our loss is light, while theirs is considerable. A portion of the Eleventh Corps arrived here about dark, and others are pouring through the gaps in South Mountain. We expect a decisive battle in the next few days. It may commence today, yet I hardly expect it. I wrote you in my last letter of our fight at Hagerstown. I then hoped that some of our officers would turn up, but they have not. I enclosed

6. Retreat and Pursuit—1863 121

you an account of our fight at Hanover. I believe that I have had the honor, with the 5th, of leading the first charge and fighting the first battle on free soil since the war commenced. We suffer a good deal from want of food, as our trains are all behind. This is the third day since our men are out of rations, and as their money is pretty much gone, it leaves them in a hungry condition. The officers are still worse off than the men, as we draw no rations having to forage for our grub. For two days I had nothing except two pieces of hardtack, except for a breakfast we got at a farmhouse, which consisted entirely of coffee, lettuce and radishes. When we went out yesterday my whole command was but 144 men, the first [West] Virginia 120. We have a great many men dismounted. The Army is in excellent spirits and confidant of glorious success.[27]

John Hammond, in his usual understated manner, refers in his letter to a cavalry charge that took place in the early evening of July 8 that turned this daylong spoiling attack by Stuart outside Boonsboro to the Union's favor. He merely tells how "about five P.M. ... we charged them the whole length of our line and drove them until after dark. Our line of battle was about two miles long."

Kilpatrick's contemporary biographer adds some color to Hammond's few words:

Just as the setting sun sent his last rays over the dusty battlefield, Buford and Kilpatrick were seen rapidly approaching each other from opposite directions. They met, a few hasty words were exchanged, and away dashed Buford off to the right, and Kilpatrick straight to the centre, and in less than twenty minutes, from right to centre, and from centre to left, the clear notes of bugles rang out the welcome charge, and with one long, wild shout those glorious squadrons of Buford and Kilpatrick from right to left, as far as the eye could see, in one unbroken line, charged the foe. The shock was irresistible....

Hyperbole aside, a charge by two depleted cavalry divisions, even for us today, can only be imagined with some considerable effort.[28]

Chaplain Boudrye, who wasn't a witness to this event, nevertheless described it in the regiment's history. "About sundown," he wrote, "after a brief consultation between Buford and Kilpatrick, their bugles were ringing with the order for a coordinated and united charge; and with a wild shout those invincible squadrons fell upon the enemy, driving his broken lines from the field, which he left strewn with his dead and dying."[29] In reality, neither side could claim a decisive victory in this battle of Boonsboro, although, at its end, the cavalry had driven Stuart back about three miles toward Hagerstown. But Stuart had essentially accomplished his mission of keeping the Union cavalry away from Lee's forces retreating through Hagerstown.

In his July 9 letter, Hammond refers to some of Meade's infantry as only then arriving in the Boonsboro vicinity late in the day, July 8, and he expected a decisive battle in the near future. This would happen, it was thought, once the army was massed. Then it would strike at Lee before his army had a chance to get over the rain-swollen Potomac. In actuality, even on July 9 Meade believed he was still some days away from having sufficient forces in position to carry forward a successful attack on Lee. From Washington, probably in response to some prodding by the president, General Halleck telegraphed Meade, urging him on. On July 8 Meade received the following: "There is reliable information that the enemy is crossing at Williamsport. The President is urgent and anxious that your army should move against him by forced marches."

Meade replied almost immediately and strongly:

> My army is and has been making forced marches, short of rations and barefooted. One corps marched yesterday and last night 30 miles.
> I take occasion to repeat that I will use my utmost effort to push forward this army.

After firing off this reply, Meade sent copies of Halleck's telegram to all his corps commanders, no doubt to indicate to them the pressure they were all under and the expectations of their commander-in-chief.[30]

Hammond's letter of July 9 is the longest of those he wrote during the campaign, indicating that he had some free time available that day. Also, after the Boonsboro engagement, Colonel De Forest was returned or recalled to the brigade, probably because of the death of General Farnsworth. That day he assumed command of the First Brigade, and Colonel Richmond returned to his command of the First West Virginia. The action of July 8 was essentially the last for the Fifth New York until July 12. The men rested on July 9, and on the tenth essentially held the left flank outside Funkstown as Buford's division fought with Stuart and Rebel infantry on the east side of the town.[31] By July 10, Lee had his army massed on the Potomac behind strong defensive entrenchments laid out by Lee's engineers. He expected Meade to attack. The rain that had been falling with regularity since July 4 had swollen the Potomac to a point that only a small ferry guided by a cable was able to cross the river. Lee's engineers were desperately trying to build a pontoon bridge using wood torn from the town's buildings. Jeb Stuart was still operating out in front of Lee's fortification, screening and hopefully spoiling any thrust by Meade before it got started. On July 11, the regiment merely "moved out two miles, drove in the enemy's pickets, and returned to our bivouac."[32]

On July 12, the Third Division made another attempt to clear the Rebels from Hagerstown. The division moved up to Funkstown, then headed for

Hagerstown, this time supported by infantry. Some skirmishing occurred about a mile and a half out of town, but a large fight did not develop. The Rebels had given up and left Hagerstown. The Third Division marched in and occupied the town.

By the afternoon of July 12, Meade had his army ready for an assault on Lee's position. He planned to open the attack the next morning, but his corps commanders were clearly unenthusiastic when Meade outlined the plan of attack in a council of war on the evening of July 12. To Meade's commanders the enemy positions they were being asked to assault looked remarkably like July 3 at Gettysburg, only in reverse. In any attack, the Union army would play the part of General Pickett. Noting their concern, Meade agreed that he would personally inspect Lee's defensive position the next day. And this he did on July 13.

While Meade was doing his reconnaissance, Kilpatrick and the division were in position on the right flank of the army. "Kill-cavalry" decided on a reconnaissance of Rebel positions in his front and notified the First Vermont. As the Vermonters went forward they encountered a large force moving on a road toward Lee's fortifications. Skirmishing started and, in another reckless charge, Kilpatrick ordered two companies from that regiment to the gallop. The Vermonters, going forward, were cut up in a crossfire with at least twenty-three men being killed. It was so reckless that General Meade, if he didn't see if for himself, heard about it almost immediately and sent a massage to Kilpatrick that night chastising the general for action resulting in an unnecessary loss of life. Again the Fifth New York had been lucky, having been left in camp that day.

As darkness grew on the evening of July 13, Lee's formations began crossing the Potomac on a hastily built pontoon bridge. By daylight of July 14, a division-strength rear guard and stragglers were the only Rebel force remaining in Maryland. Kilpatrick, early on the morning of July 14, realized that the fortifications to his front had been abandoned during the night. At dawn, Custer's brigade and Buford's division moved forward. Again, and inexplicably, the Fifth New York remained behind in camp. Kilpatrick, with about three hundred men, charged into Williamsport, only to find stragglers. Custer's brigade quickly proceeded to Falling Waters. Here the cavalry came upon fieldworks manned by Rebel infantry acting as a rear guard. Again, a charge was ordered and it was a replay of July 3. At first the defending Rebels thought the approaching cavalry were Stuart's men and held their fire. Then, realizing they were Yankees, they started shooting at a distance where they could not miss. Custer's men kept coming and, using sabers, tried to slash their way through. Thirty men became casualties, and as one of Buford's officers commented, "any competent cavalry officer of experience" would have known that the infantry would prevail in such a fight. Luckily, Burford's division came into the fight at Falling Waters from the east, and when his weight was added to that of Custer's, the Rebels who hadn't already escaped over the pontoon bridge were captured.[33]

The occasional correspondent of the *Wyoming Mirror*, John Jackson, reported home:

> The morning of the 14th found the Rebel army on the other side of the Potomac, except a rear guard at Falling Waters, consisting of three brigades of infantry of A.P. Hill's Corps. Our brigade picked up many straggling graybacks, minus shoes as well as respect for the confederate humbug for which they had fought. At Falling Waters the 2nd brigade of our division [Custer's] charged on their breastwork, and drove the rebels with the loss of 103 killed and 900 prisoners. We passed the latter on the road to Harper's [*sic*] Ferry, and one of them remarked to me, "You are beginning to do something for your country." In fact our infantry acknowledged that Cavalry is now worth something. In the past three weeks our division has captured more than its number of rebel prisoners. The sarcastic remark attributed to Gen. Hooker, "Who ever saw a dead cavalry man?" is heard no more. At Falling Waters twenty-eight brave men fell on our side. But it was a glorious death to die. As ever, yours for the Union, J.W.J.[34]

The Third Division was then ordered to Harpers Ferry and arrived there on July 16. There they rested and John Hammond wrote another letter home. The next day, July 17, the Fifth New York crossed the river back into Virginia and moved to Purcellville and camped. On July 20, the regiment was at Upperville, but essentially the Gettysburg campaign had ended when the troopers had crossed the river.[35]

> Harpers Ferry, July 17, 1863
>
> I have a moment to write you a few lines. We crossed to this point last night on pontoon bridges, and this morning crossed the Shenandoah into Loudon County, in pursuit of Jeff's ragamuffins. We are worn and jaded down. The cavalry has done all the work and fighting since Gettysburg. We charged into Hagerstown, Pa., on Sunday last, and held the place for two days against a large body of infantry and cavalry, hoping General Meade would attack them; but no, he waited one week from the time the advance of the rebels came into Hagerstown, which was the Monday we fought them. The result is that they have all re-crossed into Virginia. We all felt that we had them and should have annihilated them. The cavalry followed them to Falling Waters and Williamsport, and charged them behind their entrenchment. We have taken in all six to eight thousand prisoners in the last week. We recaptured Lieuts. Bryan, Merriman and Dimmick. Captains Lucas and Penfield have, without doubt, been carried across the river. We

have lost the best opportunity we ever had for wiping out the army of Virginia. We leave for Loudon County in a few moments in a heavy rain.[36]

John Hammond's thoughts in this letter are remarkably similar to those of many officers in the Army of the Potomac at this time. With Lee's army back in Virginia, and having stolen a day's march on its pursuers, nearly everyone, President Lincoln included, believed a great opportunity had been lost by the Union army. "Every trooper believed that the Army of the Potomac had the confederacy by the throat, at last, and that vigorous and persistent effort would speedily crush the life out of it," wrote one cavalryman.[37]

The main body of the Army of the Potomac, although severely bloodied in three days of fighting at Gettysburg, did pursue Lee's as best it could during the week following the battle, but rain, slop-trough roads and insufficient supplies added up to slow going for the Federals. Simply put, Lee's army had moved faster. Primarily, it was the Cavalry Corps that had done the chasing and the fighting for nine critical days as the Army of the Potomac moved to positions in Maryland to attack Lee. But by the time Meade was in position to attack, the Rebels had thrown up powerful fortifications defending their crossing points. These defensive lines had intimidated Meade's corps commanders and justifiably so. These were not squeamish men, but ones who had, just a few days before, lived a bloodbath and were reluctant for another. These commanders probably did not know the exact number of casualties their army had sustained at Gettysburg, but they had to know they were exceedingly high. Another Gettysburg, with the Federals doing the charging, could result in wounding the Army of the Potomac so severely that it may not recover. This hesitation, nearly two days in length, had by dawn on July 14 allowed Lee to get over the river and into Virginia. As Hammond indicated in his Harpers Ferry letter, the regiment was ready to renew the pursuit. However, once in Virginia, the regiment was ordered to halt at Purcellville and rest as the Army of Northern Virginia drew further away.

William P. Dye was captain of Company E of the Fifth New York. As the regiment rested as best it could at Purcellville, he dashed off a letter to his hometown newspaper in Allegany County, New York:

> Headquarters 5th N.Y. Cavalry, Percelville [sic], Va.
> July 18th, 1863.
>
> EDITOR TIMES:—Wishing to inform the friends at home of the fate of Company E, of this Regiment, and not having time to write at all, I improve the first hour's rest we have had since crossing the Potomac into Maryland, (June 27) to give you a list of killed, wounded and

prisoners in this company, which was recruited in Cattaraugus and Allegany counties.

At Hanover, Ps., June 30, 1863 2d Lieut. Elem S. Dye, killed, Allegany, Cattaraugus Co., N.Y.; Mortally wounded, 1st Sergeant John S. Trobridge, Rushford, N.Y.; Henry W. Monroe, Little Valley, N.Y.; Slightly wounded, Bradley Alexander, Farmersville, N.Y.; Newton C. Row, Friendship, N.Y.; Orson S. Keyes, Genessee, N.Y. Captured, Frank Olmstead, Allegany Co., N.Y. At Williamsport, Md., July 5th 1863, wounded by fall of horse, and captured, 1st Lieut. D.B. Merriman, Richburg, N.Y.; wounded and captured, Fred J. Ehman, Ellicottville, N.Y,; captured Fred J. Clark, Orlean, N.Y. Lieut. Merriman being too seriously injured to be moved, he was released. Wounded all doing well.

Respectfully,
W.P. Dye, Capt. Co. E, N.Y.C.[38]

During these days of riding and fighting for the Fifth New York, Chaplain Boudrye and the other Union prisoners were marching deep into Virginia. Probably on the cable ferry or in a boat, he crossed the Potomac on July 8 on his long trip to Libby Prison in Richmond. In the letter to his children of July 18, Hammond makes note of the chaplain: "The Chaplain also promised me to write your mother a few lines, when we were at Gettysburg, as I had no time to do so, and also send her a Hanover paper with the account of the gallant charge of the Fifth at that place; but as he has never been heard of since that time, we think he has been taken prisoner, as he was a good ways behind when we left that town.... The enemy being both in our front and rear, he must have been captured by them, as we lost quite a number from the division."[39]

The disappointment that bordered on bitterness as Hammond assessed the campaign was still with him on July 18. In his letter of that date he writes at length of what he sees as the army's lost opportunities:

> We had hope that Gen. Meade would have captured a portion at least of the remainder of Lee's army before crossing the Potomac, as he certainly could have done, had he the spirit of Generals Kilpatrick and Buford. They [Kilpatrick and Buford] have attacked the rebels everywhere they could find them, sometimes a success and sometimes we have been unsuccessful; yet our impudence has carried terror into the rebel ranks many times. We have suffered, but feel proud of our arm of the service.... The First Vermont charged their entrenchments at Hagerstown, and put two brigades of infantry in great disorder, and had Gen. Meade allowed one or two brigades to go to their assistance, we might have captured ten thousand of the ragamuffins.[40]

The Fifth New York wasn't in this action by "Kill-cavalry" on July 13 and almost certainly did not know Meade reprimanded the young general for getting so many Vermont troopers killed.

At the Potomac crossing, in one of the few of his comments that rise above the superficial, Boudrye refers to morale among the retreating Rebels at that moment: "The officer of the guard, taking us over, as soon as we reached the Old Virginia shore, threw his saber down on the ground, emphatically exclaiming, 'There, I'll never cross this river again on a similar expedition.'"[41]

7
Virginia in Summer, Fall and Winter — 1863–1864

> At Culpepper [*sic*], Stuart made a stand.–Planting his artillery on the hill near the town shelled us vigorously. Our brigade being in the advance received the most attention. Several shells burst in our ranks, killing one man in company F, and wounding three in company H, of our regiment.
> Gen Kilpatrick here brought up the brass band of the division, who played one or two pieces while the shells whistled over our heads for an accompaniment.—With his accustomed coolness, he rode up to where our battery was placed and ordered a charge.... Maj. Hammond who led our battalion received a wound in the hand, and two or three others were slightly wounded, in the charge.
> —John Jackson to the *Wyoming County Mirror*, September 30, 1863[1]

Chaplain Boudrye in his regimental history summarized the remainder of July and all of August for the Fifth New York. He writes that, beginning on July 20 "until September, the headquarters of the third division were near Warrenton, while picketing was performed by the regiments in rotation, along the line of the Rappahannock, opposed to Stuart's cavalry, whose headquarters were at Culpepper [*sic*]." In a letter dated July 25, John Hammond gives his wife a summary of what the regiment had been doing since coming back to the area where the Gettysburg campaign had started:

> We arrived here on the 23rd from Ashby's Gap. We Passed Gen. Buford's cavalry in front of Chester Gap.... We crossed the Rapahannock [*sic*] near Waterloo bridge, and camped at this place. Yesterday morning we attacked Hill's column near Battle Mountain. It was a desperate thing on our part, and the Michigan brigade came near being lost with a section of artillery. Hill's infantry got in our rear, and we had to cut our way out,—we saved our artillery,—and the Michigan brigade lost in killed and wounded about forty, thirty of whom were left on the field, being unable to get them off. I can assure you we made some tall trav-

eling to the rear. To-day we made a reconnoisance [*sic*] to Gaines' Cross-Road, and we are satisfied that all the rebels are past this point that have crossed the Blue Ridge.... We have made up our mind that Gen. Meade has no idea of fighting the rebels very soon, as he certainly might have got to Culpepper [*sic*] before them, if he had wished. I wish, Maria, you would get from Tom a list of the conscripts from Crown Point, as it rather pleases the boys. We have had the upper hand of the rebel cavalry since we have had Kilpatrick for a leader. Generals Stuart and F[itzhugh] Lee don't court an engagement with him.... F. Lee was to occupy this place the same night we came here, but did not see fit to dispute the point very savagely with us.[2]

The draft instituted by the Lincoln administration had gone into effect earlier, and there had been riots in New York City as a result. No doubt the boys from Essex County and Crown Point in Company H, when they saw the list of people they knew who were drafted, would have a good laugh knowing that those eligible were now probably headed for an infantry regiment with no bounty to show for it when the war ended.

Of these weeks, John W. Jackson of Company F told his hometown newspaper:

> Our duty consists in picketing the ford for several miles up and down the river. It is not dangerous duty as the pickets do not fire on each other, in fact they are on very friendly terms, often swimming across and exchanging coffee for tobacco, and holding short confabs on the state of affairs. The rebel officers do not relish this; they fear disaffection and desertion will follow. Their soldiers complain of poor food, short rations, clothing, &c., own they were badly whipped at Gettysburg. They are heartily sick and tried of the war, would be glad to have peace on any terms.

Such interaction seems to have been common during this period. Jackson goes on to relate, "Lt. Tolles has received a letter from Capt. Lucas, who accounts for the missing boys of Co. F, as prisoners with himself in Richmond. Lt. T. wrote a letter in answer, which Sergeant Nouse carried to the rebel pickets across the river, to mail." Lt. Lucas had been captured during the fighting withdrawal from Hagerstown on July 6.[3]

Captain James Penfield of Company H was captured during Lee's fighting retreat from Gettysburg. One of the regiment's officers received a letter from Penfield written in Libby Prison in Richmond. In a letter to his wife dated August 7, Hammond sees nearly the same things as trooper John W. Jackson: "I have written James this morning, and shall send it to him through the rebel pickets on the opposite side of the river. Our pickets and the rebels are very friendly, they sit on the bank and talk to each other, and swim out to each other through the river. Occasionally ... the rebels come over to our side to visit. They exchange tobacco, and so forth, for bread. All this appears very strange, when perhaps in a few hours they may be in deadly struggle to take each other's lives."[4]

Colonel Othneil De Forest had returned to command the First Brigade of the Third Division on July 9, 1863, just after the fighting at Boonsboro, Maryland, and replaced Colonel Richmond of the First West Virginia. What transpired in the subsequent weeks relative to Colonel De Forest is the most curious episode in the regiment's history, yet the record leaves only tantalizing hints as to what it was really all about. In the reorganization of the Cavalry Corps that took place just after Meade assumed command of the army, De Forest was taken from command of the First Brigade and replaced with the newly promoted Elon Farnsworth. On the day of the reorganization, June 28, De Forest was sent on "an extended leave of absence," according to one cavalry historian. In Chaplain Boudrye's history — and the only mention of De Forest at all for this entire period — the colonel is said to have been ill since June 28 and returned to the brigade on July 9, replacing Colonel Richmond, who as senior colonel in the brigade assumed command upon Farnsworth's death. These two explanations of De Forest's disappearance can be looked upon as either incompatible or meaning relatively the same thing, but suspicion surfaces in that moving Farnsworth into brigade command was General Pleasonton's doing from the moment Meade said he could put into command those officers he thought would obtain the desired result. It is difficult to believe, therefore, that De Forest's removal coincided with an illness. De Forest, in his leadership first of the Fifth New York and then the brigade, had been "consistently praised by his superiors as an energetic, intelligent officer." At the time he initially raised the regiment, De Forest was thirty-six years old; Yale educated, he had been a "broker" in New York City prior to Fort Sumter and Bull Run.[5] However, his return to brigade command in the wake of Gettysburg was a short-lived affair. The only clue in the *Official Record* comes in a brief reference to the colonel at the end of a report to General Pleasonton written by General Custer on July 18, 1863. Custer at that moment was temporarily in command of the division while Kilpatrick went to New York City to help deal with the draft riot there. Custer is reporting on the division's operations during the few days preceding July 18 and near the end says, "I will relieve Colonel De Forest as soon as Colonel Richmond returns from Frederick, Md." Obviously, Custer is replying to an order he had received from Pleasonton, reporting that he will replace De Forest with the experienced Richmond. There is no appearance of urgency about this in Custer's report. Colonel Richmond and the First West Virginia had been on provost duty at Frederick, Maryland, for about a week and would soon return to the division. However long Colonel Richmond commanded the First Brigade after his return from provost duty is not clear in the record.⁶

Somehow, the Army of the Potomac had reached out to Colonel De Forest, wherever he was at the time just after Farnsworth's death, and he had gotten himself to Boonsboro by July 9, apparently ready to resume command of his former brigade. However, between De Forest's return on July 9, Custer's report of July 18, and August 14, something happened within the command of the army and in New York City. The men of the Fifth New York probably knew a great deal about it, but little has succeeded in coming down to us. There is in the New York State Military Museum an undated newspaper clipping that from its tone appears to have been written about this time. Colonel De Forest's name is mentioned in this article, written with the intention of informing the public of an investigation then being conducted by the War Department. "For some time past, there had been a secret office established in the city [presumably New York], under the direction of Col. Olcott, for the ferreting out and exposing frauds of any and every kind against the Government," the paper told its readers. "It was in this office that the charges against General Blenker and Colonel D'Uasey were made out. Besides the charges at present against Kohnstam, there are a number against Col. De Forest, 5th N.Y. Cavalry, for defrauding the government in the purchase of horse, arms, &c." The Colonel Olcott mentioned in the newspaper had previously been put in charge of internal army investigations relating to fraud and corruption, and the cases mentioned in the article were those that were either known to the paper, and thus the public, or were being litigated. In neither Boudrye's journal nor his history, nor in the *Official Record*, is any mention made of Col. De Forest at this time or for the remainder of the regiment's existence.

Luckily for the historian, Private Richard Kenwell of Company D wrote of what he had heard in a letter to his parents dated August 27, 1863:

> You have probably heard before this of the arrest of Colonel De Forrest [*sic*] for swindling the government out of nearly $60,000 dollars by presenting false bills of sale for horses and equipments. Since the time of the organization of the Regt he had been selling Commissions in the Regt to men, some of who was no more fit for the office they hold than I would be a general. There was one of them come to our company last spring as a second Lieutenant who did not know how to mount his horse. He either resigned or was dishonorably discharged for drunkenness last summer. He left without paying his negro servant for his services. The meanest thing that I knew an officer to do was that of the Colonel [presumably De Forest] who kept $20 dollars that a poor private in our Company gave to him to get change and he never gave him either the change or bill back to him.⁷

The selling of commissions, if true, could be one reason why the attrition rate among officers during the regiment's first year of existence was so high.

In a letter home dated August 14, John Hammond makes his first mention of the De Forest affair, but gives no details: "Col. DeF–, I am told, has gone to New York under a strong guard. I don't believe he is as guilty as he is represented, as his principal accuser is the biggest villain in the country. I regret his situation very much, on account of his family."[8] The regiment's history notes, in an antiseptic list inserted by Chaplain Boudrye, that De Forest officially left the army on March 29, 1864, by "Special Order 131 A.G.O." However, prior to this date, the colonel appears to be free in New York in early March and in a combative frame of mind. He had apparently read in the *New York Times* of the indictments brought by the government against him. On March 2, 1864, there appeared in the newspaper a forthright note demanding that the *Times* correct an inaccuracy it printed mentioning the indictments and his status within the army: "Will you please state that I am still Colonel of the regiment [Fifth New York], and am not only willing but eager to meet any charges against me." Nothing else relating to De Forest written by John Hammond in 1863 has survived. Only in a letter dated April 5, 1864, did he again mention the colonel: "We have received official notification of the dismissal of Col. O. DeF — from the service, by order of the President."[9]

A civilian as of March 29, 1864, De Forest next surfaces in U.S. Circuit Court in New York, according to an article in the *New York Times* of April 24, 1864. He is there to answer to five indictments brought by the army against him and two others, Benjamin De Forest and Charles L. Rowand. However, the newspaper does not list what the five indictments were. The names of the other two defendants do not appear in any of the regiment's records, and it must be assumed they were dealing with De Forest directly from the civilian sector. The U.S. Attorney, speaking in court, is reported to have told the judge that he had reviewed in detail the investigation conducted by the War Department, including statements by deposed witnesses. Regretfully, he tells the judge, "it would be impossible, upon the evidence, whatever be its moral aspects, to procure a conviction."[10] Although the U.S. Attorney must have given his reason to the judge, in the newspaper article he is not quoted giving any particulars about the indictments or why, specifically, he does not think he could obtain a conviction. Was this deliberate on the part of the paper in that the charges were disposed of, or merely inadequate reporting by the paper's man in the courtroom? Apparently, this was the end of the legal aspects of the matter.

The former colonel had been out of the army a month at the time of his appearance in court and out nine months when General Nathaniel Banks

7. Virginia in Summer, Fall and Winter—1863–1864

wrote to Secretary of War Edwin Stanton on December 14, 1864. It was under General Banks, in 1862, that De Forest and the Fifth New York had first served. With no explanation, Boudrye included in his history the text of the note by Banks: "Dear Sir — Col. O. De Forest served under me in the Shenandoah Valley in 1862, for nearly a year. He was then colonel of the 5th New York Cavalry, and performed his duty willingly, fully, and with great energy. His regiment was the best under my command. As an officer, then and there, he showed much ability, and I do not hesitate to recommend him to the favor of the Dep't. N.P. Banks, M.G.V." There is no explanation in the record as to why Banks, obviously having been asked to write this note, is giving the secretary of war his opinion concerning the former colonel. But by his use of the phrase, "As an officer, then and there...," the politician turned general is obviously hedging his bet. Boudrye's history of the regiment covered in detail all of the activities of the Fifth New York during the time the chaplain was a prisoner in Richmond. It is curious that Boudrye, who must have learned what transpired when he returned to the command after his release, mentions Colonel De Forest only a few times in over 300 pages of text, and then only tangentially. This is unusual, for De Forest apparently led the regiment to the satisfaction of his superiors. Indeed, De Forest had been mentioned favorably in reports, particularly for his leading a wagon train to safety during the retreat from Strasburg in May of 1862. Indeed, he was considered able enough to be brought back to command the brigade after Farnsworth had been killed. It does seem that De Forest led the command well despite the small number of references to him in the *Official Record*, well enough to consider the judgment of him — "consistently praised by his superiors as an energetic, intelligent officer" — to be correct. It is speculation, but having had the U.S. Attorney declined to prosecute earlier in the year, De Forest might have been maneuvering to re-enter the army, and the note by General Banks could have been employed in his favor. It is inconceivable that the chaplain would tell a falsehood when he penned his regimental history, but he certainly could exclude. Othneil De Forest, despite his commendable leadership, is a shadowy figure in the chaplain's rendering of the regiment.

The note by General Banks recommending De Forest proved, sadly, to be an exercise. On December 17, 1864, three days after the general wrote the note, the *New York Times*, in its obituary column, reported: "On Friday, Dec. 16, after a short illness, OTHNEIL DE FOREST, late Colonel of Fifth New York Cavalry (Ira Harris Guards), in the 38th year of his age. The friends and relatives of the family, and officers of the army, are respectfully invited to attend the funeral services, on Sunday next, at 2 o'clock, at his late residence, No. 97 East 49th St."[11] This should have ended the De Forest episode, but perhaps

Banks's note or some other undisclosed maneuvering turned the situation to the deceased colonel's favor. The following citation appears in Frederick Phisterer's *New York in the War of the Rebellion*, published in 1912. Othneil De Forest was "dismissed March 29, 1864; dismissal revoked, March 14, 1866, and honorably discharged as of date of dismissal, April 11, 1866; restored to his regiment, to date September 3, 1864; died, December 16, 1864, of congestions of the brain, at New York City, commissioned Colonel, January 1, 1863, with rank from October 1, 1861, original."[12]

The brief return of Colonel De Forest in the summer of 1863 may in some way be related to the equally brief return of Lt. Col. Robert Johnstone to the regiment. John Hammond had taken command of the regiment from Johnstone on June 1, 1863, and Boudrye's history lists him as commanding the regiment until the end of August 1864. Also, nowhere in the records or the unit's history for this period is Johnstone's return mentioned. For that matter, there is no mention of the reason why command of the regiment was turned over to Hammond, except for a brief mention in the Military Service Record for Johnstone in the National Archives. In the regimental returns for June 1863, the lieutenant colonel is listed as being "Absent left in charge of convalescences at Fairfax C[ourt] H[ouse] by order of Maj. Gen. Stahel [*sic*]." Nevertheless, in a letter dated August 14, 1863, the same day Hammond reported that De Forest had been taken away, he writes:

> Lieut. Col. J — took command yesterday, he threatens all who are inimical to him to have them in arrest. You need not be surprised if you hear of my being under arrest soon, as I shall take no orders from him, after he has avoided all the labor, dangers and privations of the regiment for nearly three-fourths of a year. He commenced yesterday by putting Capt. Barker under arrest, and swearing at everybody that he dared to. He keeps clear of me. I have no idea of leaving the service, although I may leave the regiment if I can. No one can be spared from the army at the present time, and, above all, a citizen of New York.

Fortunately for the Fifth New York, this situation did not last long. On September 3, Hammond noted in a letter, "Lieut. Col. J — is under arrest." By September 6, there seems to be some form of resolution. Hammond reported home, "A court sits to-morrow for the Trial of many officers on many charges. Lieut. Col. J — is one of the unhappy subjects." At this point it appears Hammond is again in full command of the regiment. In the same letter of September 6, he writes, "Col. Davies of the Second N.Y.V.C., is in command of the brigade. He is a very strict disciplinarian, and has no mercy of officers and soldiers who is [*sic*] neglectful of duty or discipline. He is very kind to me and seems to like me much." Then he adds, "I have a terrible task on my hands after the loose, neglectful manner in which Col. DeF _ and

Lieut. Col. J _ have managed the regiment." Finally, on October 17, Hammond writes, "Lieut. Col. J. is out of the service." This apparently was the result of the trial Hammond referred to in his earlier letter.

Chaplain Boudrye's history lists Johnstone as leaving the army under General Order 104 on December 5, 1863. The regimental list in the New York State Military Museum lists Johnstone as being "cashiered" on that date with no specifics given. After piecing together the fragmentary records, one is strongly inclined to believe that somehow the tale of Col. De Forest and Lt. Col. Johnstone are related. Also, judging from his written statements regarding De Forest and Johnstone upon their return to the regiment, Hammond might be inadvertently telling us that the charges against De Forest were incited by the "biggest villain in the country," and that his later being cashiered was the result of his being guilty of the charges initially brought against De Forest.[13] It does seem curious that in the records available to us there appears to be a conscious effort by those knowledgeable of the situation to ensure that the Fifth New York's hard-won reputation as a superior volunteer fighting command did not suffer as a result of whatever Johnstone and De Forest had allegedly done.

Yet, De Forest's case does not appear to be an isolated incident, confined to New York City. The *New York Times* reported from Washington on May 1, 1864, that Colonel William Fish, in command of the First Connecticut Cavalry, was convicted of various charges of fraud against the Army, among them filing false claims for horses lost in combat that were supposedly his personal property. He was cashiered from the army, fined $5,000, and sent to prison while the fine was in the process of being paid.[14]

On September 4, the Third Division embarked on what was called Kilpatrick's gunboat expedition. The division moved down stream from Warrenton along the northern bank of the Rappahannock to the vicinity of Port Conway, attacking with artillery Rebel gunboats that were found in the river. The boats were being used by the Rebels to haul supplies from the sympathetic north side of the river, territory outside the Union army's immediate control. John Jackson later wrote to the *Wyoming Country Mirror* some of his impressions:

> The boys had often remarked, since our campaign in Pennsylvania and Maryland, that Gen. Kilpatrick had charged everything but gunboats, and our next work would be to take an *iron clad*. Little did we think how near the prophesy [sic] would be fullfilled [sic].... At 2 A.M. the 5th N.Y. with Captain Elder's battery moved down the river and at sunrise threw the first shell.... Capt. Elder then sent his compliments to the gunboats, (if they may be called such), and succeeded in sending several shells through their hulls near the water line, making them worthless for sailing purposes.

Doctor Lucius P. Woods had been the surgeon for the Fifth New York and was now the surgeon-in-chief for the First Brigade. After returning from the raid he recorded his impressions in a letter home. Kilpatrick had the horse artillery ready at daylight. "Then the flying artillery of ten guns," Dr. Woods wrote,

> supported by the old Fifth New York and First Michigan, dashed at a full run-down to the river-bank, wheeled into position, and gave the Rebels a small cargo of hissing cast-iron, which waked them up more effectually than their ordinary morning call. They soon came to their senses, and for half an hour sent over to us what I would think to be, by the noise they made, tea-kettles, cooking-stoves, large cast-iron hats, etc. But our smaller and more active guns soon silenced theirs, and drove the gunners away, when we turned our attentions to the boring of holes in their boats with conical pieces of iron, vulgarly called solid shot. I am sure I can recommend them as first-class augers, for they sank the boats in time for all hands to sit down to breakfast at half-past nine o'clock.... We were absent from camp three days, and had only nine hours' sleep.[15]

Of more significance was the movement of the Cavalry Corps that began on September 12. In the days previous to this, General Lee had detached James Longstreet's infantry divisions and sent them west to add weight to General Braxton Bragg's army as it fought to hold Union forces from advancing in the vicinity of Chattanooga. General Meade, finding out about Longstreet's departure, was determined to take advantage, and ordered the Cavalry Corps to cross the Rappahannock. As part of the Third Division, the Fifth New York crossed the river at Kelly's Ford, while the other two divisions crossed further up stream. They bivouacked, and the next morning the three divisions moved forward, with Kilpatrick moving down the Orange and Alexandria Railroad in the direction of Culpeper. As the Federals moved, driving Stuart's pickets before them, the Rebel cavalrymen were ordered into a defensive position outside of town. The First and Second divisions of the Cavalry Corps attacked the left and center of this position as the Third division, having further to travel, approached the right flank. When he got to the field, Kilpatrick ordered an immediate attack on this flank. Stuart, now confronting pressure on three sides and outnumbered, began a withdrawal to the south, heading for the Rapidan. The Fifth New York's part in this action is captured by Chaplain Boudrye:

> Not long into this equal contest, when Kilpatrick's artillery was heard thundering in the enemy's right flank and rear, on the road from Stevensburg, whither he had led his swift squadrons. Under this well directed fire the enemy fell back into town; and, before he had time to reform his line, and in spite of a heavy fire from his artillery, the Fifth New York and the First Vermont, with detachments from other regiments, charged into the streets of the town, capturing three

Blakely guns, and throwing the boast [host] of chivalry [Rebel cavalry] into a perfect rout. They hastily retreated in the direction of Pony Mountain and Rapidan Bridge, whither they were pursued closely by our victorious boys. Several prisoners fell into our hands.

In that Boudrye was at this time ensconced in Libby Prison, his account of this action, obviously, was conjured up, probably from verbal accounts related to him long after the fact. Actually, the Cavalry Corps followed Stuart until he reached the relative safety of the Rapidan river bank and supporting lines of Lee's infantry and artillery. The decision was made by the Federals not to press further without their own infantry support, and a withdrawal was initiated to a point out of Rebel artillery range.

At some point on September 14, the regiment was in action in the vicinity of Culpeper Court House, and John Hammond was wounded slightly. In a letter dated September 15 and written by Major Amos White, he says that Hammond cannot hold a pen because he "had the first joint of this forefinger on his right hand broken." On September 19, Hammond was able to again hold a pen and got off a note giving his account of the action:

> The Fifth lost one man killed and five wounded, on Sunday at Culpepper [sic], and ten missing. The Fifth charged the rebel battery four times and were repulsed, owing to their using canister and grape on us, and to their superior numbers. Four horses were killed by one shell, cutting six legs clean from their bodies. Our brigade, however, captured three pieces of artillery. The weather is cold and wet. Captain [Augustus] Barker was mortally wounded near Kelly Ford day before yesterday. I suppose he is dead before this. He was shot by a guerrilla. You will excuse this short letter, as I can't use my forefinger. It is doing well, and I think I shall save it. I have not lost an hour's duty with it.[16]

Skirmishing went on over the next few days before the cavalry retired to the Rappahannock. The total casualties sustained by the Fifth during this period were two killed, eight wounded, and fourteen missing. The early regimental history lists the date of Captain Barker's death as September 14, but both Hammond and an unnamed newspaper report say it occurred on the 17th. As reported in the newspaper as part of an obituary, on September 15 the Fifth New York moved from

> Hartwood Church and crossed to the Southern Side of the Rappahannock. Capt. Barker was left behind in charge of troops picketing the river, and on the 17th, while on the march to rejoin his regiment, as he was riding with a single man some distance in front of the column, he was fired upon by guerrillas concealed in the adjourning wood. Two balls took effect, one in the right side and the other in the left breast, each inflicting a mortal wound. He was immediately carried to the house of Mr. Harris Freeman, near Mount Holly Church, about one mile from the Ford. From this gentleman and his family the dying soldier

received the most tender attentions. Everything in their power was done to alleviate his sufferings, but he survived his wounds only twelve hours.[17]

On September 21, on Meade's order, another two-division cavalry action pitted the First and Third divisions against Stuart. Meade ordered a reconnaissance to the west to determine the location and strength of Lee's left flank. Kilpatrick moved to the village of Liberty Mills while Buford's division headed for Gordonsville. Stuart quickly became engaged with Buford, who chose to fight dismounted. Kilpatrick, possibly hearing the firing, came upon Stuart's rear and was about to attack, but Stuart beat him to it, no doubt remembering his forced retreat from Culpeper a few days previously. Turning from facing Buford, Stuart crashed into Kilpatrick's First Brigade and the Fifth New York, knocking them back. Fighting intensified now as Buford pressed what had become Stuart's rear and Kilpatrick, gaining a measure of unit cohesion after the initial Rebel assault, held his ground. Now in the jaws of a two-division vise, Stuart had to retreat again. No one in the Fifth New York was lost in this action at a place called by contemporaries Brookin's Ford.[18]

On September 29, 1863, John Hammond, his finger apparently much better, wrote what was for him a long account of the Fifth's last couple of actions. It was addressed to his children, which probably accounts for the unusual amount of detail he put into it:

> General Buford, with a portion of Kilpatrick's division and one other brigade, returned from the expedition Wednesday last to Madison Court House and the south branches of the Rapid Ann [sic]. We fell in with Stuart's cavalry near Madison. Buford attacked them in front and drove them all day. We moved on their right flank and crossed the Rapid Ann [sic] in the rear of the rebels. When they found they were cut off they attacked us with great fury, taking prisoners of the Second N.Y.V.C., and wounding some sixty men. We killed of the rebels ten or twelve, and took about a hundred prisoners. I was complimented, as well as my command, by Brig. Gen. Davies, for having my regiment so well in hand at a time when some of our regiments were in a good deal of confusion. Greatly to my mortification, this army is going to fall back to the Potomac. I could never have believed two weeks ago that we should have been here at this time. It is very disheartening to the cavalry, who have done so much hard work and fighting since Gettysburg, to have to turn back. You will probably see in the papers that Gen. Custer took three guns when we came into Culpepper [sic]. Gen. Custer's brigade never took a gun. The Second N.Y., of our brigade, took them, and the Fifth N. Y. had tried to take two more, but we were repulsed, charging four several [i.e., separate] times. Gen. Custer undertook to take the same guns that we did, and with no better success. We are now encamped nearly on the same ground where we fought the rebels one week ago last Monday. We were attacked by very superior numbers both cavalry and infantry, and had to fall back to this place, where we made a stand and drove them back. Capt. Elder

had got his cannon into position on a small hill in our rear. It had got to be almost night, and we were very hard pressed to hold our ground. When Capt. Elder opened on the rebels, firing his shells over our heads into the rebels, this gave us all new courage, for we did not know that he was near to support us. Cheer after cheer went up from our brave lads, as they sang out, "There goes old Elder," meaning his shell, which he was firing over our heads into the rebel ranks. Our men now charged upon the rebels,—the brave Kilpatrick leading part of them,—and we were left masters of the field; darkness coming on we went into camp, and the Fifth N.Y. has remained here ever since.[19]

As Lee had to detach troops and send them to the western theater, now Meade, too, was obliged to send two of his infantry corps to help prop up the Chattanooga campaign. And, as Meade had done, Lee learned of it and moved. For October 8, Boudrye noted in his history an overview of the Union Army's situation at this that time: "While we were thus picketing and scouting along these streams [tributaries of the Rapidan and Rappahannock], living sumptuously on a country that had not yet been impoverished by the march of armies, Gen. Lee, whose army lay mostly south of the Rapidan, crossed the river, moved to Madison Court House, and by a rapid flank movement on our right, compelled us to beat a hasty retreat, which was continued until Gen. Meade's main army occupied the heights of Centerville."[20]

On October 9, Meade ordered out the cavalry to scout toward the Rapidan. Brigadier General Henry E. Davies, in command of the First Brigade of the Third Division, had two of his four regiments out on picket from Russell's Ford to Grigginsburg the next day. The two other regiments, held in reserve, were in camp at a place called Brown's Store close by James City. At daylight on the morning of October 10, the Fifth New York was hit by the Rebels at Russell's Ford and driven back along the road to James City. It was a fighting withdrawal until the men reached a defensive position thrown up by General Davies. Here the New Yorkers formed a skirmish line in front of Davies. Typical of Boudrye, he recorded in his history not the essentials of the fighting but the disrupted morning routine of the regiment. "Our men," he noted, "were compelled to leave their palatable breakfasts of roast lamb, sweet potatoes, fine wheat bread, milk and honey, &c., with which the country abounded, and to attend to the stern and always unpleasant duties of a retreat, with the enemy pressing heavily upon us." The bounty of Virginia wasn't satisfying only the Fifth New York in this period. Willard Glazier of the Second New York, a regiment that would see a lot of action in the next few days, also had his breakfast interrupted on the morning of October 10. "It was early in the morning," he later wrote, "and steaming breakfasts of roast lamb, sweet potatoes, bread, milk, and honey were left untasted as our pickets were driven in with the intelligence that an attack in force was being made in our front."[21]

When the Rebels came within range of Elder's battery in Davies's defensive position, they opened on them. The Rebels withdrew but sporadic gun fighting continued the rest of the day. In Davies's opinion, written into his later report and quite correct, this attack was made by the Rebels to mask an infantry movement in the direction of Woodville, Virginia, an element of Lee's flanking move. By nightfall, the Rebels withdrew except for occasional probes of the Federal line. Early the next morning, October 11, the regiment was ordered to fall back to Culpeper Court House. The First West Virginia was ordered to take a separate route to the Court House and was attacked while detached from the rest of the brigade. The Second New York was ordered to their assistance and the two regiments together drove off the Rebels and eventually reunited with the brigade. From there the brigade continued the retreat, this time to Brandy Station, while the Rebels continually harassed the Second New York while it acted as rear guard.[22]

Near Brandy Station, a general cavalry fight developed with several charges and countercharges. Davies reported, "A description of the engagement is hardly practicable, as it consisted of a series of gallant charges made wherever the enemy appeared, in a manner that proved both the individual gallantry and the thorough discipline of our troops." During this fight, Major White of the Fifth New York supported Elder's battery with a part of the regiment. The harassing fire by the battery caused the Rebels to charge. White and his men shot it out with the Rebels at close range before driving them off. After this, the first brigade, along with the Second, continued its retreat to the river.

It was here another attack was made by the aggressive Fitz Lee and his cavalry command, one more fierce than any since the action began. Boudrye, again writing with no firsthand knowledge and more than a drop of drama, explained what supposedly happened:

> This was a situation to try the stoutest heart.... Forming his force in three lines of battle, [Kilpatrick] assigned the right to Gen. Davies, the left to Gen. Custer, and placing himself in the centre, advanced with terrible determination to the contest. Having approached to within a few hundred yards of the enemy's lines. His band was ordered to strike up Yankee Doodle, to whose inspiring note was added the blast of scores of bugles, ringing forth the charge. Fired with a sort of frenzy. And bearing aloft their colors, this band of heroic troopers shook the air with their battle cry, while their drawn and firmly grasped sabres flashed in the light of the declining sun. Gen. Custer, pulling off his cap, gave it to his orderly, and thus led on the charge, while his yellow locks floated on the breeze. Ambulances, forges and cannon, with pack train, non-combatants and others, all joined to swell the on-flowing tide, before which the Rebel lines broke in wild alarm.

7. Virginia in Summer, Fall and Winter—1863–1864   141

With this counterattack successful, the Fifth New York along with the rest of the division moved back to the Rappahannock and crossed in the darkness that had now descended on the scene.[23] It should be noted that it was probably Custer who ordered the band to play "Yankee Doodle," as he was noted to have done so on several other occasions during the war.

Boudrye continues: "His [Kilpatrick's] division soon after joined that of Buford, and together they engaged the enemy in a series of brilliant charges, which materially checked his [the enemy's] advance. At night they recrossed the Rappahannock in safety." In actuality, it was mostly the Second Brigade that did the charging, aided by a brigade of Buford's coming in from the direction of the river crossing. "It took three or four attempts, the last made in darkness, but the Wolverines [Second Brigade] broke through, joining Buford along the south bank. After some further difficulty, both divisions succeeded in fording the river to safety." In this action, two men were wounded and four captured from the Fifth New York.[24]

On October 12, the regiment and brigade moved to Bealeton Station, and the next day the command moved the Buckland Mills, getting there at 1 A.M. There the command went into camp with pickets thrown out in all directions. For the next few days, movement and skirmishing with the Rebels was the order of business for the Fifth. On October 14, they moved to Sudley Spring, on October 15 to the north side of Bull Run. October 16 saw the Rebels advance in the direction of Groverton, and the cavalry had to drive them off. The next day, the brigade moved in the direction of Thoroughfare Gap, scouting, and Davies reported Rebels moving in his direction through the Gap. While this was going on, Meade had concentrated his forces on high ground in the Centerville vicinity, possibly hoping for an attack by Lee against a strong, entrenched position reminiscent of Gettysburg. But Lee looked at the defensive position, and possibly remembering those days in July, decided not to attack. Instead be began a retrograde movement back behind the Rappahannock. The Fifth New York had at some point arrived at Fairfax Court House by October 17 and was able to rest briefly. John Hammond was able to compose a letter to an unnamed recipient that included his assessment of the situation from his level of command:

> I got me a pair of boots here. Have been nearly barefooted for some time. Otherwise am pretty well to do for clothing; have not had my clothes off since I last saw you, except to change them. The army is all back. We hold the country from the front of Manassas to the Blue Ridge; should not be surprised if we had another campaign in Maryland and Pennsylvania. I hope so. Good Country to live in. We have had rough work from ten days past. Lost some men and many horses. Capt. Rider is a prisoner. Our men are rough, tough and full of fight. We get a little tired at times; think our generals don't fight enough but are confi-

dent of results, such as will make us all proud of having been the defenders of our Union. We have five hundred men here of our brigade with unserviceable horses, and some without horses.[25]

In the afternoon of October 18, the Fifth and the rest of the First Brigade skirmished with the Rebels and drove them from Gainesville.

When Lee withdrew, Meade followed, slowly, with the cavalry out in front. October 19 saw the Third Division, with "Kill-cavalry" leading, setting a brisk pace, no doubt the commander wanting to accumulate some more glory before winter weather limited his opportunity. The division headed south from Gainesville with Davies and the First Brigade in the lead with Custer's Second Brigade following. At the suggestion of Fitz Lee, Stuart was to turn his command and attack the Third Division as Lee hit it in the flank. There was too much of a gap between the two brigades because Custer had stopped at the Buckland Mills crossing of Broad Run while Kilpatrick and the First Brigade continued on. The attack on Custer while stationary prevented riding to support Kilpatrick's and the First Brigade that was some distance ahead. Then Stuart's full weight fell on the First Brigade. It became a desperate situation by that afternoon and Kilpatrick abandoned his glory quest and ordered Davies to run for it with what was left of his brigade. Each command within the brigade was now to act on its own and it was about five miles back to the crossing of Broad Run. During the fight and then the desperate run for safety, the First Brigade lost 238 during this action; the Fifth New York had two killed, five wounded, and reported ten troopers as missing. The Rebels had won the day, allowing General Lee's infantry to retire unmolested. Stuart's men ever after referred to this engagement as the Buckland Races.

Surely, Kilpatrick should have known that all of Stuart's cavalry would be covering Lee's retirement. But all contemporary commentary on Kilpatrick and all the evaluation of his actions assert that he was glory hunting this day. Perhaps a serious victory could be gotten cheaply to supplement his supposed postwar political ambitions. The separation of the brigades allowed Stuart and Lee to attack and defeat in detail a better-armed and -equipped cavalry division. Kilpatrick's written report of this action has been called by historian Stephen Z. Starr "a masterpiece of obfuscation." To describe the defeat and running retreat as a slow retirement, in Starr's words, "called for an attitude toward the truth out of the reach of any ordinary man." Boudrye, who was not there, tries to gloss over the action: "Kilpatrick marched through Groverton and Gain[e]sville, meeting the enemy in overwhelming force at Buckland Mills. Had it not been for great skill and daring his entire command would have been annihilated. As it was, he narrowly escaped, saving all his guns, but leaving some of his men in the enemy's hands."[26]

Captain George Morton, a company commander in the First Brigade, had an opinion concerning the actions of the regiment during this period that he passed on to this father on October 27: "Yours of the 23rd came to hand Monday, and I was glad to hear from home. I think our regiment has had its share of the fighting for the last two months with General Kilpatrick, though I can't say it has amounted to much, as we fight and get driven back by the Rebels one day, and the next day we fight, lick and drive the rebels; and this is about the amount of what we have been doing the last two months, and are likely to do for the residue of the campaign, unless our depleted regiments are filled up." One cavalry historian has noted of Buckland Mills: "The outcome was wholly attributable to Judson Kilpatrick's penchant for sending his command into territory teeming with enemy troops for the sake of professional advancement — a reprise of Farnsworth's charge on a larger, more disastrous scale." A contemporary, however, noted, "This was a critical situation, but 'Kil' (as the general is familiarly styled among us) seemed to comprehend it in a moment.... Kilpatrick is supposed by some to have unnecessarily exposed himself, in which he suffered his first defeat, though escaping with a remarkably small loss."[27]

Davies, commanding the First Brigade, later reported about this galloping retreat in words that do not convey the severity of the situation and illustrate to the historian that official reports, written after the firing has stopped, do not always tell to fullest of stories: "The firing in my rear growing heavier, I took the responsibility of countermarching my command, returning toward Buckland Mills, at the same time directing the Second New York Cavalry, which had the advance, to hold their ground for some time and then retire slowly, covering my rear." Riding hard to about a mile from Buckland Mills, the brigade was then attacked by Rebel infantry, and the Fifth New York was sent to check their advance with their repeating rifles. The brigade then crossed Broad Run, moving in the direction of Hay Market. There the brigade was again attacked by what was thought to be Fitz Lee's cavalry, which were driven off with Kilpatrick personally leading attacks against his Rebel opponent.

After this hard day of fighting, the command retired to Gainesville and went into camp for the night. The next day in a letter, John Hammond did not use words equal to conveying the serious situation the command had ridden through: "We have had constant skirmishing and fighting since I last wrote you. Our army has again moved southward, and stretched from Thoroughfare Gap to Manassas Junction. Our division had a fight yesterday near Buckland Mills. We ran into a trap and were completely surrounded by Stuart's cavalry and Lee's infantry. We, however, cut our way out with a loss of only about one hundred men and officers. We are resting today."

In his report, Davies expressly wrote of the actions of one of the Fifth's officers in the days preceding the Buckland Races: "I would also refer to Lieutenant Boice," Davies penned, "...who, at the request of the general commanding division, made, while the command lay near Sudley Spring, two scouts to Thoroughfare Gap and to Aldie obtaining much valuable information which at the time was forwarded to headquarters." The information spoken of was probably the report received by Meade that Rebels were moving through the gap for an attack on his army. Lieutenant Theodore A. Boice had joined Company A from New York City in 1861 as a sergeant. Promoted to lieutenant in December 1863, he became captain of Company B in December 1863. Boice was one of the early recruits to the regiment who went on to prove fit for command. He would eventually lead the regiment in the fall of 1864.[28]

Chaplain Boudrye later commented in his history on the grand picture as he understood it at this time. Despite having been in Libby Prison as summer turned to autumn, the chaplain did seem to grasp the import of the events the regiment had lived through during this period. "It is quite singular to remark how these great armies had been swinging like huge pendulums during the present season. In June they swung from the Rappahannock, Va., to the Susquehanna, Penn.; then back to the Rapidan, afterward almost to the Potomac, then back to the Rapidan again. It is encouraging to notice that the swing of the Rebel army toward the north, shortens at every move, giving indications of its waning power."[29]

The result of a summer and fall filled with moving and fighting was that Lee and Meade, by November, were back essentially on the Rappahannock line the armies had occupied in May, facing each other across the river. What the contestants had to show for all the effort were two long casualty lists stretching from the spring into the fall. General Lee had lost a battle and lost men and equipment that were becoming ever more difficult to replace. General Meade had won a battle and lost men and had a cavalry corps that if not yet a fully integrated component of his armed force, it was close to becoming one.

On November 7, Meade crossed the Rappahannock in force and Lee was forced to retreat, moving toward the Rapidan River. The Union forces had crossed the Rappahannock at two points, Kelly's Ford and Rappahannock Bridge. The Third Cavalry Division tangled with Wade Hampton's cavalry to the east of these crossing points that day. The next day, November 8, the rest of the cavalry corps crossed the river and attacked the rear of Lee's army as it was retreating to positions behind the Rapidan River. It was a fighting withdrawal for Lee, and at one point in the pursuit a Rebel battery was firing at the approaching Union horsemen. John Hammond led a portion of the Fifth New York in a swift flanking movement and caught the Rebel battery in a killing fire.

In his history, Boudrye included a newspaper report, written by an unnamed correspondent for a New York paper attached to the brigade. His reporting covers what he witnessed on November 8:

> There was no very severe fighting, it is true, but the ease with which the enemy were driven from his position, and the short duration of the fight, were mainly attributable to the adroitness used in the disposition of our forces, and the intense eagerness and animation with which out men went up to the attack. A battery of the enemy which occupied a commanding position at Stevensburg, right in the line of our advance, was started off at a double quick, almost without firing a shot, by sending a regiment round to the right, which came in upon it from an unexpected quarter, and threw the gunners into instant alarm for the safety of their guns; and when they had taken up a new position and were busily shelling our troops coming up in front, Major Hammond, commanding the regiment just mentioned, with about twenty men, again compelled them to decamp by coming under cover and unseen to within easy carbine range of them, and thus picking off the artillerists.[30]

John Jackson described what he saw from his point of view regarding this action:

> Our regiment, on Saturday, Nov. 8th, distinguished itself, in taking possession of this town, (if a few deserted houses with huge chimney's attacked can be called a town). Acting as dismounted skirmishers in the advance of the brigade succeeded driving the enemy's skirmishers to their battery and their guns from a strong position from which there were shelling the column as it emerged the woods.— One of their regiments attempted to make a sabre charge, but were repulsed with the loss of several killed and wounded.... Our boys kept up a running fight with the enemy's rear. Three times Gen. Davies sent orders for them to halt, as he had only orders to take and hold the town, but it was dusk before they would give up chase. Gen. Kilpatrick, Gen. Davies, and other officers who saw the affair, said it was the most brilliant dismounted cavalry fight of the War. Our loss was confined entirely to horses.

Jackson finishes his letter by moving to another, and important, subject reflecting on the Fifth's situation in November 1863: "The nights are cold and frosty—days pleasant for December. The roads are in excellent condition. Yesterday we had soft bread and dried apples issued to our regiment, luxuries which we are generally strangers to. May we receive more such."[31]

John Hammond, writing home from Stevensburg a few days later, spoke at some length about this action. In devoting so many words to it, the normally reticent Hammond probably thought it showed his command in a favorable light:

Our boys got their blood up so, that it was only after Gen. Kilpatrick had ordered me to halt them three times that I could do so. The rebels had a splendid position, and shelled us severely with their English eighteen-pounder Blakely guns. The Fifth have the credit of making one of the most splendid and reckless cavalry fights of the war. One of our boys had an eighteen-pound shell pass through the entire length of his horse, bursting after it came out. He picked himself up very coolly, and said he didn't care so much for the horse, but didn't want to be scared to death in that way. I could not see where the scared was on his part. As we were fighting past a house, the woman of the house made a great outcry, as follows, "O, here comes those terrible Yankees of Kilpatrick; they say he is a devil from hell," etc., etc. We hope to do something worthy of our name soon, as we are tired of so many delays, and the weather is exceedingly cold.

The Fifth New York patrolled, picketed and occasionally skirmished with Rebels after the Southern army got over the Rapidan. In his usual style, Boudrye noted in his history one of the more important events occurring in the regiment this November: the arrival of the paymaster. On November 21, "the paymaster appeared with his greenbacks, and though the rain had fallen almost incessantly none have been heard to murmur. Whatever trouble or difficulty the soldier has, pay-day is sure to take it all away — at least if his accounts are all right." Boudrye's journal entry for the same day gives us a little more insight into this small event. "At 12 midnight, the Pay Master arrived and all were paid. I received but one month's pay, $118.00. The boys were quite cheerful, as they always are when their greenbacks come. Rain or shine, they never murmur on that day. There being no sutler nor any opportunity for drunkenness, the camp was very orderly. Gambling prevailed to some extent, as usual, but all quietly."[32]

Robert E. Lee now had his army south of the Rapidan in a defensive stance. With maneuver each day becoming more difficult and each day colder than the one before, his position could, if left alone, remain static through the quickly approaching winter. But General Meade and the Army of the Potomac, with the approval of Washington, attempted one more offensive before the weather closed in. It was to be an attack on the right flank of Lee's army that was anchored on a Rapidan tributary called Mine Run.

Chaplain Boudrye had returned to the regiment on November 14, and on November 23 noted in his journal: "Just before night and through the evening, there were indications of a general movement of the Grand Army of the Potomac. Some cavalry regiments, pontoons and other wagons with infantry were passing on toward the river.... we received orders to sound reveille at 5 tomorrow and be ready to move at 6½."[33] After a rain delay lasting two days, the move started again on November 26. The only role for the Fifth New York is this operation was a feint at several crossing points on the Rapidan

7. Virginia in Summer, Fall and Winter—1863–1864

The 18th Pennsylvania Cavalry in the winter of 1863–1864, in a typical winter camp — log huts with tent canvas stretched over the top and with fireplaces and chimneys constructed with any material readily available (Library of Congress).

upstream from where the main attack was targeted, an effort to distract Lee from the movement intending to come in on his right. "Reached the river (Rapidan) at Morton's Ford. The hills on the opposite side of the river were filled with Rebels," the chaplain noted, now once again an eyewitness. "Considerable shelling took place. More or less firing during all the day, yet no one was hurt."[34]

The next day, November 27, there was again contact with the enemy. The division crossed the river at Raccoon Ford early that morning after finding that Lee's infantry had withdrawn. Instead, the New Yorkers along with the rest of the Third Division found Fitz Lee and his cavalrymen in force. The firing started at once and on this day, Kilpatrick decided on a retreat. Boudrye said, "Our boys were compelled to return very soon." This must have been more of a fight than is suggested in either Boudrye's journal or history. Private Loren F. Packard, Co. E, this day was cited for heroism that resulted in his being awarded the Medal of Honor. Pvt. Packard had enlisted from the town of Cuba in Cattaraugus County during the initial call to the colors. On this November day it was noted "After his command had retreated, this soldier, voluntarily and alone, returned to the assistance of a comrade and rescued him from the hands of 3 armed Confederates."[35]

The regiment remained in the general area of Morton's Ford for several days, bivouacking among trees just out of artillery range while the Mine Run campaign unfolded downstream. After its initial demonstration at the opening of the operation, the regiment patrolled and did picket duty until December 3, when it was ordered into camp at Stevensburg. Meade's attempted maneuver and attack became merely an inconclusive exercise, bogging down as Lee quickly moved to counter the Union thrust at his flank. After all the fighting and bleeding of that summer and fall, this operation by Meade and his army seems, overall, to have been a sluggish, half-hearted affair. The troops had had enough fighting for one year.

Winter Quarters

Chaplain Boudrye, captured on July 5 and sent to Libby Prison in Richmond, was released in a prisoner exchange on October 7 and sent by boat to New York City. He took a train home to Kinderhook, New York, and started a thirty-day furlough. By November 14 he was back with the regiment and immediately resumed his duties. In his journal he comments on the regiment at this time, four months removed from his last being with it:

> Reached my Regiment near Stevensburg, Culpepper [*sic*] County, Va., after considerable difficulty and fatigue in finding them. The boys are looking well and in good spirits and appeared very glad to welcome me among them. Some change had taken place here in officers and men. Nearly all faces are familiar. Many have been killed, taken prisoner and died of disease. The change is very apparent. My brother Charles of Co. H still survives the dangers and privations of a long and perilous campaign.... It rained hard this evening. I took quarters with our Adjutant, formerly Sergeant Major.

Farquin Chapman, Company D, was captured at nearly the same time as the chaplain and was probably held at Belle Island near Richmond. He was exchanged in October and sent to a parole camp at Annapolis, Maryland. He wrote home from there of his experience: "I was a prisoner 85 days and I got along well untill [*sic*] that last 3 weeks I was there. Tha [*sic*] gave us a small busket [*sic*] and a smaller pease [*sic*] of meat twice a day. We had tents but had to lay on the ground. Having no blankets when we got here this morning tha [*sic*] put me in the Hospital. Everything is as clean and nice as you please.... The Doct says that I have the eremitting fever but will be well in a few days. I know I shall for I have a good appetyte [*sic*].... When I was taken my weight was 168 now I weigh 129 lb."[36]

For December 17, Boudrye penned what is a typical description of winter and living essentially outdoors:

> A cold rain which partially froze as it fell upon the tree tops, commenced during the night and has continued nearly all day, making one of the darkest days since

7. Virginia in Summer, Fall and Winter—1863–1864   149

I came to the regiment. Mud is deep and plentiful. We suffer from the cold. By spreading hay on the ground inside our tent, we make ourselves pretty comfortable beds for the night. About eleven (11) P.M. the regiment returned from picket, muddy, wet, cold and hungry.... Our camp looks anything but pleasant tonight. However, each one appears cheerful and the campfires dispelled the darkness with their lurid light, notwithstanding the heavy rain falling. Such days' and nights' experiences must long be remembered by the soldiers.[37]

After the Mine Run operation, both armies generally recognized the onset of winter. The cold and rainy weather, and thus the roads made quagmires, conspired against large troop movements. And the men were generally worn down by nearly six months of marching from the Rappahannock to Pennsylvania and back again to the Rapidan River. Each regiment in the Cavalry Corps was assigned a campsite, and it was near Stevensburg that the Fifth New York settled into its winter quarters. Picket duty along the Rapidan and scouting in the region was rotated among the division's regiments. The first priority for the men at this time was to secure adequate shelter. And as this was their third winter living in the open, a basic pattern to winter camp had emerged.

When not out on picket or patrolling, the men busied themselves building or improving their quarters. "The sound of the busy ax and hammer is heard from dawn till dark, and our camp begins to assume the appearance of a city of mushroom growth," wrote John Jackson to *Wyoming Mirror*. Trees were cut and hewed into logs. A crude hut was constructed, roughly twelve by seven feet in area, and about as high as there were logs available. Over this was stretched the men's shelter half tents supported by poles. The walls were chinked with mud, of which there was an endless supply. A crude fireplace with a chimney was built to provide a semblance of heat. If bricks were available and could be pried from some substantial edifice in the vicinity, a fireplace could easily be put in the structure. Otherwise, simple rocks and sticks were employed and a chimney built, slapped together with liberal amounts of mud. If there was material for a door or window, so much the better, but usually there was only a door made from a blanket or shelter half stretched over the opening. Pine boughs usually served as flooring if planks or other material was not handy. "Nearly every man has suddenly become a mason or carpenter, the hammer, the axe and the trowel are being plied with utmost vigor, if not with the highest skill. Many of us, however, are astonished at the ingenuity that is displayed in this department." Looking at period photographs of these constructions and knowing of the dampness and cold of winters in this region, it is surprising that attrition from sickness during these months did not equal or exceed battle casualties. Usually, up to four men would inhabit these accommodations, sleeping on pine boughs or hay if there weren't boards ripped from nearby buildings to fashion cots. Chaplain Boudrye's journal contains numerous references to suffering from the cold during this, his first full winter in the field. And then there was the mud. In wet weather and for days thereafter, whenever men and horses moved on the open ground of the campsite, slop from inches to feet deep prevailed. Comments concerning this condition are as numerous as those speaking of the cold. For the regiment's horses, crude constructions were thrown up to at least keep them out of the wind, if not the cold. The attrition among horse is not recorded, but there certainly had to be a number that didn't survive these months. And by the arrival of spring, the animals that did live had to have lost considerable weight and strength as a result.[38]

Most regiments built one facility to serve as a common room. The Fifth New York during this winter, and at the prodding of its chaplain, built a chapel. But this structure no doubt served many other purposes as well. With the arrival of raw recruits that winter, recruits with absolutely no previous training, sergeants had to instruct them in at least the rudiments of caring for themselves, their equipment and their horses. Officers occasionally received further tactical instruction also and the chapel no doubt doubled as an advanced training center when not in use for Boudrye's religious services.

Generally this winter, when not on picket or out scouting, the men did have some hours during the day to themselves. These were mostly spent reading, writing letters or, perhaps, studying a subject of interest. Boudrye spent many hours during this period in an attempt to learn the German language. The men of the regiment, based on the chaplain's comments, were loosely divided into two groups. First there were those who regularly attended his services, either formal Sunday church or preaching he gave during the week. There were also an indeterminate number of troopers who attended regular classes he gave in "phonography," a subject we would today call phonetics. Although this appears to have been a hobby with Boudrye, this instruction was possibly provided to help improve the letter-writing skills of the less formally schooled men of the Fifth. And temperance was a matter close to the chaplain's heart. During this winter he incessantly preached at meetings in the chapel about the evils of drink and the benefits of sobriety. By winter's end, over one hundred men from the Fifth New York had signed a temperance pledge Boudrye circulated.

The second rough category or group of men in the regiment consisted of those not partaking in the above. These men certainly read whatever books were available, but probably not the religious tracts the chaplain was always handing out. They wrote letters home, devoured newspapers and magazines

7. Virginia in Summer, Fall and Winter—1863–1864   151

as soon as they were distributed in camp, but they also played cards and took part in other forms of gambling, a ubiquitous pleasure that was so frowned upon by the chaplain. Popular with all the soldiers of this era were the illustrated news weeklies such as *Harper's Weekly Magazine* and *Frank Leslie's Illustrated Newspaper*. Perhaps the popularity stemmed from the pictures, drawings sometimes done by artists traveling with the army. The reporting contained within, however, was not always accurate. "Cavalrymen alternately laughed and groaned at illustrations showing them riding straight at the enemy in perfect order at a gallop on fierce-looking horses while firing their carbines with one hand and waving their sabers with the other. Even so good an artist as Thomas Nast portrayed a trooper who had skewered his enemy with such force that the blade of the saber protruded six inches out of his adversary's back."[39] And this category of trooper drank whiskey when it could be purchased from sutlers. It is likely these men took part in glee clubs or participated in minstrel shows and other such activities that were organized to occupy their off-duty hours.

General Kilpatrick had a large hall built at his headquarters that was used as a theater and for amateur shows performed by the Dialectic Society

General Kilpatrick, fourth from the left with hands in pockets, and members of his Third Division staff during the winter of 1863–64, Stevensburg, Virginia (Library of Congress).

of Stevensburg, an organization he started and encouraged. The *New York Times* reported in February 1864 that the Society had "for its special objective the instruction, as well as amusement, of the Third Cavalry Division and their friends, particularly the ladies, now visiting them." The building was reported as being sixty by twenty-four feet, not including the stage that included all the "paraphernalia" for theatricals. It could accommodate about 300 and included a full-length painting of Kilpatrick on one wall and a painting of the Goddess of Liberty on the other. A few days before Washington's Birthday, a minstrel show took place that included troopers from the Fifth New York. In attendance was Kilpatrick, "accompanied by his staff and several ladies; Col. Ulric Dahlgren, and officers and men representing every regiment of the Third Division. Barring the usual faults incident to a first performance by non-professionals, a very cold night and a smoky stove, everything passed off in a satisfactory manner." As reported in the newspaper a few days later, one of the original songs performed that evening included the following lines:

> Out of the way of the Third Division,
> Kilpatrick desires a slight collision
> With the noted corps called Stuart's legion.
> If they're any where about the region....
> For there's no one to love, none to caress,
> Any Southern guerrillas or any such mess;
> And they'll find when they've come we've a nice little pill
> Manufactured by Spencer and sent them by Kil.[40]

In addition to the theatrics, companies and sometimes regiments fielded baseball teams if the ground was dry enough. And as there probably had been since the cavalrymen obtained horse, racing, accompanied by wagering, was a prime off-duty activity. "Generals Custer and Kilpatrick had a race course where they used to devote some time to the sport of horse racing. There were in the division a number of blooded and speedy animals, and not a little friendly rivalry was developed in the various commands when the merits of their respective favorites were to be tested on the turf." The betting on this activity was probably held within days of the paymaster's appearance in camp.[41]

As for the paymaster, his arrival in camp was, theoretically, to be on the first of the month, but only on a few occasions did this actually happen. Boudrye almost never fails to note in his journal the arrival of this man or his receiving money from the men to express home to their families. By far the most common comment in the letters of the men of the Fifth New York to their relatives concerns the amount of money the writer has sent home to help their families. And typical of Boudrye's journal entries about the pay for the troopers is the following, dated November 22, 1863: "At 12 noon, Majors

Hammond and White, Lieut. Waugh and myself along with two men, went to Brandy Station to Adams Express office. Together we expressed about nine thousand ($9,000) dollars. I had 46 packages amounting to ($3,704.00). I sent seventy-five ($75) dollars to my wife. In all, we had 132 packages."[42]

Veteran Volunteers

It was clearly known in Washington in the autumn of 1863 that those men who had enlisted for three years in 1861 would become eligible for discharge at various times in 1864. Also clear was that the war, barring the unforeseen, would drag well into the coming year. The War Department formulated a plan and announced it in December 1863. For its time it was a generous re-enlistment program with the hoped-for goal of retaining as many experienced soldiers and regiments as possibly. On December 4, Chaplain Boudrye commented on this in his journal: "Considerable ado was made today to ascertain how many men of this regiment would be willing to reenlist under the orders for 'Veteran Volunteers.' Of 327 men, 205 gave in their names for veterans. Considerable feeling is unleashed in the enterprise. The boys feel well and are enthusiastic."[43]

Under the terms of the War Department's offer, if three-quarters of a given regiment re-enlisted for another three years or the duration of the war, that regiment would be kept intact, would retain its officers and would be designated a "Veteran" regiment, with an indicative chevron on the uniform of each re-enlistee. And there would be a $402 bounty paid by the United States and a thirty-five-day furlough. As can be imagined, and as indicated by Boudrye, this announcement started a buzz in the Fifth New York that would last into the coming year. There were probably any number of forces working on the troopers considering re-enlistment, as there had been with their initial enlistment in 1861: patriotism, group pressure and so on. The difference now was that these men were experienced, had seen what fighting entailed, and could get out of harm's way if they desired. Someone else could do the fighting. This or they could bring the experience gained in countless actions big and small to go forward and finish the job once and for all.

The historian of Union cavalry notes that the furloughs and large bounty were indeed factors that influenced the numbers who re-enlisted that winter. But there was one other dynamic at work: "The result of the individual and group soul-searchings and debates was precisely what one could have predicted: the factor that seemed to weigh as much with the men as did patriotism, the furlough, and the bounty, was the personality, influence, and competence of their officers."[44] Boudrye, in his journal, seems to indicate, however, that the two hundred and five men who re-enlisted as veterans didn't change their minds, committed as they were and were anxious to take the furlough, whether the regiment reached the three-quarters requirement or not. On December 7, he noted, "We are now a regiment in great suspense, not knowing whether we are to be relieved and go home on furlough or whether we are going back to Fairfax C.H. to do picket on the grounds we occupied last winter."

Trooper John Jackson also commented on the re-enlistment campaign. He told the *Wyoming Mirror* in January 1864, "The only subject engrossing attention is that of re-enlistments as 'veterans.' About 180 of our regiment have been mustered in as such, receiving their $100 (old bounty), and the first installment of their new bounty. They are now waiting for their promised furloughs.... Their patriotism is not dead nor yet diminished. They love their country none the less for having made sacrifices and suffered hardships to insure an honorable peace — and undivided Union." And despite concern about the need for three-fourths of the regiment to re-enlist, it does appear that the army was thinking at that moment that there indeed would be a Fifth New York in 1864.

The same day Boudrye wrote of waiting for the expected furlough, December 7, the regiment was reinforced. "This evening eighteen (18) new volunteers for N.Y. City were brought to us," Boudrye reported. "We had quite an interesting time with them. The night was cold. They slept by our fire with their guards, a detachment of the 4th Delaware Volunteers. The recruits are mostly foreigners."[45] These men, called volunteers by Boudrye, were either coerced "volunteers" or draftees, as indicated by their being "escorted" to a forward area. That they were foreigners to Boudrye indicates that these men might have been scrounged from the immigrant slums of New York City by one means or another. Or perhaps they were recruited in some fashion as they stepped off the boat from Europe. Still, they might have been thought to be bounty jumpers: men who enlisted, collected all or part of the bounty the state was paying, and then deserted, to repeat the process elsewhere. Throughout this winter and into the spring the Fifth New York periodically received reinforcement, new recruits and generally volunteers from New York State. These men would have to learn fast.

The re-enlistment effort continued through December. On the December 12, Boudrye recorded, "A great effort is being made to secure at least ¾ of the men of this regiment to re-enlist under the General Order for re-enlisting 'Veteran Volunteers.' If this number can be secured, I'm quite certain the regiment will, within ten (10) days, be furloughed for thirty (30) days and ordered home before the holidays. The number working to reach the minimum is 22. It is thought the number will soon be reached."⁴⁶ It was reached. Overall, the re-enlistment program was a success both in the regiment and in the Army of the Potomac. In all, 212 men re-enlisted in the Fifth New York. Most of these were formally mustered in on January 1, 1864.

A month before, John Hammond had written in a letter home his impression of his men at this stage of the war. He could not have been surprised at the number re-enlisting. "They are rough, but that true, manly courage which leads them to bare their breasts in defense of their country, sometimes so affects me that I can scarcely restrain my tears.... And the spirit that they manifest," he said of the Fifth New York veterans, "the desire to fight this fight to the bitter end, is beyond anything I ever expected to realize."⁴⁷ The Fifth New York would exist for another eighteen months. But it would not be going on furlough until it finished one more mission.

The Kilpatrick-Dahlgren Raid—1864

Regardless of the winter weather, guerrilla activity in the region continued, and when on picket duty, the Fifth New York had to be constantly alert. For January 19, the regiment's history recorded a typical occurrence. The cavalry corps this winter was located in what could be call a peninsula, lying between two rivers, the Rapidan to the south and the Rappahannock to the north. Pickets had to watch in all directions because the "territory ... between the rivers abounds in thick underbrush and deep ravines, through which guerrillas creep up and attack our pickets. Patrols are sent out daily from the picket reserve, on the main roads to the fords of the rivers, to drive out any force of the enemy that might seek to advance upon us from that direction. To-day our patrol was attacked by a considerable force concealed in bushes by the road side. Under very great disadvantage, our boys defended themselves as best they could, but suffered quite severely. This was near Ely's Ford, Rapidan." On January 22, the same thing happened. "Our boys were out again patrolling toward the Rappahannock, and were attacked by bushwackers near Ellis' Ford. As on the 19th inst., one man was killed, several wounded and captured. Among the latter were several veterans, who were daily looking for their 35 days' furlough promised in their reenlistment. They will have a dreary furlough in southern prisons."⁴⁸

On February 6, the entire Third Cavalry Division saddled up and crossed the Rapidan for a thirty-five-mile reconnaissance. They returned the next day. After that, things in winter camp settled back into a routine, at least for a couple of weeks. Finally, on February 26, the veterans were approved for their furloughs and no doubt started packing for home. But as Boudrye recorded, the order "had not been in camp thirty minutes before they were sent for from brigade headquarters. They are doubtless detained for some wise purpose, but many fail to *see the point*."[49]

The point was that General Kilpatrick had received approval for a plan that has been attributed to him in the histories written of this period of the war. "The whole division under Kilpatrick," the regiment's history notes, "accompanied by Col. Dahlgren, who was entrusted with a very important position in the expedition, set out on a great raid to Richmond."[50] It was February 28, and the chaplain noted in his journal, "Orders were issued this morning to have the regiment ready to march at a moment's notice with 5 days' rations — light marching orders.... The regiment left for a grand raid at about 5½. It appears General Kilpatrick is to command a very large force of cavalry, I think, the largest which has as yet been under the command of one man during the war. The whole force moved toward Culpepper [*sic*] Mine Ford about 7½."[51]

Six days before getting this order to move, many elements of the Army of the Potomac had held celebrations honoring the birthday of George Washington. General Kilpatrick hosted a party at his headquarters near Stevensburg that evening. But just prior to the party, the division hall was used for a series of patriotic speeches given by certain invited guests. It can be speculated that the important guests were at least aware some kind of effort was in the offing and spoke in the hope of providing encouragement. "The Hall was gaily decorated with the red, white and blue, the battle flags of Gens. Kilpatrick, Custer and Davies, and the standards of the different regiments in their respective commands." There were speeches by Senators Howard of Michigan, Wilkinson and Ramsey of Minnesota, and Congressman Kellogg of Michigan. Finally, Kilpatrick spoke, denouncing Copperheads, "who, even in the halls of Congress dared cry Peace! Peace! When there is no peace — when traitors, only three miles from where he now stood were straining every nerve to destroy our nation and overturn the principles on which it is founded." There was much applause, "after which the invited guest[s] repaired to Gen. K's headquarters to partake of the entertainment for the inner man, there provided." The *New York Times* reported, "The proceeding over, the whole company proceeded to Gen. Kilpatrick's quarters, where after partaking of a supper, prepared under the personal supervision of Mr. Sires, the efficient and popular purveyor at this post, dancing was indulged in to music furnished by Capt. Perkins' amateur minstrel company, until a late hour."[52]

At a point earlier in the month, the ever-ambitious Kilpatrick had traveled to Washington to peddle his plan to the administration and had received at least tacit approval. No doubt orders were already being drafted and supply requisitions written, as the party at his headquarters got under way. This night was devoted to remembrance of a general who had become president, a transition that General Kilpatrick considered for himself, particularly after the hoped-for success of his plan. The affair at Kilpatrick's headquarters included all the division's officers, those wives visiting their husbands in winter camp, and the contingent of officials from the capital. Chaplain Boudrye, if invited, makes no mention of it and probably did not attend, one reason being that the teetotaling Kilpatrick saw to it that his guests were liberally supplied with strong refreshment. One guest remembered the party as a loud and merry affair with Kilpatrick "as active as a flea, and almost as ubiquitous."[53]

The next day the Second Corps held a review for the guests who had attended from Washington, and the Third Cavalry Division took part. "It was the greatest thing of the kind I ever saw," Boudrye recorded in his journal that night. Besides Generals Meade and Pleasonton, on the reviewing stand were several senators and Secretary of the Navy Gideon Wells. "[B]ut not least," Boudrye noticed, were "a large number of ladies. There were at least one hundred (100) I think. Several were on horseback, presenting a very interesting appearance with their long flowing robes in flashing colors and their waving brilliant ribbons. General Meade looks quite aged and looked upon us with spectacles."[54] The review ended with the Third Division engaging in "a noble mock charge, a thundering, yelling, gallop across the dead grass of the plain, troopers rising in their stirrups with gleaming sabres extended, all very stimulating for the visiting ladies."[55]

But behind the party and parade was the plan, conjured up as bold and brash as Kilpatrick himself. According to John Hammond, "Kill-cavalry" had been mulling over the idea for some time. In a letter home dated November 11, 1863, Hammond says, "Gen. Kilpatrick wants to take his cavalry and go to Richmond, and release our officers and soldiers imprisoned there. We think we can do it, but the powers that be don't think it is best."[56] The Rebels would not be expecting such a deep strike in winter weather, Kilpatrick and his staff probably argued. Although the plan was not really approved by Cavalry Corps commander Alfred Pleasonton, "Kill-cavalry's" immediate superior, it was eventually by General Meade, but only after he learned of the sentiments in Washington regarding it. Indeed, the particulars seemed to have intrigued President Lincoln as well as Secretary of War Edwin Stanton. An order came down from Meade's headquarters on February 11 that Kilpatrick "proceed to Washington and report to the President, as requested by the latter." When in Washington, therefore, Kilpatrick must have explained the plan in detail and gotten an approving nod, either from Lincoln—details of his interviewing Kilpatrick are not documented—but more likely from Stanton. It was to be a raid in division strength on Richmond with its primary purpose being to free prisoners of war held there, an estimated 15,000. Also, along the way, the command was to distribute throughout the territory traversed, copies of Lincoln's recently issued amnesty proclamation.[57]

In its simplest terms, Kilpatrick's plan evolved into a two-pronged thrust at the Confederate capital. "Kill-cavalry" would lead the main body of the division around the right flank of Lee's positions on the south side of the Rapidan and approach Richmond's outer defenses from the east and north. Once there, he and his command would occupy the defenders while a smaller, second contingent, having circled the capitol to the west and from across the James River, entered the city from the south. It was thought that the Rebels, being so occupied with the threat from Kilpatrick, the smaller and more mobile force entering from the south could rush Belle Isle and Libby Prisons, free the prisoners, and lead them out and to safety without encountering any significant resistance. This accomplished, the division and smaller force would reunite and return to Federal lines above the Rapidan or retire to the lines held by General Butler down on the Virginia peninsula. While all this was happening, copies of Lincoln's proclamation would be broadcast in the hopes that many citizens and, hopefully, many more soldiers would take advantage.[58]

The smaller raiding party, it turned out, would be led by Colonel Ulric Dahlgren, the same cavalryman whose semi-independent command had fought within sight of Kilpatrick in Maryland in July during Lee's retreat from Gettysburg. Newly promoted to colonel, Dahlgren had learned of the plan in Washington in the days just prior to its beginning and had hurried down to Kilpatrick's headquarters to volunteer. It seems Kilpatrick was not put off by the obvious security leak Dahlgren's appearance signified, and probably because he knew the colonel from the summer's campaign where he had lost a leg, nevertheless offered him command of the smaller raiding force that was to liberate the prisoners. Alternatively, it could be Kilpatrick himself had solicited Dahlgren's participation while he was in Washington selling his plan for the raid. No documentation has come to light explaining the sudden appearance of the one-legged colonel at Kilpatrick's headquarters. Although Dahlgren was as much a glory hunter as Kilpatrick, he appears to have gone about it in a less obtrusive manner. However, his involvement in the raid, at least to the Rebels in Richmond when they learned of it, seemed to include one additional agenda item beyond posting proclamations and freeing prisoners, or so it seemed at the time.[59]

"Orders were issued this morning," Boudrye noted in his journal, trying not to be disappointed for it meant no furloughs until after the raid. "Many

7. Virginia in Summer, Fall and Winter—1863–1864

and some larger sum of money were left with me to express and the keep till their return, by the men going out on this raid."[60] The chaplain was not included in that portion for the regiment that participated in the raid.

From the beginning, all seemed to go according to plan. An infantry corps would demonstrate along the Rapidan, and a large cavalry formation under Custer would let itself be seen by the Rebels moving out to the west, all to divert the eyes of the enemy from Kilpatrick's flanking maneuver on Lee's right. The maneuver worked. Dahlgren with between 500 and 600 men went ahead of Kilpatrick to Ely's Ford, getting there at 11 P.M., February 28. "We crossed the river, and a party of the Fifth New York Cavalry, under lieutenant Merritt, and Hogan, the scout, captured the enemy's pickets, 1 officer and 14 men, belonging to a North Carolina regiment of cavalry."[61] Kilpatrick, about an hour behind Dahlgren, was across the Rapidan and through Spotsylvania Court House by morning of February 29. Here Kilpatrick halted for a time while Dahlgren and his men got a good head start on the longer trek to Richmond.[62]

Chaplain Boudrye, in his regimental history, included a lengthy account by one member of the Fifth New York, who with about forty men from the regiment, was with the Dahlgren column. He was Lt. Henry A.D. Merritt of Company K. Merritt was captured during the raid and his account of it was written after his escape from prison and return to the regiment, some time in the winter of 1864–65. Dahlgren's command included details from the Second New York, First Vermont, First Maine and Fifth Michigan as well as the Fifth New York. In all, the colonel led what were considered the best men from these regiments. The captured Rebel pickets at Ely's Ford were sent back to Union lines, and several men from the Fifth New York were detailed for this duty. Boudrye might have encountered these prisoners later in the day as he was going about his duties nearby in the Fifth New York's Camp. "Returning, I met a company of 'Johnnies' consisting of three officers and eleven men, captured just across the river last evening," he noted on the 29th.[63]

Up ahead, Dahlgren led his command to Frederick Hall Station, the advance being those from the Fifth New York who were still with him. When they reached Frederick Hall during the afternoon of February 29, the command found parked in the vicinity eighty-three pieces of Rebel artillery. It was tempting to attack and destroy a significant portion of Lee's artillery component, but it was heavily guarded and any action would reveal Dahlgren's presence within Confederate lines and possibly preclude any continuation of the mission. The cannons were bypassed.

With the men from the Fifth New York still leading, the command approached a house and found that a Rebel court-martial was in progress. Those within the house were quickly captured, and included a Rebel colonel, two majors, other officers and about thirty men. These prisoners were guarded and marched along with the column. However, during the night, as the column continued on its way, the captured Rebels escaped. This was to Dahlgren's relief, because having to guard them all the way to Richmond and beyond would only slow the command down.

As they moved on and it grew dark the weather turned. Heavy rain and wind slowed progress toward the expected James River crossing point. The Fifth New York's Lt. Merritt picks up the story:

> We now learned that we were about three miles from Dover Mills, and ten miles below Columbia Mills [the proposed James River crossing point]. The guide, a negro, had misled us during the night, and, to obviate the delay of retracing our steps, Col. Dahlgren, on the representations of the negro that an excellent ford was to be found at Dover Mills, concluded to cross at that point. After two hours' halt we moved again on, and soon reached Dover Mills, but only to meet discouragement. The negro had deceived us, no ford existed at this point nor any means of crossing the river. He then stated that the ford was three miles below, this obviously false, as the river was evidently navigable to and above this place, as we saw a sloop going down the river.
>
> This man was sent from headquarters to guide us and was considered faithful and reliable. I afterwards learned that he came into our lines from Richmond, in company with several officers who escaped Libby Prison. He was born and had always belonged in the immediate vicinity of Dover Mills, was very shrewd and intelligent, and it would seem impossible that he should not know that no ford existed in the neighborhood. Col. Dahlgren had warned him that if detected acting in bad faith, or lying, we would surely hang him, and after we left Dover Mills, and had gone down the river so far as to render further prevarications unavailing, the colonel charged him with betraying us, destroying the whole design of the expedition, and hazarding the lives of everyone engaged in it—and told him that he should be hung in conformity with the terms of his service. The negro became greatly alarmed, stating confusedly that he was mistaken, thought we intended to cross the river in boats, and finally said that he had done wrong, was sorry, etc. The colonel ordered him to be hung—a halter strap was used for the purpose, and we left the miserable wretch dangling by the roadside."[64]

Bruce Catton, in *A Stillness at Appomattox*, identifies the victim as "a boy named Martin, the property of Mr. David Meems, of Goochland."[65] Merritt's statement about Martin's leading escaped prisoners from Richmond cannot be verified in relation to Catton's explanation. While at Dover Mills, Dahlgren ordered a detachment to burn the buildings there along with the canal boats docked there.

Just prior to this episode, Colonel Dahlgren had visited the house of

Confederate Secretary of War James Seddon and had been entertained and given refreshment by his wife — the secretary was at work in Richmond — who had been acquainted previously with the Colonel's father, a Union admiral. After Dahlgren left the house, the slaves on the property, Merritt reported, began looting the house and set fire to the barn, no doubt thinking that their freedom was now at hand. But this was not the case, and Merritt, it appears, tried to stop it with little success, going so far as to stop some troopers from joining the destruction and apparent robbery. Merritt reported that he stopped one trooper carrying away silverware, saying it "all apparently [was] plaited [and] was of a very cheap description, of a pattern found in every shop window. If Mrs. Seddon's plate and jewelry were all of the same character and value, she will be able to replace them without difficulty and at very slight expense." The plantation's slaves then fell in with the column as it set off.[66]

Without being able to cross the river and approach Richmond from the south as planned, Dahlgren followed the road along the river and came at the city from the west. It was now that the command could clearly hear Kilpatrick's guns booming in the distance, away to the north. At about seven miles from the outer edge of the city, Dahlgren sent out two messengers to locate the general and inform him of his arrival. The messengers never returned and don't seem to have reached Kilpatrick. Nevertheless, the colonel decided to probe the city's defenses. But before doing this he ordered the column followers off, sending them to Hungry Station in the care of a Signal Corps lieutenant named Ruben Bartly, who was also to try to find Kilpatrick.[67] Lieutenant Bartly never got to Kilpatrick's position. If he had, he would have found the general and his division frustrated before the city's defenses and contemplating withdrawal. Merritt continues, "Arrangement being completed, at dusk, we moved down upon the enemy's pickets, who hastily retired, evidently in surprise." A gunfight developed at a second line of defenses and the command, fighting both on foot and mounted, pressed them, advancing to the outskirts of the city. "Here we encountered a heavy force formed in line of battle. It was now dark and the gas lights burning. We were inside the city limits.... But the force in front was soon found to be too great for us to contend with."[68]

Dahlgren ordered a withdrawal, and the command moved toward Hungry Station. From there Dahlgren decided to make for Gloucester Point and get within the lines of Butler's army on the peninsula. The column crossed the Chickahominy and encountered a Rebel ambulance train bringing wounded back from fighting with Kilpatrick's force, somewhere out ahead of him. "For some time they were not aware of our character, but were loud in their boosts that they had driven off Yankees — their surprise was ludicrous when Col.

Dahlgren informed them that we were Yankees, and asked 'if they did not think they were a nice lot of fellows.'"[69] Dahlgren let the ambulance column go on its way and continued on toward Butler's lines. Now there began skirmishing with probing elements of Rebel cavalry sent in pursuit of these Yankees.

It seems it was here that Dahlgren's command became divided into two portions. On the retreat from Richmond, Dahlgren assigned as the rear guard that portion of the Second New York that was with the column. The captain of this detachment said in his report, "He [Dahlgren] proceeded to the point where we first struck the plank road; here the column halted. After some time, becoming anxious as to the reason, I sent forward Lieutenant Mattison ... who reported that the column had become separated; that Colonel Dahlgren and Major Cooke with about 100 men had gone on, and the rest of the column had lost sight of them in the darkness. I sent out scouts in all directions, but could hear nothing of them." This portion, the larger of the two, succeeded in making contact with Kilpatrick's command before it got within Butler's lines. The others, with Dahlgren, is reported by Merritt to number only about seventy men in all by 6 P.M. on the evening after the skirmish on the outskirts of Richmond.

The column stopped at a creek near Kings and Queens Court House. There they rested and fed their horses before moving on in the darkness and rain. Merritt reported that on that dark night:

> The first evidence of the enemy's being in advance was the absence of three men sent upon picket a short distance ahead of our halting place. Very soon after the discovery we were challenged.... Col. Dahlgren had ridden to the head of the advance guard a moment before we were challenged by the enemy.... I responded to the challenge by demanding, "Who are you?" The word was repeated and the colonel immediately called out, "Surrender or we will shoot you" — and snapped his pistol, the cap only exploding. The next instant a heavy volley was poured in upon us. The flash of the pieces afforded us a momentary glimpse of their position stretching parallel with the road about fifteen paces from us. Every tree was occupied, and the bushes poured forth a sheet of flame.

It was this firing that killed Dahlgren, although Merritt didn't see it, and the colonel made no sound after attempting to fire his pistol.[70]

The seventy or so cavalrymen now had to fight their way out of the ambush and did so, with Merritt's account not mentioning Dahlgren for some paragraphs. The command broke into groups of three or four men and scattered after breaking off from the ambush, each group attempting to gain Butler's lines. Merritt was captured and it was the next day when he learned "the particulars of Dahlgren's fate."[71]

> His body was found perforated with five bullets, and his death had been instantaneous.... The best joiner in the neighborhood had been employed to make the coffin.... It was an after thought which doubtless eminated [sic] from Richmond,

to disinter, and heap wrath and indignity upon the senseless corpse of a dauntless foe. We were subsequently informed that the body had been mutilated before burial by a Lieut. Hart, 7th Virginia cavalry, who severed one of the fingers to possess himself of a valuable ring worn by the colonel, but the act was regarded as so disgraceful, that several soldiers of the same regiment who witnessed the act and informed us of it, said that the scoundrel deserved to be shot.[72]

Merritt concluded his account of his part in the raid with the following: "I would be improper to conclude this paper without lauding to the good conduct of the men of the Fifth New York. Through the entire raid their behavior elicited frequent and earnest commendations from Col. Dahlgren, and reflected credit upon the regiment." Fourteen men from the Fifth New York were captured during this portion of the raid, with one, Sgt. John Hardy, of Company I, dying in Andersonville Prison.[73]

Controversy followed Colonel Dahlgren in death, and the tale remains one of those unsolved—perhaps unsolvable—mysteries of the Civil War. It may never be definitively known whether the story of the raid emanated from Richmond as a propaganda campaign directed against the Yankees by an increasingly weakened Confederate government in the hope of boosting morale, or whether the idea for the raid originated with Dahlgren himself, or with Kilpatrick, or with any number of would-be helpful hands in Washington. In fact, an operation similar to the one Kilpatrick and Dahlgren had attempted had been made by General Butler in February. It also had as its primary purpose the freeing of prisoners, but additionally aimed at destroying the principal military targets within the city, as well as the capture and removal to Federal lines the Confederate President Jefferson Davis. The Rebels had learned of the plan from a Union deserter who had been under a death sentence and had escaped to Richmond. Based on this intelligence, the Rebel forces were deployed in such a way as to forestall the planned rush by Butler's men on Richmond.[74] Now, in March, documents supposedly found on Dahlgren's body listed as the primary purpose of the raid, not the freeing of prisoners and the like, but the burning and sacking of the city and the murder of Jefferson Davis and his cabinet. It has never been determined with certainty whether the documents were authentic or forgeries planted on the colonel by enterprising Confederates.

When this news reached the local press, the Southern public was outraged. Confederate Secretary of War Seddon sent General Lee copies of the papers allegedly found on Dahlgren. The secretary inquired of the general whether the prisoners captured from Dahlgren's command should not be hanged. Lee advised against it, fearing retaliation, but under a flag of truce, he forwarded the papers to General Meade on the far side of the Rapidan.

With them went his own inquiry as to their validity, asking Meade whether murder had been added to the Federal arsenal. By return communication, Meade assured his opponent that no one commanding the raid or under his command, or in the Federal government, had ordered anything of the kind. All the officers and men riding with Colonel Dahlgren who returned were asked whether they were instructed to burn Richmond and kill the Confederate leadership. All denied that the colonel ever so ordered them or even spoke of any such intention while they were under his command. In that this small raiding party never did get within the city, this inquiry appears academic. Dahlgren, if he had gotten within Richmond, might have only then ordered the burning and killing.

When the news hit the Northern press, flames of righteousness were fanned to equal the outrage in the South. In the end nothing really came from this episode other than its contribution to a further hardening of attitudes, which were already quite solidified after three years of fratricidal war. Even before the raid, John Jackson of the Fifth New York noted a change in attitude among the troopers he came in contact with. In January 1864, he noted, "The politics of the Army of the Potomac has undergone great changes.... Soldiers are convinced the rebels have forfeited all rights and privileges that the Constitution guaranteed them." Of course there had been killing from the beginning, but the coming campaigning season would witness even bigger, more vicious and bloodier encounters than the nation had yet dreamed could occur.[75]

One is inclined to believe that more than a modicum of blame for this failed effort resides with Judson Kilpatrick and his undeniable thirst for glory and the recognition and promotion that would inevitably follow. Although having a sort of romantic spirit about it, the raid was a worthless grasp for glory resulting in the waste of good men, horses and equipment. Even if initially successful in freeing the prisoners held in Richmond, how could it be expected that a large cavalry column could navigate its way back to Union lines while shepherding thousands underfed and ill-clothed men over many miles of muddy winter roads? It was a matter of luck that only a portion of the Fifth New York was included on the raid and only a small portion of those were captured.

While Dahlgren and Kilpatrick were marching on Richmond, it appears from Boudrye's journal that the portion of the Fifth New York remaining along the Rapidan were still doing dangerous picket duty. In his journal, Boudrye notes that on March 4, at least a portion of Companies C and D were out in the dark along the Rapidan: "Last night or this morning, one of our picket posts was attacked near the Rapidan River. One man, Elijah Johndro, Co. C, was killed; it is said too, after he surrendered and Mr. Edmund Barber, Co. D, had a ball graze the top of his head and another shot which it is feared broke his leg. I saw him as he was brought through camp on his way to the hospital. The body of the other was also brought in camp." Boudrye assisted in the services for Johndro and says that Barber had his leg amputated, but survived.

On March 11, John Hammond and several men from the regiment got back to camp from the raid. The next day, "just before dark, our whole regiment arrived in camp making the welkin ring with their shouts of joy. Only about 20 men of our regiment were lost, all of them captured. I believed none killed. It is remarkable small loss when we consider that our regiment occupied the post of honor and danger, being in *the van* as the command advanced to within about two miles from Richmond and they covered the retreat in returning."[76] Actually, the chaplain is in error about the regiment's participation in the raid. Only forty men from companies I and K rode on the raid.

While Colonel Dahlgren had led the abortive thrust at Richmond and it prisoners, Kilpatrick had gotten to within five miles of the city at 10 A.M. on March 1. A few hours later, skirmishing as he went, he was within one mile. Here something happened that led the general to falter. Resistance to his advance on the city had gone from skirmishing to nearly full scale fighting. Kilpatrick's after-action report contains "uncertain language," and others appear to have believed that it was here he "lost control" of the situation. General Meade is later quoted as saying that Kilpatrick "made no serious attempt to enter" Richmond, if indeed that had been part of the plan. Colonel James H. Kidd, commanding the Sixth Michigan, wrote later that the general "appeared to be overcome with a strange and fatal irresolution." The division shot it out with the city's defenders for the remainder of the day and then retired to Mechanicsville in the darkness, after sustaining sixty casualties, killed and wounded.[77]

For his part, Kilpatrick reported later only on the route he had taken to Richmond and the railroad infrastructure he destroyed on his way. By about 1 P.M. on March 1, Kilpatrick says he was within a mile of Richmond. "Here considerable force of infantry with artillery effectually checked my advance.... I ordered my entire force, and after thoroughly examining the enemy's position, determined to attack, believing that if they were citizen soldiers I could enter the City."[78] Some of the Fifth New York was dismounted as skirmishers and sent forward. More dismounted cavalry followed. A barrier in the road was captured and Kilpatrick ordered up his artillery and extended his line right and left. The general "was about to order an advance of the whole line, when I discovered that the enemy was rapidly receiving re-enforcements, not only infantry but artillery. Feeling confident that Dahlgren had failed to cross the river, and that an attempt to enter the city at that point would end in a bloody failure, I reluctantly with drew my command at dark crossed the Meadow Bridge over the Chickahominy, and ... went into camp near Mechanicsville."[79] This is essentially all Kilpatrick has to report concerning his approach and fight at the gates of Richmond, and given earlier and lengthier reports of action his command had fought at other places, notably Gettysburg, one is suspicious. Therefore, there can be a certain degree of credence given to the remark by Colonel Kidd of the Sixth Michigan concerning "Kill-cavalry's" "fatal irresolution."[80]

In the vicinity of Mechanicsville, the command had no sooner bivouacked when Wade Hampton attacked with a detachment of his command numbering about 300 men. It was snowing and dark and this small force succeeded in scattering the Third Division as it made its retreat down the peninsula toward General Butler, skirmishing as it went. They were exhausted when they got within Butler's line and knew they hadn't accomplished what they had set out to do. Some track had been ripped up and railroad buildings burnt along with a few bridges, but the command had lost "340 men, 583 horse, 594 rifles and carbines, 516 pistols, 505 sabers, and a large quantities of miscellaneous gear." The division was sent back by boat to the Potomac and had to march down to Stevensburg and its camp, where Boudrye and the other men of the Fifth New York who had remained behind welcomed them.

One of Meade's staff officers, knowing Kilpatrick, commented on the return of the general: "Behold my prophecy in regard to Kilpatrick's raid fulfilled. I have heard many persons very indignant with him ... that he is a frothy braggart without brains and not overstocked with desire to fall on the field.... These charges are not new and I fancy Kill has rather dished himself." This company of indignation presumably included General Meade after reading the inquiry from General Lee.[81] In closing his report of the raid, Kilpatrick noted, "Several thousand of the President's amnesty proclamations were scattered throughout the entire country, and I am satisfied that if Colonel Dahlgren had not failed in crossing the river, which he did either through the ignorance or treachery of his guide ... I should have entered the rebel capital and released our prisoners."[82] The evaluation by Stephen Starr of Kilpatrick's after-action report concerning the charge on July 3 at Gettysburg still applies: "shabby and disingenuous."

That portion of the Fifth New York that was engaged in the raid was shipped by transport to Alexandria, arriving there on March 10. The next day the regiment began marching for Stevensburg, getting there on March 12, a day after John Hammond. Also on March 12, word came to the regiment's headquarters that the furloughs for the veterans had been ordered. The next day, Boudrye reported, "This has certainly been the day of preparation. Nearly two hundred (200) are going (there would have been a few more if none had been wounded nor captured since reelisting)."[83] The men left for home on March 14, with Boudrye going to Washington, to collect his pay—$231.92 for January and February—and then traveling by train to New York. Although Boudrye was not eligible to re-enlist as a veteran, somehow he got a furlough too.

During his leave, Boudrye, in addition to spending time with family, was invited to speak about his experiences, both in the army and about conditions in Libby Prison. A newspaper account included in his journal says, "Mr. Boudrye is a very impressive speaker, and his experience is [as] interesting and rich as any army or prison experience we have ever heard." On his return trip, Boudrye stopped in Brooklyn to visit "my friend Emile Portier of Company F of our regiment, whose life, he says, I saved at the battle of Hanover last June. We had a very affectionate meeting." After two days with Portier, Boudrye returned via Washington to the regiment.[84]

While the veterans and Boudrye were on thirty-five-day furlough, the regimental history is a blank. The chaplain resumes his chronicle on April 22. "Our division of cavalry, with a large force of infantry, appeared in a review before Lieut. General Grant, on the Plains of Stevensburg. The army is very enthusiastic over its commander-in-chief. Some change had recently taken place in our Calvary. Gen. Kilpatrick had been assigned to a larger command in the west, and Gen. John [James] H. Wilson succeeds him. Gen. Davies is also removed to some other position, and Col. McIntosh commands the first brigade, which is now composed of the 18th Pennsylvania, 1st Connecticut, 2n New York and 5th New York."[85] In actuality, Colonel John McIntosh did not assume command of the First Brigade until May 6, during the Wilderness Campaign.

It was now springtime, 1864; Lee's army was just across the Rapidan, and with Ulysses S. Grant as the new commanding general, there had to be a new fight. For the Fifth New York the next two months would be the most severe thus far in the war.

8

Across the River — 1864

I suppose we may call this the lull before the hurricane, which little short of a miracle can avert. There is Grant, with his utterly immovable face.... He evidently means to do something pretty serious before he gives up.
— Diary entry of Theodore Lyman of General Meade's staff

Artillery fire commenced early in the morning and continued all day — terrible towards evening. A continuous roar. What suspense. God grant that we may be successful. May He give wisdom and grace to our leaders, strength and nerve to our men and victory to our cause. We must be successful, for it must be that the right is on our side. I would give anything to know and witness how goes the battle. A very warm day.[1]
— Diary entry of Luman Tenney, Second Ohio Cavalry, May 30, 1864

"I determined to hammer continuously against the armed forces of the enemy and his resources, until by mere attrition, if in no other way, there should be nothing left to him but submission."[2] In its simplest terms this was the plan for the campaign against the Confederate armies beginning in the spring of 1864. Now a lieutenant general and in command of all Union forces, Ulysses S. Grant wrote this summary. His language is as concise as his plan was to the point. In Tennessee and northern Georgia stood another army under General William T. Sherman. This army had the same orders: to push deep into Georgia, destroy the Confederate army in the field, and capture Atlanta. In this way, Grant hoped to end the war that year, if not that summer. But the bloodletting that came to be in Virginia in just the months of May and June was undreamed of by the participants, men who thought themselves immune to nightmare after suffering Antietam and Gettysburg. In this Virginia springtime, two armies would clash and clash again, twisting and turning in a death struggle covering a hundred miles, all in a period of six weeks.

"Day by day, as we watched the smoke ascending from the camp fires of the Rebel army just across the rapid river, we had gathered a fresh inspiration, and we knew that but a short journey would bring us face to face with our confident enemy, whom we expected to drive before us."[3] So wrote Chaplain Boudrye of the days just before the beginning of what would become known generally as Grant's Overland Campaign. It was spring, the weather growing more pleasant each day. Arguably, and generally noted in overview histories of this period of the war, the Army of the Potomac was rested and ready for the coming campaign. Although there were noted deficiencies within some units, the Fifth New York was as ready as it could be, given its time on the picket line that winter and living in a rude camp in cold, wet weather. The strength the command would need had been recovered through furloughs, adequate supplies of food through the winter, and new equipment and recruits. Beneath the surface the Fifth New York had acquired an attitude that would be carried into the field in the coming campaign. A large proportion of the men, the core of the command, were now "veteran volunteers," most having re-enlisted during the winter while their ranks had been augmented with new men who had received at least a semblance of training since showing up at the regiment's camp. At the beginning of April 1864, the Fifth New York reported 36 officers and 979 enlisted in the ranks. As for their attitude and outlook about the coming season, their early history records that they were confident and believed that the coming campaign would be successful, and that 1864 would see the end of the war.[4] But deeper still there was a determination among the now "veteran volunteers" bred in part by the shared experience of two years in the field. With the arrival of new and untried recruits and draftees to the regiment, it was understood, if unspoken, by these veterans that the Fifth New York was *their* regiment. In speaking of the Army of the Potomac as a whole, Bruce Catton has ably summarized this unspoken attitude as it had evolved by the spring of 1864: "The army had put its stamp on all of its infinitely various members. It had produced a type, at last, and the volunteers had become the old-timers — rusty in a worn uniform, wearing his forage cap with its broken visor tugged down over his eyes, tolerant of high authority but not especially respectful of it ... taking eventual triumph for granted, but fully aware that he himself was the man who was appointed to pay for it."[5]

As for the Rebels, it was reported during the winter that a steady stream of deserters got themselves across the Rapidan River, having read in Northern papers smuggled through the lines or heard via the army grapevine of Lincoln's Amnesty. During the cold and wet winter their morale appeared to be as bleak as the weather, the result of poor and inadequate food and little warm clothing. The *New York Times* reported in February, "That a Confederate collapse is

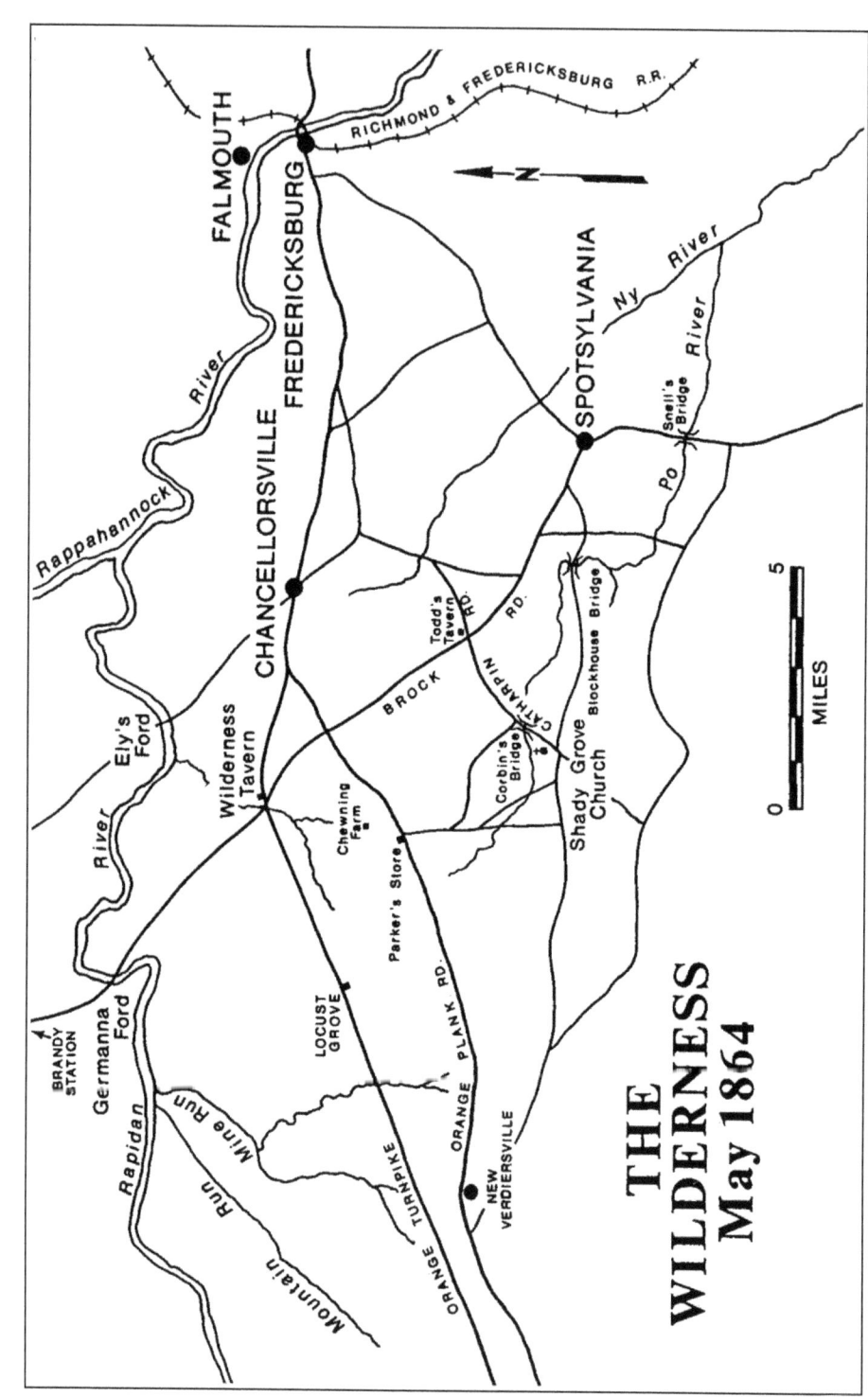

near at hand the rebels here believe, and nine out of ten with whom I have conversed of late, do not hesitate to assert such to be their belief, the remaining one-tenth are silent and sullen, waiting — hoping without hope — like Micawber, for something to turn up to give new life to the cause of secession."[6]

Chaplain Boudrye returned to the regiment from his furlough on April 19, two days after Brigadier General James H. Wilson took command of the Third Cavalry Division. In March, General Grant had come east, been promoted and placed in total command of all Union forces. Inevitably, there would be changes with a new man at the top. In a reorganization of the Army of the Potomac undertaken by Generals Grant and Meade, Alfred Pleasonton was taken from command of the Cavalry Corps and replaced with Major General Phillip Sheridan. Sheridan had served with flair and distinction under Grant in the western theater, and it was Grant who placed him with the cavalry. Judson Kilpatrick, whose stock appears to have lost value after the unsuccessful raid on Richmond during the winter, would, after some delay, be shifted to command cavalry under Sherman in the west. Newly promoted Brigadier General Wilson took his place.

At odds, however, with Boudrye's somewhat optimistic view of the regiment that spring and despite the veteran attitude the Fifth had acquired, there was a report by the Cavalry Corps' inspector general regarding the First and Third Divisions. The contents of the report may have been known prior to its formal submission and may have helped speed Kilpatrick's departure. The language employed in the inspector's report includes phrases such as "large deficiencies," "considerable disorganization," "demands much care and attention," and the most damning of all, the Third Division was "not in a condition to perform active duty with credit."[7] This last comment was more in reference to the division's horses than the unit as a whole. Nor was this all. The commander of the First Connecticut Cavalry reported that he had eighty-five men who had "formerly served in the enemy's cavalry, being deserters who took the oath of allegiance, and on entering our service were assigned to his regiment. He has no confidence in them, has them dismounted now in camp, and is very anxious that they should be sent to the rear, as they would be summarily dealt with if captured by the enemy, and therefore could not be relied upon in action."[8]

A few days after taking command, Sheridan reviewed the Cavalry Corps. It was the horses, their haggard condition, that immediately drew his attention. He found "the men were ... good and satisfactory, but the horses were thin and very much worn down by excessive and ... unnecessary picket duty." He informed General Meade that the extensive picketing the various regiments were called upon to perform was wearing on the animals to a point that they could not stand for long the rigors of a campaign. He requested that the cavalry only picket the fords on the Rapidan and that infantry be employed to cover the remainder of the army's perimeter, an arc of about sixty miles of Virginia countryside. Sheridan had other suggestions for his commanding general at this time concerning the use of cavalry as a separate combat arm, and their discussion on this subject and the Corps' horses has been described as stormy. But Meade seems to have acceded to Sheridan concerning the horses.[9]

As for the Third Division's new leader, James H. Wilson was, like Kilpatrick, another of those "boy wonders" of the Civil War, a general barely four years removed from West Point. He had graduated from the academy sixth in the forty-one-member class of 1860 and was now twenty-seven. According to those acquainted with him, Wilson stood five feet ten inches tall and wore a "light complexion and a pinched face." Wilson had served on Grant's staff in the west the previous year and taken part in the Vicksburg and Chattanooga campaigns. But leading a cavalry division would be his first combat command. From February 1864 until assigned to the Third Division, Wilson had served as chief of the Cavalry Bureau in Washington, an organization set up to see that the cavalry's needs were expeditiously fulfilled while containing cost. At the Bureau, Wilson had made significant improvements, particularly in procedures for the procurement of horses for the mounted forces, and his recommendation that the cavalry adopt the seven-shot Spencer carbine.

Arguably, the adoption of the Spencer by the Calvary Corps was the most significant technical enhancement made by the army during the war. It gave cavalry formations overwhelmingly superior firepower even over Rebel infantry units of significantly greater size.[10] In a letter written by Wilson much later, after seeing the weapon used against the Rebels, he wrote, "There is no doubt that the Spencer carbine is the best fire-arm yet put in the hands of the soldier, both for economy and maximum effect physical and morale. Our best officers estimate one man armed with it equivalent to three with any other arm. I have never seen anything else like the confidence inspired by it in the regiments and brigades which have it. A common belief among them is if their flanks are covered they can go anywhere."[11] The report of the Inspector General on the Third Division, dated April 17, includes the following: "The commander of the Fifth New York Cavalry ... has given the Spencer repeating carbines a fair trial in action and considers them a capital arm."[12]

The placing of Wilson in command of the Third Division was Grant's idea, despite Sheridan claiming in his *Memoirs* that the appointment originated with him. In his *Memoirs*, Sheridan remembers: "At my request he [Wilson] was selected to command the Third Division. General Grant thought highly of him, and, expecting much from his active mental and physical abilities, readily assented to assign him in place of General Kilpatrick." "From the first ... he [Wilson] demonstrated a sternness ... a determination to exact respect, order, and discipline ... which some of his subordinates felt was akin to an obsession," writes Wilson's biographer. But Wilson knew he had only a short time before the start of the campaign, and with Sheridan's approval, drove the men of the Third Division, getting them in shape for combat operations.[13] Wilson admitted in his memoirs that he found the division "badly run down" on taking command, the "horses over worked and exhausted, its equipment and clothing nearly used up, and ... weapons dirty and out of order." There were

General James H. Wilson, commander of the Third Cavalry Division during the Overland Campaign (Library of Congress).

3,436 troopers in the division but only 2,692 had horses. Further, thirty-four men had disabled horses. The deficiencies Wilson found were immediately addressed and remedied as best as could be before the division moved at the beginning of the campaign.[14] Wilson later wrote, "At the first morning inspection, I found but few officers attending stable call, while all routine duties were so poorly performed that I felt obliged to put one colonel in arrest and to admonish the rest that radical improvements must be made at once if they would save themselves from a similar fate."[15]

By May 2, 1864, whatever deficiencies an inspector's eye might have noted in the Fifth New York had been corrected. On that day, John Hammond, now a lieutenant colonel, received a note from First Brigade commander Colonel T.H. Bryan: "Col. The commanding general of this division desires me express to you his gratification at the military deportment and soldierly bearing of your command at the division review to-day. He considered your regiment, in every particular, by far the finest on the field, in which opinion I heartily concur."[16]

Across the river the Army of Northern Virginia had more serious deficiencies to confront; indeed, the entire winter had been a time of near starvation and weather-induced hardship. General Robert E. Lee had written the Confederacy's president several times during the winter in a tone that was near to pleading. With his words, the general is reflecting the difficulty facing the Rebel government as it entered the fourth full year of war:

> My anxiety on the subject of provisions for the army is so great that I cannot refrain from expressing it to Your Excellency. I cannot see how we can operate with our present supplies. Any derangement in their arrival or disaster to the railroad would render it impossible for me to keep the army together, and might force a retreat to North Carolina. There is nothing to be had in this section for men or animals. We have rations for the troops for today and tomorrow. I hope a new supply arrived last night, but I have not yet had a report. Every exertion should be made to supply the depots at Richmond and at other points. All pleasure travel should cease, and everything be devoted to necessary wants.

And privately to family members, Lee was saying during the winter, "I have had to disperse the cavalry as much as possible, to obtain forage for their horses, and it is that which causes trouble. Provisions for the men, too, are very scarce, and, with very light diet and light clothing, I fear they suffer.... I received a report from one division the other day in which it stated that over four hundred men were barefooted and over a thousand without blankets."[17]

In this springtime prior to crossing the river, the Army of the Potomac, the Third Division and the Cavalry Corps as a whole had to be reorganized as a result of the replacement of Kilpatrick by Wilson. The inconvenience stemmed from the fact that Wilson was junior in rank to Brigadier Generals Kilpatrick, Custer, Merritt and Davies. The date of one's commission in a particular rank was no small matter to Civil War officers, especially among generals. Whatever the reason behind Wilson's placement in a combat command on April 7, beyond the vague reference to his "active mental and physical abilities," by April 14 he still had not taken over. There is an interesting exchange of telegrams between Sheridan and Wilson, who appears to be waiting at Grant's headquarters for some resolution to Kilpatrick's status. On April 14, Sheridan was telling the staff at Grant's headquarters, "General Wilson having been directed to report to me, I am very much embarrassed in his assignment to the Third Cavalry Division of the Cavalry Corps, as General Kilpatrick, commanding the division, ranks him. General Kilpatrick is anxious to be transferred to the west; is it possible to do so?" The next day, April 15, Wilson replied directly to Sheridan from Grant's headquarters: "General Grant has not returned, will be back this P.M. General Rawlins [Grant's chief of staff], says no doubt he will make the order we wish. Suppose you make my order and sent it over." That order, transferring Kilpatrick to General Sherman in the west, was made that same day. Then, on April 16, Wilson telegraphed Sheridan, "Telegram received. I start over immediately." At this point the quick reshuffling of the Cavalry Corps began as Wilson arrived to take over the Third Division. Custer's Second Brigade, therefore, was transferred from the Third to the First Division, replaced by the brigade led by Colonel George Chapman. Merritt, who had been temporarily commanding the First Division, reverted to command of the Reserve Brigade, and Davies, in command of the First Brigade, transferred from the Third to the Second Division. The First Brigade of the Third Division, to which the Fifth New York belonged, was assigned to Colonel Timothy Bryan. Two days into the campaign, Colonel John McIntosh replaced Colonel Bryan as commander of the brigade. Colonel McIntosh would lead it through the summer. Also, the Third Division gained by the return of the First Vermont, a veteran regiment, and to a lesser degree by the addition of the Twenty-second New York, a formation described by Wilson as being "so green that no one else wanted it."[18]

Despite the worn and haggard state of its horses and equipment, after two years in the field, the Fifth New York was not only confident, it was experienced — a veteran outfit that had learned its trade by trial and error in its first year of existence. Lieutenant Colonel Hammond had been in command of the regiment for nearly a year and was now a familiar commodity. He was trusted, not only by his men, but by his immediate superiors. The Fifth New York, given the above and everything culled from the record available to us, was probably in as good a shape for field operations as it could be at the beginning of May 1864.

When he returned to the regiment, Chaplain Boudrye quickly slipped back into his customary duties and his ongoing efforts to improve the men's morale. The day following his return, Boudrye spoke to those gathered at the regimental temperance meeting. "Spoke and was followed by some others who presented some facts on the subject which came under their experience. The meeting was very enthusiastic. Three signed the pledge.... The number of signers is now 164. This is a great success. The interest is increasing. Men preaching to each other and the cause becomes self serving and increasing."[19] But there was a darker side. On April 23, Boudrye went to the division's guardhouse to visit Private John Crowley of Company A. It was a part of the chaplain's duty to visit prisoners, and he recorded his impression that evening:

"Saw one of our men ... who is sentenced to be shot next week, Friday. Crime — desertion. He is a poor miserable man. He weeps as he speaks of his family and says 'Whisky' [sic] is the cause of his trouble. He stands ready to sign the pledge now." Boudrye visited Crowley again the next day, bringing him his mail. Two days before Crowley's scheduled execution, Boudrye saw him again. "Tried to cheer Mr. Crowly [sic], who is somewhat downcast, at the approach of the day of his execution and no tiding of his reprieve." Apparently some appeal must have been winding its way through the legal machinery of the Army of the Potomac, but the chaplain gives no details.

The next day, April 28, the day before his execution, there was good news of Crowley. Boudrye wrote in his journal, "I saw Mr. John Crowly [sic] who had been pardoned or rather had his sentence commuted from being shot to hard labor on the Dry Tortugas for term of service. He was a happy man and grateful." John Crowley was 27 years old when he enlisted in New York City in February 1864. As a cavalry trooper, Crowley apparently lacked whatever it was that kept so many others at the task. He deserted in March "from Stevensburg, Va; was retaken, and sent to Dry Tortugas by sentence of court-martial." Some days earlier, General Meade had been given permission by Lincoln to commute desertion death sentences to imprisonment on Dry Tortugas.

Crowley was indeed lucky, but others were not. Meade's power to pardon did not include at least one soldier in the days prior to the beginning of the campaign. At about this time, the chaplain observed the grim reality of the army's discipline. "Went to witness the execution of a private, Co. L, 19th Mass. Vols. He was hung by the neck, till he was dead. The arrangement of the troops and the music were very imposing and impressive. The execution was bad, on account of the scaffold being too low, or the rope too long, as that the feet of the man struck the ground as he fell. It was a solemn and impressive hour, one I had never before witnessed nor as I hope to see another."[20]

On April 29, the regiment broke winter camp and moved into bivouac closer to First Brigade Headquarters. In the little direct testimony of those in the Fifth New York at this moment there seems to be an almost unspoken knowledge that the coming campaign would take many lives. In a brief note written at 8 P.M. on May 3, John Hammond told his wife, "Maria, I hope to write you in my next a victory gained by our arms that shall make the hearts of all loyal people glad; but none can tell the events that are to come." One trooper did speak of his apprehension to Chaplain Boudrye. His journal for May 3 includes the following: "Just before leaving, a young man — Charles Don Smith, Co. M — came to my quarters, put a splendid gold ring on my finger which exactly fitted, saying, 'I may be killed rather than you. If we

8. Across the River—1864

both survive, return it to me about the first of October next. If I die, send it to Miss _____.' (I have her address). Inside the spring is a hair braid and Isabella engraved, neither showing when the ring is closed. I shall not soon forget this sudden move." Charles D. Smith was later captured and probably sent to Andersonville Prison, but he is not listed in the regimental history as having died there. In this manner the chaplain and the Fifth New York began the campaign it was hoped would end the war.[21]

This morning was different and almost everyone sensed it. It was different because this day's operation was historic, as had been that third day in Pennsylvania the year before, or the one next year further down in Virginia at a place called Appomattox. Speaking of May 4, Bruce Catton captured the sense of it:

> The men of this army left books and letters behind them, and in these there is a remarkable testimony that the men who marched away from winter quarters that morning took a last look back and saw a golden haze which, even at the moment of looking, they knew they would never see again. They tell how the birds were singing, and how the warm scented air came rolling up the river valley, and how they noticed things like wildflowers and the young green leaves, and they speak of the moving pageant which they saw and of which they themselves were part.... It would never be like this again, and young men who were to live on to a great age, drowsing out lives of old soldiers in a land that would honor them and then tolerate them and finally forget them, would look back on this one morning and see in it something that came from beyond the rim of the world.

The Fifth New York Volunteer Cavalry was moving. "Thus the months of winter glided by, till vernal grasses and flowers came to festoon the graves on battle-fields over which the contending hosts had wrestled for three years." This was how one participant remembered the beginning of General Grant's campaign. Chaplain Boudrye noted: "At two (2) A.M., we were on the march. The stars shown [*sic*] brightly and the air was chilly. We traveled quite rapidly, passing by infantry and artillery. Reached the Rapidan at Germanna [*sic*] Ford at day break. Considerable cavalry forded. Pontoons were laid and at 6½ the first artillery arrived. No resistance was made by the Rebels who have disappeared." It appears that Chaplain Boudrye was riding at the rear of the division when he recorded these observations. Further back, a staff officer, as yet unfamiliar with the horror of this war's bloodletting, was moving toward the river that early morning. Yet instinctively he seems to be aware of the "golden haze" of this Virginia springtime, perhaps trying to avert his mind from what was to come. Later he recalled, "The glad May air was full of spring. Dogwoods with their open, enwrapped blossoms ... violets and azaleas, heavenly pale little houstonias ... here and there beautify the pastures and roadsides of this part of old Virginia, were all in bloom, and the dew still on them."[22]

The mission of the Third Division was to lead two infantry corps across the Rapidan and into the woodlands known as the Wilderness, a tangle of second growth pine and briars, the same wilderness where General Hooker had come to grief a year before. It was then to move southeast to Wilderness Tavern, scouting ahead of the advancing infantry and covering the roads that converged at the tavern. Lee's army was then in camp in the vicinity of Orange Court House and any reaction by it would come from either the south or west, or both. The division was over the Rapidan by 6 A.M., followed closely by the Fifth Corps. By noon the division had reached and secured the area around Wilderness Tavern, and Wilson had sent out patrols on the roads to the west and south, particularly out along Orange Turnpike. The probe sent along the Turnpike to the west encountered some Rebel skirmishers some distance out, exchanged fire with them, and then slowly returned. When the Fifth Corps arrived at the tavern, Wilson's orders were to then move south to the Orange Plank Road and then slightly west to a place called Parker's Store. The infantry were to follow the next day. By 2 P.M. on May 4, Wilson's troopers were at Parker's, a place deep within the Wilderness, and again patrols were sent out on the narrow roads leading south and west looking for movement by any of Lee's formations.[23] All seemed to be going as planned. However, when Wilson moved off from Wilderness Tavern, so did his scouts, those who had earlier skirmished along Orange Turnpike, and it is unknown whether this information was passed on to the arriving infantry. The infantry did not replace them with pickets. As a result, there would be little advance warning of the attack the Federals would receive the next morning.

While most of the division rested in the area surrounding Parker's Store, the Fifth New York was sent probing to the west along the Orange Plank Road. Approximately five miles down the road, the New Yorkers encountered Rebel pickets. Shots were exchanged and the pickets retired further west. It didn't seem, Colonel Hammond reported, that there was evidence of a larger force behind the pickets within any reasonable distance. At 7:40 P.M. Wilson reported to Meade's headquarters that his patrol had gone "to within 1 mile of Mine Run, on Orange pike, skirmishing with small detachments of the enemy." The Orange Turnpike leads to the Wilderness Tavern, and here, Wilson seems to be reporting on patrol activity he ordered earlier while still at the Tavern. The approximate five miles traveled by the Fifth to the west after arriving at Parker's Store, on the Orange Plank Road, places the regiment encountering Rebels at or near a place called New Hope Church. No doubt Hammond reported his exchange of shots with Rebels to Wilson, but whether Wilson reported it to headquarters is unknown. The Fifth New York stayed in position near New Hope Church that night and returned to Parker's early

8. Across the River—1864

the next morning. In probing to the west, Hammond had not followed the retreating pickets after exchanging shots, and this was probably a mistake. If he had, the Fifth New York would have detected the advance of a Rebel infantry corps.[24] On the other hand, the Fifth New York might have precipitated the Battle of the Wilderness a day sooner and with the Army of the Potomac in less of a position to react effectively. As it was, the regiment that night was within rifle range of the Rebel advance.

As he understood his orders for May 5, Wilson was to lead his division south from Parker's via a road that would connect with an east-west thoroughfare called Catharpin Road. Once there, the division was to advance west to a place called Craig's Meeting House, about eight miles from Parker's Store. Again the command was looking for movement by the enemy toward the Union army. By 5 A.M., the Fifth New York had returned to Parker's Store to rejoin the division. But Wilson ordered Hammond and the regiment to remain at Parker's and continue to scout to the west until relieved by Fifth Corps infantry advancing from Wilderness Tavern. When relieved, it was to follow and catch up with the division at Craig's Meeting House. Wilson also reported at this time to Meade: "My pickets report nothing new from the enemy this morning."[25]

The New York troopers rekindled campfires and started to boil their coffee while Company I, under Captain William B. Cary, again advanced west along the Orange Plank Road. If Cary and his men found the enemy, he was to report and to try not to become heavily involved. As had happened at Hanover the year before, the Fifth New York would be among the first to become engaged in another of the war's epic battles.

Captain Cary and his men, heading west, crossed a stream and, following the road, climbed a rise in the ground. Over the rise, directly to their front, was the advance of Confederate General A.P. Hill's infantry corps, and the shooting started at once. "The Captain, a resolute man as you can readily see looking into his steady dark eyes, dismounted his men, formed them as skirmishers across the road and notified Hammond." Cary was now in a brief holding action as he waited for a response from the rest of the regiment. Getting this news from Cary and probably already hearing the firing, Hammond sent some reinforcements to Cary and ordered the rest of the regiment to prepare to receive an infantry attack. The men of the Fifth threw up barricades of fence rails, and the horses were moved to the rear. Even with reinforcements, Cary was steadily driven back down the road to Parker's Store, his company firing its Spencer carbines as they went. As the Rebels advanced and closed in on the area of Parker's Store, the entire regiment became engaged. The Fifth New York was in a fight for its life. A staff officer of the Fifth Corps,

Washington Roebling, had ridden up to the area around Parker's as the Rebels drove in Cray's skirmishers. Roebling, who later in life would supervise the construction of the Brooklyn Bridge, apparently was scouting the terrain over which the Fifth Corps would march that day. He quickly found the commander, "and Hammond told him that perhaps he could hold on fifteen minutes longer, whereupon Roebling hurried back."

Corporal D.H. Robbins of Company H later recalled that morning. He wrote, "The Johnnies must have had an early breakfast, for they came tumbling thru those jack pines and persimmon trees in almost a solid line, no doubt thinking a few cavalrymen would be a decent breakfast for them." Experienced as were the bulk of these troopers, it was clearly evident at this moment that the Fifth New York was in serious trouble. Trooper L.J. Lichtenberg later remembered, "Our regiment ... formed in a small clearing ... on the left side of the road, fronting the enemy.... Shots, at first a few, but rapidly increasing, were heard on the picket line. Company after company was dismounted and sent to participate in the fun." Corporal Robbins remembered, "Col. Hammond addressed us, and instructed that we were to expected to hold our position as long as possible, we having already formed a line and counted off by fours and thrown up a slight barricade of [fence] rails before the Johnnies showed up." Every fourth man took his own mount and the horses of the other three and led them to the rear.

The men of the Fifth New York, behind any cover available, kept up the firing. What happened next, and for the next several hours, was a direct result of the regiment having been equipped with the seven-shot Spencer carbine. Corporal Robbins remembered, "Our sevenshooters work sharp and it was almost impossible not to hit our mark." Because of the rate of fire coming from the Spencers, the Rebels thought they had encountered a much larger force than just one cavalry regiment. But it was a losing situation. "There were 10 Johnnies to one of us," Robbins recalled, "but we blocked the whole line in our front in no time; but the rebel lines on both left and right swept right past our flank, and in a few minutes were making things buzz from all sides, and we were obliged to skip out for our horses." The regiment fell back about a quarter of a mile and again deployed to receive the infantry advance. At this point the initiative shifted over to the Rebels. Robbins continues, "The Johnnies, having been reinforced, they poured the cold lead into us in great shape, and some of our best officers and many men and horses went down in a heap. We had to break to the rear again, leaving our dead and wounded in their hands." At the end of this second withdrawal, the troopers came upon the lead elements of the advancing Union infantry and "they laughed at us when we told them that the woods were full of Johnnies just back of us." The

8. Across the River—1864

infantrymen advanced, Robbins says, and "in a few minutes the roar of musketry was continuous."[26]

Chaplain Boudrye described May 5 as "warm and dusty" and "one of the most laborious I ever experienced." He had spent the night with the division's train back at Wilderness Tavern. "At 7, with a small guard, I left Wilderness Tavern and escorted the Headquarters wagon toward Parker's Store where the Regiment lay during the night. As we approached the place, we heard skirmishing and as I came up to the boys there were some of them wounded. I entered into caring for them."[27] It was now about 10 A.M. and the Rebels were moving past both flanks of the regiment. Hammond had ordered the men back to their horses and moved about a quarter of a mile along the road toward the Tavern. There he established another defensive line facing west while hoping, no doubt, that Fifth Corps infantry would arrive soon. Boudrye put a wounded man on his horse. "I led the horse for about three miles, having to run about ¼ of the way." By noon he was back at Wilderness Tavern helping the Fifth New York wounded in a field hospital the Fifth Corps had established there.[28]

Boudrye continues: "Having sent word to General Meade that a heavy column of infantry was advancing and that he would 'check them as long as possible,' Col. Hammond kept the regiment well in line, encouraging the men with his presence. Many of the men were dismounted, and their Spencer carbines made the dense woods ring, and told with fearful effect upon the enemy. Prisoners, afterwards ... swore that a whole brigade must have been in their front. Fighting ... and compelled to fall back before superior numbers, we nevertheless held them at bay for five hours, until relieved by a portion of the 6th Corps."[29] In actuality, Hammond led the Fifth New York in another fighting withdrawal along Orange Plank Road to where it intersected with Brock Road, a point about a mile to the southeast of Wilderness Tavern. It was now early afternoon and by this time the chaplain was helping at the hospital. Also, by this time the Battle of the Wilderness was fully opened, with Union and Rebel infantry engaged from the area north of Orange Turnpike and continuing south to Orange Plank Road.[30]

Finally, with Fifth and Sixth Corps infantry now up in a defensive line and receiving the Confederate attack, the Fifth New York, nearly out of ammunition, retreated about a mile to the rear. The chaplain gives the casualties as thirteen killed, twenty-two wounded, and "24 known to have been captured, besides 15 or 20 from which tidings have never since been heard." Included in his history is a statement by a reporter for the *New York Herald*. Presumably it appeared in the paper within days of the battle: "The Fifth New York was detached from Colonel McIntosh's command for duty under the immediate orders of General Meade. This was a compliment well earned by its gallant conduct at Parker's Store. It is under the command of Colonel Hammond, one of the best officers in the service." John Hammond later wrote his wife that in this action, "We fought Hood's division for five hours, holding them in check until the infantry came up.... We lost some forty or fifty men in killed and wounded."[31] The mention of Colonel McIntosh is an indication that the newspaper reporter was fully aware of the events, at a minimum having talked with the participants.

On May 5, McIntosh had been sent by Sheridan to catch up with the Third Division and take command of the First Brigade from Colonel Bryan. McIntosh had traveled as far as Parker's Store, probably riding along with the group that included the chaplain. Arriving at some point in mid-morning, he found the fight was already in progress. He wasn't able to reach the First Brigade until the next day. If Roebling had hurried back to obtain infantry support for the Fifth New York, that support hadn't arrived as yet to prevent the regiment from having to fall back. At 11 A.M., McIntosh dashed off a note to those further to the rear and gave his location as "on the plank road, about 3 miles from Parker's Store." McIntosh reported, "I met this morning a picket force of about 400 cavalry stationed at Parker's Store.... After a gallant resistance, and when all their ammunition was expended, they were forced back by heavily superior numbers. I have remained with them. We are now formed at the junction of the Parker's Store road and the Chancellorsville road without ammunition. We want a strong infantry, and I understand General Crawford is on my right. As yet he has given no help. He should extend his line at once across the Parker's Store road." In his later report McIntosh wrote, "The regiment did itself great credit and sustained its high reputation" during the action at Parker's Store on May 5. By late afternoon, the regiment had been relieved and ordered to report to General Meade. Upon reporting, the regiment went into bivouac near Wilderness Tavern as the battle raged to the south and west through the remainder of that day and into the night. Arguably, the engagement fought by the Fifth New York on May 5, 1864, standing by itself with only carbines against infantry in the thousands, was the regiment's finest hour.[32]

While Hammond and the Fifth's troopers fought through the morning and early afternoon, Wilson, with the rest of the division, became heavily engaged with Confederate cavalry on Catharpin Road in the vicinity of Craig's Meeting House. It was about 8 A.M. when the division was hit by Rebel cavalry, with the First Vermont initially being driven back before turning, reforming lines and charging the Rebel horsemen. The brigade, still led by Bryan, drove the Rebels about two miles beyond the Meeting House. By 2 P.M. Colonel George Chapman's Second Brigade was meeting stiff resistance

8. Across the River—1864

from reinforced Rebels and was, in turn, driven back along the road until horse artillery could be deployed to counter the Confederate surge.

At this point in the day, Wilson and the division were essentially cut off from the army whose flank it was supposed to be protecting. A move was essential to disengage from the believed-superior Rebel force that was attacking them front, and in rear as well, and to re-establish a position relative to Meade's army. Wilson decided on a mad dash to the northeast that focused on a place called Todd's Tavern. Rebel cavalry was seen in every direction as the division moved desperately to separate itself from impending disaster. Some hours before, Meade had become aware that contact with Wilson had been lost. He ordered Sheridan to move Gregg's Second Cavalry Division in the direction of Todd's Tavern in the hope that contact with Wilson could be made. Gregg's division got to the area of the Tavern and prepared either to receive an assault or to make one. To the relief of everyone in the Third Division, they met Gregg's command as they galloped disorganized into the area of the Tavern. Relieved, they fell in behind Gregg's men as he counterattacked the pursuing Rebel cavalry, driving them back. The Third Division had gotten itself into the first of several tight spots under its new commander, but had managed, somehow, to ride and fight its way to safety.

It had been a discouraging day for the division, but another lucky one for the Fifth New York. They had fought and suffered severe loses, but hadn't been in the large and nearly disastrous running fight with Wilson and the rest of the division. The Third Division was discouraged, as reported by a Michigan officer who saw them that day and who had been in the same brigade with both the Fifth New York and the First Vermont that winter. The Michigan and Vermont regiments had been close, to a point that the men from Michigan called the Vermont regiment the "Eighth Michigan." After Craig's Meeting House and all that they had been through this day, the First Vermont moved slowly through the lines of Gregg's Second Division. "They were moving to the rear," the Michigan officer wrote,

> and seemed much chagrined over their defeat and declared that they did not belong to the Third Division, but were the "Eighth Michigan."
>
> "Come along with us," called one of the Michigan troopers to the First Vermont.
>
> "Wish we could," they replied.

This was their reflection after a day of combat under James Wilson, their new commander in his first action in command.[33]

By nightfall of May 5, Wilson and the rest of the division fell into bivouac to the northeast of Todd's Tavern after having fought Rebel cavalry most of the day. In the bivouac that night the men kept their carbines ready for use because their opponents were resting on their arms not far away. General Wilson's division had survived a tough day of fighting in which the Fifth New York had been entirely separated from the command. New to divisional command, James Wilson no doubt had learned a good deal about leading combat operations. But the troopers in the ranks were decidedly unimpressed. And this impression would only grow in the coming weeks as the veteran regiments became acquainted with their new commander. Samuel Gilpin of the Third Indiana, part of the division, confided in his diary later in the campaign, "General Wilson is not popular with the command. No one doubts his bravery, but, he had no experience as a Cavalry Commander. Our Brigade will not fight under him as they did under 'Old Johnny Buford.'"[34] In defense of Wilson, it might be noted that although this was his first combat posting, he was a new face to these men and an officer who demanded discipline from those falling under his command. This was not so with Judson Kilpatrick. He had seen a good deal of combat before commanding the division, had become familiar to the men by the time Wilson arrived, and was in no way a disciplinarian.

Presumably, General Meade, at some point after Wilson returned within Union lines or the next morning, told Wilson that the Fifth New York had been ordered to his headquarters. On the morning of May 6, the regiment was "ordered from the left to the right wing, just in time to prevent the stragglers from our broken lines passing far to the rear. After our position was reestablished we rested for the night."[35] All through the daylight hours, indeed well into the darkness of May 6, the Battle of the Wilderness went on, with both sides suffering on a horrific scale.

Early the next morning, May 7, Hammond received an order. "Gen. Sedgwick directs (in accordance with orders from headquarters Army of the Potomac and General Grant) that you move forward and remain as far as possible near Germanna Ford, and report immediately any movement of the enemy. Be sure that no force of the enemy crosses the plank road without notifying General Sedgwick at once."[36] "This morning early," Boudrye wrote in his journal for May 7, "we were sent out to Germanna Ford to guard our extreme right wing. Never in my life have I seen such a waste of property as could be seen in this road, especially near the Ford, where [there were] blankets, overcoats, jackets, blouses, guns and ammunition, etc., etc. I picked up several canteens which I distributed among the men." The infantry, as it marched into the Wilderness on May 4, had thrown away many of the items individual soldiers carried, in order to lighten their load as battle neared. This, the usual refuse remaining after a serious engagement, is what Boudrye recorded seeing in his journal. Boudrye continued:

8. Across the River—1864

Until about 2 P.M., only a few 'Rebs' had been seen though one shot came very near a small squad of us as we sat by the roadside between our videttes and reserve. At two, the 'Rebs' came down upon us with artillery, cavalry and infantry. I was within plain sight and gunshot of the Rebel skirmishers as they came out of the woods on the opposite side of the clearing where we were resting. A few balls whizzed among us and their battery was opened upon the command which consisted of the 25th N.Y. and ours. The former Regiment broke at once and nothing was left us, but to retreat which we did very precipitously, down the river, going as far as Ely's Ford, returning to the place we left this morning. We lost only two or three men in this skirmish. Our horses have been almost entirely without feed, except the new grass, all the day.... We were much fatigued on arrival at our halting place, about dusk. Soon after this, an immense cheering took place along our lines, commencing on our right and round to the left, making a welkin ring and the hills resound.[37]

The cheering was the response of the troops in the line to the news that they were to move and it was not back, back over the river they had just crossed, but to their left. They were not retreating. The order had come down to advance. General Grant was not General Hooker of the previous year. The movement was beginning at once.

After the retreat to Ely's Ford and the Rebels having not pursued, Hammond marched the regiment back to the Germanna Plank Road. On the way Hammond received notice from Sixth Corps headquarters that he was to take command of the 22nd New York and 2nd Ohio Cavalry regiments and picket in force the road leading to Germanna Ford. Hammond did this, detailing the new regiments under his command while most of the Fifth New York went into bivouac. It was then that the cheering was heard and a movement by the army to its left was begun.

During the early evening another order from the Sixth Corps reached Hammond detailing what he was to do on May 8. "You will please remain with your command near the old Wilderness Tavern, until you are notified by Maj. Gen. Hancock, that his corps and pickets are withdrawn. Gen. Hancock's pickets are to be withdrawn at 2 A.M. (two o'clock A.M.) Upon being so notified you will follow the 2d Corps."[38] The Fifth New York, with the two other regiments, was going to cover the rear of the Army of the Potomac as it attempted a flanking movement against Lee. At 8 A.M. that morning, the regiment followed the Second Corps down the road to Chancellorsville and went into bivouac. On May 9, the only action by the Fifth New York was a reconnaissance sent to Ely's Ford.[39]

It was also on May 9 that Sheridan began his raid in the direction of Richmond, a movement designed to coax Jeb Stuart's cavalry away from Lee's army and into a fight with his Cavalry Corps. The Fifth New York and the other two regiments remained with the Army of the Potomac under Meade's orders. The day before, May 8, Sheridan and Meade had their famous confrontation at the latter's headquarters. The result was that the Cavalry Corps would become what Sheridan had advocated since taking command: a semi-independent combat arm, able to move, raid and fight at a distance from the main army. The two generals had argued over an order Meade had given directly to one of Sheridan's divisions without his knowledge. Beyond that, Sheridan strongly advocated, in language bordering on insubordination, and in a tone not to Meade's liking, that his corps be relieved from guarding supply trains and screening duties and cut loose from the army so that it could find and fight the enemy. Later in the day, Meade reported the "conversation" to Grant, who, rather than calling Sheridan to account, allowed him to do as he asked. Sheridan lost no time. He and his corps moved away from the army and toward Richmond early the next morning, May 9.

For the next several days, the Fifth New York performed picket duty on the right flank of the army and generally tried to rest and feed the horses. Meanwhile, another major and bloody engagement, the Battle of Spotsylvania Court House, raged to the east as Grant's flanking movement was countered by Lee. For the days between May 9 and 11, Boudrye's journal speaks of grazing horses and the warm and dusty weather. He can clearly hear the heavy artillery in and around Spotsylvania Court House, as rumors of all kinds circulate among the troops. The weather had indeed been dry, and when it rained on the evening of May 11, the men greeted it with relief. It rained well into the next morning, May 12, and Hammond and his regiment were ordered to move to Chancellorsville while the fighting at Spotsylvania continued. "The fields and woods show signs of Hooker's great battle here a year ago. Bodies and bones of unburied men, and those only partially buried, may be found on every hand." At one point during the day, Boudrye rode toward the sound of the guns and found it eight miles distant and a place where rumors swirled with greater intensity than in the rear.

The rain continued into May 13, and the Fifth New York stayed where it was. It moved up to Meade's headquarters then next day and camped. May 15 saw Hammond's command move further to the left, to a place called Massaponax Court House, where there was a brief skirmish before it bivouacked for the night. At some point on May 12, John Hammond had time to write a few lines. "The battles of these eight days' fighting have been the most severe ever witnessed, and the killed and wounded will be immense.... Never has such desperation and determination been exhibited since the world was. I hope soon to write you from the James River." And again on May 14, he says, "The loss on both sides will far overtop anything in the annals of war.... This is a horrible country to fight in ... everywhere being about as closely covered with dense forest as it is out about Long Lake in the Adirondacks.... We are encamped on the same ground where Stonewall Jackson was killed, and where he turned Gen. Hooker's flank. The ground is dotted with graves and human skulls & bones. While I write I am sitting on the grave of some poor fellow."[40]

The Fifth New York was ordered on May 16 on a reconnaissance across the Ny River and skirmished with a large force of entrenched Rebels before coming back to its camp. On May 17, orders came directly from Meade: "Colonel: Your dispatch reporting a superior force of the enemy at Guineas [sic] Station received. I send you Lieut. Col. Chamberlain, 1st Massachusetts, with 1,200 men from Dismounted Corps. You will take command of these men and endeavor to drive back the enemy's cavalry and destroy the depot at Guineas. Also advance on their right flank and ascertain all you can of the enemy's position and force."[41] The command went forward and found the Rebels posted on the banks of the Po River. Although there was a skirmish, Hammond retired and no doubt reported his findings to Meade. It wasn't until May 21 that the Fifth New York moved on Guineas [sic] Station and encountered Rebels. The regiment pushed them back through Bowling Green and then to Milford Station, where a bigger fight began. "The regiment behaved handsomely in this fight, which resulted in the capture of six officers and sixty-six privates, and the dispersion of the entire force which guarded the station. In the depot were found some stores of the Rebel quartermaster and commissary, which were readily appropriated."[42] The next day the regiment moved further on, going to New Bethel Church by day's end.

During the days spent in bivouac while the infantry was fighting in the area of Spotsylvania Court House, the Fifth New York had received some reinforcements in the form of dismounted men. Chaplain Boudrye's journal contains a comment on two of them, dated May 19: "Just after dark two of our boys, Crum, Co. B. and Davis, Co. F. deserted and were caught on their way to the Rebel lines by our pickets. They were both recruits and had been here but two days. This created a great excitement among us. Crum is said to be here under a fictitious name. They are hard cases. Davis boasted that he had jumped two bounties before by desertion and that he would jump another. They were sent to General Patrick [Provost Marshal]."[43] Bounty jumping and desertion, although not a critical source of lost manpower within the army, was still a problem. One can only speculate on the possible fate of Crum and Davis, however, having decided to desert during combat operations.

Boudrye spoke of the fight at Milford Station on May 21 as being severe. The Fifth New York lost one man killed and five wounded. "John Vandemark,

Co. G. who was killed, was buried with appropriate ceremony. There was a large collection around the place. He has two brothers in the same company who were present. It was an affecting time." May 23 was another day of movement as General Grant again tried moving to his left in an effort to flank Lee's army. The command was approaching the North Anna River in the afternoon when it ran into Rebel pickets and entrenched artillery. Another fight was soon underway. Boudrye was riding with the advance as the fighting started and reported that three men from the Fifth New York were wounded, "one mortally, B.F. Washburn, Co. H. He had been a neglector of religion and was very profane. But in this trying hour, he clung to me most ferociously, unwilling I should leave him for a moment. He also desired to have me pray for him, which I did. But he said to me, 'Chaplain, it is too late,' I went and prayed over him.... He was placed in one of the 5th Corps ambulances. He will probably not live more than 3 hours or till sundown."[44] Prayers had their influence, since Washburn survived. In his history, Boudrye comments on the fight at the North Anna as being "desperate" and a "general engagement" that went on until 9 P.M., "ending with a terrible cannonade."[45]

The next day the regiment crossed the North Anna by moving to the west from the area where the fight of May 23 had taken place. On May 25, the regiment was at the Virginia Central Railroad and "our men are effectually destroying. The fire of the ties, culverts and bridges makes a line of lurid light smoke along the evening sky."

The regiment rested the next day. But early in the evening "we were joined by the division, just returned from Sheridan's great raid, which commenced with the opening of the campaign." Actually, it began on May 9 and resulted primarily in the Battle of Yellow Tavern, where Rebel cavalry commander Jeb Stuart was fatally wounded.[46]

For the next few days the Fifth New York, reunited with its division, marched and skirmished at the periphery of the Army of the Potomac as Grant maneuvered, trying to lure Lee out from behind entrenchment and into battle. The regiment's history for these days speaks respectfully of the weary horses that were breaking down after carrying their riders since May 4. For May 28, Boudrye comments on the horses: "For want of forage and rest many horse gave out by the way. It is wonderful how long these faithful animals carry their riders with their kit, even after overtaxation of muscles has nearly destroyed them. On they plod fearful of being abandoned by their mates, until strength has entirely departed, and they quiver beneath their load, and would fall, if not relieved." When a cavalry horse could go no further or simply fell down, "these 'played out' horses are invariably shot, lest they might fall into the hands of the enemy, and, in a few weeks of care, become serviceable." During these few days of movement at least fifty horses collapsed belonging to the Fifth New York. The riders had no choice but to shoot them to prevent them falling into Rebel hands. Then the men followed the regiment on foot.[47]

By May 31, the division was advancing on Hanover Court House. The next day, the whole division became engaged with Rebels. The fighting moved past the Court House and on to Ashland Station and to a pair of railroad bridges over the South Anna River. The Second Brigade was to burn the bridges while the First, with the Fifth New York, battled a brigade of Rebel cavalry.

> Several times our boys were partially surrounded, but the ceaseless fire of the carbines and the grape and canister of the artillery, mowed fearful gaps in the enemy's lines, and strewed the ground with slain. While gallantly riding up and down our lines, directing the operations and encouraging the men, Major White of the Fifth, received a dangerous wound through the body, which was feared would prove fatal to his valuable life. Col. Hammond received a bullet, which flattened upon his scabbard, but cracked the bone just above the ankle joint.... When the force fell back, Dr. Armstrong volunteered to remain with Major White, who could not be moved. This noble act was never forgotten.

Of this action, Hammond told his wife the scabbard "saved my leg. It made me limp a little."[48]

Major White was captured in this action but recovered from his wound. Later, it appears he was exchanged and returned to the regiment, eventually ascending to command it the next year. The Fifth New York had no one killed in this action but fifteen were wounded and twenty captured. In one of the longest letters John Hammond wrote during the war, he explains to his wife what happened at Ashland:

> Gen. Grant has issued a complimentary order to our brigade, and it is said to have been one of the most desperate cavalry battles of the war. Our loss was heavy, and the rebels suffered terribly. Our men fought like demons. We were completely surrounded, and it was a matter of life and liberty, or death. We drove them and rejoined our army. Our orders were to burn and destroy the bridge on the Virginia Central and the Fredericksburg R.R. on and about the South Anna and its branches. It is very gratifying to the old soldiers of the Army of the Potomac, to have officers and men, from Gen. Grant down to private soldiers, say they never saw any real fighting until they came here.

Then Hammond goes on to the action of June 3: "Our division had a fight here yesterday of the most terrible nature. We had two colonels wounded. Colonel Preston, of the First Vermont Cavalry, was killed. A braver man never lived. We lost largely in officers in the line, but we drove them and whipped them so that they were glad to get back. We have perfect confidence in our ultimate success, but 'tis at a most terrible sacrifice. We are tired and exhausted, but our will is inexhaustible. Gen. Lee made an attempt, last night, to break through our lines, but was repulsed and driven back with slaughter."[49]

There had been little rest on June 2, but in the evening the division again got ready to move. The next day, June 3, would bring another fight with the Rebels, this time at a place referred to in the record as Salem Church. Rebel cavalry advanced, trying to capture a supply train passing in the vicinity. Chaplain Boudrye recorded in his journal what Hammond later wrote to his wife. This attack was driven off, but Lt. Colonel Preston, commander of the First Vermont, was killed. It was quiet for a while, and then, "just before dark, a severe attack was made on a portion of our line by Rebel infantry. I never knew Cavalry to keep up a more brisk fire." Again the Spencer carbines had helped win the day.

On June 4, Col. Hammond ordered Boudrye to take the letters the men had written to the rear and pick up any mail that had come for the regiment. Boudrye went to Third Division headquarters and while there he heard or was told — it is unclear in his journal — something General Wilson had said, possibly referring to the fight of the previous day. In his journal, it was recorded thus: "Meanwhile, General Wilson said the 5th N.Y. Cav. was the best Cavalry Regiment in the service and that he would not lose Col. Hammond for any amount of money." And expanding on the point, Boudrye added another record in his journal that he heard at nearly the same time. "A soldier remarked to his fellow the other night, both members of another regiment whom I overheard 'that no man in the Fifth Cavalry New York need ever be ashamed to say he had been in the army.'"[50] Boudrye return with the mail and does not say if he related what he had heard to Hammond or anyone else. Probably, the chaplain was unacquainted with Isaac Gause of the Second Ohio, a regiment riding in the Fifth's brigade. In later years Gause remembered the same period of time, saying: "The Fifth [New York] had the right stuff in them, as they afterwards proved to the satisfaction of all that knew them."[51] The next few days were spent quietly, on picket duty on the right flank of the army.

On the same day the Third Division and the Fifth New York had fought at Salem Church, General Grant had ordered a frontal assault on the entrenched Rebels at Cold Harbor. The attack was a failure, excessively expensive in lives and long regretted by General Grant for ordering it. It was after this bloodletting that Grant decided to move the Army of the Potomac south and across the James River. It was to be another attempt at flanking Lee. But this time the design was to capture the city of Petersburg and cut the railroads coming from the unoccupied South that supplied both Richmond and the

Rebel army. At the same time, Sheridan would take the First and Second Division and ride to the north and west of Richmond, cutting the railroad coming into the Rebel capital from the Shenandoah. Sheridan moved on June 7. On June 11 and 12, he fought Rebel cavalry at Trevilian Station, while Wilson's Third division remained with Grant's forces, covering the army's right flank and screening the move forward to the James River.

The next few days were spent picketing as Grant disengaged from Lee and moved toward the river. On June 11, the First Brigade was called out on a move toward Cold Harbor. At Shady Grove they encountered Rebel infantry. The brigade charged them and drove them back into entrenched positions. "Our boys behaved gallantly in the charge, some of them urging their horses over the fortifications. A few of them never returned." More picketing and screening for the army followed. The division was now slowly moving to the James River. On June 15, another engagement with Rebels was fought at White Oak Swamp, and the Fifth New York lost two killed, eight wounded and four captured.[52]

During the night of June 16–17, the regiment reached Wyanoke Landing on the James. Early on the morning of June 17, at a point about a mile from the landing proper, "we cross the James on the longest pontoon bridge I ever saw. It was a pleasant sight. The river was filled with floating crafts of almost every kind, which lay upon the still waters in great beauty." The regiment then continued in the direction of Petersburg. Finally, the division went into camp near Price George Court House. "The heat today has been exceedingly oppressive and the dust very annoying."[53]

The Union army's crossing of the James River effectively ended Grant's Overland campaign and marks the beginning of the Petersburg campaign. And this campaign would be like the one gone before, trying and taxing the troopers of the Fifth New York to the extreme. Having sent Sheridan with two cavalry divisions raiding to the northwest, it had been the Third Division that had effectively hidden from General Lee the move by the Army of the Potomac to and across the James River. General Lee could only suspect that crossing the river, seizing Petersburg and cutting the rail lines was Grant's intention. The suspicion was confirmed on June 15, when a small Rebel force was just able to hold off the Union's lunge for the city.

The historian of the Union Cavalry has summarized for us what had gone before, and although speaking in terms of the entire Third Division, he might well be quoted here to apply directly to the Fifth New York as it found itself on June 17, 1864:

> As the only body of mounted troops left with the army, the Third Division was kept fully occupied protecting its advance to the James.... After a week of almost

continuous marching, scouting, picketing, and skirmishing in the midsummer heat, the division was exhausted. Wilson had to report of June 17 that for several days he had been without forage and on short rations, that his men had been on duty without a break for three days and nights, and that he needed desperately a short rest, so that he could unsaddle his horses, draw supplies, and allow his men and animals a chance to recover.

Permission was granted.

As bone-tired as he must have been, John Hammond penned a letter home on June 17, written "South Side, James River, Ten miles from Petersburg, Va." This would be his last letter home until after the next episode in the life of the regiment and it gives us an estimate of affairs as he saw them at that moment: "Our division have covered the rear of our army in crossing the Chickahominy and James Rivers," Hammond wrote his wife. "We have had some severe fighting to hold the rebels in check, as they had an idea we were whipped and were going home down the Peninsula, in which idea we encouraged them. We flanked them, and their line of communication for supplies is in our hands.... Our loss, since we crossed the Rapidan, is about fifty-seven thousand; theirs is about the same."[54]

9
Wilson's Raid — 1864

We then drove down the Richmond & Danville R.R. and for 47 miles we burned every foot of the Road, every bridge culvert, Station and storehouse. We left a long track of flames behind us and at night it was one of the most magnificent sights I ever saw.
—Lt. Charles Greenleaf to this parents, July 4, 1864[1]

At 3½ we left this place and traveled. That last bivouac, I will name Gold Pen bivouac, for there I lost my pen, which I have had more than a year in all my wanderings. Just one year ago today at 6 o'clock A.M., I was captured by the Rebels. I thought much upon it. At sundown, we came to a house where I learned that our men were not far away. At 9 o'clock we were halted by Yankee pickets and were soon among our friends! Oh! What a moment of gladness was that to our hearts.
—Chaplain Boudrye, July 5, 1864, on return from Wilson's Raid[2]

"From the beginning of the Wilderness Campaign to the end of the war a year later, Grant's constant desire was to have broken up the railroads from the north, west, and south that kept the people of Richmond and Petersburg alive and brought General Lee the food and supplies he needed to keep fighting."[3] By the evening of June 16 at the latest, the Army of the Potomac had come to rest before Petersburg, a junction where rail lines from the west and south merged and continued on to the Confederate capital. Since the start of the campaign on May 4, the Army of the Potomac had fought three horrific battles and countless skirmishes, marched one hundred miles, and suffered along the way an estimated 50,000 casualties. Grant had little choice after crossing the James River but to invest Petersburg after his initial lunge to capture the city failed. The Confederates' meager forces were just able to hold Grant on the city's outskirts to the east and southeast, saving the railroad lines supplying the city from being cut. Knowing well the exhausted condition

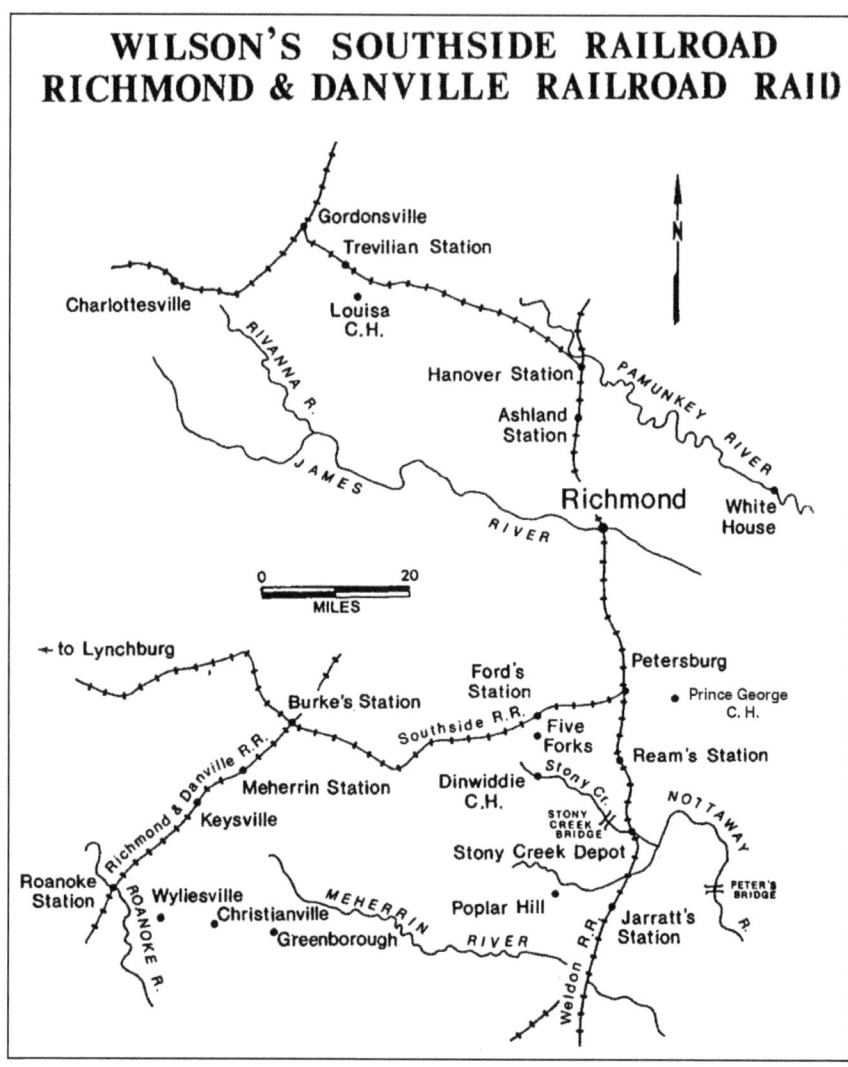

of his force, Grant could do little else as Lee moved quickly to reinforce and defend this vital junction. With the exception of cavalry on both sides, a campaign of movement became static. Trench warfare began, similar to the Western Front of World War I fifty years hence. On the rail lines coming from further south, the Weldon Railroad, and from the west, the Southside Railroad, moved the trains with munitions and rations, all that was between Lee's continued resistance and defeat, and Grant knew it. An attempt to cut these lines was the obvious strategy, and it was to this work that General Wilson and his Third Cavalry Division were assigned. The cavalrymen were to break the rail

9. Wilson's Raid—1864

lines so thoroughly that Lee's forces would surrender just before they starved to death.

In its camps around Prince George Court House after June 17, the Third Division rested as best it could and wrote supply requisitions. Rations, clothing, forage and ammunition were needed badly. "This is the first hour of rest we have had in four days," John Hammond wrote when he had a moment. In his letter dated June 17, he reflects on the campaign he had passed through. "I suppose many at home think we ought to have cleaned out the rebel army before this. It cannot be done but by wearing them out and maiming and killing them. Of course we suffer in like ratio; but there is more of us in the north, so we shall eventually win the day.... If any of the people in the north think we are slow, let them come on; there is room for all."[4]

When he was told of the proposed raid, Wilson asked for another day's preparation, until early on June 22, to get his command ready. The request was granted. Another request was for at least part of General August V. Kautz's small cavalry division from the Army of the James to be included in the command, to add combat power to the strike. This request was also granted. This was a fortunate addition because Kautz, in May, had led two raids against the railroads in the same area where Wilson was headed. Kautz was familiar with the country.[5] Also, in discussion with Meade's headquarters about the raid, Wilson expressed concern about the location of Wade Hampton's cavalry. Hampton was now in command of the Rebel mounted forces after the death of Jeb Stuart. Wilson was assured that Sheridan and the rest of the Corps would keep the Rebel cavalry occupied. At this time the Cavalry Corps commander was beginning his return from his own raid with the First and Second Cavalry Divisions to the northwest of Richmond. Also, Wilson was told that Union infantry would be moved into position to keep open the roads his command would most likely use on returning from the raid. In both instances, Wilson's assurance came from General Meade's chief of staff, General Andrew A. Humphreys. As it turned out, neither of these assurances was fulfilled.

In was in the afternoon, Tuesday, June 21, when General Wilson got the official word from Meade's headquarters. "I received instruction from Major-General Meade ... to move with my division and four regiments of General Kautz against ... railroads for the purpose of destroying them, and to continue my operations till driven from them by a force of the enemy so strong that I could no longer contend with it successfully."[6]

Oppressive heat and humidity had settled over the Army of the Potomac as it invested Petersburg, and the next day, June 22, was the first day of summer. Meade's chief of staff later recalled, "No rain fell from the 3d of June to the 19th of July, a period of forty-seven days. There was no surface water; the springs, the marshes, the ponds, and even streams of some magnitude were dry. The dust was several inches thick upon the roads and bare plains, and the passage of troops or trains over them raised great clouds of fine dust." Cavalrymen riding in their wool tunics and pants would fare no better than the thousands with shovels digging trenches before the city. As the digging went on, so there was activity among the cavalry regiments on the periphery of the army.

There would be two columns. The first was led by Kautz, with his familiarity of the countryside, and the second, the Third Division, now temporarily under the command of Colonel George Chapman, the ranking brigade commander, as Wilson assumed overall command of the two divisions. The orders filtered down, division, brigade, regiment, company, to each man. Everyone in the Fifth New York knew late that afternoon, June 21, if the requisitioning and other activities hadn't already raised suspicions, they were again going into enemy territory. One can picture sergeants, then officers in the Fifth, moving among the troopers, checking equipment, seeing that their Spencer carbines were clean. Blacksmiths looked at the shoes of the horses. Whatever available meat there was in camp roasted over that evening's campfires. Each man had been issued five days' light rations, cooked bacon, hardtack and coffee. Everyone carried 100 rounds of ammunition. The Third Division had an artillery component of twelve guns and Wilson sent six with Kautz. Each column would be followed by a wagon train carrying a little more food and a lot more ammunition. Behind these were at least thirty ambulances with surgeons and medical orderlies.[7]

Chaplain Boudrye rode on the raid and what impressions he wrote are available to us in his journal. However, there was also Roger Hannaford, Quartermaster Sergeant of Co. M of the Second Ohio, part of Colonel McIntosh's First Brigade. After the war Hannaford wrote an extensive account of his experiences and observations during the raid. This material was gathered and edited by cavalry historian Stephen Z. Starr, who used it in his history of Union Cavalry. In that the Second Ohio was in the same brigade as the Fifth New York, Hannaford's words can provide additional color and insight into what was happening to the New Yorkers during the next ten days.

Estimates of the strength of this combined force vary, but not fewer than 5,000 cavalrymen, and possibly as many as 5,700 troopers, went on the raid. Wilson had roughly 3,435 men in his division at the beginning of the Overland Campaign and the Fifth New York counted 979 men on the roaster in April. In the campaign thus far, the Fifth had lost by mid–June approximately 122 men, not counting those dismounted. This is about twelve percent of the regiment's strength as counted in April.[8] General Kautz counted 2,414 horsemen in his command at the beginning of the raid.[9] Even by the standard of another century, Wilson was leading a considerable mounted force, one that could create great havoc if it were not interfered with by a similar mobile force. Roger Hannaford gave his impression dated June 21, when word of the coming raid first circulated. As quoted by Starr, Hannaford recalled: "Every body seemed in a hurry. The surgeons were examining the men & all not fit were being sent back to City Point; there were ... rations to be drawn, also requisitions to be made out for clothing, then drawn and issued. The butchers were killing beeves, the Q[uarter] M[asters] were running around wildly ... broken down horses [were] being condemned & turned over to the Q[uarter] M[asters] and it was plain to be seen some move was to take place."[10]

A cavalry force of this size, riding four abreast on a road, must have stretched for miles. Union cavalrymen by this stage of the war were well aware that maneuver was a key to success, and Wilson allowed for spacing with the Third Division marching behind Kautz a few miles to the rear. If one column was attacked, the other could maneuver in support. Scouts rode out ahead of both columns ranging from a few hundred yards to a mile or more. The last company of the last regiment in both columns was responsible for making certain the Rebels didn't slip into the rear unnoticed and attack.

Moving at a walk, but in the extreme heat and humidity of this Virginia summertime, a horse with a rider would become tired after several hours. During the raid, men in the column frequently had to dismount and walk with their mounts. But still, by the second afternoon into Rebel territory, horses began dying of heat exhaustion. In that afternoon's heat, losing horses at an increasing rate, Wilson sent out parties on either side of the column's route to impress horses from neighborhood farms. This practice would continue as Wilson moved about south central Virginia.[11]

The most common comment written into the record after Wilson returned from the raid concerned the heat. Nearly every unit commander's after-action report stresses the heat and the effect it had on the men. One unit's report said, "The work of these two last days, performed under a burning sun and over hot fire, was extremely exhausting and many of the men have not and never will recover from its effects." A trooper riding with the Eighth New York remembered years later, "Many of the men of the Eighth New York, who lived through the war and to get home, died a few years after, from the hardships of the raid."[12] Certainly the heat was having an effect on the horses. Also, there couldn't have been any significant rain during the week Wilson was going about his business. Dirt roads beneath any significant rain immediately turned to slop troughs as thousands of horses marched on them. Of the heat much is said, but the record speaks not a word about muddy road conditions; hence, dry weather.

Sketch by A.R. Waud of Wilson's Raid, June 1864. The railroad crossties are torn up, stacked and set on fire. The rails are then heated and bent. In foreground two officers take a break with coffee boiled over the fire (Library of Congress).

About ten miles south of Petersburg is Reams Station on the Petersburg and Weldon Railroad. Kautz's troopers arrived there in mid-morning, June 22, and burnt the depot and wood supply and ripped up the track on either side of the station for some distance. It wasn't until 2 P.M. that Wilson and the Third Division got to Reams, with Kautz already moving west, on his way to Ford's Station on the Petersburg and Lynchburg Railroad (called the Southside railroad). It was at Reams Station that the first contact with Rebel scouts was made. The scouts weren't looking for a fight, but trying to determine the size of the cavalry force moving in its territory and where they might be headed next. Chaplain Boudrye recorded the sighting by the Rebels saying only one "bushwacker" was seen firing on the rear of the column.[13]

From Reams the Third Division moved through Dinwiddie Court House and on to the vicinity of Ford's Station. Samuel Gilpin of the Third Indiana wrote of what he remembered as he marched in enemy territory this day. "The 3rd Cavalry Division with command all under Wilson, started early on a raid. Crossed the Petersburg, Weldon and Raleigh R.R. at Reams' Station, which was destroyed, at 11 A.M. where the Enemy shelled us while passing, and following in our rear, fought our Brigade vigorously to 'South Side' R.R. near Dinwiddie C.H. which we reached in the night."[14]

At Dinwiddie, Wilson's division was again probed by Rebels, but they were driven off. Kautz, as reported by Wilson, "had pushed on rapidly to Ford's Station, where it captured two trains of cars with locomotives, burned the depot, water-tank, and woodpiles. The First Brigade of my division was kept employed from the time it reached the [rail]road till late at night in tearing up and burning railroad track, and details from the entire command were kept at the work of destruction till a late hour at night."[15] Chaplain Boudrye, who seems not to have been riding with the regiment proper but with the supply train, nevertheless got to the area of Ford's later in the day and recorded, "The burning of the depot and cars made a lurid light upon the heavens." Finished with Ford's, Kautz's men headed west down the railroad ripping up the track, piling up crossties and setting them on fire. Then the iron rails were laid on the burning ties and heated until they warped. Troopers would sometimes take the heated rails and bend them around trees, increasing the difficulty of their being straightened and reused. Kautz's column didn't stop working until midnight. Then the men collapsed on the ground where they were and slept soundly, the reins of their mounts wrapped about their arms. Before sunrise, Kautz was again moving west along the Southside road, headed in the direction of a rail junction called Burkeville.[16]

During the day, June 23, Wilson's column followed Kautz but was delayed, taking a wrong turn as it marched westward. A Confederate cavalry brigade under Rooney Lee had arrived in the vicinity and shadowed Wilson's force. When the opportunity arose, Lee slipped into the area between Wilson and Kautz. This was the first indication that Sheridan was not occupying all of Hampton's cavalry force. Regaining his bearings, Wilson halted about noon at a rail depot called Blacks and Whites so the column could quickly cook up something to eat. Before leaving they burnt the depot's storage shed. Later that afternoon the Third Division, once again moving and ripping up track as it went, ran into Rooney Lee's men at Nottoway Court House, about four miles east of Burkeville, which Kautz was burning. As Wilson tells the story, "Chapman's [Second] brigade, in advance, attacked them with spirit and drove them some distance. The rebels were re-enforced and in return compelled Chapman to fall back to the railroad. They attacked with great vigor, but were repulsed. Chapman was then re-enforced by the Fifth New York [from First Brigade], but it being by that time quite dark, and the troops fatigued by their labor and marching, I determined not to renew the engagement till I could hear from General Kautz. The rebels having been severely handled by Chapman's brigade remained quiet during the evening and night."¹⁷ "We had quite a number wounded who we bring along with us in our ambulance train. Only three wounded in my Regiment that I know of," Boudrye recorded that evening.

It was a bigger fight than Wilson makes it sound in his report. One of the units involved in this action was a sister regiment of the Fifth New York. Major Edmund M. Pope of the Eighth New York reported, "June 23rd was engaged with the enemy on the railroad at Blacks and Whites' suffered a loss of 30 killed and wounded, among whom was Captain Mcnair [sic] killed and Captain James A. Sayles missing, supposed killed. We were engaged in the charge which drove a largely superior force across the railroad, and it is believed that the enemy suffered severely in the fight. We held the ground until morning and withdrew without molestation." The Fifth had two men wounded in this action.¹⁸ The casualties reported by Pope speak volumes about the size and violence of the fight the Fifth New York was called into. The Fifth stayed on the skirmish line throughout the night. And Trooper Gilpin of the Third Indiana also left his impression of June 22 and 23: "Terrible hot weather. Burned two engines and trains at Fords Station. Continued marching towards Burkesville [sic] Junction completely destroying the R.R. as we advanced and burning Stations, Coal and Tobacco houses, etc. Took dinner at Black and White. W.H.F. Lee's Cavalry attacked us near Nottoway C.H. cutting us off from Kautz. A Vigorous fight ensued in which our Brigade lost 90 men killed and wounded. The fight continued during afternoon and night. Bivoucked [sic] in line of Battle."¹⁹

The next day was as hot and humid as the one before. Movement was slow, but the work on the tracks acquired an organized routine. Colonel McIntosh's First Brigade reported that whenever tracks or a depot was encountered, "the men were at once put to work burning the depot, tanks, tracks, trestle-work, and wood in all directions. The men worked cheerfully, and by piling fence rails over the railroad iron lengthwise with the road and burning them the rails warped by expansion and the ties so destroyed as to compel the entire reconstruction of that part of the road."²⁰ It went on like this all day and into the night. While part of the command toiled in the sun, other troopers shot it out with Rebel cavalry that continued to probe and fire at the Yankees.

The Third Division caught up with Kautz at Meherrin Station about ten miles southwest of Burkeville. From there the column continued on in the direction of Keysville, another ten miles to the southwest. There the command rested for the night. From Burkeville to Keysville, approximately twenty miles, everything associated with the railroad was destroyed in a systematic manner. As recalled by Sgt. Hannaford:

Each Regiment was given a certain distance to burn, and when it was finished they would pass on until they again came to the front where another distance would be allotted to them.... It was a most terrible hot day, and carrying fence rails & wood a distance was no desirable work.... After our portion would be finished, we would put fire to the piles ... and march forward through fire & smoke and under a broiling sun a mile to a mile and a half where another [distance of track] would be allotted to us.... A great part of the way we could find no water, and many of the boys began to give out.[21]

The Fifth New York engaged in this work on June 24 and into June 25. It can be safely assumed that the majority of track between Meherrin and Keysville was destroyed, as well as that from the latter station onward to Roanoke Station, in excess of twenty-five miles on the maps of today. According to Col. McIntosh, June 25 "was excessively hot, and the men were completely exhausted by their continued hard work on the railroad.... I detailed the Fifth New York and one regiment from Chapman's brigade (the First Vermont) to complete the destruction of the railroad down to Roanoke Station, where we arrived about 6 P.M." Charles Greenleaf of the Fifth New York, now a second lieutenant in Company B, told his parents after the raid that his men worked on the railroad in this section of Virginia "for 47 miles we burned every foot of the Road, every bridge culvert, Station and storehouse. We left a long track of flames behind us and at night it was one of the most magnificent sights I ever saw. We went to Roanoke Station more than 100 miles from our army."[22]

Roanoke Station was located on the Staunton River, upwards of fifteen miles from Keysville, and Kautz's column rode into the area during the afternoon of June 25. There the Weldon Railroad crossed the river on a long wooden bridge. If the bridge could be burnt, rebuilding it could take the Rebels considerable time. On the south side of the river, two forts situated on a high bank on either side of the track had a clear field of fire across to the open and flat bottomland the railroad embankment crossed to reach the bridge. This bottomland had been planted with wheat that on this day was almost ready to reap. The Rebels on the south side of the river had at least six cannons aimed at the approach to the bridge as well as plenty of local militia and some infantry deployed in rifle pits. Despite the open country that had to be crossed to reach the bridge, Wilson thought the burning of at least part of the structure was a prize worth having and ordered Kautz's command to make the assault and set the bridge on fire. There being no cover, the veteran cavalrymen knew this assault was semi-suicidal. Nevertheless, two assaults were made and the Rebels on the opposite bank repulsed both. According to Sgt. Hannaford, Wilson was held responsible for "many a brave mans life was uselessly lost here." Another trooper in the Second Ohio had by this time reached another opinion about Wilson's leadership during this period. Isaac Gause noted there was a "lack of confidence that prevailed throughout the whole command."[23]

Wilson tried finding a ford both upstream and down from the bridge by which to turn the Rebel position, but there was none. Eventually, he concluded the bridge was "so effectively covered that we could not get closer than seventy-five yards. The place was found to be impregnable." To his credit, Wilson had tried using his own cannons to dislodge the Rebels across the river, but to no avail. Although it was the men commanded by Kautz who suffered most in this action, Wilson had not endeared himself to the men of his division by the way he conducted this action. Wilson reported, "The wheat was so high and the sun so hot that many men fainted.... I decided to give up trying to carry or turn the defenses, and to take the back track as soon after dark as possible." While Wilson focused on the bridge, Rebel horsemen had been harassing the rear of the long column. In his memoirs, Wilson wrote that it was here, trying for the Roanoke Bridge, that he decided that the mission as a whole had been completed and that it was time to get back to his own lines. The command had now, by Wilson's estimate, about two hundred wounded men to care for and transport in the ambulances rolling with the column. Consulting his maps, Wilson decided to head east to a place named Jarrett's Station on the Weldon Railroad. From there he would move north, passing within two miles of Stony Creek Station and then on to his lines. "[W]e silently took the road at midnight, passing noiselessly under the enemy's guns not over four hundred yards away, and pushed on till daylight, when we found ourselves at Wyliesville with no enemy in sight." This was June 26, and by its close the command was well past Wyliesville. June 27 was spent marching north and by noon of the next day the column had crossed the Nottoway River at a place called Double Bridges on its path to Stony Creek.[24]

At the time Wilson turned back toward his lines, he was unaware that more than one detachment of Rebel cavalry had been sent to stop him. Wade Hampton had been ordered down from the Richmond area by Robert E. Lee himself, having previously disengaged his command from contact with Sheridan's mounted divisions. General Lee knew better than anyone what was at stake if the rail lines were permanently severed. Wilson's men were exhausted after days of fighting and wrecking, their horses nearly "play[ed] out," as Hampton's command moved to block any retirement into Union lines. In his report, Wilson wrote what he believed at the time. "Having completed the work assigned to me, under cover of night I withdrew my command.... The enemy no longer pressing upon us."[25] As he stood now, on June 28, to the south of Stony Creek, Wilson was occupying an empty country, with no one about "except negroes from who we learned that the enemy had a small force of infantry at Stony Creek Depot, supported by two small detachments of cavalry.... As the direct road ... [back] to Prince George Court House passes two miles west of Stony Creek Depot ... I sent a small detachment to clear the way for the main column."[26] No doubt Wilson was thinking of making a quick two-mile detour to burn the depot before crossing back within his lines. But by the time Wilson had received and digested this intelligence and had sent forward his "small detachment," the situation had changed. Hampton's cavalry had moved into the area, and if not equal in numbers to Wilson, there were now enough Rebel horsemen to give the Yankees serious trouble.

The action in the vicinity of Stony Creek started in mid-afternoon, June 28, and lasted into the next day. The Fifth New York was in the thick of it from the beginning. The casualty record for the regiment is bracketed for the days June 22 through June 28 and totals three officers and ninety-one men as going missing during that period. This was the largest loss of men in one action that the regiment would sustain during the war. As for the confusing hours of fighting near Stony Creek, the record provides little concerning the numbers involved or the direction the fighting took at a particular point. In the time that passed before reports were written, exact details and actual dispositions within the First Brigade and within the Fifth New York itself must have become clouded with specifics either forgotten or more likely going unrecorded.

Wilson had thought there was only a light force spread around Stony Creek Depot and the road intersection leading to it and he had reacted accordingly, sending a detachment forward to sweep it out of the way. "The advance guard, under Captain Whitaker, of my staff, found the picket posted as I expected ... and by spirited dash drove it toward the depot.... The success had scarcely been reported before the enemy received reenforcements and in turn drove back the advance guard to the head of the Column. Colonel McIntosh hastily dismounted his brigade and attacked the rebels with great spirit, driving them back." Riding near the end of the brigade column, trooper Gause of the Second Ohio remembers: "At three o'clock the sound of battle indicated that the contest was no ordinary skirmish." The odds, building against Wilson over the previous six days, were now fully turned against his command.

During the dismounted attack by McIntosh and the First Brigade, "a few prisoners were taken, from who we learned that the advanced part of Hampton's cavalry had just arrived from Richmond. Although it was night a fierce fight ensued, lasting to nearly 10 o'clock, the enemy making several determined attacks, but gaining no ground. It was at once apparent that the prospect of penetrating their line at this place was by no means flattering and that a new route must be chosen."[27] The Fifth New York had been fighting dismounted, using its Spencer carbines to repel probes by Rebels in at least regimental strength. The fighting spread outward into the fields and woods bordering the intersection, with Wilson on the road coming from the south and the Rebels using the one leading directly to Stony Creek Depot.

The First Vermont, in its history, included the following that might well apply to the New Yorkers who were fighting alongside them:

> In resisting this attack the Vermont Cavalry was dismounted and threw up some slight breastworks in a ploughed field, and held the enemy in check at that point with the help of about sixty men from the Second Ohio. The regiment was then advanced in the darkness, while the artillery was advanced firing canister over the heads of the men.... The worst of the fighting was over before midnight, but throughout the night the enemy would occasionally feel of the line, and fusillades of carbine, and often discharges of artillery, would break out along the lines.[28]

"It was evident, however," Wilson wrote later, "that we were up against a sufficient force to hold both the railroad and the Stony Creek Bridges."

His maps indicated to the general that the best alternative was to move west and then north, back in the general direction of Reams Station, a place he believed would now be occupied by Union infantry. He ordered Kautz's command off, sending it silently on the road leading away from Stony Creek and toward Reams.

> This made it necessary to confront Hampton till daylight, and with intermittent charges and counter charges it was a night of unusual peril and excitement. The enemy, feeling that he had us in his toil, made three successive attacks on our dismounted line nearly a mile long. I lay with my Staff in the edge of a clear field personally watching and directing the defense. Of course, we got no sleep, and when a courier came about daylight with a dispatch from Kautz saying that the road was clear to Reams Station, I withdrew all the men except the rear guard, remounted, and pushed rapidly to the left [west] and north.[29]

The rear guard Wilson left behind was the Second Brigade.

Colonel John B. McIntosh, commanding the First Brigade, reported that his men withdrew first, and the Second Brigade, with Colonel Chapman leading, found "that the enemy had turned his left flank and was on the road in his rear, pushed to the right with that part of his brigade which he could collect together and by a circuitous route rejoined the command with a large part of his brigade near Reams' Station."[30]

"There was a great crowd moving," Boudrye wrote in his journal.

> The Rebels hearing us move made a terrible attack on our pack train, just behind myself and party, where they captured, as is reported, nearly all the 2nd

Brigade ... and a large part of their train.... Moved as rapidly as we could.... Crossed Stony Creek a second time and soon came upon a portion of the road we traveled a week ago today and arrived within 2 miles from Reams Station. It then seemed good to be so near our lines, not more than 9 or 10 miles. But our hopes were soon frustrated. About 12 noon, it became evident that a very superior force was before us.[31]

Meanwhile, the rear guard, fighting a holding action, was in trouble. Major Pope of the Eighth New York reported, "At daylight on the 29th were attacked by a largely superior force of the enemy, and after a brief engagement were flanked and attacked by a direct line in our rear. With great difficulty a large portion of the command regained their horses, many were cut off from horses, and a large number (about 700) are still unheard from, supposed captured. Large number of men were obliged to throw away carbines to enable them to effect escape to their horses. The whole command was badly broken up." One of Major Pope's troopers, Henry Norton, perhaps writing later in a journal, remarked, "Fighting all last night near Stony Creek Station ... and this morning had to get up and dust out to save ourselves from being captured. The rebels came down onto the regiment with a large force and came near taking us all prisoners. They captured a large number of men. The most of us saved ourselves by putting spurs to our horses and scattering around the country, by running our horses and taking cross road."[32] The Second Brigade, less those captured in this fight, caught up with the First Brigade at about noon in the vicinity of Reams Station.[33]

Earlier when Kautz's men approached Reams it was discovered that the area around the station was teeming with Rebel infantry supported by artillery. The Union troops thought to occupy Reams were not there. In fairness, Union infantry had tried during the previous week to move in that direction, but the Rebels repelled the thrust and a second try was not attempted. Shooting between Kautz's command and the Rebels started immediately and continued while Wilson and the First Brigade came up. Trooper Gause of the Second Ohio observed a concerned expression on Kautz's face: "He kept a close watch on the road where the head of Wilson's column must appear." When the First Brigade got the Reams, the Fifth New York joined the fight and suffered its only recorded casualties here, other than those bracketed in the record as being captured. One trooper, Corporal Keyes Davenport of Company L, was killed and three others were wounded in this action.[34]

By early afternoon, Wilson's entire command was in place in a field west of Reams with Kautz's men in contact with the Rebels. What remained of the Third Division's Second Brigade had arrived also, riding away from one fight and into another. Hampton had quickly moved his cavalry to the area and

Wilson saw that he was about to be confronted on three sides by the Rebels. He was faced with a difficult choice: either attack in an attempt to break through to Union lines he knew were to the north, or retreat. Initially, his instinct was to attack, and he ordered the First Brigade to do so, but Colonel McIntosh either talked him out of it or Wilson himself took a closer look at the force in his front and decided against it. For his part, McIntosh reported that he had looked at the terrain and advised Wilson against an attempt at breaking through. Regardless of how Wilson decided to retreat rather than attack, one is reminded of a similar situation nearly one year before, in Pennsylvania, and thinks of what Kilpatrick would have done had he still commanded the Third Division. Wilson would retreat, leading the command first to the west, then south, then east back to the Jarrett's Station vicinity. Then he would move further east and into Union lines by the extreme left flank of the Army of the Potomac, a wide circle on the map that added many miles and two days to the expedition. Wilson gave the orders to get ready. Every man was to take from the supply wagons as much ammunition as he could carry before they were set on fire. The artillery pieces were spiked. Near a small stream, the ambulances were gathered together under the care of the surgeons to become prisoners.[35]

It is at this point that the Third Division became more disorganized than it already was. The Second Brigade led the way in the retreat, but just before the First Brigade could follow, there was an attack on it by Rebel infantry from the west. McIntosh left the Fifth New York and the Second Ohio in place and led the First Connecticut and Second New York in an attempt to check the attack. The attack was stopped by this quick move but the two halves of the brigade were now separated. McIntosh at this point followed Wilson and the Second Brigade on a movement "made in a cloud of suffocating dust, and lasting during the afternoon and night."[36] Meanwhile, the Fifth New York and the Second Ohio remained behind and could do nothing else but follow Kautz and his division in their attempted escape. Thus the route followed by the Fifth New York is different from that of the bulk of the division, the one most cited in histories of this raid.

Kautz later reported that when it was time to move and follow the Third Division, he couldn't, presumably because of enemy action in his front or the attacking Rebels from the west that McIntosh had engaged. He reported later, "Finding that I could not get to the stage road [west], I immediately determined to turn the enemy's left [southern] flank and thus seek to enter our line. This was done with opposition. We crossed the railroad between Reams' Station and Rowanty Bridge and reached our line soon after dark."[37] Kautz understates what he accomplished, and it is left to Sergeant Hannaford of the

9. Wilson's Raid—1864

Second Ohio to relate to us how this escape was executed. Hannaford later wrote:

> The side [on which the Rebels] had not attacked us was very swampy, and any person looking at it would judge it impossible for the cavalry to push themselves through such a tangled, swampy jungle. But it was our only chance.... So in we plunged.... As first we entered it, the[re] sat our old Colonel [Kautz] and not one of our Regiment but felt infinitely better when they understood he was in command; he was sitting [with] leg thrown over his horse's neck, and seemingly as cool as though the situation was perfectly agreeable. He had a pocket map of Virginia spread on his knee, while in his left hand he was holding a mariners compass, and was looking at the sun.... then ... he pointed out the course.[38]

The ride took seven hours, but by 9:30 P.M., Kautz and the Fifth New York were within Union lines, where he immediately reported to General Meade, saying, "This afternoon ... we were surrounded and overpowered." He couldn't report with certainty whether Wilson's division was still intact and retreating or had ceased to be.[39]

It took Wilson until July 1 to get back within Union lines after a trek of 125 miles, to the west, then south, then east, back to the Blackwater River. For days afterward, stragglers from his column continued to wander in, singly

General Kautz's Cavalry returning from Wilson's Raid. Note the solitary black refugee walking with the column (Library of Congress).

or in small groups, mostly on foot. Chaplain Boudrye had been with the wagon train during the retreat from Stony Creek and was now riding with the column. He became separated, he says, from his horse crossing a creek in the quick retreat from Reams, and another horse he acquired soon gave out. By the evening of June 29, he was on foot with two others from the regiment and they decided to try to make their lines together. It wasn't until July 7, after days of wandering generally in a northeasterly direction, sleeping in thickets and avoiding contact with roaming Rebels, that the three men made contact with pickets of the 3rd New Jersey Cavalry and safety. By then the Fifth was in camp at Lighthouse Point on the James River, recovering as best it could. On July 8 Boudrye finally caught up with the command.

As for the retreat from Reams Station, the chaplain noted that the Rebels followed Wilson and the command closely. As Wilson's command moved, they became disorganized to a point where individuals were acting on their own. Crossing Stony Creek on the afternoon of June 29 became a wild scramble to escape capture. "Our men were demoralized. Many had thrown away or lost their arms and all they had.... We were in no shape to resist the foe.... As the enemy approached us, he increased his fire, until every column was broken and each undertook to escape as best it could. And such a sight!"[40]

John Hammond recorded his impressions on July 2 in a long letter home. These are the only known sentences left to history by the commander of the Fifth New York concerning the raid:

> We are encamped on the James River, a few miles below City Point. Arrived here last night from a raid on the Petersburg and Lynchburg, and on the Richmond and Danville Railroads. We have been gone ten days, marching night and day in the most intensely hot sun and dust such as you never saw. We have traveled about three hundred miles; passed through eleven counties, and destroyed effectively about fifty miles of railroad, destroyed depots, two locomotives with trains, a large amount of cotton and tobacco.... We have lost probably a thousand men, two thousand horse, fourteen pieces of artillery, twenty-seven army wagons, fourteen ambulances, and about two hundred and fifty of our wounded were left in the rebels' hands.

After this, Hammond provides a rare glimpse at and impression of the contrabands, or runaway slaves, who increasingly followed the column as it moved through the countryside. "You cannot conceive how they flock into our columns from the first to the last day, of every description, from little babe at the breast in the mother's arms, up to gray-heads."

As for the Fifth New York, he writes, "I never saw men and officers so completely worn out. Some were deranged with want of rest, sleep and food.... Our men for the last three days, when drawn up in line of battle, would drop down and go to sleep, and nothing but beating them severely with a sabre would wake them." And finally, he speaks of the Rebels. "It is said that some of the rebel prisoners taken by us stated that Gen. Lee was determined on the capture of every one of us, he was so terribly incensed at the havoc we had made in his rear. But, thank Heaven, we are back again, and our loss in men may prove much less than I have stated, as many are yet coming in. Sergeant Chillson was wounded, also Corporal Joseph Wooster; both, I think, slightly, as they were able to ride their horses."[41] The next day, July 3, John Hammond was promoted to colonel.

Historians down the years, when they have chosen to speak of Wilson's Raid, have given the operation mixed reviews. One concluded, "A cavalry raid ... tried to cut Richmond's remaining three railroads. Though the Yankees managed to break all three, in these actions many exhausted veterans and inexperienced new troops of the Army of the Potomac performed poorly."[42]

Wilson's own report merely lays out the facts as he knew them and is remarkably free of boasting. He wrote, "During this expedition the command marched 335 miles, 135 between 2 A.M. on the 28th and 2 P.M. of the 31st of June [July 1st]. During this interval of eighty-one [sic] hours the command rested from marching and fighting not to exceed six hours."[43] Colonel McIntosh of the First Brigade added in his report, "They marched by day and night with little rest and little to eat, working under a broiling hot sun destroying railroad, and yet no murmuring was heard."[44]

The Fifth New York, already spoken of by Wilson as one of the best regiments in the army, must have performed well on the raid. Otherwise a professional soldier like Wilson, despite his relative newness as a general officer, would not have mentioned the regiment's commander by name in his report, a special accolade. Wilson said, "Col. Hammond of the Fifth New York ... and many other officers are specially worthy of commendation for their gallantry and uniform good conduct."[45] The phrase "uniform good conduct" in this context can only be taken to mean that the men under Hammond's command performed well.

Later historians evaluating the raid as not fulfilling the hopes of the general who had ordered it perhaps took their cue from General Grant. Writing years later in his memoirs, Grant summarized the matter with a somewhat neutral comment. "Meade sent Wilson's division on a raid to destroy the Weldon and South Side Roads.... Wilson got back not without severe loss, having struck both roads, but the damage done was soon repaired."[46] This is somewhat at variance with what Grant said at the time to Generals Sheridan and Meade, as Wilson's troopers were limping back to their lines. Those later who have written of the raid have often quoted Grant as using the word "disaster" in describing the outcome of the expedition. But in a note written on July 1,

Grant, speaking to Meade, when quoted in full, reveals his true contemporary thinking on the matter. "I regret the disaster," he wrote, "but the work done by Wilson and his cavalry is of great importance. I understand from Kautz's description that it will take the enemy several weeks to repair the damage done the South Side and Danville roads."[47]

Sheridan, Wilson's immediate commander, wrote later in his memoirs that "the benefits derived from this expedition...were considered by General Grant as equivalent for the losses sustained by Wilson's defeat, for the wrecking of the railroads and cars was most complete, occasioning at this time serious embarrassment to the Confederate Government." However, in the same sentence, Sheridan adds his own view of Wilson's performance, saying, "I doubt if all this compensated for the artillery and prisoners that fell into the hands of the enemy in the swamps."[48] Obviously, something was going on under the surface between Sheridan and Wilson at that time, and it was still there years later when Sheridan wrote his *Memoirs*. In all probability it had to do with the assurances Wilson had received from the Army of the Potomac's chief of staff that he would find Union infantry holding open the road(s) he would use to return to the army.

Indeed, in his own memoirs, written long after both Grant's and Sheridan's, and therefore getting in the last word, Wilson devoted an inordinate amount of ink to an elaborate discussion concerning his belief that he would find Union forces and not Confederates in the vicinity of Reams Station. And the weight of evidence in the record seems to support his contention. Attacked on three sides by Rebel infantry and cavalry that June morning, Wilson quickly penned a note and sent it with a staff officer and about forty men from Kautz's division to Meade's headquarters. Somehow, this detachment managed to slip through the fighting and got to Meade in the late morning of June 29. The note — obviously asking for help and quickly — told Meade where he was and what he was up against. This moved Meade to contact Sheridan. He ordered Sheridan, now returned from his Travellian expedition, to head for the fight and extricate Wilson's command. Sheridan later claimed that he moved as soon as he got the word of Wilson's situation. But the contemporary record, ambiguous at best, nevertheless reflects little aggressive movement or any degree of concern by either of the two cavalry divisions under Sheridan's direct command at that moment. Wilson isn't a perfect historical character by any means and was new to combat command, but he was then and afterward justified in thinking that Meade's infantry had essentially let him down by not gaining control of Reams Station during the week he was working behind enemy lines. Perhaps Sheridan thought his troopers too far distant to be of immediate help to Wilson, or his horses too worn down after his own activity in the days just prior to June 29. But one cannot help thinking that Sheridan's force did not move to help with anything like deliberate speed. Only by 7 P.M. on the evening of June 29 did Union infantry from Sixth Corps chase the Rebels out of the Reams area while Sheridan's cavalry was still marching in that direction. Even if he had known that his messenger had gotten through to Union forces, before that help arrived Wilson's command would have had to remain in contact with the Rebels at Reams for upwards of seven hours, in a contest with what he justifiably considered a greatly superior force. He chose a scrambling retreat rather than remaining where he was and facing outright defeat on a field he hadn't chosen.[49]

Be that as it may, all the contemporary records that have come down to us testify that Wilson's men and the Fifth New York performed their duty in regard to the railroads to the letter. Even a neutral summation by Grant, much later in his *Memoirs*, about the cavalry's toil in the sweltering Virginia countryside is certainly better than an evaluation of a lesser degree by someone even further removed from the event. After-the-fact estimates of those who came later must be balanced against contemporary "uniform good conduct" and the numbers cited relating to miles of track destroyed and ancillary buildings burned.

As for the interruption of Confederate supply lines, one can speculate on the precise meaning of Grant's use of the phrase the "damage was soon repaired." In that the Army of the Potomac was invested before Petersburg from the northeast to the southeastern side of the city for the remainder of the year and into the next, "soon repaired" can mean many things. Besides burning stations, auxiliary buildings and sawmills that cut wood for railroad ties and fuel for steam-driven locomotives, Wilson's men destroyed upwards of sixty miles of track, burning the crossties and heating and bending the rails. When he got back, Wilson estimated that it would take forty days to repair that distance of track alone, even if the materials were readily available.

How long did it actually take the Confederates to repair the damage done by Wilson and his raiders? It has been suggested that only days were needed to throw down new tracks and get the trains rolling. This seems an overly optimistic appraisal, however. It assumes that at this stage of the war the Confederates had a ready supply of crossties and rails, enough to cover an estimated sixty miles of roadbed, and a road gang large enough to do the job in mere days. This eventuality is unlikely within the context of the Confederate economy in 1864, and the straightening of thousands of twisted rails, if it could be done at all, would have consumed weeks, not days. In fact, it took the Confederates nine weeks — sixty-three days — to lay new crossties and rails. Only then did the first supply train manage to enter besieged Petersburg.[50] During those nine weeks, Lee was forced to haul supplies by wagon from outlying areas where trains had to stop as repairs slowly went forward. This was a logistical effort much slower and less efficient than if the rail lines had not been cut. Much later, in his memoirs, Wilson summarized correspondence between Confederate leaders concerning the precariousness of supplying General Lee's forces while the railroads remained broken. If quoted correctly by Wilson, the supply situation confronting Lee was near desperate in the immediate aftermath of the expedition. Further, Robert E. Lee, thinking at the time from a strategic perspective, clearly saw that the raid "was the grimmest of all warnings that a superior Federal cavalry force at any time might interrupt and destroy communications on which the very existence of the army depended."[51]

As for the human cost, calculations vary, as they do with the exact number of Union troopers involved. The best estimate comes from the commander. "The loss sustained by the entire command was about 900 men, killed, wounded, and missing. Twelve field guns, 4 mountain howitzers, and 30 wagons and ambulances were abandoned and fell in the enemy's hands," Wilson reported.[52] On July 4, Charles A. Dana of Grant's staff (and also a back-channel informant for Secretary Stanton on matters internal to the army in the field) wrote the secretary in Washington, "I have just come from Wilson's cavalry camp.... Wilson estimates his total loss at from 750 to 1,000 men, including those lost by Kautz's division. Of these some 600 were killed and wounded in fair fighting, of which there was plenty from the beginning.... And he had destroyed all blacksmith shops where the bar might be straightened out ... and all the mills where scantling for sleepers [railroad ties] could be sawed." In his history of the Fifth New York, Chaplain Boudrye details the unit's losses on the raid that included a total of three killed, seven wounded and ninety-four men captured. It is interesting to note that in the engagement at Stony Creek on June 28, where it has been thought the bulk of the ninety-four men were captured, he counts only six going missing on that day. During the fighting at Reams Station the next day, a total of forty-eight are listed as captured. Then, curiously, for June 29, Boudrye counts another twenty-four men captured at Stony Creek. This citation comes after his reporting the numbers at Reams Station. It might be that all the men engaged at Stony Creek on June 28 were not able to withdraw, either because they didn't get the order early on the morning of June 29, or because they were in no position to withdraw at that time and had to surrender. It either case, the regiment sustained its largest number of captured while riding with General Wilson.[53]

In retrospect, it appears that to have thoroughly starved both Petersburg and Lee's army, Grant would have had to totally surround the city, not allowing the Rebels to escape. In July of 1864, Grant simply didn't have the resources in men to do this. The raid by Wilson was the logical alternative.

Confederate Cavalry Commander Wade Hampton had led the Rebel cavalry in the fighting in and around Stony Creek and Reams Station. His report might contain a kernel of accuracy as to Wilson's losses. Hampton had no reason to exaggerate in that the numbers he put in the record are significant from a weakened Confederate perspective. "In the fight ... and during the following day [June 29] the enemy lost quite heavily in killed and wounded. We captured 806 prisoners, together with 127 negroes — slaves. My loss was 2 killed, 18 wounded, and 2 missing."[54] After a thorough reading of the record, and considering the past record of the units involved, Wilson's Raid was a well executed operation, accomplishing precisely what it was designed to do, and was all that could be mounted at the time. Audacious though it was, the cost had been high. Conservatively put, the raid cost fifteen percent of the force engaged (killed, wounded and missing) for a nine-week partial interruption of Confederate supply. For the Fifth New York, in its four-year existence, this operation was the most difficult and costly of the war.

Beyond Sergeant Hannaford and others in the division, General Wilson, despite his short tenure with the Army of the Potomac, had his detractors in the officer corps. He may have been a strict and demanding commander, but it remains something of a mystery why he was so disliked by George Custer. Probably it had to do with rank. Custer had been a brigadier general for over one year at the time of the raid, while Wilson had only been promoted to that rank in the spring. Yet Wilson led a division while Custer still commanded a brigade. Seniority in the army during the Civil War was in many cases a raw nerve among the officer corps. George Custer, an officer destined to become vastly more famous than Wilson for all the wrong reasons, was at this time commanding a brigade in the First Cavalry Division and had known Wilson at West Point. Another of those "boy wonder" generals of this war, and certainly more dashing and flamboyant than Wilson, Custer had also on occasion led his men into tight situations during his year in brigade command, as Wilson had just done. Still, why such animosity between them comes down the years is impossible to explain. Writing to his wife on July 1, and having only second-hand knowledge of the raid, Custer said, "The papers have no doubt informed you of the disgrace brought upon a *portion* of the Cavalry corps by the upstart and imbecile Wilson." Custer implies in the letter that Grant had Wilson promoted to general only because he had been on his staff in the western theater, stating that the new general was in reality "an inexperienced and untrained officer." "But enough of this," Custer writes with disgust. But

Custer wasn't finished. In the next sentence, "You cannot imagine what a blow this humiliation is to our esprit-de-corps, and to the pride each member of the Cavalry falls in our organization ... and now to have this imbecile (in Cavalry), this Court favorite tarnish our fair fame is discouraging to say the least. We of the 1st and 2nd divisions have the consolation of knowing that we were in no way connected with it."[55] Writing when he did, it seems likely Custer didn't know whether Wilson was dead, alive or captured. But in all likelihood he hoped that Wilson was done as a division commander, thus opening a leadership role to be filled by the person he thought most qualified.[56]

There remains one almost forgotten, yet interesting and telling subplot to the raid. Although it is mentioned in diaries and journals some kept at the time, the almost total lack of reference to it in after-action reports of unit commanders illustrates for us the contemporary view of the army at that time regarding slaves, freed or being freed. Perhaps because it had happened everywhere the cavalry had ridden behind Rebel lines, it was no novelty by 1864. Charles A. Dana, in a note to Secretary Stanton while he was waiting for Wilson to finish his complete report, wrote, "Very many contrabands came off with the column. No particulars are yet reported, but the raid seems to have surpassed all others ... in damage inflicted on the enemy."[57]

While Wilson's troopers were moving about the Virginia countryside, slaves living on or near the route of march left their homes, individually and in family groups, and followed the column. No doubt, like those who followed Dahlgren and Kilpatrick the previous March, they thought that by following they might walk into free territory, someplace where they could begin a new life. The Union commanders had made no provision for any such eventuality and made no claim whatsoever to the slaves that freedom was at hand merely by walking behind them. To men like Wilson, his was solely a military mission. Wilson and his men questioned slaves for possible intelligence about Rebel movements in a particular area, but made no allowance or accommodation for a group that grew to a throng as the command moved across the landscape. At points along the route of march it was estimated that upwards of 1,000 slaves attached themselves to the column, either marching with it or following at a distance. Wilson offered no encouragement, no food or direction in getting them over to Union lines.

Indeed, during the confused retreat from Reams Station, it was reported that some runaways captured by Rebel cavalry were murdered and the Union troopers did nothing to protect them. The First Vermont's history recorded the following concerning an incident during the retreat from Reams Station:

9. Wilson's Raid—1864

At the double bridges over the Nottoway, which was reached in the night, a terrible scene took place. Some 1,200 colored fugitives from slavery had accompanied the column. With these were hundreds of dismounted troopers. General Wilson placed a guard at the bridges and allowed no men on foot to pass till the mounted men had crossed. These had not all filed over the bridge when the enemy rode up and opened fire on the helpless mass of unarmed men. The bridge at once became filled with a mass of footmen, black and white, mingled among the horsemen. Many were pushed over its sides, and fell upon the rocks or into the stream below. The enemy shot and sabred the negroes without mercy. Most of them not killed were surrounded and retaken, some 200 only succeeding in crossing the river and keeping up with the cavalry column.[58]

Whether or not an individual soldier thought by mid–1864 that the war was one to free slaves, the Union Army's mission remained the same: to defeat the enemy in the field and thus reunite the seceded states to the Union. In the reports filed throughout the division upon its return, there is no mention of people trailing the column and seeking freedom. This in itself illustrates their contemporary thinking and outlook.[59] Wilson only mentions it years later in his memoirs.

Only the contemporary Southern press, reporting on the raid, speaks of runaways. An exception, also, is Chaplain Boudrye in his journal, a rare instance of heightened observation, yet colored by his innate patriotism. For June 28, and at some point after the fact, he recorded his observations of the people following the command. "The contrabands begin to increase in number," he began.

> Long will they remember this journey. How many points of interest they prescribe, which at times, excited my admiration, at other times, my tears. There were the hapless maidens, very fine in appearance, perfectly destitute of everything, except one and that, the Hope of Liberty. This was the circle of all their thoughts. For this idea the old gray-haired slave, and lame at that, was carrying his grandchild on his arm and on his head by turns. The mother with babe ten days old clinging to her breast, traveled through woods and brisk heat and dust, toward the guiding star. There is no end to the interesting tales they have to tell.

In Sergeant Hannaford's words, in an account written long after the fact, there were so many slaves moving with the column that it formed its own "Negro Brigade," and Wilson sent officers to make them march in cavalry fashion.

And this depopulating of the region through which Wilson moved had its effect, one in addition to the interruption of supply lines. While no officer thought to mention it in his report, Hannaford saw it and made note: "We ... did an immense deal of damage and destroyed large [quantities of] supplies of all sorts.... We passed over that portion of Virginia just as the wheat harvest was or should have been in progress, and by disarranging the labor, most of which followed us, an immense ... loss must have been the result.... it may be said [that] on each side of our line of march for at least twenty miles we stripped the country of its able-bodied labor in its time of utmost need."⁶⁰ The exact number of freedmen who got within Union lines with Wilson's command can never be precisely known.

The South's military leaders reacted to Wilson's railroad raid as they had to others that had gone before. It was a part of war, hopefully to be prevented or defeated, but war nevertheless. On the other hand, the Southern press had a different view of the matter. Charles A. Dana, again writing to Stanton in Washington, related the following:

> The Richmond Examiner of Saturday claims that they have taken 500 prisoners from Wilson's command, including 250 wounded, 16 cannon, and between 500 and 700 negroes of all sizes and sexes, 35 wagons, 33 ambulances. Many of the negroes were dressed in the finery of their masters and mistresses. The captured soldiers were loaded, according to the Examiner, with stolen watches, silverware, and ladies' and children's clothing. The papers argue, in a bitter article two columns long, that they ought not to be treated as prisoners of war, but as bandits and assassins.

That there was thievery committed cannot be denied. John Hammond even refers to it in a letter written on July 17. However, he is careful not to mention names or units, and it is clear that talk on this subject was current at this time and place. He writes, "But this stealing women's clothing, jewelry and a thousand other things, not necessary to the cause, and appropriated by private individuals is most damnable."⁶¹

The Southern press of the time was notorious for spewing flaming rhetoric at Yankee invaders, not to mention occasionally exaggerating a fact or a figure. But whether realizing it or not, Dana was reporting that at least some hundreds of runaways failed to gain what they took to be freedom as Wilson's column moved about. No doubt there was also some appropriation of private property was made by men in the column as it traveled the countryside. Nevertheless, the fact remains that the Union prisoners taken on the raid, whatever the exact number, were treated no differently from others taken in battles or similar raids.

The Fifth New York officially reported that ninety-four men were missing after returning from the raid. If this figure is accurate, the number represents approximately ten per cent of the regiment, based on the sketchy manpower figures cited in its history.⁶² And Wade Hampton was reporting a figure of about 800 prisoners after the raid. Clearly, it might never be known what number of men Wilson lost on the raid, but for the Fifth New York it was the most severe loss it would experience. But what happened to those men of the Fifth New York who were captured? Little is known generally, but one representative case can be detailed, that of Corporal George Lamb of Company L. He was captured during the fighting on June 28 at Stony Creek and eventually shipped to Andersonville, arriving there in mid–July. He never recorded any details of his capture other than the place and date. Either he was fighting, ran out of ammunition and was overrun, or was retreating and somehow captured. Alternatively, Corporal Lamb could have been one of those spoken of by General Kautz, whose words about his own men during the raid could conceivably be applied to some men from the Fifth New York. In his after-action report Kautz noted, "For nine days the men had been constantly in the saddle, or engaged at ... destroying railroads.... The men were so much fatigued that every exertion of the officers was necessary to keep the men awake, even under the fire of the enemy. Many men were captured in consequence of falling asleep by the railroads."[63]

On returning from the raid, the Fifth New York was probably a little better off than the other regiments of the division. They didn't have to scramble for another two days, but got within Union lines that evening, June 29. For the first two weeks of July the regiment rested and no doubt requisitioned clothing, equipment and forage. Chaplain Boudrye reported, "Many of our men were disabled by the raid and have been sent to hospitals, and many dismounted fellows have gone to Camp Stoneman, at Geisboro Point, D.C."[64] The Geisboro Point facility near Washington was the primary distribution point for remounting and equipping cavalrymen in the eastern theater. During this period, there was some light picket duty, but generally the regiment was recovering from the raid. John Hammond wrote home on July 18, "We have been having a long rest, some ten days now, with the exception of doing picket during for three days near what is called Old Church.... There was a little creek near us called Powell's Creek ... the men found that there were a great many fish in the creek, and they caught a great many.... There are a great many large, black snakes in the water, but they being perfectly harmless the men do not mind them at all. We have some real, genuine copperhead snakes here, which we have quite as great a dislike to as have the loyal people of the north for copperhead traitors."[65]

At the end of July, the Army of the Potomac was finishing preparations for what would come to be called the Battle of the Crater. A mine shaft had been excavated by soldiers from the Pennsylvania coalfields from their trenches, beneath no man's land and under the Rebel trenches and fortifications. The end of the tunnel was filled with tons of explosives. The plan was to explode the mine and for infantry to exploit the inevitable break in Rebel lines. A full breakthrough would follow in which the Army of the Potomac would capture

Petersburg and, essentially, finish off Lee's army. The First and Second divisions of Cavalry Corps were sent to a position on the right flank of the army to create a diversion that might be exploited and to move, with infantry, on Richmond if the breakthrough succeeded. On July 29, Wilson and the Third Division moved to the left flank. When the explosion occurred the next day, Wilson was to attack to his front, preventing Rebel reinforcement from that flank moving to support the fighting at what would be the breakthrough point at the crater. "The dawn ushered in with a terrible explosion and cannonade, making the earth tremble beneath our feet," Boudrye recorded on July 30. The division got ready to move forward, but its attack was called off when it was clear that the infantry surge at the crater had become a disastrous failure. On August 1, the Fifth New York marched back to its camp.[66] The next chapter of the regiment history would begin in a few days.

10
Autumn in the Shenandoah — 1864

> My health is not very good I am troubled with a Diherea [sic] have had it some time hope I shall be better soon. We had a great day here yesterday the most part of our Brigade of Cavalry went out on the Berryville and Winchester Pike Road meeting the enemy. About three miles from B'ville driving in their Pickets for about 3 miles and at last Capturing most part of a Regiment one Colonel 2 majors 1st Lewtenants [sic] 9 Second Lts and 148 non commissioned officers and privates.... The Boys returned in great glee they had done the thing so easy and nice and with such small loss.
> — Pvt. Merlin Hopkins, Co. A, to his mother, September 14, 1864[1]

It remains today as beautiful a place as America has to offer. The Shenandoah of 1864 was a valley of well-tended, independent farms, raising a variety of grains, sheep and cattle. Scattered mostly along a macadamized road, the valley pike, its north-south axis, were small towns supporting the surrounding farms. In the late summer of 1864 and unlike the land to the east of the Blue Ridge Mountains, now nearly desolate after three years of marching armies and battles, the Shenandoah had remained relatively untouched by war. It would not remain so after the arrival of General Philip Sheridan and his Army of the Valley. The Fifth New York had operated there in 1862 and there had been plenty of fighting up and down the valley that year, but that fighting had not wrecked the farms or towns except in the immediate area where the actions had occurred. Now the Fifth New York was going there again as part of Sheridan's force, and the Shenandoah would be its home until the end of the war.

Lee had used the valley as a thoroughfare into Maryland and Pennsylvania in both 1862 and 1863, and there had been serious fighting around the town of Winchester as the Confederates moved north towards Gettysburg. But militarily, the valley's strategic importance was its open northern end leading directly to the loyal states above the Potomac and the volume of foodstuffs it could provide Confederate forces under Lee's command. The valley was a granary, a breadbasket for the men resisting General Grant on the far side of the Blue Ridge.

And the Civil War of 1864 was not the war of 1862. By that spring and summer the war had taken the chivalry, the civility of army against army, if it could be called that, out of the military equation. If the war was going to be won and the Union restored, not only must the Rebel armies be defeated but the properties that sustained them — the farms and livestock — had to be denied them, eliminated, as a means of support. As for the will of the people supporting the Rebel cause, this will to resist had to be crushed. Sheridan and the Army of the Valley came to the Shenandoah in August 1864 to accomplish all of the above. The Shenandoah would feed no more of Lee's men and the army inhabiting the valley would be defeated.

The Fifth New York spent the bulk of July 1864 resting and refitting after the arduous weeks of marching and fighting from the Rapidan to Petersburg and the wrecking of the railroads south and west of that city. The horses particularly needed attention, new shoes and goodly amounts of forage, as well as simple rest to allow the animals to gain weight and strength. Every man in the regiment needed new clothes and shoes, while many pistols and carbines had to be requisitioned. There was some picket duty, but basically rest was in order prior to the mine fiasco before Petersburg on July 30.

It had been nearly a month since the Fifth New York limped back from Wilson's Raid. Now, in the first week of August, with the regiment rested and re-equipped as best it could be while in the field, orders came down. With the Third Division, the Fifth New York was to move to another field of the conflict, Virginia's Shenandoah Valley. In mid–June, General Lee had sent General Jubal Early with his infantry corps to the Shenandoah to check the threat posed to the railroad lines there by Union General David Hunter as he moved south in the valley as part of Grant's overall campaign against his opponent's forces. Early accomplished his mission, and Hunter retreated westward into West Virginia, leaving the Shenandoah open to maneuver all the way north to the Potomac. Early quickly took advantage and moved north without serious opposition.

Lee had seen an opportunity to throw his enemy off balance as he contended with Grant in front of Petersburg. By July 6, Early and his command were over the Potomac and in Maryland, near Frederick. On July 9, Early defeated a Union force along Monocacy Creek, thus leaving the way open to Washington. By July 11, Early was standing before the fortifications northwest of the capital, contemplating whether to attack the city. Just in time the Sixth Corps arrived from the Petersburg front to bolster the capital's defense, sent

10. Autumn in the Shenandoah—1864

up by Grant after urgent calls for help by the government. There was probing by Early that developed into moderately serious fighting before the city defenses. This was enough to convince Early not to launch an all-out assault. Instead, he retired, heading back to Virginia.

Meanwhile, Grant decided to establish a strengthened command in the Shenandoah that could deal with Rebel forces there once and for all. Grant was determined to end the valley's role as a Rebel granary and permanently gain control of the region for the Union. The Sixth Corps would be augmented with additional infantry commands and substantial cavalry to accomplish the mission. Grant decided on General Phillip Sheridan as overall commander for this operation that, over the next several months, would become a sub-theater of the war in the east. Sheridan's orders from Grant with regard to Early were simple: he was to "follow him to the death." To help accomplish this, Grant gave him the First and Third Cavalry Divisions from the Petersburg front.

There is confusion concerning when the Fifth New York got the word that it was moving. Boudrye's journal indicates that the regiment was moving towards the City Point embarkation on August 3, and his history says that they got their orders on August 5. General Wilson got the word on August 4 to begin moving toward the transports that would carry the division north. The First Division boarded transports and sailed first. Late on August 5, the Fifth New York along with the rest of the division began loading its horses and equipment. "The embarkation was tedious and laborious. Every horse had to be unsaddled and his pack, saddle and equipment tied into a blanket. It was difficult to get some horses in, as they were unused to going into such dark holes in the hull of a ship. One man could not do the work alone. At length, we got all the horses and forage necessary." The next day the regiment sailed. "After reaching Chesapeake Bay, I saw a school of porpoises, a thing I had never seen before.... Our horses packed tightly, so tightly that many could not be reached for feeding or walking, must suffer terribly. It is quite likely that some will not survive their griefs."[2] Most of the regiment reached Geisboro Point about noon by August 7. Unloaded from the transports, they went into camp. The regiment spent the next few days near Geisboro Point, no doubt trying to secure new horses for those still worn out, remounts for the dismounted, and more new equipment.

Not having mentioned it in his journal at any time prior to August 12, Chaplain Boudrye now admits what appears to be an attempt to transfer out of the Fifth New York. Without explaining any motives, Boudrye committed to his journal, "Today, Colonel Hammond refused recommending me for the position of Post Chaplain, as he does not want to part with me." It might be assumed the "Post" was Geisboro Point, the largest cavalry remount and supply depot in the east. "He said he was much pleased with my labors and did not see how he could spare me. He said that in all things, the interest of the Regiment would be consulted first. He finally said that at some future time, paying deference to Mrs. Boudrye's feelings, he might consent to have me leave the Regiment, if I could in anywise better my condition."[3] The chaplain gives no further explanation, why Mrs. Boudrye is mentioned, or what his "condition" might have been. One is left merely to speculate on what Boudrye was trying to do. In all likelihood he had simply had enough of the cavalry life and his wife wanted him either home or posted to a less dangerous position. But it was not to be; the Regiment, with the rest of the division, was moving later that same day.

"About 9 [P.M.], the whole Division began to pass through Pennsylvania Avenue. I fell in with my Regiment. We marched up river, crossing Chain Bridge and at midnight stopped about 2½ miles on the Pike to Leesburg."[4] In the regiment's history, Boudrye wrote, "We were now to enter upon a field of operations the glory of which would eclipse all that the cavalry had yet accomplished." Stated after the fact, this was not clairvoyance but his accurate conclusion after witnessing events in the Shenandoah over the next months. The Fifth New York, in this period, would reach its highest level of accomplishment.

On August 13, the division was told to escort a colonel carrying dispatches to General Sheridan, who was already in the valley preparing his campaign. The march, obviously quickened because of the dispatch courier, passed through Drainsville and Leesburg, and then through Sincker's Gap that night. There were reports of Mosby and his raiders prowling near the Gap, but the division pushed through without incident. Of the Gap, Boudrye remarked:

> It was near midnight. The moon shone beautifully, gilding the mountain tops, making the groves and woods wear that somber weird appearance which generally fills with awe. This aspect was doubly thrilling in our case, as we expected that from every nook or dark crevice of the rocks would flash the weapon of an enemy.... I cannot describe all my emotions nor the beautiful scenes through which I passed and which passed through me. The scene of the beautiful Shenandoah Valley, filled with the hazy light of the moon, as we looked upon it from the summit of the hill or gap, was perfectly enchanting.

After crossing the Shenandoah River and going through Berryville, the division got within Sheridan's lines in the vicinity of Winchester at about 3 A.M., August 14. The Fifth New York had covered seventy-five miles in twenty-two hours, according to its history.[5]

The dispatch rider reported to Sheridan and the regiment, after resting, rode through Winchester and on to a place the chaplain calls Milltown, but is probably the small community of Millwood, a few miles southeast of Winchester. On August 16, the regiment marched to Berryville, where the division had gone after a scout to Ashby's Gap. During this time Sheridan and the bulk of his army had advanced to the area around Cedar Creek, approximately sixteen miles south of Winchester. But by the next day, Sheridan was falling back toward Winchester, pressed by the Rebel force commanded by General Early. The Fifth New York, along with the division, was covering this retirement. The Fifth New York, picketing at a place called Petticoat Gap, could see the Rebels advancing as it grew dark on August 17.

> [F]rom a high hill near Milltown [Millwood], our artillery opened upon the advancing column of the enemy. In consequence of our line's retreating on the Valley pike, before we could be appraised of the fact, the Rebels entered the town, thus flanking us completely. No time was lost, however, in falling back over the hills, northwest of town, passing through the embankments of Fort Milroy. We rejoined our forces on the plain below, and together we continued retreating toward Summit Point, on a dirt road, east of the pike. About midnight we halted for rest not far from Wadesville.[6]

The advance to Cedar Creek had been Sheridan's first attempt to engage Early and defeat his command. Despite bringing a larger force to the field than his opponent, Sheridan cautiously retired when he encountered the Rebels. The dispatch rider the division had escorted into the valley had brought to Sheridan intelligence from Grant saying that Early had been recently reinforced with two infantry divisions and one of cavalry from the Petersburg front. Hence Sheridan's caution in that if he advanced up the valley, this new force might threaten his rear and supply line. Sheridan and his army retreated and Early followed, skirmishing with them for three days. Early maneuvered his forces for the next several days before retiring himself, going into positions at Winchester. By August 22, Sheridan had moved to Halltown, resting his men and contemplating his next move. Both armies leered at each other over the intervening territory until mid–September as the cavalry picketed, scouted and probed the surrounding countryside.

The Fifth New York took part in engagements on August 23 and 25. The action of August 25 as described by Boudrye involved both cavalry divisions and took place near Kearneysville Station. "Seldom are forces so suddenly and furious engaged. The artillery of both parties was immediately brought into position, and the hills resounded with the rapid discharges of screaming shell and sweeping grape and canister. Before the quick firing of our Spencer, and our swift charges, the enemy's column at first recoiled and gave us a decided advantage over him. But we were at length compelled to retreat before superior numbers, that were lapping around our flanks." The regiment eventually was ordered across the Potomac and into bivouac along Antietam Creek with the rest of the division. Charles Greenleaf, some of whose letters home have been included here and who was now a lieutenant commanding Company A, was one of the five men killed in action on August 25.[7] It was thought by Sheridan that the advance by the Rebels was another crossing of the Potomac for yet another excursion into Maryland, but going only so far, Early retired back in the direction of Winchester.[8] The Rebel threat dissipated as quickly as it had appeared.

By August 28, the Third Division had re-crossed the Potomac, headed toward Charlestown. Boudrye comments on the regiment's arrival in Charlestown, calling it a "very rebellious village." On entering the town the division's band "struck up the air of Old John Brown, and played lustily as they marched through the streets, where but a few years past gathered the chivalry to witness the execution of Old Ossawatomie [sic]."[9] Here Boudrye is referring to the radical abolitionist John Brown, who, after attempting to incite a slave insurrection in 1859, was tried and executed in Charlestown. Osawatomie refers to the anti-slavery settlement in Kansas where Brown lived prior to committing a massacre of pro-slavery settlers in the territory in 1856. "In the ears of the very people who witnessed the execution ... this music must have sounded rather harshly. To us, it was more inspirational."[10] The regiment them moved on to Berryville that day and went into camp.

"Up to this time our work in the valley has been very discouraging. It had been constant marching and fighting, but always retreating." This was how the regiment's history spoke of those weeks in August after first arriving in the Shenandoah. "The Rebels had had things nearly all their own way. However, we had prevented their crossing again into Maryland; and now, for some reason, they were falling back to the line of the Opequan [sic] Creek."[11] This is how Boudrye saw the situation on the ground on August 28, and it wasn't radically different from how Washington and Grant saw it too. Since taking command of operations in the Shenandoah in early August, Sheridan had maneuvered and engaged Early's forces, but nothing decisive had occurred, no victories and no removal of the Rebels from the northern end of the valley.

During these weeks, the Fifth's old nemesis, John Mosby and the guerrillas he led, were frequently and lethally ambushing Union patrols and couriers in the vicinity of Sheridan's army. When they could, these irregulars would capture horses, supplies and weapons. That the war had become something quite different by the late summer of 1864 is evidenced by the intensity and bitterness of the struggle against Mosby and his men in this period; it had become nearly an eye-for-an-eye affair, where prisoners may or may not survive a march into captivity. The enmity between the two sides was so severe that a vengeful and exasperated Sheridan, with encouragement from Grant, ordered that if any of Mosby's men were captured they were to be hanged on the spot. Also, all males thought to be in sympathy with Mosby or capable of bearing arms were to be arrested and sent to Fort McHenry. All the grain and horses in the area surrounding the Union army were to be confiscated in the hope of denying the guerrillas a means of sustaining operations. Probably with Sheridan's approval, General Wilson, on September 5, ordered Captain Theodore Boice of the Fifth New York to his headquarters for "special duty."

In his memoirs Wilson says that he created a unit within the Third Division whose chief mission was reconnaissance. "I detailed Captain Boice, one of my best officers," to command the unit, Wilson wrote, adding that "so long as I remained with the division, [the unit] was used to my entire satisfaction." The choice of Theodore Boice may have stemmed from an exploit the captain reported two days previously. As Wilson notified Cavalry Corps headquarters, while on reconnaissance, "Posting his men to wait his return, he [Captain Boice] approached the camp-fires of the reserve of the Rebel [picket] line near Stephensburg [sic] and listened to the conversation of some of the officers, by which he learned that they were acquainted with our force and expected a battle to-morrow, saying they had three divisions to our two."

With the order out for Boice to report, Wilson then ordered up some men for the captain to command. "Brigade commanders will send in the names of five of the most daring and enterprising men in each regiment to be under the command of Captain Boice for Special Duty. These men will be selected with care and only such will be recommended as can be sure to be a credit to their regiment and the division in every particular." This special duty contingent was referred to as "scouts," and those coming from the Third Division numbered between forty and fifty. As it turned out, these men "were probably the toughest daredevils in the army." When deployed, their job was intelligence gathering, counterintelligence and counterterrorism. They wore Confederate uniforms and some developed Southern accents. When they rode out of Sheridan's lines, they were on their own, and if not killed outright, would be hanged by Mosby if captured. Intelligence seems to have been gathered and the information used to some degree by Sheridan, but the real exploits of the "scouts" can only be guessed at from the scant mention of them either at the time or afterwards.[12] It is interesting that there is no record that Captain Boice ever filed a written report on his unit's activities. Given the level of guerrilla violence at this time, there can be little doubt that the "scouts" from the Third Division paid Mosby sympathizers and the residents of the countryside he controlled back in their own coin and with interest.

One of the most memorable events to take place within the Fifth New York in the year 1864 occurred on August 30. The chaplain wrote of it at length in his journal that evening:

> This morning, unexpectedly and to our great sorrow, Colonel Hammond was also discharged. Before leaving for the front, the Regiment was formed in a hollow square and the Colonel took leave of us. He undertook to speak to us, but was choked by emotion. He rode forward to the officers who were together in front and center, and shook hands with us. He then rode to the rear of us before the men, addressing them a few words, ending with "God Bless You." With three loud cheers for Colonel Hammond proposed by Lt. Col. Bacon, he passed out of the square and left us to weep. There were few dry eyes among the officers. When the Regiment moved out, I cannot say, but I have never felt so badly since I came to the army. I felt as though a great life had gone from me. It seemed as though I could not have it so. But the Colonel told me this morning that his family needed his presence at home and he intended to go directly to them. For this I could give him up — We moved southward.[13]

John Hammond had led the Fifth New York for fifteen months, through Hanover, Gettysburg and the retreat, in the Overland Campaign and on Wilson's Raid, as well as numerous other actions. He had been with the Fifth New York since it came into being, and as a unit the regiment would not have another leader to equal him. He was at the end of his three-year enlistment, and of the exact nature of the family matters so in need of his attention at home, no mention is made in the record. But a remarkable series of documents coincident with his leaving the regiment are there for the reading.

Hammond had submitted his request for mustering out near the end of his enlistment, and General Wilson, commanding the division, could do nothing but regret it. Wilson's endorsement is dated August 30, and was forwarded to Sheridan's Cavalry Corps Commander, General A.T.A. Torbert. "Col. Hammond," Wilson wrote, "is a most valuable and worthy officer and has served with great credit to himself and benefit to the service — but the regiment would be left in the hands of a good officer [Lt. Col. William P. Bacon] should he be mustered out, while the reason urged by Col. Hammond for his leaving service are of so grave a character as to deserve the serious consideration of the major general commanding the department." For his part, Torbert also had to approve Hammond's request, but in doing so said the following: "I am constrained to approve this application under the circumstances but I am pleased to mention from personal observation that he is one of the most accomplished officers I have known in service, and the country can ill afford to lose the services of such an officer at this time."[14]

10. Autumn in the Shenandoah—1864

Whatever the situation within the Hammond family, the colonel left the regiment and went directly to Crown Point, New York. But that doesn't appear to be the end of it. General Wilson, the next day, wrote to Hammond, his words no doubt designed to entice the colonel back to at least the regiment. "I am sorry you took your final farewell from the division without letting me see you again," the general wrote.

> I cannot, however, allow your absence to prevent me sending after you my sincere regrets at losing you, and my best wishes for your prosperity and happiness.
> It is no flattery to say, your loss cannot be repaired in the command except by your return to it, and I must hope for the its sake and *the cause*, that circumstances may so shape themselves as to allow you speedily to rejoin us with increased rank and authority.
> There may be something personal in it, but your absence gives me special pain. Our cause, the country's, needs not only support from stout arms and brave hearts, but that of every pure and moral nature in the land. When one such as yourself leaves the service, there is, therefore, a double loss, with more than the ordinary difficulties to overcome in repairing it. There are plenty of men who wish to advance themselves, but few that are worthy of the places to which they aspire.
> In writing you this letter permit me to assure you the sentiments I express are shared by Gen. Sheridan as well as by every member of my staff.
> With sentiments of the highest regard, I am, Colonel, Very Truly your Friend, J.H. Wilson[15]

General Wilson, dangling a brigadier general's star, didn't entice Hammond back the regiment. But if he had, there can be little doubt, given a combat record three years in length, that Hammond would have received the promotion, probably to brigade command, and deserved it.

Nor was this all. Boudrye, in his history, includes a letter sent to Hammond's hometown newspaper, the *Essex County Republican*. The chaplain says in his history, "Its contents were approved by those who had been the colonel's military companions." It is a long recitation of Hammond's eminent qualities as a leader and clearly came from Boudrye's pen. Publication of the letter may have been the first time the citizens of Essex County and Crown Point had read that their local son "was no wanderer from his men, nor a lover of ease at the expense of duty." Also, his men honored him for this and many other qualities, in part "because in all his promotions he never forgot their wants, nor stood aloof from them."[16] This is high praise for any officer in any war, and in the Civil War an accolade few others were accorded.

Immediately after the formal departure of Colonel Hammond from the regiment, the Fifth New York, with Lt. Col. William Bacon in command, marched to Berryville with the Eighteenth Pennsylvania. The command bivouacked there that night and the next day, August 31. The next day, September 1, Boudrye noted, "We spent the day on status quo. Some of our men who went out foraging, were captured. The 18th Pa. went out on a scout and had a little brush with the Johnnies. At least four (4) men were wounded." One of the men captured on September 1 was John W. Jackson, the Fifth New York's occasional correspondent to the *Wyoming County Mirror*. Jackson was twenty-eight years old and a "veteran volunteer." Born in Fishkill, New York, he had settled in Wyoming County and been a farmer before joining the regiment in 1861. There would be no further letters to the newspaper. Jackson was sent to the prison camp in Salisbury, North Carolina, and died there of disease on January 28, 1865.[17]

The first two weeks of September was more of the same, maneuvering and skirmishing, picketing and more maneuver. Lt. Col. William Bacon now led the Fifth New York. Although General Wilson thought that the regiment would be left in capable hands when Hammond went home, something appears wrong. Bacon had joined the regiment in October 1861 and had served with it since. In his journal, Boudrye for September 12 writes, "This evening, Lt. Col. Bacon received his discharge from service, term of three years being expired. He expects to leave soon." However, the regimental history lists Lt. Col. Bacon as resigning his commission effective September 12. No explanation is given for his short tenure in command. It is doubtful General Wilson would have allowed an officer to assume command with the knowledge that he would be leaving in less than two weeks.

In the same journal entry Boudrye mentions the following: "We were up late, i.e. officers, and made application to Governor Seymour, New York State, to commission Major White a Colonel...."[18] There is no mention of this in the regiment's history. On this same day, September 12, Major Abram H. Krom assumed command of the Fifth New York. Abram Krom had enlisted in August 1861, and recruited a company in Tioga County, New York. He was mustered out of service at the end of his enlistment on October 19. Captain Theodore Boice, now promoted to major, possibly the result of his work with the division's "scouts," would lead the regiment for the next several weeks. Abram Krom led the Fifth New York for only a brief time, but well. The date of his departure, curiously, coincides exactly with the day of the last major action of the Shenandoah campaign, the Battle of Cedar Creek.

Since its arrival in the Shenandoah, the Fifth New York had been in nearly constant motion with what can be described as incidental action along the way. Typical of the kind of work being done during this period is a comment from Henry Norton of the Eighth New York on the events of September

7. "On a reconnoissance [sic] toward White Post and Winchester by the whole Third Division. Got up quite a fight within about four miles of Winchester, upon the west side of the Opequan [sic] creek. Our cavalry were driven back." A few days later, on September 13, would begin a period of extensive campaigning that would last over a month.

"We got orders to be ready to move at 8 with light marching orders," Boudrye wrote that day.

> Our quarters were left standing.... We went down on the Winchester Pike. Struck a few Rebel pickets at Lime Grove Ridge. Drove them rapidly across the Opequan [sic]. Drive and captured everything before us, to within two miles of Winchester, where we surrounded and Captured the 8th S. Carolina Vol., taking their battle flag, their Colonel, and 16 officers and about 150 men. We did this work and returned with our prisoners, losing only one man killed and two or three wounded. All done in eight hours. The 2nd Ohio and 3rd New Jersey did most of the work. Reached camp at 4 o'clock.[19]

In fact, this action was part of an effort by Sheridan to probe the whole of the Rebel line in the vicinity of Winchester. The entire First Brigade, still commanded by John McIntosh, recently promoted brigadier general, was involved in this action. McIntosh had ordered a charge, which crossed a creek and quickly captured the Rebel pickets. The general didn't stop but moved on, breaking through a line of infantry and swallowing up the South Carolina infantry regiment. The Second Ohio and Third New Jersey were sent in on the flanks by McIntosh while he maintained pressure in front with the rest of the brigade. It was the flanking regiments that captured the Rebel battle flag in some woods where the Johnnies attempted to hide it. As was the custom, Corporal Isaac Gause of the Second Ohio was awarded the Medal of Honor for retrieving the flag.[20]

In camp that night the Fifth New York was celebrating. As recorded by the chaplain, the reason for the celebration—not previously mentioned in either the journal or the history—went back to Wilson's Raid. "At Reams Station last June," Boudrye wrote, "we lost or rather left, our battle flag and the order had been that this Brigade should have no flag until it had captured one. Of course today's capture was hailed with loudest applause." For the day, therefore, September 13, General Early lost an infantry regiment and the First Brigade got its flag back. Small as the return of a unit's flag may appear, it was of significance to the men of the Fifth New York. To the nineteenth-century soldier the capture of an enemy flag meant victory. The chaplain noted, "There had been cheering in our camp all the day and throughout the evening.... There was a large gathering of officers and men at our headquarters this evening which engaged in singing. While the airs sung were beautiful and well executed, the sentiment was not always the most prepossessing to a Christian mind. Hence, the singing sounded better from a distance."[21]

There was relative quiet for the next several days, the regiments probing and scouting towards the Winchester area. During this time Sheridan had met with Grant and gotten approval for a major move, an attack on Early in his positions around Winchester that had as its object the destruction of his force. The Battle of Opequon or Winchester, on September 19, 1864, was the result.

Wilson's Third Cavalry Division was to lead the attack along the Berryville Pike in advance of two infantry corps. The pike crossed the Opequon Creek, and in the pre-dawn hours of September 19, the division crossed it unopposed. From there the pike went through Berryville Canyon, a ravine leading to high ground where the Rebels were assumed to be deployed in strength. Because this was the same place that McIntosh had advanced on and captured the regiment of Rebel infantry on September 13, Wilson gave his brigade the lead. The Third Division was to seize a foothold beyond the ravine in advance of the infantry. It was thought the Rebels would have stationed a strong picket force along the road through the ravine and General McIntosh sent the Second and Fifth New York into it, both mounted and dismounted, to clear them out.

But resistance was only encountered at the western end of the ravine. This was a North Carolina infantry regiment positioned behind breastworks and fence rails. The Second and Fifth New York charged into them with Spencer carbines blazing, driving them back several hundred yards before the Rebels were able to turn on them and deliver a stout volley. The Rebels then quickly recovered and counterattacked, headed for the lost entrenchments. "A fierce melee of charge and countercharge ensued, in which both sides put forth their best effort. Every man of the division became sharply engaged and ... few orders were necessary.... we had to hold the captured entrenchments ... till our infantry arrived, and hold them we did."

In other accounts of this action it was mentioned that batteries of horse artillery were engaged from near the western entrance of the ravine. During this action, two more attacks were made and repulsed, one in which General McIntosh was wounded. Then, in a third charge the three regiments, Fifth and Second New York and Eighteenth Pennsylvania, with artillery support, drove the Rebels into a wooded area bordering the pike. It was now about 7 A.M. and infantry and wagons were clogging the narrow road through the ravine, delaying the quick follow up Sheridan had planned after the initial strike with Wilson's cavalry. The North Carolina infantry had put up a stubborn resistance, allowing Early to bring up reinforcements. By the time Union infantry got through the clogged ravine and went forward to press the attack, the Rebels, although driven a considerable distance, now had artillery support. The cannons began dueling.

At some point during these early morning hours, as the infantry formed and prepared to make their assault, the Third Cavalry Division moved to the south, blocking Sensenney Road and any attempted flanking movement by the Rebels. Prior to noon, Sheridan ordered an all-out assault that, delivered in coordination with other attacks to the north and northeast of Winchester, drove Early's command before it. The Fifth New York and the division saw no further action after moving into a blocking position south of the battlefield.[22]

Chaplain Boudrye saw the event of September 19 this way: "[T]he whole force of Infantry and Cavalry and Artillery all moving at 1½ or 2, on the Pike to Winchester." The Third Division was attacking from the east or near the right end of the Rebel line:

> The 2nd N.Y. led the advance, the 5th followed that. At the crossing of the Opequan [sic] River, the Johnnies gave quite a volley from the high hill in front. One bullet struck so near Dr. Armstrong and myself as to splatter sand very freely in our face, while other bullets whizzed too near to be interesting. The command "Charge," the enemy was driven from his strong position. The Regiment moved rapidly up the Pike [Berryville Pike leading to Winchester] and met the Rebs in strong force behind breastworks near woods on a crest of hills. This was the beginning of a great battle. Cavalry skirmished with Infantry all day.... For a time, the enemy's artillery was so accurate and rapid, and his resistance so obstinate, that I feared for the result. But as our infantry poured in rank on rank, and fought as only heroes can, the enemy began to fall back.[23]

Actually, it was McIntosh who led the entire First Brigade in an attack on Rebel breastworks on the crest of a ridge beyond the ravine and pushed them off it. Then, by moving to the left, the Sixth Corps moved forward to the attack while other elements of Sheridan's army were pushing in on Early all across his front.[24] "About 2 P.M., their grand skedaddle commenced, made it a disastrous day for the Johnnies of this army."

Boudrye lamented, "General McIntosh, commanding our Brigade, had his right leg broken, so that amputation below the knee was necessary. This is a great loss to us. In our Regiment, we had fourteen (14) wounded.... We had three or four killed.... Our Regiment made five (5) distinct charges and was at work all day." As the infantry had taken control of the action in this sector of the field, Wilson's followed his orders and led the division on a move south, to block another road running into Winchester. And later, "Toward night, we began the close pursuit of the Johnnies on their right flank. Passing through Kearnstown.... We drove the Rebs not less than Ten (10) miles...."

They left caissons and ambulances burning behind them with many of their dead also falling into our hand."[25]

Wilson's Third Division was trying late that afternoon to move south of Winchester and cut the Valley Pike and, therefore, block the route of retreat for Early's force. Given what the general faced in such a maneuver and the small size of the division, historians generally excuse him for not cutting the pike and, essentially, putting Early in a position where surrender had to be considered. The division faced "desperate resistance" through "ravine, stone fences and rough country," as well as growing darkness. Early's force might have been bottled up and captured if everything had gone as hoped. Instead, now in darkness, there was only some small success. Prior to 10 P.M., the division was "picking up prisoners and capturing his impedimenta." However, the darkness "made it impossible to distinguish friend from foe."

Finally, Wilson ordered the command into bivouac about five miles south of Winchester.[26] It had been a successful day, a long and hard-fought day. The battle of September 19 had been a combined arms attack upon the enemy. The weight and the numbers had favored Sheridan's attack. But the Union cavalry and infantry moved to the attack in a coordinated manner, each element of the force recognizing and fulfilling its role in the overall plan. More than one contemporary realized this almost as soon as the gunsmoke dissipated. This was the way to defeat the enemy, the model for future engagements. The employment of cavalry in battle had evolved considerably since 1861. Officially, the regiment lost four killed, eleven wounded and two missing.

In the darkness, Early's defeated command trudged south on the Valley Pike through Strasburg and on to Fisher's Hill, fully twenty-two miles from Winchester. Fisher's Hill is more ridge than hill and runs east to west across part of the valley to the west of the pike. Here Early positioned his remaining men in prepared breastworks, confident he could hold the position. The next day, September 20, Sheridan's army took up positions before Fisher's Hill as the general closely surveyed the strong defensive position. It took until September 22 for Sheridan to organize his attack, a flanking maneuver on Early's positions from the west while demonstrating in his front. But prior to this, Sheridan had issued orders for the movement of the cavalry divisions of Wilson and Merritt. He could see that if successful in driving Early from Fisher's Hill his retreat south could be blocked by cavalry that had moved down the Luray Valley, crossed one of the gaps in Massanutten Mountain, and re-entered the Shenandoah near New Market, about thirty miles beyond Fisher's Hill. Possibly, if such came to be, Early would then be caught in a vise, between Sheridan's cavalry blocking further retreat and his infantry pursuing him. Early's force would be crushed. On September 21, General Torbert sent two brigades

10. Autumn in the Shenandoah—1864

of Merritt's to join Wilson's division to accomplish the move down the Luray Valley. Early could see this possible movement as well and sent Fitz Lee's cavalry into the Luray Valley to block the Union maneuver there. This done; Early concentrated on defending the Fisher's Hill position.

On September 20, Wilson was already in position to move into the Luray Valley, knowing the Rebels were position to defend it. The next day, before being reinforced by Merritt, Wilson pressed forward. Using early morning fog and the massed bugles of the division blowing the charge, the division spooked the Rebels into withdrawing further south. They retreated to a place called Gooney Run, one of the narrowest sectors of the Luray Valley.[27] "We crossed ... [the North branch of the Shenandoah River] and met the Johnnies just across the South Branch," Boudrye wrote. "They had an admirable position and rifle pits just made, or rather making, for we drove them even from their spades and picks which lay in the trenches when we came up to them."[28]

Boudrye continues:

> We pursued him rapidly through Front Royal, and halted to feed our horses in the corn field beyond the town. At three P.M. we moved up the Luray pike to Ashbury Church [Gooney Run]. This is exceedingly romantic, with the broad, clear river on one side, and the lofty precipitous rocks on the other.
> At the church we halted, and received one of the most fearful shellings, through which we ever passed, from Rebel batteries posted on a high, commanding hill. Several regiments of the brigade broke before this fire, but the Fifth New York received high commendation for standing firm. We built our bivouac fires by the church at night.[29]

Late that day Torbert, with Merritt's brigades, joined Wilson. One of Merrit's brigades was sent on a flanking maneuver on the west side of the South Fork of the Shenandoah, but it was spotted by the Rebels and they retired further down the valley. The next morning, September 23, as Sheridan's army was assaulting Fisher's Hill, Torbert crossed Gooney Run and followed. "We followed them to Milford creek, where we found them strongly entrenched in an impregnable position. All day we skirmished and fought with them. The Fifth New York was engaged till night, when the division fell back, and left us on picket."[30]

When Sheridan heard the next day that his cavalry had been blocked in the Luray Valley, he was irate. Early, defeated and driven from Fisher's Hill, was retreating southward. If the cavalry could only cross over Massanutten Mountain and get to New Market, the campaign might end there. September 23 saw the Union cavalry retired northward in the Luray Valley, abandoning the ground it had won. When it stopped near the Manassas Gap Railroad, it learned of Sheridan's victory of the day before. The announcements of victory "were read to the division, and the air was rent with the vociferous cheering of our men," Boudrye commented. But Torbert, in overall command, knew he had not fulfilled Sheridan's plan. By marching at night, Torbert and the cavalry command returned to Milford.[31]

In his later report, Torbert made the best of it, speaking about the block the Rebels threw at him and hoping no doubt that it might lessen Sheridan's ire. Torbert described the Rebels at Milford on September 22 as having a line "resting on the Shenandoah, which runs so closely under [the] mountain it was impossible to turn it, and their right rested against a big mountain ... their line very short, and the banks of the creek so precipitous it was impossible for the men to get across in order to make a direct attack. In addition to their naturally strong position they were posted behind loophole breastworks, which extended clear across the valley. Not knowing that the army had made an attack at Fisher's Hill, and thinking that the sacrifice would be too great to attack with that knowledge, I concluded to withdraw."[32] This explanation didn't change things with Sheridan, who, even years later, described Torbert's move up the Luray Valley that September as "impotent."[33]

On September 24, the Fifth New York, with the rest of the cavalry command, was back at Milford Creek. The Rebels were gone from the impregnable position that blocked the valley. With Merritt's men leading, the column pressed forward toward the gap in Massanutten Mountain. "They saw few Johnnies until near Luray. There quite a skirmish took place, the Rebs fleeing like sheep. We captured nearly 100 men." The Fifth New York then turned into the gap through the mountain leading to New Market, with the men tried and hungry. But it wasn't until the next day, September 25, that they rode through to New Market. By that time, Early's retreat from Fisher's Hill had already passed New Market. The chaplain seems to have missed the point of the maneuver, getting to New Market at least a day late. In his journal he noted, "About 10, we arrived in the vicinity of New Market where we met our supply trains. This was a blessing we had long sought.... We went into camp in the woods half a mile from town.... Just after dinner, we had 'Boots and Saddles.' Our march was up the valley. We traveled to Harrisonburg where we set up camp about 11 o'clock."[34] Sheridan's plan to crush Early had misfired, and thus the campaign went on.

September 26 saw the Fifth New York and the division continue down the pike to Staunton, arriving at dark, after a march Boudrye says was thirty-one miles, but in reality is closer to twenty. "In Staunton, we captured considerable Rebel ammunition and arms which we destroyed."[35] The regiment was detailed the next day to escort General George Custer, who had been assigned to lead the semi-independent cavalry command that had been led

10. Autumn in the Shenandoah—1864

by General William Averill. There was a small skirmish with Rebels near Mount Meridian on the way to the camp of Custer's new command. That afternoon, while the Fifth was escorting Custer, the Third Division had passed through Fishersville and arrived at Waynesboro, where the train depot was burned and tracks ripped up. Rebel cavalry attacked, drove in the pickets, and forced a withdrawal to Spring Hill at dawn on September 28.[36] The Fifth New York spent the day following the division to Spring Hill via Staunton, a trip that lasted all night.

On September 29, Sheridan began a retrograde movement back the way he had come, having concluded that Early and his force was thoroughly defeated. The Fifth New York was the rear guard as the cavalry and infantry column headed north. Along the route north, horses were now giving out, and a few replacements were appropriated from civilians along the march. At about noon, the cavalry column reached Bridgewater, where part of the Fifth went into camp and part set up a picket. All that morning the Rebels had been snapping at the rear element of the column as it moved north.[37] All of September 30 the regiment remained in camp. It rained all day October 1, and the Fifth stayed in place, resting and attending to the horses.

On September 30, however, a change in command of the Third Division took place. While the Fifth New York had been escorting General Custer to his new command, Sheridan acted on instructions from Grant to send either General Torbert or General Wilson to command part of Sherman's cavalry in the west. Apparently without hesitation, Sheridan chose Wilson for the post. George Custer would now be quickly reassigned from his small cavalry command to take over the Third Division. One can assume that Sheridan was probably relieved to lose the less experienced Wilson. Also, sending Wilson west relieved the potential for conflict between the two young generals resulting from their mutual dislike of each other.

Although nowhere mentioned by Boudrye in his writings, the Third Division had not enjoyed the high level of morale that other cavalry divisions had obtained during the five and a half months Wilson had been in command. The division had failed to gain a "reputation" while under Wilson. The men thought of him as "unlucky," remembering no doubt the second day in the Wilderness and the raid in June on the railroads. In short, the troopers never developed a confidence in Wilson. Writing years later, Wilson's close friend, Charles A. Dana, had considered him at this time to be "thoroughly companionable." But he was impatient. "In consequence he is unpopular among all who like to live with little work. But he has remarkable talents and uncommon executive power, and will be heard from hereafter."

Custer was altogether a different matter. From nearly the moment he assumed the division's leadership, it was "Custer's Division" and would be until the surrender at Appomattox the following April. "The boys liked General Custer," Henry Norton of the Eighth New York recalled, "there was some get up and get to him. He used the saber a great deal, which the boys of the Eighth New York liked."

In defense of Wilson's tenure in command, all Civil War generals made mistakes and suffered casualties, some horrific, but he successfully completed the missions assigned to him. Overall, in a war were thousands were gunned down in attacks in which the slightest accommodation to stealth and/or maneuver might have significantly lessened the work of the gravediggers, James Wilson fares reasonably well. He was certainly not without faults, but he didn't repeat mistakes. His successor was of a more dynamic stripe and led the division well through the remainder of the war. Afterwards, he would lead other cavalry commands until that summer day twelve years hence on the high plains within sight of a meandering stream called the Little Bighorn.[38]

October 7, 1864, Custer leading the Third Division troops during the burning of the Shenandoah that was ordered by General Sheridan (Library of Congress).

James Wilson moved on and, in the western theater, was successful. In the waning days of the war, in March of 1865, he would lead the largest cavalry raid of the Civil War, commanding of 12,000 troopers, against the remaining Confederate industrial infrastructure in Alabama. His opponent in Alabama was the much-heralded General Nathan Bedford Forrest.

The morning of October 2 was quiet, but just past noon the Rebel cavalry again was probing the rear guard as established by the Fifth New York. They threw cannon shells at the regiment before being charged by the New Yorkers and driven off. The regiment stood picket during that night and the next day, eventually being relieved from the duty as rain curtailed activity on both sides.

What was to become known as the "burning" began on orders from Sheridan on October 4. "But I have looked upon the most awful scenes I ever witnessed," Boudrye wrote that evening.

> We then received orders to report to Captain Lee, Provost Marshal of the Division, to destroy the whole country round about, by fire, in retaliation of the murder of Lieut. Meigs, son of Major General Meigs, last night, by citizens of this vicinity. When I learned the work we had to do, I was heartsick! At 3, the work commenced and the black curling smoke rose toward the pure heavens. I pleaded to be relieved from accompanying the regiment, but Major Krom would not release me. Capt. Barker, Co. H, was put under arrest for refusing to go. Flanking columns were sent out into the country, burning everything they found, while the main column passed on the Pike, announcing the terrible news to the panic-stricken people. The horror that prevails cannot be imagined nor described. Two hours were given the villagers to get out of their houses, and the column marched toward Harrisonburg, burning all the buildings as they went, except one, where lay a sick woman.... Such a duty, I hope, our Regiment will never have to perform again. The influence on the Command is very demoralizing.[39]

The chaplain's summary and the reason for the destruction ordered by Sheridan he wrote in his journal are reasonably accurate. The murder of Lt. Meigs had set it off and it was Sheridan, and he alone, who ordered the burning. In his history, Boudrye says that the regiment had orders to burn everything within a three-mile radius of the town of Dayton and the town itself. Sheridan himself ordered a radius of five miles and his reason was that the people responsible for Meigs's murder, he believed, were from the immediate area.[40] The Fifth New York was getting ready to burn Dayton when timely counter-orders arrived from Sheridan telling them not to burn the town. There are indications that many of Sheridan's subordinates thought the burning of private homes was going too far and his orders were eventually modified. But this was after sowing seeds of hatred, if they hadn't been there already, that would remain in the valley for generations.[41]

The Fifth remained in camp the next day, October 5, no doubt relieved not to have to be a part of any further pacification operations. "Had a good bath in the creek," Boudrye wrote.[42] Sheridan ordered the retirement to the north to start again on October 6, and the burning was to continue, but this time only barns and mills, not people's homes. Also, all livestock was to be rounded up and driven along with the troops, to be used as a welcome change in their diet. "The cavalry as it retired was stretched across the Country from the Blue Ridge to the eastern slope of the Alleghanies [sic], with orders to drive off all stock and destroy all supplies at it moved northward."[43] The Shenandoah, long a granary and a source of fresh meat for Lee's forces, would not be such any longer. Sheridan's object, as written into Boudrye's history, "was to prevent the enemy's ever returning to subsist his army on this fruitful country."[44]

Sheridan, on October 7, summed up what he had accomplished. He reported that his command in the Shenandoah had burned 12,000 barns and more than seventy mills and had taken 3,000 sheep, 4,000 head of cattle and many horses. If he knew the number of houses burned, he didn't report it. Sheridan was literally leaving the valley with nothing that could possibly support Lee or the rebellion in the future, not to mention the local inhabitants. This was total war as Sheridan understood it, taking from the people who supported the enemy's forces in the field. Many troopers in the division, and no doubt some in the Fifth New York, either disobeyed the burning orders outright or found a way not to carry them out. The lone expression of disobedience in the record kept by Boudrye was that related to the arrest of Capt. Barker. Acknowledging the clear military necessity of denying the enemy the means to subsist, however, does not lessen the severity of the deed. Sheridan's action remains one of the clearest examples of what the Civil War had become by 1864: a war to a bitter, unconditional end.

And this wasn't all. As the Fifth New York moved north, the Rebels continued to nip at the rear of the withdrawing column. "At Root's Store on the North Shenandoah River, a large force came upon us, before which we were compelled to fall back with some loss in prisoners. This was quite a smart skedaddle. Our Regiment lay on a skirmish line this evening," Boudrye wrote on October 6.[45]

The movement north continued the next day. The Fifth New York was traveling on what some histories call the Mountain Road — also called Back Road — to the west of the Valley Pike. The column was again attacked with the loss of one man killed, along with the capture of forges and ambulances by the Rebels. In addition to the one man killed, officially the Fifth New York had four wounded and four went missing on this day. General Thomas Rosser, the commander of this Rebel cavalry, followed the Third Division and claimed to have captured about fifty prisoners in this action. The next day, October 8, the regiment reached Fisher's Hill and the continual nipping at the rear had gone on all the while the command was moving. That night the regiment was again on picket duty.[46]

By the close of October 8, Sheridan had had enough of the chewing at his rear by Rebel cavalry. In no uncertain terms he ordered General Torbert, the cavalry commander, to do something. In his *Memoirs*, Sheridan phrased the order, in all probability without the colorful language he used at the time, in these terms: "I told Torbert I expected him either to give Rosser a drubbing next morning, or get whipped himself.... I also informed him that I proposed to ride out to Round Top Mountain to see the fight."[47] Thus ordered, Torbert had the word carried to Custer's and Merritt's divisions.

Confederate cavalry by this stage of the war, indeed since its defeats at Yellow Tavern in May and the action at Trevilian Station in June, was becoming a shadow of its former self. Outnumbered in men, its weapons deficient or obsolete and its horses deteriorating and sickly, Rebel mounted formations simply were no longer a match for Federal cavalry in full-scale combat. And any losses they suffered could not be made up. The action ordered by Sheridan on the evening of October 8 would prove this conclusively.

The morning of October 9 saw both Union cavalry divisions attack the trailing Rebel cavalry. The Battle of Tom's Brook was the result. Beginning at 7 A.M., it would continue until after darkness fell on the Shenandoah. The Fifth New York with the division, having been traveling on the Back Road, was assigned to attack across Tom's Brook to the south of Fisher's Hill, while the First Division would strike down the Valley Pike. The Third Division would be attacking the cavalry force led by General Thomas Rosser, a West Point classmate of Custer's. The division's horse artillery was deployed, and fired at the Rebel cavalry that had massed on a hill south of Tom's Brook. This firing had "varying Success" during the morning hours, and then at about noon, the division's new commander, George Custer, ordered the charge.

And Custer led the charge personally, riding with the Fifth New York. In his history, Boudrye says Custer "ordered the bugles of the entire line to sound the *advance*, and leading the Fifth New York in person, he made a dash on the enemy's central position.... Our color bearer, Sergeant Buckly, Company C, displayed his usual bravery, bearing our flag close by the side, and, at times, ahead of the general's. With a shout and a dash, with thundering artillery and gleaming sabres, with trusty carbines and Yankee grit, our boys scattered the enemy before them."[48] Of course, there was much more to it than that. But the scattering of the Confederate cavalry formations that attempted to resist the attack cannot be doubted. Three other regiments from the First Brigade made the charge with the Fifth New York: the Third New Jersey, Eighteenth Pennsylvania and Second Ohio. After they crossed Tom's Brook the fight was joined, and at one point the brigade was forced back across the brook. But Custer had kept the artillery firing and eventually got flanking support from a brigade from the First Division that crashed into the Rebel right flank. This second push couldn't be stopped. The Fifth New York attacked in the center, and meeting stern resistance, Custer moved the Eighteenth Pennsylvania and two regiments of the Second Brigade on a flanking maneuver to the Rebel right.

There is an account of this action as seen from the Second Brigade's First Vermont that is less stylish than the chaplain's but gives us a slightly better picture. That regiment's historian says the following:

> As soon as the brigades were fairly in position, Custer attacked in one sweeping charge. It was first a walk to the skirmish line, then a trot, then a gallop, then a wild rush of shouting troopers with waving sabres and frantic horses. The charge was so sudden and rapid that the enemy's fire of artillery and small arms took little effect, and before Rosser knew what had happened, his position was carried. Its supports broke before they were fairly struck, and the entire force fell back half a mile to a belt of woods. Here Rosser re-formed his line and his battery opened and soon Custer's advance fell back before a counter-charge made by Rosser, which, however, was checked by Custer's artillery. Custer then re-formed his division; and in a second charge swept all before him, taking all of Rosser's guns, caissons, wagons and ambulances, and following him on a run, for twelve miles, to Columbia furnace.[49]

This movement, described by the First Vermont, turned the action into a rout, as the Rebels broke and began riding off in any direction where there were not blue horsemen. "The enemy seeing his flank turned and his retreat cut off broke in the utmost confusion and sought safety in headlong flight," Custer reported. "The pursuit was kept up at a gallop by the entire command for a distance of nearly two miles."[50] "The country south of Tom's Brook was open, a magnificent place for a cavalry fight [with] room to deploy, smooth ground to ride on, and the rail fences [gone]."[51] The two Union divisions outnumbered the Rebels about three to two, but the action continued for about two hours, with separate, small-unit actions occurring in every direction. During the running retreat, the Rebel groups would occasionally turn and offer resistance, but there were too many Yankees riding down on them.

According to Boudrye, who had to have received eyewitness accounts within hours, the Fifth New York chased the Rebels to Columbia Furnace, several miles south along Back Road. "We pursued him [the enemy], capturing about 100 prisoners, the whole train, which they did not burn, and six pieces of artillery, which they had no time to spike.... General Roisser's [*sic*] private valise with his best uniform and private papers were captured by a Sargt. of our Regiment. General Custer awards much praise to the Old Fifth for the valiant deeds they performed."[52] This pursuit became known in the Union Cavalry thereafter as the Woodstock Races and covered a distance, it was said at the time, of about twenty miles from the Fifth New York's starting point that morning.

Not written in the reports of this action, but reported years later in the history of the Third Indiana Cavalry, was an interesting note. The six guns captured during Rosser's retreat were the same guns that Wilson had spiked and then abandoned before his hasty exit from Reams Station on June 29. In the intervening weeks the Rebels had put them in working order and transferred them to the Valley for use against their former owners.[53]

Over on the Valley Pike, the pursuit by the bulk of Merritt's division continued all the way to Edinburg.[54] A like number of prisoners, wheeled vehicles and guns and caissons, were captured in this route. "Our Division lost only about ½ dozen killed," Boudrye recorded, "28 wounded and perhaps one dozen prisoners.... The Rebs had many killed and wounded. After our days work, we returned to the north of Tom's Brook where we camped for the night." The Official Record of casualties within the Fifth New York in this action was listed as four wounded and one missing.[55] The Fifth New York, deservedly, remained in camp all the next day. And General Sheridan was pleased. He had watched the action from atop Round Top, probably, until the chase was over the horizon.

The next move came on October 11, with the Fifth again covering the rear of Sheridan's army, as it continued the retrograde to the north. "Our Regiment brought up the rear of the entire army," Boudrye wrote, "no enemy appeared. We went through Strasburg and pitched in the field not far from Cedar Creek, on the north side." October 13 saw the Fifth New York sent on picket to reinforce another unit that had skirmished with probing Rebels. The next day the regiment scouted south to Lebanon Church, skirmishing with picketing Rebels. They returned by that evening, apparently without any intelligence of Rebel forces again moving forward. They were on picket again on October 15.[56] The final engagement of the campaign was only a few days in the future.

11
Cedar Creek —1864

> On the 19th Sept ... we gave the Rebs a sound thrashing; on the 19th Oct ... we routed them as never a large army was routed. "No refuge could save, the hireling and slave, From the terror of flight or the glower of the grave." The number 19 has become with us a symbol of good, at least of victory. Tonight, our men were much scattered, busy taking care of the spoils they had taken.
> — Chaplain Boudrye in his journal, October 19, 1864[1]

Sheridan left his army on October 15, traveling to Washington by train for meetings with Secretary of War Stanton. His army was in camp on the north side of Cedar Creek with the Fifth New York doing picket duty along the western flank. Despite defeats at Winchester and Fisher's Hill, the retreat far down the valley and the loss of a large body of cavalry in the action at Tom's Brook, the fight had not entirely gone out of General Early. In the days after Tom's Brook, Early led his force forward, his infantry re-occupying the old Fisher's Hill line. There he began fashioning a plan for a renewed attack, believing he still had a chance to push the Yankees out of the valley. From an observation post on the northern end of Massanuttin Mountain, on October 17, the entire Federal army could be seen in all its dispositions north of Cedar Creek. A surprise attack on the Union camps might not merely succeed, but could start a domino-like event that possibly would end with the Federals at or over the Potomac River. Also, it had been reported to Early that a Yankee cavalry division was camped in an isolated position along Back Road to the west of the Union army. There was a possibility that what remained of his cavalry could "gobble it up," a sliver of revenge for Tom's Brook.

Early sent General Rosser and his command to do just that. The Rebel cavalry marched there on the night of October 16 and were in position at dawn to attack the supposed Yankee camp at first light. In the predawn darkness Rosser's men advanced and found what had been a divisional camp empty,

11. *Cedar Creek—1864* 243

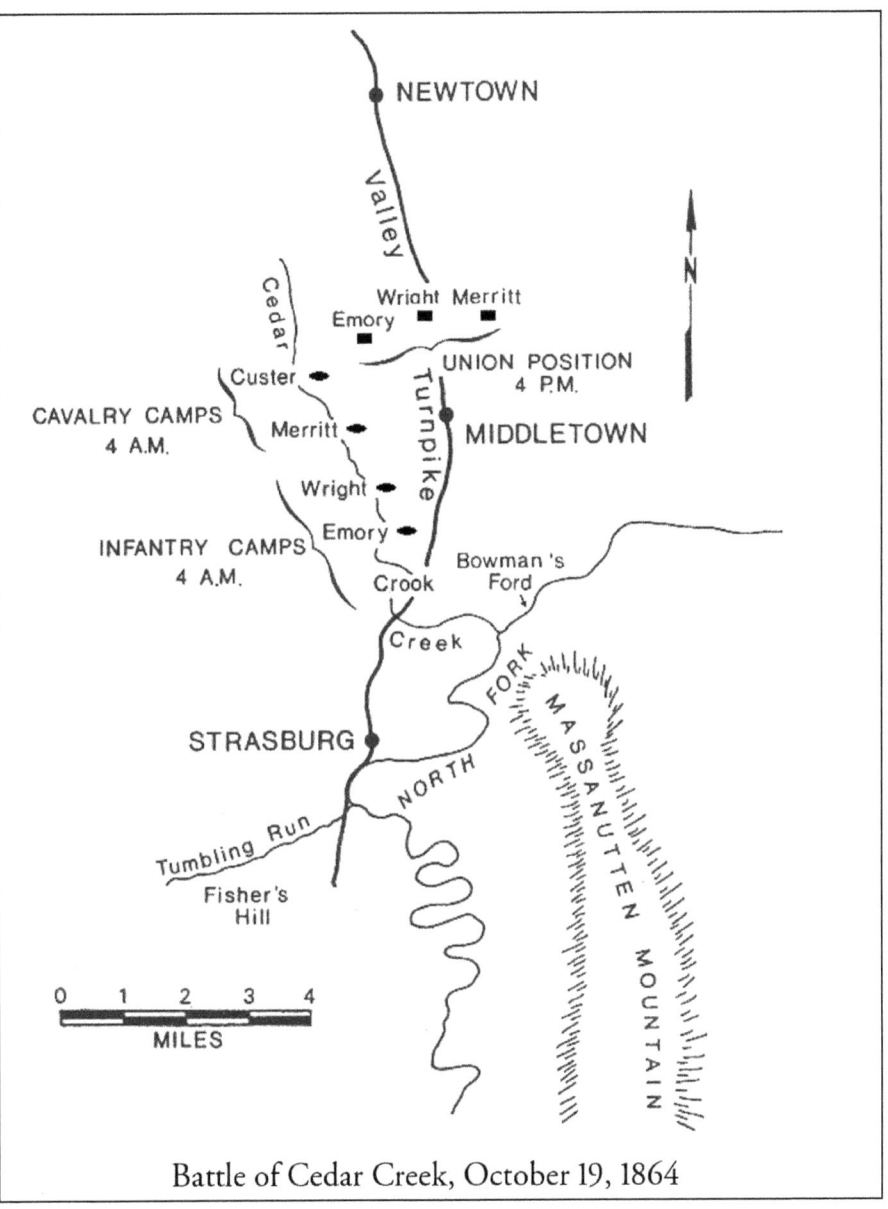

Battle of Cedar Creek, October 19, 1864

except for the pickets and the picket reserve of the First Connecticut. A quick and confused action followed, in which the commander of the picket, a major, and twenty-five troopers from the Connecticut outfit were captured.[2] Boudrye wrote in his journal for October 17, "This morning about 3, one reserve of our pickets, 1st Conn. were grabbed by a large Rebel force. Among them was

Major Marcy, Commander of the Regiment and about 40 men.... One prisoner who our boys captured, reported that the main object of the expedition was to gobble up the 5th N.Y. Cavalry. They owe us a great grudge and will do us all injury in their power."[3]

The Fifth New York spent October 18 in camp as Early, undetected, prepared to advance in the coming darkness and attack at dawn the next day. The Fifth New York, with the rest of the division, was camped on the extreme right flank of the army during the night of October 18–19, with the infantry corps echeloned along the creek to the east. The New Yorkers were at the farthest point removed from where the planned Rebel infantry blow was to fall. As envisioned, Early's attack would hit the easternmost infantry corps and fold it back against the next in line. Then his troops would push both back into the third. The surprise attack, it was hoped, would allow Early's men to drive the Yankee soldiers from the field and start them on the journey north. If in their haste to withdraw the Yankees left behind supplies and equipment, so much the better. After the burning and destruction Sheridan had visited on the Valley in the past weeks, there was certainly a degree of revenge inherent in the plan. It was a complex and daring plan, but for Early the situation demanded that it be tried, despite his depleted force and given the ever-weakening state of the Confederacy in general at that moment.

"It was a perfect night, bright and clear. The moon was full, the air crisp and transparent. A more serene and peaceful scene could not be imagined," wrote a Michigan cavalry officer in the Third Division. In the moonlight Early's men threaded their way forward, fording the north Fork of the Shenandoah at Bowman's Ford, and in the morning fog, predictable over the river at this time of year, formed to attack. "Every facet of this exceptionally bold and complex plan — without question one of the most intricate plans of the Civil War — worked to perfection."[4] On the Union right flank, where the cavalry divisions were positioned, General Rosser's men demonstrated with a probing attack on the Union pickets as dawn approached. But no determined attack seemed to be coming from that direction. During the long night, "a heavy fog had by this time settled down upon the valley," the Michigan officer later remembered. Then the real attack started. "The first streaks of dawn began to appear, and it soon became evident that the cavalry attack upon the right flank was but a faint [sic] and the real danger was in another quarter. Far away to the left, for some time, volleys of musketry had been heard. With the roll of musketry was intermingled, at intervals, the boom of cannon."

When the Rebels attacked, coming out of the fog, they hit the Eighth Corps camped on the left of the main Cedar Creek line. Most of the Yankees were still sleeping in their tents. In minutes an entire Union infantry corps essentially dissolved, and those not killed, wounded or captured were running northwest into the slowly forming lines of the next Union corps. This was the Nineteenth Corps, and it quickly stood to defend itself. However, the rush of the retreating Eighth Corps men, the speed of the Rebel advance, and the confusion in the dense fog caused some units to break, with the inevitable cascading effect on the corps as a whole. The third corps in echelon was the Sixth Corps, and it had some minutes to prepare for the onslaught racing at them out of the fog. The Sixth Corps' left flank had been compromised by the speed of the Rebel advance, forcing it to engage in a fighting withdrawal to the northwest from where it had been camped. This withdrawal didn't stop until they were beyond Middletown, the next town to the north on the Valley Pike. Eighteen pieces of artillery had been lost, left where they stood in the infantry camps, as well as untold numbers of small arms. According to Boudrye, it was "nine o'clock, and our lines had been driven back about three miles, and disaster had followed every step. A deep gloom had settled upon the army."[5]

Many of the Union soldiers had thought that the year 1864 would see the end to the war. At least it was thought so in the Virginia springtime now four months in the past. Now it was October, the beginning of a perfect Indian summer day as the sun dispersed the fog that had risen in the night. And it was October, the fourth October of the war, and here were the Rebels again, winning again. Would it ever stop? So far, it was a spectacular victory for Early and his weary command and it was still only mid-morning. There was still plenty of daylight left to finish the job. The scene revealed that some Rebel units were still pressing the Yankees toward Middletown. But the Rebel ranks were somewhat thinned by stragglers who were now roaming about in the three abandoned infantry camps along Cedar Creek, picking up rations or rummaging among the tents for loot. This scavenging was seriously weakening the offensive punch the Rebels could bring to bear on the nearly defeated Yankees.[6] It was now about 10 A.M. For reasons known only to General Early — but not to us even after a century and a half of analysis — the crushing advance turned into an inexplicable lull that could only favor the Federal troops, retreating northward on the pike, or as they formed confused defensive lines near Middletown. One of his Early's subordinates, General John Bell Hood, suggested to Early about this time that he renew the attack so that the victory would be utterly complete. "No use in that," Early is reported as responding, "they will go directly." But they didn't go.[7]

It had been 4 A.M. when the cavalry pickets along Cedar Creek at the extreme northwestern end of the Federal line were probed by Rebel cavalry under Rosser. Soon after came the sound of gunfire from the main Rebel attack to the east. Both Union cavalry divisions were soon to horse, but nothing happened. A few units were sent to stem the flood of Union infantrymen running out of the fog. But it wasn't until sometime between nine and ten that morning that General Torbert was ordered to move his cavalry to what was then the left flank of a retreating army, to a place north of Middletown across the Valley Pike. In Custer's opinion, formed after the action, this move saved the army from being flanked by the Rebels and thoroughly defeated. Custer, of course, was unaware of Early's prediction at about the same time that the Yankees would "go directly."

While Early's surprise attack was rolling forward, Sheridan, who had spent the night in Winchester on his return from Washington, heard the cannon firing early that morning. At once he started galloping down the pike toward his army. Along the pike he and his escort were soon meeting Yankee stragglers from the battle and began urging them back to the fight with oaths that were both "in character but also more in keeping with the time-honored cavalry standard of rhetoric."[8] It was most likely about 10:30 A.M. when Sheridan arrived at the Union line north of Middletown. By this time the flow of soldier-refugees had been stopped, and his army had straightened itself into a semblance of a position, preparing to receive a renewed Rebel attack. But by his presence, his riding through the ranks, showing himself on the field and ready to lead them, Sheridan elevated the army's morale to a point where it could go over to the offensive. The inexplicable stall by Early coupled with Sheridan's arrival had, therefore, swung the initiative in the engagement to the Union. At this time, the Fifth New York's history says, "loud cheering in the rear, taken up by centre and front, announced that the hero of the Shenandoah had arrived upon the field of carnage. His black charger, reeking with foam, and covered with dust, had brought him in quick haste from Winchester."[9]

Sheridan ordered the Third Division back to the right flank and Merritt's division to the left for the counterattack he was organizing. Boudrye, in his history, quotes Sheridan as saying, "Custer, I can trust you with the work of driving back this force," meaning any Rebel cavalry that might be encountered on the right flank. Custer in his report says that at about 11 A.M. he was ordered to the flank to "take charge of affairs on the right."[10] Although Boudrye doesn't mention what reply Custer gave to Sheridan, one can only assume it was an enthusiastic affirmative. Before noon the division had deployed on the right flank and shortly thereafter elements of Rosser's cavalry attacked. This attack was beaten off by three regiments from the First Brigade and thereafter settled into scattered carbine fire supported by some artillery.

The next few hours passed as Sheridan organized his infantry for a counterattack. At 4 P.M. Custer could see Sheridan's advancing infantry corps to

11. Cedar Creek—1864

his left. His choice was either to renew the attack on the Rebel cavalry to his front with the division, or charge along the right flank of the advancing infantry and capture the bridge over Cedar Creek in an effort to cut the Rebels' line of retreat. He chose to leave three regiments to deal with Rosser and turned the remainder of the division toward the bridge. They went forward. As they galloped, the Rebels became aware of what Custer was attempting. Custer later reported how "the enemy, already broken, now gave way in the utmost confusion."[11] By the time Custer approached the bridge over Cedar Creek he could see it was already in the possession of horsemen from Merritt's division and, indeed, some were already across creating havoc among rear elements of the Rebel force.

Custer, leading the Fifth New York and First Vermont, moved up stream and forded the creek. From there they charged into an infantry formation that was trying to stem the flood of Yankee cavalrymen. "The bugles again sounded the charge, and with a cheer rode straight for the foe. It was a maddening time. The Rebels delivered one fierce volley, and the next instant the pitiless sabres of our men and the iron heels of the horses were doing their work. For three miles the charge continued, the bloody ground, the broken muskets, the dead and wounded, told its ferocity."[12] With pistols and sabers the Fifth New York rode among the enemy, firing and slashing.

The account written by Custer of the action beyond Cedar Creek says,

> The Fifth New York was moving on the left and near the pike, the First Vermont on a parallel line and to the left. As soon as the nature of the ground was favorable both regiments quickened the gait to a trot, and when within short pistol range of the enemy's line charging simultaneously upon his front and flank. Hearing the charge sounded through our bugles the enemy only stood long

Custer leading the charge at Cedar Creek, October 19, 1864 (Library of Congress).

enough to deliver one volley, then, casting away his arms, attempted to escape under cover of darkness. This was the last attempt the enemy made to offer organized resistance. That which hitherto, on our part, had been a pursuit after a broken and routed army now resolved itself into an excited chase after a panic stricken, uncontrollable mob.... prisoners were taken by hundreds, entire companies threw down their arms, and appeared glad when summoned to surrender."[13]

"From that point well into the night his [Custer's] men and Merritt's enjoyed a cavalrymen's dream, a grand and glorious chase after the enemy, who were fleeing south along the Valley Turnpike."[14] They rode among the teams pulling wagons and shot the horses while ordering Rebels to drop their weapons and surrender.

A mile or more down the pike, Custer halted but ordered the Fifth New York and the First Vermont to continue on while he organized the trailing regiments of the division. The Fifth New York went through Strasburg and on to Fisher's Hill, capturing everything it encountered. "The darkness of the night was intense, and was only relieved here and there by the light of a burning wagon or ambulance, to which the affrighted enemy in his despair had applied the torch."[15] "Before the pursuit ceased, halted by exhaustion and the darkness, sixteen hundred prisoners had been taken, the eighteen guns captured by Confederates in the morning had been recaptured together with twenty-five to thirty of Early's guns, and nearly all his transport was smashed, burned, or in Sheridan's possession."[16] Those Rebels not captured slipped away in the dark and marched thirty miles south to New Market, getting there the next day. Sheridan wrote to Grant, "For ten miles on the line of retreat the road and country was covered with small arms thrown away by the flying rebels.... Forty-eight pieces of captured artillery are now at my headquarters. I think not less than 300 wagons and ambulances were either captured or destroyed." One trooper from the Fifth New York claimed to have run through two teamsters handling a Rebel baggage wagon and then turned it around and drove back to camp.[17]

Merritt's cavalry had charged on the left and crossed Cedar Creek, where they "pursued the enemy up to the foot of Fisher's Hill. Had one half hour more of daylight been left, it is probable that but few of Early's men would have escaped, but knowing the country, and aided by darkness, they broke for the fields and woods, and though our cavalry were miles ahead of them, thousands got away and joined Early in his lines of Fisher's Hills during the night. Their artillery was captured all along the road, across Cedar Creek, as well as ambulances and wagons in great numbers."[18]

As for the Fifth New York, Boudrye included the following in its history:

11. Cedar Creek—1864   249

Received from the Fifth New York Cavalry, commanded by Major A.H. Krom, twenty-two pieces of artillery, fourteen caissons, one battery wagon, seventeen army wagons, six spring wagons and ambulances, eighty-three set of artillery harness, seventy-five sets of wagon harness, ninety-eight horses, sixty-seven mules, captured in action in the battle of the 19th of October, 1864 on Cedar Creek, Va. A.C.M. Pennington, Jr. Colonel Commanding Brigade[19]

Not mentioned in the above receipt were two battle flags captured by the regiment in this action. Sergeant David S. Scofield, regimental quartermaster, captured the flag of the 13th Virginia Infantry, and Corporal John Welch of Company D recaptured the flag of the 15th New Jersey Infantry that the Rebels had taken that morning. Both Scofield and Welch were awarded the Medal of Honor.

In the days following the battle, Custer and officers of Merritt's cavalry division argued over who had captured all those pieces of artillery. On the face of it, Custer made a good case for the credit going to his division. Also, he had the receipt signed by his brigade commander, Colonel Pennington, specifically noting the Fifth New York's contribution to the mass of Confederate materiel the regiment brought back from beyond Cedar Creek.

When the grand pursuit stopped at some point during the night of October 19–20, the men of the Fifth New York trudged back to the camp they had left that morning. After whatever sleep the troopers could manage, after exalted talk of the great victory won that day, the regiment was ordered on a reconnaissance late the next morning. "We went to the high hill beyond Tom's Creek finding no enemy and returned."[20] What was left to General Early as an organized force was retreating much further south along the Valley Pike.

The Fifth New York spent the next two days on picket duty along Cedar Creek. It was at this time that Major Krom turned over command of the regiment to Theodore Boice, now promoted to major, most likely as a result of his leadership of the "scouts." This must have been a confusing time because according to the record, Major Krom's term of service ended on October 19, and it is certain no change in command occurred during the Cedar Creek battle. Technically at least, between October 19 and 21, Captain Elmer Barker, presumably no longer under arrest for refusing to burn buildings ten days before, was in command of the regiment and is listed as such in the record. Officially, Major Boice took command on October 21.[21]

The battles fought and won in the Shenandoah Valley in September and October, coupled with the capture of Atlanta by the forces under Sherman, invigorated Northern morale after the horrific carnage of the Overland Campaign and the stalemate before Petersburg. What had appeared to the president early in September as a likely defeat at the polls turned in November into an

Custer's presenting Rebel battle flags captured during the Battle of Cedar Creek at the office of the secretary of war (Library of Congress).

election victory over the former commander of the Army of the Potomac, George McClellan. The troops were already predisposed towards Lincoln at least from the previous winter, as commented on by John Jackson. In January 1864, Jackson was already looking forward eleven months. "Who will be our next President? This question is being agitated around the campfires. At present 'Honest old Abe' appears to be the favorite in the army. Many who formerly voted the democratic ticket are coming out strongly in his favor." New York State had made provision of its soldiers to vote in the field.

Curiously, there is no mention in either Doudiye's journal or history of Lincoln's candidacy, of the troopers voting in the field, or even that there was a national election. On Election Day, November 8, "we heard 'Boots & Saddles' and by daylight, our Brigade had its tents struck, camp broken and ready to move. Moved to the Pike, touching it at Middletown. Moved down to about one mile from Kernstown and stopped in the field." Because there is nothing mentioned in the available record, it is unclear whether the men of the Fifth New York were able to cast votes in the election of 1864, but given the comments of men within the regiment and the known results from other units, it is probable that Lincoln would have secured a large majority from the Fifth New York. Whatever the Fifth's situation, Union soldiers able to vote in the field went overwhelmingly for Lincoln.

The *Western New Yorker* reported in October that fifteen members of the Fifth New York had arrived home at the end of the three-year enlistment. The paper had talked with Sergeant G.D. Lawrence of Company F and reported his view of the coming election. "Serg't Lawrence reports that the soldiers of Sheridan's command ... are going with their General for Lincoln and Peace through the unconditional surrender of the Rebels. Of the 15 who came home 14 are for Lincoln. Serg't Lawrence says that McClellan's ... failure to spurn the base surrender platform upon which he was nominated, and the notorious bad hands into which he has fallen have arrayed the soldiers against him in a body." A further example of the troopers' support for the president is seen in the voting by the Second Ohio, another regiment in the Third Division. An officer in the Second Ohio noted in his diary, "The decisive day of the nation. If the cause of the Union prevails today, Liberty and union will be ours forever. God grant the right success.... Voted. 201 for Lincoln 4 for McClellan. Glorious for the 2nd Ohio."[22]

As another winter approached for the Fifth New York, the confidence they had felt that spring as they prepared themselves to jump the Rapidan and pitch into the Rebels, if it had wavered at all during the hard riding and fighting of the spring, summer and fall, had returned by November. In a letter home that November, one of the regiment's officers wrote, "Since it has been decided that 'Uncle Abe' is to be our commander-in-chief for another term, we all feel confident that the rebellion will shortly be put to an end to, and we shall see all hands be able to give up fighting and return home under a government where there will no longer be as there now is."[23] The war would continue into 1865 and would be a fight to the finish on Lincoln's terms.

12

The Final Months —1865

> We don't have any fighting this winter but I've been through every one of them battles that you have read about in the papers and had 2 horses killed, yet I have come through without being wounded at all.
> — Pvt. Hiram Graves to his mother, January 18, 1865
>
> I know just how you feel poor woman for you son.... The regt. was out by where he was missing ... & they found Hiram buried right whare [sic] we had the battle.... The man that buried him buried him as good as he could.
> — Corp. James Shoney to Mrs. Graves, June 28, 1865[1]

Most of the month of November 1864 saw the Fifth New York scouting and on picket duty in front of the army that was now camped in the Kernstown area. The chaplain's journal contains a typical note of the unit's activities during this period. On November 11, he wrote, "We remained on picket until about 3 P.M., at which time we were relieved by the 2nd Ohio. Just before reaching camp about 4 miles from Winchester, we heard the firing of an attack on the 2nd Ohio, shortly after which we left. Our Regiment charged upon them and drove them back. The Ohioans captured four (4) prisoners. There was some skirmishing by the Pike until dark. We lay on the ground without tents. It was quite chilly." The next day the contact with the Rebels continued and the First Brigade moved to the action. "The Brigade went out after them," Boudrye recorded, "and drove them at least four miles beyond Cedar Creek, making about 12 miles. In some places they made some resistance and fought pretty well. The Colonel of the 2nd N.Y., Hull, was killed with one man, 1st Conn. The 5th N.Y. had only one man wounded, though at one time it was completely cut off, having gone further than any of the Regiments. We inflicted more injuries to the Rebels than they to us."

On November 21, there was a reconnaissance in force up the valley by the Second and Third Cavalry Divisions. The next morning was "clear and cold and somewhat windy. We left early, up the valley. At Edinburg, we struck their pickets. Captured one man. Just beyond Mt. Jackson, we met the Rebels in force on Road's [Rude's] Hill in a favorite position. We drove them out as desired, but had a severe conflict before getting away. Their Cavalry did nothing, except as their Infantry followed them close. They tried to flank us, but made bad work of it. We had only about 35 wounded and about 6 killed in the whole force. Just before dark, we got back to Woodstock, where we camped.... It was hard, as we had most of the fight this P.M."[2] After this action, the Fifth New York's role in the war would change. It would be another instance where the regiment's luck would play a role.

"This is our National Thanksgiving. Chicken and turkey were sent to the soldiers, not to officers. I did not get any," Chaplain Boudrye wrote on Thanksgiving Day, November 24, 1864. The regiment was in camp outside Winchester. Two sentences later, he says, "This evening we received an order detailing the Regiment as General Sheridan's escort, to report to his headquarters tomorrow at 9 A.M." At the appointed time the Fifth New York took up its new duties at Sheridan's headquarters at Kernstown.[3]

The move to Kernstown was uneventful, as was most of the month of December. On December 4, the regiment marched to Harpers Ferry escorting a herd of cattle, and didn't get back until the night of December 7. It snowed, the wind blew and it was cold for several days, and it was only the beginning of winter months, the regiment's fourth winter. On December 12, Boudrye received a letter from his wife enclosing a picture of his newborn son, a son he had yet to see. Two days later, on December 14, Sheridan moved his headquarters to Winchester and the Fifth set up camp on a hill on the northeast side of town. The next day the paymaster arrived with two months' pay. The chaplain collected money from the men and sent it home for them over the next two days. On December 16, three troopers were killed near camp when a brick wall of a burnt-out building collapsed. They had been taking bricks from the wall to build a fireplace for their winter shelter.

Now the escort for General Sheridan, the Fifth New York did not take part in the large cavalry raid that began on December 19. General Grant had been urging Sheridan to mount a raid to cut the Virginia Central Railroad in the vicinity of Gordonsville. Initially hesitant to commit to the raid because of the changing weather and road conditions, Sheridan finally ordered his First and Second Divisions to cross the Blue Ridge and strike at the railroad. These two divisions, under General Torbert, met enough Rebel resistance to make them retire back to Kernstown without cutting the tracks. At the same time, the Third Division, under Custer, had assigned to it the role of moving to Staunton and from there cutting the James River Canal. This operation was stymied too by the Rebels, who attacked the division in its bivouac north of the canal in the pre-dawn hours of December 21. This action convinced Custer to retire back to Kernstown.[4]

Christmas was uneventful within the regiment, each trooper probably secretly wishing he were somewhere else. No doubt the chaplain looked at the picture of his newborn son, a wish also offering itself up. "A merry Christmas to some, I trust, rather lonely for me," Boudrye wrote on December 25. "At eleven (11), I attended service at the Episcopal Church. Generals Custer and Sheridan were present."

On December 19, Colonel Amos H. White, possibly as a result of the officer's petition to the governor, took over command of the regiment from the recently promoted Lt. Col. Boice, who remained second in command. Colonel White had joined the regiment as a Lieutenant in September 1861 and was one of those officers, like John Hammond, who had proven himself capable over time. He had been absent from the regiment, recovering from the wound he received during the Overland Campaign in the spring. On New Year's Day, 1865, the chaplain wrote, "Spent much of the P.M. with the officers of the Regiment in the Colonel's tent. It was about half past 10 when I retired, disgusted at the carousals of drunken officers and men around me." The rain, snow and wind continued for the next two weeks. On January 10, Boudrye received a fifteen-day furlough and started for home. He returned on January 27.[5]

February brought no letup in the severe weather with the chaplain still living in a tent. Boudrye, writing during this period, is less enthusiastic about his role with the regiment than in former months and hardly a day passes without some negative mention of the weather.

Although the regiment was Sheridan's escort, the Fifth went on reconnaissance twice during the month, on January 10 and again on January 23, to Edinburg. These excursions included some skirmishing with Rebels, but nothing came from it. In both cases the command marched back to camp. And nothing of significance for the Fifth was happening in their cold and wet camp, where the primary activity after daily caring for the horses was keeping warm and drawing enough rations. There was snow in February, evidenced by a notation from the Fifteenth New York Cavalry. "February 17th.— The regiment had a snowball fight with the 8th New York cavalry, and the next day turned their attention to the 1st Vermont cavalry, driving them out of their camp and causing them to surrender."

However, there were plans being made by Sheridan and his staff. The Fifteenth New York recorded, "On the 24th and 25th of February the regiment was busily engaged in sharpening the sabers an indication that hostilities were soon to begin." The entire division was issued a five-day ration of pork and hardtack, along with a ten-day supply of coffee and sugar. Then General Custer reviewed the entire division. For each horse, thirty pounds of forage was issued. Boudrye recorded, "The order is to have the whole effective force of the Regiments ready to move at 6 tomorrow morning. The Colonel thinks I had not better go. Considerable excitement prevails in camp." The next day, he wrote: "This morning, the Cavalry force of this Department, having been reinforced recently, left on some important expedition. As General Sheridan accompanied the force, our Regiment had to go as escort." The Fifth New York, numbering thirty-eight officers and 778 men as of January, rode south on its last major combat operation.[6]

By March 2 Sheridan had led the First and Third Cavalry Divisions, with other attached mounted units, through the Valley southward to Staunton. It was known by Sheridan that General Early and his small force of about 2,000 men were in the Waynesboro vicinity, aligned in a defensive position and waiting out the winter weather. Sheridan, outnumbering his enemy about five to one, was eager to move on Early's force, and it was the Third Division that moved it. The resulting action at Waynesboro was planned and executed by George Custer using only his own command. As the Fifth New York was designated escort to Sheridan, they remained with the general, who was not present at Waynesboro when Custer attacked. This is evidenced by the fact that Boudrye speaks only of the division in his regimental history and not of the Fifth New York specifically, as he would have if it had taken a direct part in the fight. Of the division, he says, "Our men swept around this ill-starred army and enveloped them like a fish in a net. Gen. Early's staff and nearly his entire force fell into our hands, making a total of about 1,400 prisoners. His artillery, camp and garrison equipage and stores were either appropriated to our own use or destroyed, mostly the latter."

Another account of the action at Waynesboro speaks of Custer leading a frontal assault on Early's positions. As this assault went forward, four regiments, two on each side, struck the Rebel flanks. "Both flanks of the enemy were turned and our men were in the rebel rear before they knew how it was done," recorded the historian of the Third Indiana. Another account has three regiments of the Third Division sent on a dismounted flanking attack into Early's left rear, firing their Spencer carbines as fast as they could. This was followed by a frontal assault by other elements of the division that quickly made the small Rebel force run in confusion. General Early and only a small remnant of his command escaped capture in the action. This event essentially cleared the Shenandoah of organized Confederate military, although some Rebel cavalry and guerrillas would continue to roam the valley.

The prisoners, as many as 1,400, perhaps fewer, were rounded up and the Fifth New York, along with several regiments with the smallest number of men, those whose horses were "played out," and dismounted men, were assigned the task of escorting them back to Winchester, a distance of about 100 miles. Only those men of the Fifth New York who were orderlies on the general's staff, messengers and color bearers remained with Sheridan as he crossed the Blue Ridge, continuing his ride, one that would eventually reunite him with Grant in the Petersburg area late in March, 1865.[7]

The escort for the prisoners almost equaled the number of captured Rebels, about 1,200 men from both the First and Third Divisions. The command started for Staunton on the morning of March 3, with the Fifth New York in a familiar position, covering the rear of the column. The road was muddy all the way until the column gained the Valley Pike at Staunton. Once in Staunton, the commander of the column, Col. John L. Thompson of the First New Hampshire, requested the town's citizens to provide food for the prisoners. Only a feeble attempt was made by the townspeople, so Thompson appropriated the necessary supplies from Staunton's insane asylum and started on his way north. At about noon on March 6, the column was at Mount Jackson, looking at the swollen North Fork of the Shenandoah River. They would wait until the next morning to attempt a crossing, allowing for the water level in the river to fall overnight. After the first elements of the column crossed, they had to engage and drive off a Rebel force of about 200 that was waiting on the north side of the river. After this, the command, in groups of fifty and sixty, started wading the river.

While this went forward, the Fifth New York was still guarding the rear. "At Mt. Sidney a considerable body of Rosser's men made their appearance, and attacked the rear guard. They were repelled after a brief skirmish.... Occasional shots were exchanged with these pursuers, who hung on our rear, all the way. At Lacey Springs, their numbers having been increased, they made quite a demonstration."[8] Again at New Market another demonstration was made. Now on March 7, as the command was crossing the Shenandoah, Rosser's cavalry made a determined attempt to gain release of their comrades. Rosser, with about 300 men under his command, charged down Rude's Hill toward the column. The regiment, commanded by Lt. Col. Theodore Boice in place of the furloughed Col. White, made a stand and beat off this first attack. The Rebels regrouped and tried again as the prisoners looked on.

> Col. Boice ... suddenly changed direction, held his men in good line, each receiving fire until the enemy had approached within a few rods, then ordering and leading the charge, fell with a crushing blow upon the enemy. The Johnnies, not expecting such a dash, wheeled about and undertook to fly, but were pre-

vented doing so rapidly on account of the mud of the field where they were. A hand-to-hand contest of unusual excitement followed, in which the most daring deeds were done. Col. Boice, having emptied every chamber of his revolver, unhorsed six Rebel troopers with the butt. The affair resulted ... in the capture of thirty-five of his [Rosser's] men, the killing of quite a number, and the dispersion of his entire force.

When it was over, Rosser had lost ten men killed and an estimated twenty-five had now joined the prisoners marching toward Winchester.

It was in the action at Rude's Hill that Hiram Graves of Company M was killed. Graves, according to the regiment's early history, was the last trooper from the regiment killed in action during the war. Colonel Thompson reported, "Lieutenant-Colonel Boice ... whom I had put in charge of those from the Third Division, deserves high commendation. He covered the rear during the entire march. His repulse of the enemy in the two assaults at Rude's Hill was brilliant. The prisoners could not withhold their commendation, but shouted with our men."[9] Offhanded as this last sentence by Colonel Thompson appears, it is indicative of the sentiment within the Rebel ranks by March 1865. Even the most die-hard Confederate by this time could see that the war was lost and would soon, somehow or other, be ending.

The column marched into Winchester the next day with all the prisoners. Now back in their winter camp, the Fifth New York fell under the command of General Winfield Scott Hancock, temporarily in charge of the forces remaining in the valley.[10] On March 13, "The Regiment went on a reconnaissance to Berryville. Deserters from the Rebel lines are daily coming in our own, giving themselves up." Quite possibly this ride to Berryville was the last combat patrol of the Fifth New York in the war. On April 3, "swift telegrams announce Gen. Sheridan's victorious battles below Petersburg, and the fall of Richmond! Batteries rend the air with their salutes, and bands of music fill the intervals with joyful airs. The evening has been made luminous with fireworks from the signal tower on Logan mountain, and bonfires in the streets."[11] This was how Boudrye described the news arriving in Winchester of the Union victories around Petersburg that forced General Lee to abandon his positions near the city and begin the retreat that would end at Appomattox. Those few troopers of the Fifth New York who rode with Sheridan and Custer would be the only men from the regiment to be near at hand for the surrender of General Robert E. Lee. For them, it would be the end of their direct participation in history.

It was midnight, April 9, and the cannons started firing all around Winchester. General Lee had surrendered to Grant earlier in the day. "Aroused from their slumbers, the soldiers and some citizens rush to Gen. Hancock's headquarters, a happy, almost crazy throng.... bells ring, bands discourse patriotic music, flags are paraded through the streets, and the multitude grows hoarse with cheering. The whole night is filled with jubilation."[12] The war in Virginia had ended.

The rest of the week was uneventful, at least until late that Friday, Good Friday, April 14. The next day the chaplain wrote: "The news of the assassination last night of President Lincoln and Wm. H. Seward and perhaps others, has filled our hearts with sadness and gloom. Thus, the bitterest cup is tendered to the lips of the people in the middle of their rejoicing over the past victories and their buoyant hopes of the speedy return of peace and prosperity." This is how Boudrye reacted to Lincoln's death in his journal. There is little else recorded in his journal for that day except the words, "We anxiously await particulars. The day has been cold and stormy."[13] The chaplain never set any "particulars" in his journal or any other thoughts concerning this tragedy. When the comments and thoughts of so many others within the regiment could have been recorded, if for no other reason than to refresh his later memory, the chaplain wrote nothing of the assassination of President Lincoln, and it is our loss.

Essentially, this was the end of the Civil War for the Fifth New York Cavalry. The regiment stayed in camp at Winchester until May 4. On this day the command started on one last expedition, the purpose of which seems to have been to show the flag in the southern end of the Shenandoah and to discourage any lawlessness by ex–Rebels. With a brigade of infantry, the Fifth New York marched toward Staunton at a leisurely pace. The march headed out "resembling more a picnic, than an assemblage of warriors," as the chaplain phrased it. The first night on the Valley Pike the regiment camped at Cedar Creek. "How different this move from that of a year ago across the Rapidan. Had quite an interesting Negro banjo concert and dance in camp this evening." Arriving at Staunton on May 9, they set up another camp. "Staunton is so peculiarly situated that you cannot see it from any distance until you arrive upon it. It is like a bird's nest, carefully hidden. It is noted for its fine public buildings, viz. Asylum for lunatics, one for orphans, one for deaf and dumb."[14]

Boudrye had already begun gathering records relating to the regiment's history he contemplated, and clearly his thoughts had turned to the project. "About three miles north of Harrisonburg, in the first heavy skirmish of the Regiment in May, 1862, one man was killed, the first victim of the Regiment to die this cruel way. About three miles north of New Market, in a charge of the Regiment on Rosser, March, 1865, one man was killed also, probably the last victim. The martyrs lie buried where they fell, by the roadside. The Regiment commenced its work in the valley, ends it in the valley and only 18 miles between its first and last engagements, though nearly 4 years intervene." The regiment's camp was within walking distance of Staunton and it appears that nothing of particular interest was done there for few days. But there was trouble. "Last night, Wm. Criddle, Co. B, a pioneer, was murdered near town. He was intoxicated and is reported to have had money with him. He had none, when found. He was struck on the back side of the head with a stone though the skull was not fractured."[15] Nothing is mentioned as to whether the assailant was ever discovered.

During the days in camp, Boudrye continued to collect and organize regimental statistics. The regiment stayed in the Staunton area until May 19. "At 1½, nearly the whole Regiment went out with two day's rations and forages to Lexington for Ex-Governor Letcher."[16] The Chaplain gives no reason for the order coming down to arrest or detain the former Virginia governor who had been in office during the secession crisis of 1861. Probably, the regiment wasn't told.

"It is remarkable," Boudrye wrote while in Staunton, "how readily paroled Rebel soldiers affiliate with us, and how anxiously those who are not paroled seek their papers."[17] In the few comments he makes about ex-soldiers and civilians he meets during this period, Boudrye seems not to have encountered any noticeable resentment or sullen defiance by what had to be considered at that moment in time a defeated army and people. It could be that the people were uncertain of what could happen to them with Federal troops living among them and went about their business gingerly, purposely keeping their true sentiments hidden.

There was, however, one mild exception. It was only while attending church on May 11 that Boudrye encountered rebellious sentiments. Given the chaplain's elliptical writing, the reader of his journal is left without any real details or pertinent quotations. "At 11, I attended Church at Fort Defiance, Rev. Mr. Bowman. They continued with their views of hate to the Yankees and the Union, at least, such is the undoubted appearance."[18] Boudrye was acquainted with the Reverend Mr. Bowman, having encountered him three times before. In July 1863, while a prisoner, he had been marched through the Staunton area on his way to Libby Prison and met Bowman. At the time, "I called on Rev. Mr. Bowman, where many harsh words were spoken to me because of my relation to the hated Lincoln Army." Then in September 1864, as he was again riding with the Fifth New York as it operated in the area, Boudrye called on Bowman, and given the chaplain's demeanor, his call was not to cause any offense. Boudrye reported, "I called again, at which time Mr. Bowman feared I would retaliate on him, acknowledging that his only speaking their cause looked badly, but thought that Providence was on their side and that in their extremity, God would deliver them." Then, for a third time, Boudrye met with Bowman, during the regiment's occupation of the area in May 1865. It was May 9 and the chaplain reported in his journal, "Mr. Bowman said but little. I did not stay long.... These tribunals represent the progress of ideas and events during the past few years."[19] For the chaplain, this was rare perception recorded in his journal. Defiance and hate in 1863 had turned, in a year, to mere faith in ultimate deliverance and finally, within months, to the resignation of the conquered whose sentiments could only find vent on Sunday from the sanctuary of a pulpit.

On the same day Boudrye was making this observation, orders came down the chain of command. All men whose terms of service would expire prior to October 1 were to be mustered out immediately. The Fifth New York would lose 175 troopers. "Among those ... were many of my old friends. Some of them wept like children on bidding us goodbye."[20]

The regiment remained in Staunton until June 12. Relief came in the form of the Twelfth Pennsylvania Cavalry, and the New Yorkers were ready to march north that same afternoon. They marched up the Valley Pike at a slow pace to save on horseflesh. The weather was warm and the command marched mostly in the evenings or early morning. They arrived near Winchester on June 15 and went into camp, a place they called Camp Hammond. As soon as he got settled, Boudrye applied for leave. He gave no reason for this in his writing. Leave was granted and he hurried home. He returned to the regiment on July 8, in time for the final scenes in the unit's saga. During his absence, the regiment had apparently received word that it would soon be mustered out of service and various arrangements had to be quickly completed, including disposal by sale of the unit's horses. In addition, before the mustering out, Boudrye pre-sold 388 copies of his history for a total of $1,135.00. This helps explain why the first edition of *Historic Records* was published a mere three months after the regiment was disbanded.[21]

The celebrating started in the evening, July 14.

> Lighted candles were placed on the tents or just before them and on trees. Individuals climbed trees, each Company vying with the others to have the highest light. Bonfires and torches were made of old bags and blankets, suspended on trees or carried on poles, emitting a glaring light. What the boys call bitches were also made by filling a frying pan with fat and dripping bagging into it for a wick. The pleasantries of the night contributed much to the beauty of the entertainment. After a while, battalion after battalion came out with lights in hand and cheered the following officers: Col., Lt. Col., Majors Barker and Merritt, Dr. Armstrong and the Adjutant. A small party went and cheered Jos. A. Phillips for the sake of getting whiskey. They succeeded. The entertainment closed with

the hanging of Jeff Davis in effigy on a tree and burning the remains, where he was pronounced dead. The enterprise commenced at 8 and closed at 11½.

The next day was Sunday and the chaplain preached his last sermon to the regiment at a well-attended service.

There was a good deal of packing to be done, and on Tuesday, July 18, a final roll call and dress parade were held. Then the regiment marched on foot to Stevenson's Station and boarded the train, headed home.[22]

> Head Quarters Fifth N.Y. Cavalry
> In the Field near Winchester, Va.,
> July 18th, 1865
>
> In compliance with orders from the commanding general the regiment will leave Stevenson's Station this P.M. at three o'clock, en route to New York city, for final discharge.
> Transportation will be furnished for officers' horses to place of muster out. The regiment will march for the depot at twelve P.M. Every officer and enlisted man will be in camp to march promptly at that hour. En route home and until final discharge, it is earnestly hoped the regiment will sustain its good name.
> After four years of hardship and honor you return to your state to be honorably mustered out of service and to return once more to a peaceful life among your friends and loved ones. In a few days you will be scattered and the Fifth New York Cavalry will be no more. The hardships you have endured; the comforts of which you have been deprived; the cheerful and prompt manner in which you have always done your duty, and the successes you have met with on the battle field, have won the admiration of every general officer under whom you have served. Surpassed by none, equaled by few, your record as a regiment is a glorious and honorable one.
> May your future lives be as prosperous and as full of honor to yourselves, as the past four years have been to your country, to your state and to the Fifth New York Cavalry.
> A.H. White
> Col. Comd'g
> 5th N.Y. Cavalry[23]

The regiment took the train to Harpers Ferry and then on to Philadelphia. By the afternoon of July 20, they were in camp on Hart Island in Long Island Sound waiting for the paymaster. Alphabetically, the companies were paid off. The first nine companies left with their money on July 25. The next day the remaining three companies received their pay, "and the Fifth New York Cavalry was no more, except in story."[24]

Epilogue

> Wherever we have been ordered we have done our duty and our whole duty.
> —John Hammond, 1863

> I preached probably my last sermon to the boys of the old Fifth, at least in the field, Text Cor. 16, 13, last clause in the verse.... The train moved off at 3 and we bade adieu to our camping ground. Officers and men demonstrated their joy in songs, etc. Train moved slowly.
> —Chaplain Louis N. Boudrye, July 1865[1]

As they had first gathered on a New York island as volunteers and fitfully organized themselves into what became a fighting command, so the Fifth New York again found itself on an island, gathered this time, for the last time, as a now veteran regiment with four years of history to be told.

"The Fifth New-York Cavalry, (Ira Harris,) 517 men, Col. A. White, commanding, arrived at the Battery Barracks yesterday morning, from Winchester, Va., and proceeded to Hart's Island, where they will be paid off. The Fifth was recruited in this city in the Summer of 1861, and was encamped on Staten Island for several weeks, where the men were thoroughly drilled. On taking the field the regiment was one of the best equipped and best disciplined in the army, and has always done efficient service."[2] This was how the *New York Times* reported the return of the Fifth New York, nearly four years removed from recruitment.

The men waited several days on Hart Island in Long Island Sound for the paymaster to arrive. By July 26 all the men had gotten the back pay that was owed and their bounty money. In addition to the original bounty, at least $75 of the initial enlistment incentive from New York State, there was the federal bounty paid to the "veteran volunteers" for reenlistment in 1864. With this transaction completed, the regiment now fades into the haze of history.

With the money in their pockets, the men probably took boats back to

Manhattan, and if they weren't from the city, they boarded trains to their homes across New York State. They got home to the great relief of their loved ones and started new lives or resumed former ones. It is probable they didn't realize as yet what they had done. That would come in time. Theirs would be a new nation, vastly different from the one they had been part of before volunteering to ride with the Fifth New York Cavalry. In any case, somewhere, someplace, within each man, there had to be a latent sense of accomplishment, especially for the "veteran volunteers" of the summer of 1861.

Chaplain Boudrye ended his history of the Fifth New York on July 26, 1865, with the men scattering for their homes. The next chapter in his history is a compilation of statistics covering the four years of the regiment's existence. In the brief introduction to this chapter, however, he includes another rare, yet heartfelt insight, one that later historians of the conflict have had to confront for upwards of fifteen decades. He speaks of the often-encountered lack of complete and accurate data for organizations like the Fifth New York. Here Boudrye is speaking of the importance to the historical record of his inclusion of the many tables and numbers in the story of the regiment. "Were the historian supplied with such data from each regiment, which has participated in our terrible struggle, an incalculably interesting and valuable history of this rebellion might be compiled at no distant day. But it is to be feared that in many instances not even the number much less the names, of our noble defenders, who have fallen in the conflict, will ever be known to posterity. While it is a noble thing to die for one's country, it is an ignoble thing for survivors not to chronicle the deeds and names of their less fortunate companions."[3] The chaplain, in his labor at gathering regimental statistics, perhaps unknowingly did future historians a great favor. The tables and statistics included in his history proved essential for any telling of the Fifth New York's story.

Fifth New York troopers who had survived being prisoners at Andersonville or at other Confederate prisons were probably already home by July of 1865, released just prior to or upon the formal surrender of the last Confederate armies. As an example, there is the record of Corporal George H. Lamb, Company L, who was captured during the engagement at Stony Creek in June 1864. From July of 1864 to April 1, 1865, he had endured the hell that was Andersonville Prison Camp. He was released in a prisoner exchange only nine days before the war in Virginia ended. Transported to Jacksonville, Florida, and put on a boat, he was landed at a parole camp for former Union prisoners established at Annapolis, Maryland. There he received $28.15 in back pay and then sent to his place of "enrollment." This meant home to Cornwall, New York. Almost certainly, after ten months in Andersonville, he was probably underweight, and his general physical condition would have inhibited his ability to perform any kind of duty with an active cavalry regiment. Besides, his family had been actively seeking information about George while he was a prisoner. The day after his parole from Andersonville, his mother was still writing, inquiring about his fate.

> Cornwall April 2 65
> Genl. Hoffman
>
> Dear Sir
> Through the kindness of Genl [illegible] I was in
> Formed of your Position hopeing [sic] you may give me Some tidings
> of my long lost
> Son George H. Lamb of Co. L 5th N.Y. Cavalry taken in the Wilson
> Raid later [sic] part
> Of June 1864. Since that time I have had no tidings from him. Eny
> [sic] information
> Concerning him will be thankfully received by his Mother.
> Mrs. Susan Lamb
> Cornwall Landing
> Orange County
> N.Y.
> P.S. he was supposed to be sent to Florance [sic] S.C.[4]

There is no record that Mrs. Lamb's request was answered or for that matter how she knew that her son had been taken prisoner, except that the regiment, after listing Corporal Lamb as missing, may have written to her after returning from the raid. On June 30, 1865, Corporal Lamb was officially mustered out of the cavalry. And on the same day the regiment was traveling back to New York City, on July 19, Corporal Lamb received the remaining $75 of his enlistment bounty. It is unlikely he was on Hart Island when the rest of the regiment was paid off.[5]

The experience of Corporal Lamb can be considered typical of this group of surviving Fifth New York cavalrymen, of which there were twenty-one officers and 572 enlisted. How many of these were still in captivity at the time of surrender is not recorded, although during the course of the war a few had escaped and made it back within Union lines, and some had been exchanged during periods when this was practiced. According to the records gathered by Chaplain Boudrye, of the ninety-nine prisoners of war who died in captivity, sixty-three died at Andersonville. A further ten men "Died from the Effects of Prison Life." Further, Boudrye listed five more men as "supposed" to have died in prison. Typical is the case of John Morse of Company B. His parents had been inquiring about him since they had stopped getting his letters. Like George Lamb, Morse had been captured during Wilson's Raid and sent south. Finally, in June of 1865 the family received a letter from L.H. Whittlesey of the First New York Cavalry. "Your son, John Morse, Co. B, 5th N.Y. Cavalry was sun struck on the 1st day of September last year at Andersonville Prison, Ga. And died on the 5th of that month. He was unconscious, or became crazed, from the first of September, when he was injured until his death."[6]

Although all prison camps, North and South, were squalid affairs, Andersonville became notorious. It wasn't long after it opened that the camp resembled something from a later century rather than strictly a place to hold combatants from further participation in the war. Exchanges of prisoners between the armies had stopped, and with the great campaigns being waged in 1864 by both Grant and Sherman, Andersonville quickly filled to overflowing. With this came starvation and disease. A Southern lady seeing Andersonville for the first time noted in her diary that "the horrors of the stockade have so enraged them [Yankees] that they will have no mercy on this country, though they have brought it all on themselves, the cruel monsters, by refusing to exchange prisoners. But it is horrible, and a blot on the fare [sic] name of our Confederacy.... on the first of December, 1864, there were 13,010 graves at Anderson." What this lady had seen, however briefly, seems to have made an impression. A short time later she wrote of Andersonville again: "The Yankees themselves are really more to blame than we, for they won't exchange these prisoners, and our poor, hard-pressed Confederacy has not the means to provide for them, when our own soldiers are starving in the field."[7]

A more detailed description of Andersonville was recorded by Dr. Joseph Jones, sent on an inspection of the camp in the late summer 1864. On September 22, Dr. Jones wrote of what he had seen to his mother:

> You can form some idea of the extent of the field when I mention the facts that there are at this time five thousand seriously sick Yankees who are dying at the rate of more than one hundred per day; and almost all the well Federals — or those considered well by contract — are suffering from diarrhea, dysentery, and scurvy.... Over thirty thousand men have been crowded into the confined space of twenty-seven acres, without a single shade tree and with scarcely a tent to keep off the rays of the Southern sun. From the crowding and filthy habits and condition of the men, their system in many cases has been so deteriorated that the smallest abrasion of the skin, as the rubbing of a shoe or the pricking of a small splinter or even mosquito bites, have taken on the most frightful gangrene, and in the hospital of the Confederate military prison over two hundred amputations have been performed for slight injuries followed by the most rapid and frightful gangrene. This day I visited two thousand sick within the stockade. Only one medical officer was in attendance upon these suffering and seriously ill patients.... I hope that my labors may be the means of mitigating some of this suffering.

Epilogue

Dr. Jones then offers his opinion on why prisoners should be treated with the care they were obviously not receiving at Andersonville. "When men surrender, the true policy ... should be to treat them in such a manner that surrendering in battle will have no terrors. The fear of great suffering in imprisonment only renders our enemies more vindictive and more stubborn in battle."[8] Curiously, Dr. Jones's official report to the authorities contained no recommendations on how the dire situation at Andersonville could be improved.

The official records are slightly at variance with the chaplain's history. Officially, 17.5 per cent (104 men) of those from the regiment who were captured died while in prison. In the regiment as a whole, sixty-six had died in combat, twenty-seven later of wounds received, while 193 succumbed to disease. In excess of eighteen per cent of the men passing through regiment died during its four years of service and nearly twenty-five percent were wounded.[9]

Although the percentages presented here are based on the original full complement of men initially assigned to the Fifth New York, 1,064 in all, there never was a time during the war when it even approached this full complement. This was due to a variety of reasons. If the numbers in the reports are taken as correct, the closest the regiment ever came to a full complement, 1,007 men in the ranks, was reported on the muster rolls for April 1865, and this was at the war's end. On average there were significantly fewer men in the ranks — an average of 622 with the two highest totals discarded — at any given time. But this average of 622 is in itself deceiving, not taking into account men on detached service, dismounted, sick and in the hospital. Also, the number absent without leave or having deserted, in some fashion, has to be considered, but there is no accurate way of doing this. In April 1862, as an example, the regiment reported 911 men on its rolls. Then in July 1862, the same muster roll reports only 607. Where did over three hundred individuals go? There certainly were no combat actions during these three months that resulted in the loss of 304 men.

On July 22, 1862, John Hammond complained in a letter home, "The force of our cavalry companies is very much reduced in numbers. They certainly have not more than one-half what they had when they crossed the Potomac. We are still worse off for effective men. There must be at least 250 men of our regiment off on sick leave and absent without leave; and then there are the deaths, some killed and some wounded, and good many discharged for sickness and disability; and ours is but a specimen of the whole grand army of the north." The muster roll for the month of July 1863 lists 534 men in the ranks. However, on July 1, the regiment was, and had been, in the field engaged in active combat operations. Indeed, it would remain in such a mode for almost the entire month.¹⁰ The reported number cannot be considered at all accurate, especially in light of the fact that John Hammond on July 9 wrote his wife that he had only 144 men left in the regiment. And here Hammond is probably speaking only of troopers who were still mounted.

Suffice it to say, the number of men in the regiment at a given moment cannot be stated accurately, and the losses sustained by the Fifth New York over the course of the war — killed, wounded, missing or lost to disease — while heavy, are not truly reflected in its records as reported to brigade and division. They can only be labeled as numbers reported "officially." As an example, the unnamed trooper killed by the men from Elder's battery after he had shot one of their own on the night of July 5–6, 1863, was not recorded or reported anywhere in any record kept by the regiment. To extrapolate only for discussion purposes here, the numbers of men in any given Civil War regiment can only really be considered estimates for any given point during the war.

The strength of the Fifth New York at any particular point during the conflict must take into account desertion. In the New York Adjutant General's Report published in 1895 and relating to the regiment, there are 319 individuals listed as deserters during the regiment's existence. However, a considerable number of names are listed more than once due to clerical errors. These names are usually followed in the report by the word "borne," taken to mean that the name is in the list more than once. Spelling differences in names recorded at different times and places by different clerks, as well as the inclusion of a middle initial as opposed to the same name without an initial, can account for a number of discrepancies.

Instances of desertion from the regiment occurred at all times through the war. However, there appear to be three significant spikes in the numbers at particular times. The first occurred during training at Camp Scott on Staten Island. As an example, William Aiken, Company F, enlisted in the Fifth New York on September 9, 1861, and deserted from Camp Scott on October 25. It can be assumed that there was something in the training — however rudimentary — that was not to his liking. Perhaps it was the horses, the care and feeding thereof, or possibly riding at a speed greater than a walk. Also, there is the case of William Barber, Company H, who enlisted from Crown Point under the initial recruitment by John Hammond in September 1861. Barber deserted on November 1 before the regiment left for Maryland. It seems unlikely Barber would ever again be welcome in the town where the regiment's best commander resided.

The second surge in desertion appears from the record to have occurred in the spring of 1862 after the regiment was deployed to the Shenandoah

Valley and had seen its first combat. This is clearly evident in the Adjutant General's Report after the Fifth's retreat through Winchester and across the Potomac at the end of May. Chaplain Boudrye, not one to dwell on a negative, even makes note of it in his history. The command was demoralized after retreating all the way from Strasburg, and "many of the boys took advantage of their sojourn in Maryland to take *French* furlough."[11]

The spring of 1864 saw another rise in desertion. One can speculate on the cause or causes for this. Given what these men had already seen and lived, it is reasonable to assume that their knowledge of the coming overland campaign and its inherent causalities caused a number of troopers to reconsider their role in the conflict and then to act on it. Among others, there was Jeremiah Bogardus of Company M. He never came back from his veteran's furlough that had been an important part of the re-enlistment program the previous winter. Thomas Frenyer of Company B took his veteran's furlough apparently with no end date.

Through the war, other troopers deserted from hospitals after being wounded. Some went home rather than going, as ordered, to the dismounted camp at Giesboro Point in Washington. And there were a few men who left while the regiment was outfitting there early in August 1864, before deploying again to the Shenandoah.

Other examples of desertion include nineteen-year-old John Brown of Company B. Brown enlisted in August 1861 and deserted "to the enemy" on February 15, 1864. There had to be a story behind this. Given the date of his enlistment, Brown, if he had re-enlisted during the winter, would have received a veteran's furlough that spring. And why go over the river and not try to make his way home to New York? Edgar Boylston, Company E, is listed as deserting at Hanover, Pennsylvania, on June 30, 1863, apparently while the regiment was engaged with Jeb Stuart's cavalry. John Moore enlisted in New York City in July 1861. Formerly a sergeant in Company A, but busted to private for some unknown reason, Moore walked away from an "insane hospital" in Washington in 1863. Also, there were a number of men who enlisted in the regiment but never reported for duty; these were listed as deserters, as were a small number of men who left early for home after the Appomattox surrender and the fighting had ended, yet before the regiment left Winchester for New York. These individuals had to know they would be forfeiting their bonuses and back pay.

Finally, there is one last class of deserter. In addition to James Ames, "Big Yankee," who deserted and joined Mosby's command, there was Benjamin Major of Company B. Major went over to the Rebel raider two days after Ames on February 12, 1863. At least three troopers from the Fifth New

York besides "Big Yankee" deserted to the enemy while the regiment was in the field. Each instance of desertion contains a story, a motive or a reason why these men took such an action, and it would be of real interest to us, help us in understanding this era and these men, if we could somehow learn what drove them. But their motives are among those things lost to history.[12]

John Hammond went home to Crown Point at the end of August 1864, to his wife and two small children. There never surfaced to our eyes the reason for his not re-enlisting at the end of his three-year term other than the vague reference of his being needed at home. There is no doubt about his continued devotion to the Union cause. In one of his last known letters from the field, Hammond summarizes his thoughts in light of his experiences since the beginning of the 1864 campaign. On August 9, he tells his wife: "You possibly hear, dearest, many growlers about our not winning all the battles, and that our cause is hopeless.... One who cannot withstand reverses is not worthy [of] the great cause we are fighting for. All will be well yet, although the sacrifices and trials are great."[13] If Hammond had remained with the regiment, or returned to it, it is with high degree of certainty that he would have been promoted to brigadier general in the field. In fact, after the war he was promoted to brevet brigadier general for service in the conflict.

Hammond returned to the family business, the Crown Point Iron Works, serving as president for the next twenty-five years. He was also president of a local railroad, the Whitehall and Plattsburg, and took a hand in politics, being twice a delegate to the Republican National Convention. In 1879 he was elected to Congress on the Republican ticket and served until 1883. His memories of the war and the regiment must never have been far from his thoughts. One of the horses he rode during his three years with the regiment, named Pink, he took back to Crown Point with him. The horse was a hearty Vermont-bred animal that lived to the age of thirty-one. Hammond, obviously Crown Point's first citizen, had a twelve-foot monument erected in the Village Park to honor Pink, and it was set facing the Crown Point Soldier's Monument. In 1886, it was dedicated. On July 1, 1888, Hammond attended the twenty-fifth anniversary ceremonies at Gettysburg, where various regimental monuments were dedicated and veterans from both sides returned and relived experiences of three epic days. Hammond was clearly the most influential man in his community and was from war's end always referred to as "General." He was active in the veterans' organizations, such as the Grand Army of the Republic, that were influential in the decades after the war in keeping issues concerning veterans in the public — and Congress's — view. It was said of him, "Any Union soldier with a clean record he was a friend of, and he could not do too much for him." John Hammond, Brevet Brigadier General of Volunteers, late commander of the Fifth New York Volunteer Cavalry Regiment, died at home on May 28, 1889, at the age of sixty-one. Fittingly, his funeral in Crown Point was held on Memorial Day.[14]

Chaplain Boudrye returned home to Kinderhook, New York, and finished his *Historic Records of the 5th New York Cavalry*. After, he became a traveling minister and lecturer. He and his wife, Pearlie, and their six children remained in New York until 1890. The family then moved to Chicago to be near his son John, who practiced medicine in that city. As he got older, the chaplain's health problems, attributed to his wartime service, became more severe. Possibly, this was among the reasons for the move closer to his son, the physician. In 1888 he applied for and received a veteran's disability pension of $10 per month. Chaplain Louis Boudrye died on January 3, 1892, of pneumonia brought on by his prolonged illnesses. Pearlie continued to receive a widow's pension until her death in 1917.[15]

Veterans of the Fifth New York formed an association after the war. The 5th New York Veteran Volunteer Cavalry Association held a meeting each year at least through 1892, when they met in Washington. There a memorial was written honoring the late Chaplain Boudrye and forwarded to his family. Louis Boudrye, said the memorial, "had endeared himself to the [regiment] by his untiring devotion to their interests as individuals, as well as an organization, who during the dark days of bloody conflict of civil war, shared with them the shadows and hardships of battle, march and camp, whose hopeful words and kindly administration to the wounded and dying on many a battlefield had dispelled the darkness and smoothed the way to the Great Beyond for many a dying hero, a man everywhere true and loyal to the God he loved, and the church in whose ministry he was a self denying and faithful laborer."[16]

The Fifth New York Cavalry was a citizen-soldier military unit, like so many others in wars since, every man called or coerced to the colors in a time of national crisis. There was much more to life in the Fifth New York than what has succeeded in coming down to us from the contemporary records. It has to be that much was deliberately filtered so as not to offend the uninitiated civilian or family members who might read or in some way be exposed to tales of the regiment's exploits, on and off the battlefield. Simply put, always there was cursing, by men and officers, some of it quite creative, as well as off-color lyrics to songs. There was drinking on a heroic scale when liquor could be had, despite Chaplain Boudrye's efforts at enlisting the men in his temperance campaign. And there was carousing, most often by officers loose in the whore-infested city of Washington. But also, there were unnamed heroes among these cavalrymen, more than the records speak of. And there were scoundrels, thieves, shirkers, cowards, drunkards and some traitors among them. But during the four long years of war the majority of the many hundreds of men who passed through the regiment, those who were not coerced into it, were merely young — or nearly young — men who knew they were needed for a cause. Their efforts and the risks taken would help in some small way in keeping the Union together and bring at least a semblance of freedom to millions who had never known it. It was a nation's war and they did the fighting and dying, leaving us precious little of who they were, what they believed and why most needed to be there.

These troopers, these citizens in uniform, of the Fifth New York were not acting in a vacuum. There were hundreds of other volunteer regiments doing the same thing at the same time, some more, some less ordinary than the Fifth Regiment of Volunteer Cavalry from New York. They had known nothing in 1861, neither how to handle a horse, how to fire a gun nor how to start a campfire in the rain so that coffee could be boiled. They learned their trade, mostly by doing it in the field. The officers who were to lead them were culled so that there remained only those who knew what they were doing, those whom the men would follow. Through the war's first two years the regiment's proficiency improved to a point that by the spring of 1863, the Fifth New York could be considered a formation bordering on the professional. This level of consistent performance was maintained until the end of the war.

And the regiment as a whole had been lucky in war. Although its complement of troopers had been severely depleted during the Gettysburg campaign, chiefly as a result of lost horses, it had not suffered the casualties of other mounted formations in the great battle. It had not been part of Farnsworth's ill-fated charge. The regiment had been in the defenses of Washington during the Battle of Brandy Station in June of 1863, had not been included when the Cavalry Corps rode to Yellow Tavern the following year. Only a few of its troopers rode with Kilpatrick and Dahlgren on Richmond. It was only during Grant's Overland Campaign and on Wilson's Raid that the regiment lost significant numbers.

On the boats departing Hart Island that day in midsummer 1865, each veteran of the Fifth New York Cavalry carried with him his back pay and bounty, and at least an unconscious sense of pride in having been part of such a command. And perhaps somewhere, also unconsciously, the former cavalrymen sensed that their contribution would remain profound, not only for the remainder of their lives, but for untold generations to come. Many of the men of the Fifth New York would live well into old age. But these years would be a vastly different age from the one that had preceded it, the age that required the creation of the regiment of which they were now veterans. The Civil War amplified and accelerated the industrialization that had been the economic force operating on the nation in the thirty-odd years preceding the war. There had been abolitionism and territorial expansion, but it was gradual shifting from an agrarian society to an industrial one, along with the increased speed of communications and availability of transportation over distance, that most clearly defines the period before the war. Then the war came and there was no turning back. Emerging from the war, the process continued, only faster. By the turn of the century at the least, and well within the lifetimes of these veterans, the United States was poised to become the most potent industrial nation on earth, one based on capital investment and free labor. What the men of the Fifth New York received for their bleeding and years of hardship was a new, free nation, still with its faults, but nevertheless one purged of slavery and positioned to be the most free of all nations.

At the risk of restating the obvious, during their four years of war and among the accomplishments of a seasoned, disciplined mounted force, the men of the Fifth New York helped remake a phrase occurring in our language, one so common it goes quite unnoticed. As the Southern writer and historian Shelby Foote often noted, people before the Civil War were apt to say, "the United States are." After it was over, they said, "the United States is."

Chapter Notes

Preface

1. *In Memoriam: John Hammond* (Chicago: P.F. Pettibone, 1890), p. 63.
2. Quoted in Stephen Z. Starr, *The Union Cavalry in the Civil War*, vol. 2: *The War in the East from Gettysburg to Appomattox, 1863–1865* (Baton Rouge: Louisiana State University Press, 1981), p. 265. One might add to the general's comments those reports by unit commanders that deliberately molded the facts included in such a way as to deflect blame from them for not achieving what they had set out to do. This topic, as it relates to the Fifth New York Cavalry, will be discussed in the text.
3. James H. Wilson, *Under the Old Flag*, vol. 1 (New York: D. Appleton, 1912), p. 565.

Chapter 1

1. James Moore, *Kilpatrick and Our Cavalry* (New York: W.J. Widdleton, 1865), p. 104.
2. Ray Allen Billington, *The Far Western Frontier, 1830–1860* (New York: Harper and Row, 1956), p. 38.
3. Starr, *Union Cavalry*, vol. 1, p. 65, n. 12. This new cavalry regiment became the Sixth U.S. Cavalry.
4. Starr, *Union Cavalry*, vol. 1, p. 66; Edward G. Longacre, *Lincoln's Cavalrymen: A History of the Mounted Forces of the Army of the Potomac, 1861–1865* (Harrisburg, PA: Stackpole Books, 2000), p. 2.
5. Longacre, ibid., pp. 2–3.
6. Samuel Carter, *The Last Cavaliers: Confederate and Union Cavalry in the Civil War* (New York: St. Martin's Press, 1979), p. 9.
7. Louis N. Boudrye, *Historic Records of the Fifth New York Cavalry*, 2nd ed., (Albany, NY: J. Munsell, 1868), p. 17; Starr, *Union Cavalry*, vol. 1, pp. 77–78. De Forest's first name is spelled incorrectly in Boudrye's history.
8. George S. Forbes, *Leaves from a Trooper's Diary* (Philadelphia: privately issued, 1869), p. 8.

9. James M. McPherson, *The Battle Cry of Freedom: The Civil War Era* (New York: Oxford University Press, 1988), p. 309; Morris Schaff, *The Battle of the Wilderness* (Boston: Houghton, Mifflin, 1910), p. 15.
10. Roy P. Basler, ed., *The Collected Works of Abraham Lincoln*, 9 vols. (New Brunswick, N.J.: Rutgers University Press, 1953–1955), vol. 8, p. 332.
11. Taken from *Final Report on the Battlefield of Gettysburg (New York at Gettysburg)* (Albany: J.B. Lyon, 1902), New York State Military Museum, www.dmna.state.ny.us/historic.
12. Boudrye, *Historic*, pp. 287–309, p. 221; *In Memoriam: John Hammond*, pp. 4–5; James Penfield, *The 1863–1864 Civil War Diary of Captain James Penfield* (Crown Point, NY: Penfield Foundation, 1999), p. 14.
13. From Frederick Phisterer, *New York in the War of the Rebellion*, 6 vols., 3rd ed. (Albany: J.B. Lyon, 1912), vol. 2, p. 882ff. The volumes by Phisterer can be found digital form in the New York State Military Museum at www.dmna.state.ny.us/historic; Starr, *Union Cavalry*, Vol. 1, pp. 108–109; Hillman A. Hall, ed., *History of the Sixth New York Cavalry (Second Ira Harris Guard)* (Worcester, MA: Blanchard, 1908), p. 17; Boudrye, *Historic*, pp. 206–208.
14. Company L, Fifth New York Cavalry, Prisoner of War Records, National Archives, Washington, D.C.; U.S. War Department, *War of Rebellion ... Official Records of the Union and Confederate Armies*, 128 vols. (Washington: Government Printing Office, 1880–1901), Series 3, Vol. II, p. 186. Hereinafter cited as *O.R.*
15. B. Conrad Bush, comp., *Articles from Wyoming County Newspapers and Letters from Soldiers of 5th New York Cavalry* (West Falls, NY: Bush Research, 2000), pp. 20–21, 84.
16. 5th Regiment Cavalry, N.Y. Volunteers Civil War Newspaper Clippings, New York State Military Museum, www.dmna.state.ny.us/historic.
17. Quoted in Starr, *Union Cavalry*, vol. 1, p. 110, pp. 131–132; Charles D. Rhodes, *History of*

the *Cavalry of the Army of the Potomac* (Kansas City: Hudson–Kimberley, 1900), pp. 8–9.
  18. Longacre, *Lincoln's Cavalrymen*, pp. 28–33; *O.R.*, Series 1, Vol. V, pt. 1, pp. 81–82; Starr, *Union Cavalry*, Vol. 1, p. 185.
  19. Starr, ibid., p. 186; Boudrye, *Historic*, p. 206, 301; *In Memoriam: John Hammond*, p. 47.
  20. Starr, ibid., pp. 258–259; Hall, *History of the Sixth New York Cavalry*, p. 31.
  21. Boudrye, *Historic*, pp. 21–23; Bell I. Wiley, *The Life of Billy Yank* (Indianapolis: Bobbs-Merrill, 1951), p. 320.
  22. *In Memoriam: John Hammond*, p. 47.
  23. Bush, *Articles from Wyoming County*, p. 115.
  24. Starr, *Union Cavalry*, vol. 1, pp. 119–125; Longacre, *Lincoln's Cavalrymen*, pp. 37, 41–42.
  25. Longacre, ibid., p. 35; Chauncy Norton, *The Red Neck Ties or History of the Fifteenth New York Volunteer Cavalry* (Ithaca, NY: Journal Book and Job Printing House, 1891), p. 18; Willard Glazier, *Three Years in the Federal Cavalry* (New York: R.H. Ferguson, 1874), pp. 32–33.
  26. Bush, *Articles from Wyoming County*, pp. 21–22, 25, 34, 39; Glazier, *Three Years in the Federal Cavalry*, pp. 32–33.
  27. Starr, *Union Cavalry*, vol. 1, pp. 207, 197; Longacre, *Lincoln's Cavalrymen*, p. 52; Boudrye, *Historic*, pp. 202–204, 287–309, 221–223; www.dmna.state.ny.us/historic, Fifth New York Cavalry, Ralph Tolles Collection, November 10, 1861.
  28. Glazier, *Three Years in the Federal Cavalry*, p. 30. Although he was in another regiment, it is clear in reading this work that the author was familiar with Boudrye's history of the Fifth New York. Several episodes related by the chaplain are included in Glazier's work.
  29. Wiley, *The Life of Billy Yank*, pp. 221–222.
  30. Richard E. Boudrye, ed., *War Journal of Louis N. Beaudrye, Fifth New York Cavalry: The Diary of a Union Chaplain, commencing February 16, 1863* (Jefferson, NC: McFarland, 1996), pp. ix-xi, 1–6. The spelling of the chaplain's family name has changed through the years and here will conform to the spelling used in the history and journal. In the regimental list it is spelled Boudrye.

Chapter 2

  1. www.dmna.state.ny.us/historic Fifth New York Cavalry, Ralph Tolles Collection, May 29, 1862.
  2. www.dmna.state.ny.us/historic Fifth New York Cavalry, Ralph Tolles Collection, April 29, 1862; Boudrye, *Historic*, p. 24; Starr, *Union Cavalry*, vol. 1, 279; *In Memoriam: John Hammond*, p. 47.
  3. Boudrye, ibid., p. 298; George G. Benedict, *Vermont in the Civil War, 1861–1865*, 2 vols. (Burlington: Free Press Association, 1888), vol. 2, p. 541; Bush, *Articles from Wyoming County*, p. 59–60.
  4. Boudrye, *Historic*, pp. 24–25, 288.
  5. Ibid., 25–27; *O.R.*, Ser. 1, Vol. XII, pt. 1, p. 456; *New York Times*, May 8, 1862.
  6. www.dmna.state.ny.us/historic Fifth New York Cavalry, Ralph Tolles, Collection, May 8, 1862.
  7. *O.R.*, Ser. 1, Vol. XII, pt. 1, pp. 456, 523, 535–536, 564–565.
  8. Boudrye, *Historic*, p. 221.
  9. *O.R.*, ibid., p. 565.
  10. Boudrye, ibid., pp. 31–33, 34.
  11. *O.R.*, ibid., pp. 581–584, 575.
  12. Glazier, *Three Years in the Federal Cavalry*, pp. 70–71.
  13. Boudrye, *Historic*, pp. 28–31, *O.R.*, ibid.
  14. Boudrye, ibid., p. 36. Twenty-four men were captured at Barnett's Ford on July 18 1862; Bush, *Articles from Wyoming Country*, pp. 63, 65–66.
  15. Boudrye, *Historic*, p. 37.
  16. Glazier, *Three Years in the Federal Cavalry*, p. 79.
  17. Boudrye, *Historic*, pp. 37–38. In this engagement three were killed, four wounded and twenty-two counted as missing.
  18. Boudrye, ibid., pp. 36–39; 5th Regiment Cavalry, Newspaper Clippings. There is no Colonel Robinson listed as serving in the Fifth New York.
  19. Boudrye, ibid.
  20. Ibid., pp. 39–40; www.History.Army.mil.
  21. Boudrye, ibid., pp. 40–41, 221, 298; Bush, *Articles from Wyoming County*, 69, 72.
  22. Boudrye, ibid., p. 41.
  23. Starr, *Union Cavalry*, vol. 1, p. 304.
  24. *In Memoriam: John Hammond*, pp. 54–57.
  25. Boudrye, *Historic*, pp. 42–43; Bush, *Articles from Wyoming County*, pp. 75–76.

Chapter 3

  1. *O.R.*, Ser. 1, Vol. XXV, pt. 1, p. 1105.
  2. Boudrye, *War Journal*, p. 3.
  3. Ibid., p. 6.
  4. Ibid., pp. 7–9. Boudrye is either confused at this time about Hammond's status in the regiment — he did not be commander until June 1863 — or Lt. Col. Johnstone was away and Hammond was temporarily in command when Boudrye arrived.
  5. Ibid., pp. 12–13.
  6. Boudrye, *Historic*, pp. 51–52; www.dmna.state.ny.us/historic/rosters, Fifth New York Cavalry.
  7. Boudrye, ibid., p. 51; John S. Mosby, *Mosby's Memoirs: The Memoirs of Colonel John Singleton Mosby*, reprint (New York: Barnes & Noble, 2006), p. 102.

8. Boudrye, ibid., p. 51; James J. Williamson, *Mosby's Rangers* (New York: Ralph B. Kenyon, 1896), p. 28.
9. John S. Mosby, "A Bit of Partisan Service," in *Battles and Leaders of the Civil War*, Robert Underwood Johnson and Clarence Clough, comp., 4 vols. (New York: Century, 1887–1888), vol. 3, p. 149.
10. Mosby, *Memoirs*, pp. 104–107.
11. Mark M. Boatner, *The Civil War Dictionary* (New York: David McKay, 1959), p. 45.
12. Benedict, *Vermont in the Civil War*, vol. 2, p. 587; Williamson, *Mosby's Rangers*, pp. 80, 255; Jeffry D. Wert, *Mosby's Rangers* (New York: Simon and Schuster, 1990), p. 227.
13. Boudrye, *Historic*, pp. 50–53.
14. Ibid., p. 50.
15. Penfield, *The 1863–1864 Civil War Diary*, p. 31.
16. Boatner, *The Civil War Dictionary*, pp. 790–791; Edmund Wright, *The Desk Encyclopedia of World History* (New York: Oxford University Press, 2006), p. 357; James H. Kidd, *Personal Recollections of a Cavalryman with Custer's Michigan Cavalry Brigade in the Civil War* (Ionia, MI: Sentinel, 1908), pp. 96–97.
17. Boudrye, *Historic*, pp. 55–56; 5th Regiment Cavalry, Newspaper Clippings; O.R., Ser. 1, Vol. XXV, pt. 1, p. 1005.
18. Boudrye, ibid., pp. 58–59; www.vermontcivilwar.org, Hammond Correspondence; Bush, *Articles from Wyoming County*, p. 93.
19. Hammond Correspondence, ibid.; Bush. *Articles from Wyoming County*, p. 93.
20. Glazier, *Three Years in the Federal Cavalry*, p. 160; Hammond Correspondence, ibid.

Chapter 4

1. Henry C. Parsons, "Gettysburg: The Campaign was a Chapter of Accidents," *National Tribune*, August 7, 1890; Kidd, *Recollections*, p. 118; O.R., Ser. 1, Vol. XXVII, Pt. 3, pp. 425–426.
2. Bush, *Articles from Wyoming County*, pp. 93–93.
3. Penfield, *The 1863–1864 Civil War Diary*, p. 64.
4. Rhodes, *History of the Cavalry of the Army of the Potomac*, p. 31.
5. Boudrye, *War Journal*, pp. 38–39.
6. McPherson, *The Battle Cry of Freedom*, p. 330.
7. Eric J. Wittenberg, J. David Patruzzi, *Plenty of Blame to Go Around: Jeb Stuart's Controversial Ride to Gettysburg* (New York: Savas Beatie, 2006), pp. 85–86; *In Memoriam: John Hammond*, p. 18; Boudrye, *Historic*, p. 302: U.S., Congress, *Biographical Dictionary of the American Congress, 1774–1949* (Washington: Government Printing Office, 1950), www.bioguide.congress.gov.
8. Boudrye, *War Journal*, p. 40.
9. O.R., Ser. 1, Vol. XXVII, pt. 3, p. 95.
10. Boudrye, *Historic*, p. 60; Boudrye, *War Journal*, pp. 43–44; *In Memoriam: John Hammond*, pp. 57–58.
11. Henry Norton, *Deeds of Daring, or, History of the Eighth N.Y. Volunteer Cavalry* (Norwich, NY: Chenango Telegraph Printing House, 1889), p. 66.
12. *In Memoriam: John Hammond*, p. 58.
13. Edward G. Longacre, *The Cavalry at Gettysburg: A Tactical Study of Mounted Operations during the Civil War's Pivotal Campaign, 9 June–14 July, 1863* (Lincoln: University of Nebraska Press, 1986), pp. 162–163; Boudrye, *Historic*, pp. 53–63; *War Journal*, pp. 46–48.
14. Noah Andres Trudeau, *Gettysburg: A Testing of Courage* (New York: Harper-Collins, 2002), pp. 130–131.
15. Longacre, *The Cavalry at Gettysburg*, pp. 53–54; Boatner, *Civil War Dictionary*, pp. 459–460.
16. Boatner, ibid., Kidd, *Personal Recollections*, p. 165.
17. Alfred Pleasonton, "The Campaign of Gettysburg," in *The Annals of War: Written by the Leading Participants, North and South, Originally Published in the Philadelphia Weekly Times* (Philadelphia: Weekly Times Publishing Co., 1879), p. 452.
18. Longacre, *The Cavalry at Gettysburg*, pp. 161–164; Stephen A. Clark, "Hanover, Pa.," *The National Tribune*, February 23, 1888.
19. Trudeau, *Gettysburg*, p. 581.
20. Longacre, *The Cavalry at Gettysburg*, p. 56.
21. Ibid., p. 172.
22. Longacre, ibid., pp. 158–159; Boudrye, *War Journal*, p. 48; Boudrye, *Historic*, p. 64; Longacre, ibid., pp. 172–173; Kidd, *Personal Recollections*, p. 117.
23. Wittenberg, *Plenty of Blame*, pp. 72–76; Longacre, *The Cavalry at Gettysburg*, pp. 161–164, 172–173; Kidd, *Recollections*, pp. 120–121.
24. Longacre, ibid., pp. 158–159; Boudrye, *War Journal*, p. 48; Boudrye, *Historic*, pp. 62–63.
25. Boudrye, *War Journal*, p. 49; Trudeau, *Gettysburg*, pp. 130–131; Parsons, "Chapter of Accidents."
26. O.R., Ser. 1, Vol. XXVII, pt. 1, p. 1008.
27. Longacre, *The Cavalry at Gettysburg*, p. 174.
28. Boudrye, *Historic*, pp. 64–65; Boudrye, *War Journal*, p. 49; O.R., Ser. 1, Vol. XXVII, pt. 1, p. 1008; Bush, *Articles from Wyoming County*, p. 102.
29. Boudrye, *Historic*, p. 65; Longacre, The Cavalry at Gettysburg, pp. 174–175.
30. *New York Times*, August 6, 1863.
31. Longacre, *The Cavalry at Gettysburg*, pp. 175–176; Wittenberg, *Plenty of Blame*, p. 96;

Boudrye, *War Journal*, p. 49; *O.R.*, ibid., pp. 1008–1009.
32. Boudrye, *Historic*, p. 65.
33. Longacre, *The Cavalry at Gettysburg*, pp. 175–176; Wittenberg, *Plenty of Blame*, p. 93.
34. Kidd, *Personal Recollections*, p. 128.
35. *O.R.*, Ser. 1, Vol. XXVII, pt. 1, p. 992.
36. Clark, "Hanover, Pa."
37. *O.R.*, ibid., p. 1008; Benedict, *Vermont in the Civil War*, vol. 2, p. 594.
38. Longacre, *The Cavalry at Gettysburg*, pp. 175–176; Wittenberg, *Plenty of Blame*, p. 101; *O.R.*, ibid., p. 1009.
39. Longacre, *The Cavalry at Gettysburg*, pp. 175–176; *O.R.*, ibid., pp. 986–987.
40. *O.R.*, ibid., p. 992; Boudrye, *War Journal*, p. 49; *O.R.*, ibid., p. 1008; Phisterer, *New York in the War of the Rebellion*, vol. 2, p. 822ff. Officially the battle cost the Fifth New York six dead, thirty wounded and eighteen missing.
41. *O.R.*, ibid., p. 1008–1009; Kidd, *Personal Recollections*, p. 128.
42. Boudrye, *War Journal*, p. 49.
43. *O.R.*, ibid., pp. 986–987.
44. Ibid., p. 987.
45. Ibid., pp. 987–988.
46. 5th Regiment Cavalry, Newspaper Clippings; Bush, *Articles from Wyoming County*, p. 59.

Chapter 5

1. Bush, *Articles from Wyoming County*, p. 102–103.
2. Boudrye, *Historic*, p. 66; Boudrye, *War Journal*, p. 49.
3. Boudrye, *War Journal*, pp. 49–50; Boudrye, *Historic*, p. 296.
4. Boudrye, *War Journal*, p. 49; Longacre, *The Cavalry at Gettysburg*, pp. 178–179, Publication Committee of the Regimental Association, *History of the Eighteenth Regiment of Cavalry, Pennsylvania Volunteers, 1861–1865* (New York: 1909), p. 78.
5. Trudeau, *Gettysburg*, pp. 262–263, 278.
6. Ibid., pp. 330–331; Longacre, *The Cavalry at Gettysburg*, pp. 198–201; Wittenberg, *Plenty of Blame*, pp. 161–176. A detailed account of this action contained in Longacre's *The Cavalry at Gettysburg*.
7. 5th Regiment Cavalry, Newspaper Clippings.
8. Longacre, *The Cavalry at Gettysburg*, 201.
9. Quoted in Longacre, *The Cavalry at Gettysburg*, p. 232; Stephen A. Clark, "Farnsworth's Death," *The National Tribune*, December 3, 1891.
10. M. Jacobs, *Notes on the Rebel Invasion of Maryland and Pennsylvania....* (Philadelphia: J.B. Lippincott, 1864), pp. 40–41.
11. Walter Lord, ed., *The Fremantle Diary* (Boston: Little, Brown, 1954), pp. 277–278.

12. Quote in Eric J. Wittenberg, *Gettysburg's Forgotten Cavalry Actions: Farnsworth's Charge, South Cavalry Field, and the Battle of Fairfield, July 3, 1863* (New York: Savas Beatie, 2011), p. 27.
13. 5th Regiment Cavalry, Newspaper Clippings.
14. *New York Times*, July 21, 1863.
15. *In Memoriam: John Hammond*, pp. 59–60.
16. *O.R.*, Ser. 1, Vol. XXVII, pt. 1, p. 1009.
17. Ibid., p. 992. A written order from Pleasonton to Kilpatrick is not included in the *Official Record*.
18. *O.R.*, ibid.; Trudeau, *Gettysburg*, pp. 516–517.
19. Evander M. Law, "The Struggle for Round Top," in *Battles and Leaders of the Civil War* (New York: Century, 1887–1888), vol. 3, p. 327.
20. Benedict, *Vermont in the Civil War*, vol. 2, p. 598.
21. C.H. Parsons, "Farnsworth's Charge and Death," in *Battles and Leaders of the Civil War*, vol. 3, pp. 393–396; quoted in Wittenberg, *Gettysburg's Forgotten Cavalry Actions*, p. 73. This episode is included here because it has often been written into the history of this action. However, there are sources that deny that the exchange between Kilpatrick and Farnsworth ever took place. See Edward G. Longacre, *The Cavalry at Gettysburg*, p. 311, note 85.
22. Ibid., p. 394.
23. *In Memoriam: John Hammond*, pp. 60–61.
24. Quoted in Longacre, *The Cavalry at Gettysburg*, p. 204.
25. Benedict, *Vermont in the Civil War*, vol. 2, p. 599.
26. *O.R.*, Ser. 1, Vol. XXVII, pt. 1, p. 1013. Lt. Col. Preston wrote another account of his part in the charge and this was printed in the *Rutland Weekly Herald* about one month after the battle. See Eric J. Wittenberg, *Gettysburg's Forgotten Cavalry Actions*, pp. 198–199.
27. Benedict, *Vermont in the Civil War*, vol. 2, pp. 601–601; Law, "The Struggle for Round Top," in *Battles and Leaders of the Civil War*, vol. 3, p. 329.
28. *O.R.*, ibid., p. 993.
29. Benedict, *Vermont in the Civil War*, vol. 2, p. 603; Parsons, "Gettysburg"; Alfred Pleasonton, "The Campaign of Gettysburg," pp. 453ff.
30. Starr, *Union Cavalry*, vol. 1, p. 441, note 85; *O.R.*, Ser. 1, Vol. XXVII, pt. 1, pp. 1018–1019.
31. U.S. Congress, *Report of the Joint Committee on the Conduct of the War* (Washington: Government Printing Office, 1865), pp. 359–360.
32. James Longstreet, *From Manassas to Appomattox: Memoirs of the Civil War in America* (Bloomington: Indiana University Press, 1960), p. 396.
33. Longacre, *Lincoln's Cavalrymen*, p. 203; *O.R.*, Vol. XXVII, pt. 1, p. 366; *Report of the Joint Committee on the Conduct of the War*, p. 333.
34. Starr, *Union Cavalry*, vol. 1, p. 440. In no

Notes — Chapters 6, 7

history of this phase of the battle by any authority is there to be found a citation noting a written order dated July 3 from Pleasonton to Kilpatrick ordering him to attack as he did. All histories of this action merely state, "Kilpatrick was ordered." For Pleasonton's rendition of urging Meade to counterattack late on July 3, see Pleasonton, "The Campaign of Gettysburg," pp. 455–456; also Wittenberg, *Gettysburg's Forgotten Cavalry Actions*, p. 146, note 14. The Confederate Command on the ground at the time denied that the Rebels were going to attack the left of the Union line on July 3; see Longacre, *The Cavalry at Gettysburg*, p. 311, note 90.

35. *O.R.*, ibid., p. 993, 1008.
36. Ibid., p. 993.
37. Henry Capehart, "Fighting His Way," *The National Tribune*, January 3, 1895.
38. Boudrye, *War Journal*, p. 50. See also Wittenberg, *Gettysburg's Forgotten Cavalry Actions*. Sergeant Perley C.J. Cheney of the First Vermont was wounded in the charge; the ball hit his pocket watch, stopping it at exactly 5:27 P.M. Cheney survived.

Chapter 6

1. *In Memoriam: John Hammond*, pp. 59–60.
2. 5th Regiment Cavalry, Newspaper Clippings.
3. John D. Imboden, "The Confederate Retreat from Gettysburg," in *Battles and Leaders*, vol. 3, p. 429.
4. Boudrye, *War Journal*, p. 50; *In Memoriam: John Hammond*, p. 59.
5. Boudrye, *War Journal*, p. 50; *O.R.*, Ser. 1 Vol. XXVII, pt. 1, p. 994; Eric J. Wittenberg, Carla Jean Husby, eds., *Under Custer's Command: The Journal of James H. Avery* (Dulles, VA: Brassey's, 2000), p. 38.
6. *O.R.*, ibid., p. 994.
7. Capehart, "Fighting His Way"; Eric J. Wittenberg, J. David Petruzzi, Michael F. Nugent, *One Continuous Fight: The Retreat from Gettysburg and the Pursuit of Lee's Army of Northern Virginia, July 4–14, 1863* (New York: Savas Beattie, 2008), p. 71; John A. Bigelow, "Flashing Sabers," *The National Tribune*, November 10, 1887.
8. *In Memoriam: John Hammond*, pp. 59–60. Boudrye in the regiment's history puts the number of wagons at 200, while Col. Huey in his after-action report, cited by Starr in *Union Cavalry*, Vol. 1, p. 450, says there were 300. Henry Capehart, cited above, also uses the 300 figure for the number of wagons captured.
9. *O.R.*, ibid., p. 1006; Wittenberg, *Avery*, p. 39; *New York Times*, July 21, 1863; Longacre, *Lincoln's Cavalrymen*, p. 225; 5th Regiment Cavalry, Newspaper Clippings; Longacre, *The Cavalry at Gettysburg*, p. 250.
10. Boudrye, *Historic*, p. 68.

11. Boudrye, *Historic*, pp. 252–253; Boudrye, *War Journal*, pp. 50–51.
12. *New York Times*, July 21, 1863; *O.R.*, ibid., p. 1009; Eric J. Wittenberg, J. David Petruzzi and Michael F. Nugent, *One Continuous Fight* (New York: Savas Beattie, 2008), pp. 102–104.
13. *New York Times*, July 21, 1863.
14. 5th Regiment Cavalry, Newspaper Clippings.
15. 5th Regiment Cavalry, Newspaper Clippings; Longacre, *Lincoln's Cavalrymen*, pp. 256–257; Benedict, *Vermont in the Civil War*, vol. 2, p. 605.
16. *O.R.*, Ser. 1, Vol. XXVII, pt. 1, pp. 1007, 1009–1010.
17. Longacre, *Lincoln's Cavalrymen*, pp. 256–257.
18. *O.R.*, ibid., 1010. Colonel Richmond reported that the First Brigade at Hagerstown, including the Fifth New York, lost fourteen men killed, forty-four wounded and 208 missing.
19. *O.R.*, ibid., p. 1006.
20. Ibid., p. 995.
21. Stephen W. Sears, *Gettysburg* (New York: Houghton Mifflin, 2003), pp. 482–484; *O.R.*, ibid., pp. 1009–1010; *In Memoriam: John Hammond*, pp. 61–62.
22. *In Memoriam: John Hammond*, pp. 63–64.
23. Phisterer, *New York in the War of the Rebellion*, vol. 2, p. 822ff.
24. Boudrye, *Historic*, p. 69; Boudrye, *War Journal*, pp. 51–52.
25. 5th Regiment Cavalry, Newspaper Clippings; Longacre, *Lincoln's Cavalrymen*, pp. 260–261.
26. *O.R.*, ibid., p. 1010.
27. *In Memoriam: John Hammond*, p. 62.
28. Moore, *Kilpatrick and Our Cavalry*, p. 104.
29. Boudrye, *Historic*, pp. 69–70.
30. *O.R.*, Ser. 1, Vol. XXVII, pt. 3, pp. 605–606.
31. Wittenberg, *One Continuous Fight*, pp. 214–215; O.R. Ser. 1, Vol. XVII, pt. 1, p. 1007.
32. Boudrye, *Historic*, p. 70.
33. Longacre, *Lincoln's Cavalrymen*, pp. 263–269.
34. 5th Regiment Cavalry, Newspaper Clippings.
35. Boudrye, *Historic*, pp. 73–74.
36. *In Memoriam: John Hammond*, p. 63.
37. Kidd, *Personal Recollections*, p. 178.
38. 5th Regiment Cavalry, Newspaper Clippings.
39. *In Memoriam: John Hammond*, p. 64.
40. Ibid.
41. Boudrye, *War Journal*, p. 52.

Chapter 7

1. Bush, *Letters from Wyoming County*, p. 105.
2. Boudrye, *Historic*, p. 74; *In Memoriam: John Hammond*, p. 66.

3. 5th Regiment Cavalry, Newspaper Clippings.
4. *In Memoriam: John Hammond*, pp. 67–68.
5. Longacre, *The Cavalry at Gettysburg*, pp. 164, 120; Boudrye, *Historic*, p. 70; Wittenberg, *One Continuous Fight*, p. 204.
6. *O.R.*, Ser. 1, Vol. XXVII, pt. 1, p. 1001.
7. 5th Regiment Cavalry, Newspaper Clippings; Bush, *Articles from Wyoming County*, pp. 101–102.
8. *In Memoriam: John Hammond*, p. 70.
9. Boudrye, *Historic*, p. 221; *New York Times*, March 2, 1864; *In Memoriam: John Hammond*, p. 77.
10. *New York Times*, April 24, 1864
11. Boudrye, *Historic*, p. 226; *New York Times*, December 17, 1864.
12. Phisterer, *New York in the War of the Rebellion*, vol. 2, p. 835.
13. Military Service Record, National Archives, Washington, D.C.; *In Memoriam: John Hammond*, pp. 68, 70, 73; Boudrye, *Historic*, p. 221; Adjutant General Report, New York State Military Museum, www.dmna.state.ny.us/historic/civil/rosters.
14. *New York Times*, May 1, 1864.
15. Longacre, *Lincoln's Cavalrymen*, p. 223; Bush, *Articles from Wyoming County*, pp. 103–104; quoted in Glazier, *Three Years in the Federal Cavalry*, pp. 316–317; Boudrye, *Historic*, pp. 235–236.
16. Longacre, *Lincoln's Cavalrymen*, pp. 224–225; Boudrye, *Historic*, pp. 77, 213; *In Memoriam: John Hammond*, p. 71.
17. 5th Regiment Cavalry, Newspaper Clippings.
18. Longacre, ibid., p. 225; Boudrye, ibid., p. 77.
19. *In Memoriam: John Hammond*, pp. 72–73.
20. Boudrye, *Historic*, p. 78.
21. Willard Glazier, *Battles for the Union* (Hartford: Dustin, Gilman & Co., 1875), p. 317; Boudrye, *Historic*, p. 78. Curiously, Glazier's and the chaplain's description of that morning's breakfast menu, from two different regiments, closely resemble each other. In that Glazier's *Battles for the Union* was published in 1875, he probably had a copy of the Fifth's history to consult and refresh his memory while writing.
22. *O.R.*, Ser. 1, Vol. XXIX, pt. 1, pp. 384–385.
23. Boudrye, *Historic*, pp. 79–80; *O.R.*, ibid., pp. 385–388.
24. Boudrye, ibid., Longacre, *Lincoln's Cavalrymen*, pp. 227–228.
25. Stephen Z. Starr, *The Union Cavalry in the Civil War*, vol. 2: *The War in the East from Gettysburg to Appomattox, 1863–1865* (Baton Rouge: Louisiana State University Press, 1981), pp. 29–30; *In Memoriam: John Hammond*, p. 73.
26. Boudrye, *Historic*, p. 83; Starr, ibid., pp. 29–30.
27. 5th Regiment Cavalry, Newspaper Clippings; Longacre, ibid., p. 230, Glazier, *Three Years in the Federal Cavalry*, pp. 334–345.
28. *In Memoriam: John Hammond*, p. 73; *O.R.*, ibid., pp. 384–388; Boudrye, *Historic*, p. 204.
29. Boudrye, *Historic*, p. 83.
30. Ibid., p. 84.
31. 5th Regiment Cavalry, Newspaper clippings.
32. *In Memoriam: John Hammond*, p. 75; Boudrye, *Historic*, p. 85; Boudrye, *War Journal*, p. 70
33. Boudrye, *War Journal*, p. 71.
34. Ibid., p. 72.
35. Ibid., p. 72; Boudrye, *Historic*, p. 86; www.History.Army.mil/moh. Medal of Honor citations.
36. Boudrye, *War Journal*, pp. 68–69; Bush, *Articles from Wyoming County*, p. 106.
37. Boudrye, *War Journal*, p. 77.
38. Bush, *Articles from Wyoming County*, p. 120; Starr, *Union Cavalry*, vol. 2, pp. 36–37; Glazier, *Three Years in the Federal Cavalry*, p. 116.
39. James M. McPherson, *This Mighty Scourge: Perspectives on the Civil War* (New York: Oxford University Press, 2007), p. 158.
40. *New York Times*, February 28, 1864.
41. Starr, *Union Cavalry*, vol. 2, pp. 38–40; Kidd, *Personal Recollections*, p. 223.
42. Boudrye, *War Journal*, p. 70.
43. Ibid., p. 74.
44. Starr, *Union Cavalry*, vol. 2, p. 46.
45. Bush, *Articles from Wyoming County*, p. 120; Boudrye, *War Journal*, p. 74.
46. Boudrye, *War Journal*, p. 75.
47. Boudrye, *Historic*, p. 92; Starr, *Union Cavalry*, vol. 2, p. 48; Phisterer, *New York in the War of the Rebellion*, vol. 2, p. 822ff; *In Memoriam: John Hammond*, p. 76.
48. Boudrye, *Historic*, pp. 92–93.
49. Ibid., pp. 93–94.
50. Ibid., p. 94.
51. Boudrye, *War Journal*, pp. 96–97.
52. Bush, *Articles from Wyoming County*, pp. 125–126; *New York Times*, February 23, 1864.
53. Quoted in Bruce Catton, *A Stillness at Appomattox* (New York: Random House, 1953), p. 4.
54. Boudrye, *War Journal*, p. 95.
55. Catton, *Stillness*, p. 3–4.
56. *In Memoriam: John Hammond*, p. 76.
57. *O.R.*, Ser. 1 Vol. XXXIII, pt. 1, p. 552; Starr, *Union Cavalry*, vol. 2, pp. 57–58.
58. McPherson, *The Battle Cry of Freedom*, pp. 698–699. Amnesty was part of Lincoln's reconstruction plan whereby ten percent of the population of any state that seceded after the 1860 election, if swearing renewed allegiance to the federal government, could then construct a new state government and seek readmission to the Union.
59. Catton, *Stillness*, pp. 5–9.
60. Boudrye, *War Journal*, p. 96.
61. *O.R.*, Ser. 1, Vol. XXXIII, pt. 1, p. 941.

62. Catton, *Stillness*, pp. 9–10.
63. Boudrye, *War Journal*, p. 97.
64. Boudrye, *Historic*, pp. 97–99.
65. Catton, *Stillness*, pp. 17–18; Boatner, *The Civil War Dictionary*, p. 461, identifies the victim as one Martin Robinson.
66. Boudrye, *Historic*, pp. 101–102.
67. Ibid., 103.
68. Ibid., 104.
69. Ibid., pp. 105–106.
70. *O.R.*, Ser. 1, Vol. XXXIII, pt. 1, p. 196; Boudrye, *Historic*, pp. 108–109.
71. Ibid., pp. 113–114.
72. Ibid., p. 114.
73. Ibid., p. 115.
74. Starr, *Union Cavalry*, vol. 2, pp. 61–62.
75. Bush, *Articles from Wyoming Country*, p. 120; Catton, *Stillness*, pp. 17–18.
76. Boudrye, *War Journal*, pp. 99–100; Boudrye, *Historic*, p. 95.
77. Starr, *Union Cavalry*, vol. 2, pp. 62–63, note 92.
78. *O.R.*, Ser. 1, Vol. XXXIII, pt. 1, p.184.
79. Ibid., pp. 184–185.
80. Ibid., p. 185.
81. Starr, *Union Cavalry*, vol. 2, pp. 66–67.
82. *O.R.*, ibid., p. 187.
83. *O.R.*, ibid., p. 193; Boudrye, *War Journal*, p. 101.
84. Boudrye, *War Journal*, pp. 101–102, 105.
85. Boudrye, *Historic*, p. 119.

Chapter 8

1. George R. Agassiz, ed., *Meade's Headquarters, 1863–1865: Letters of Colonel Theodore Lyman* (Boston: Massachusetts Historical Society, 1922), p. 83; Luman Harris Tenney, *War Diary, 1861–1865* (Oberlin, OH: privately issued, 1914), p.117.
2. Quoted in Samuel E. Morrison, Henry Steel Commager, and William Leuchtenburg, *The Growth of the American Republic*, 2 vols. (New York: Oxford University Press, 1969), vol. 1, p. 704.
3. Boudrye, *Historic*, p. 121.
4. Ibid., pp. 120–121, 205.
5. Catton, *Stillness*, p. 22.
6. *New York Times*, February 23, 1864.
7. Quoted in Edward G. Longacre, *From Union Stars to Top Hat: A Biography of the Extraordinary Career of General James Harrison Wilson* (Harrisburg, PA: Stackpole, 1972), p. 111.
8. *O.R.*, Ser. 1, Vol. XXXIII, pt. 1, p. 891.
9. Gordon C. Rhea, "Union Cavalry in the Wilderness: The Education of Philip H. Sheridan and James H. Wilson," in *The Wilderness Campaign*, ed. by Gary W. Gallagher (Chapel Hill: University of North Carolina Press, 1997), pp. 109–110; Philip H. Sheridan, *Personal Memoirs of P.H. Sheridan*, reprint (New York: Barnes and Noble, 2006), pp. 181–182; Starr, *Union Cavalry*, vol. 2, p. 80.
10. Boatner, *The Civil War Dictionary*, p. 938; Longacre, *Top Hat*, pp. 102–103.
11. Quoted in Starr, *Union Cavalry*, vol. 2, p. 252, note 48.
12. *O.R.*, ibid., p. 891.
13. Sheridan, *Personal Memoirs*, p. 181; Longacre, *Top Hat*, p. 110.
14. James H. Wilson, *Under the Old Flag*, 2 vols. (New York: D. Appleton, 1912), vol. 1, p 372; Starr, *Union Cavalry*, vol. 2, p. 79.
15. Starr, ibid., pp. 79–80, note 27.
16. *In Memoriam: John Hammond*, pp. 5–6.
17. Robert E. Lee, *Recollections and Letters*, reprint (New York: Barnes & Noble, 2004), pp. 108–109, 105. Lee's *Letters* is a volume containing selected correspondence by the general and published by his son, Robert Jr., in 1904.
18. *O.R.*, Ser. 1, Vol. XXXIII, pp. 862, 872; ibid., Vol. XXXII, pt. 3, p. 375; Starr, ibid., p. 76; quoted in Starr, ibid., p. 82, note 35.
19. Boudrye, *War Journal*, p. 106.
20. Boudrye, ibid., p. 107–109; *Annual Report of the Adjutant General for the year 1894*, vol. 2 (Albany: J.B. Lyon, 1895), www.dmna.state.ny.us/historic; *O.R.*, Ser. 1, Vol. XXX, pt. 1, p. 918; Boudrye, *War Journal*, p. 108.
21. *In Memoriam: John Hammond*, p. 79; Boudrye, *War Journal*, pp. 111–112; Boudrye, *Historic*, p. 272–275.
22. Catton, *Stillness*, pp. 55–56; William Swinton, *Campaigns of the Army of the Potomac, 1861–1865* (New York: Charles B. Richardson, 1866), p. 401; Boudrye, *War Journal*, p.112; Schaff, *Battle of the Wilderness*, p. 83.
23. Rhea, "Cavalry in the Wilderness," pp. 113–116.
24. Rhea, ibid., p. 116; Longacre, *Top Hat*, p. 112; Wilson, *Old Flag*, vol. 1, p. 379; *O.R.*, Ser. 1, Vol. XXXVI, pt. 2, p. 390.
25. Rhea, ibid., p. 117; *O.R.*, ibid., p. 430.
26. Schaff, *Battle of the Wilderness*, p. 131; Rhea, ibid., p. 118; L.J. Lichtenberg, "The Wilderness: How the 5th N.Y. Cav. Had a Hand in Opening the Fight," *National Tribune*, September, 30, 1886; D.H. Robbins, "Who Opened the Fight n the Wilderness," *National Tribune*, May 13, 1909.
27. Boudrye, *War Journal*, p. 112.
28. Rhea, ibid., pp. 118–119, note 36; Boudrye, *War Journal*, p. 112.
29. Boudrye, *Historic*, p. 122.
30. Rhea, ibid., p. 119.
31. Boudrye, *Historic*, pp. 122–123; *In Memoriam: John Hammond*, p. 79.
32. *O.R.*, Vol. XXXVI, pt. 1, pp. 885–886.
33. Longacre, *Top Hat*, pp. 115–116; Kidd, *Personal Recollections*, p. 265.

34. Bush, *Articles from Wyoming County*, p. 133.
35. Boudrye, *Historic*, p. 126.
36. Ibid.
37. Boudrye, *War Journal*, p. 114.
38. Boudrye, *Historic*, p. 127.
39. Ibid., p. 128.
40. Boudrye, *War Journal*, pp. 116–119; Boudrye, *Historic*, p. 128; *In Memoriam: John Hammond*, pp. 79–81.
41. Boudrye, *Historic*, p. 129.
42. Ibid., pp. 130–133.
43. Boudrye, *War Journal*, pp. 119. The regimental report of New York State Adjutant General's Office from 1894 had a Henry Crum enlisted as a private in Company D and born only on regimental history and "Had no further Record." William Dave is listed as joining Company F on February 5, 1864, and was " absent in arrest for desertion at muster out of company; no further record."
44. Boudrye, *War Journal*, pp. 120–121.
45. Boudrye, *Historic*, p. 134.
46. Ibid., pp. 135–136.
47. Ibid., p. 137; Boudrye, *War Journal*, p. 123.
48. Boudrye, *Historic*, pp. 137; Boudrye, *War Journal*, p. 123; *In Memoriam: John Hammond*, pp. 81–82.
49. Boudrye, *Historic*, p. 37; *In Memoriam: John Hammond*, p. 82.
50. Boudrye, *War Journal*, p. 126.
51. Isaac Gause, *Four Years with Five Armies* (New York: Neale, 1908), p. 221.
52. Boudrye, *Historic*, p. 139.
53. Boudrye, *War Journal*, pp. 131–132.
54. Starr, *Union Cavalry*, vol. 2, pp. 176–177; *In Memoriam: John Hammond*, p. 83.

Chapter 9

1. Bush, *Articles from Wyoming County*, p. 153.
2. Boudrye, *War Journal*, p. 144.
3. Starr, *Union Cavalry*, vol. 2, p. 176.
4. *In Memoriam: John Hammond*, p. 83.
5. Starr, ibid., p. 178.
6. *O.R.*, Ser. 1, Vol. XL, pt. 1, p. 625.
7. Andrew A. Humphreys, *The Virginia Campaign of '64 and '65* (New York: Charles Scribner, 1903), p. 243; *O.R.*, ibid., 621.
8. Boudrye, *Historic*, pp. 205, 213–214.
9. *O.R.*, ibid., p. 730.
10. Quoted in Starr, ibid., p. 180.
11. Starr, ibid., p. 183, note 25.
12. *O.R.*, ibid., p. 642; Norton, *Deeds of Daring*, p. 83.
13. Boudrye, *Historic*, p. 134.
14. Bush, *Articles from Wyoming County*, p. 137.
15. Starr, ibid., p. 181; *O.R.*, ibid., p. 621.
16. Boudrye, *War Journal*, p. 134; Starr, ibid., p. 182.
17. Starr, ibid., p. 182; *O.R.*, ibid., p. 621.
18. Boudrye, *War Journal*, p. 134; *O.R.*, p. 650; Boudrye, *Historic*, p. 214.
19. Bush, *Articles from Wyoming County*, p. 137.
20. *O.R.*, ibid., p. 621.
21. Quoted in Starr, ibid., p. 184.
22. *O.R.*, ibid., p. 635; Bush, *Articles from Wyoming County*, p. 153.
23. Quoted in Starr, ibid., pp. 191–192; Gause, *Three Years with Five Armies*, p. 285.
24. Wilson, *Old Flag*, vol. 1, pp. 463, 464–465.
25. *O.R.*, ibid., p. 622.
26. Wilson, *Old Flag*, vol. 1, p. 465.
27. *O.R.*, ibid., pp. 622, 627; Gause, *Three Years with Five Armies*, p. 285.
28. Benedict, *Vermont in the Civil War*, vol. 2, pp. 652–653.
29. Wilson, *Old Flag*, vol. 1, p. 466.
30. *O.R.*, ibid., pp. 633–638.
31. Boudrye, *War Journal*, p. 135.
32. *O.R.*, ibid., p. 690; Norton, *Deeds of Daring*, pp. 81–82.
33. Starr, ibid., p. 197.
34. Gause, *Three Years with Five Armies*, p. 289; Phisterer, *New York in the War of the Rebellion*, vol. 2, p. 822ff; Boudrye, *Historic*, p. 216.
35. Starr, ibid., pp. 197–199.
36. Benedict, *Vermont in the Civil War*, vol. 2, p. 654.
37. Quoted in Starr, ibid., p. 200.
38. Quoted in Starr, ibid., p. 201.
39. Starr, ibid., pp. 201–203.
40. Starr, ibid., p. 203; Boudrye, *War Journal*, pp. 135–145.
41. *In Memoriam: John Hammond*, pp. 83–85.
42. McPherson, *Battle Cry*, p. 756.
43. *O.R.*, ibid., p. 624.
44. *O.R.*, ibid., p. 637.
45. *O.R.*, ibid., p. 638.
46. Ulysses S. Grant, *Memoirs and Selected Letters*, reprint (New York: Literary Classics of the United States, 1990), pp. 604–605.
47. *O.R.*, Ser. 1, Vol. XL, pt. 2, p. 560.
48. Sheridan, *Memoirs*, pp. 228–229.
49. Longacre, *Lincoln's Cavalrymen*, p. 291.
50. William C. Davis, *Death in the Trenches: Grant at Petersburg* (New York: Time-Like Books, 1986), pp. 56–57.
51. Wilson, *Old Flag*, vol. 1, pp. 523–524; Douglas Southall Freeman, *Lee's Lieutenants: A Study in Command*, ed. by Stephen W Sear (Old Saybrook, CT: Konecky & Konecky, 1998), p. 731.
52. *O.R.*, Ser. 1, Vol. XL, pt. 1, p. 624.
53. *O.R.*, ibid., p. 33; Boudrye, *Historic*, p. 214.
54. *O.R.*, ibid., p. 809.
55. Marguerite Meringham, ed., *The Custer Story: The Life and Intimate Letters of George A, Custer and Wife Elizabeth* (New York: Devin-Adair, 1950), pp. 110–111.

56. Longacre, *Lincoln's Cavalrymen*, p. 292.
57. *O.R.*, ibid., p. 31.
58. Benedict, *Vermont in the Civil War*, vol. 2, p. 654.
59. Noah Andres Trudeau, *The Last Citadel: Petersburg, Virginia, June 1864–April 1865* (Boston: Little, Brown and Company, 1991), p. 90.
60. Boudrye, *War Journal*, p. 136; quoted in Starr, ibid., pp. 194, 206.
61. *O.R.*, ibid., p. 33; *In Memoriam: John Hammond*, p. 87.
62. Boudrye, *Historic*, pp. 205, 214.
63. *O.R.*, Ser. 1, Vol. XL, pt. 1 p. 732.
64. Boudrye, *Historic*, p. 159.
65. *In Memoriam: John Hammond*, p. 86.
66. Starr, ibid., pp. 230–231; Boudrye, *Historic*, pp. 159–160.

Chapter 10

1. Bush, *Articles from Wyoming County*, p. 158.
2. Boudrye, *War Journal*, pp. 153–154; Starr, *Union Cavalry*, vol. 2, p. 251.
3. Boudrye, ibid., pp. 156–157.
4. Boudrye, ibid., p. 157.
5. Boudrye, ibid., p. 158; Boudrye, *Historic*, pp. 162, 163–164.
6. Boudrye, *Historic*, p. 164.
7. Boudrye, ibid., pp. 166–167.
8. Boudrye, ibid., pp. 166–167; Starr, *Union Cavalry*, vol. 2, p. 250.
9. Boudrye, *Historic*, p. 168.
10. Boudrye, *War Journal*, p. 164.
11. Boudrye, *Historic*, pp. 168.
12. Wilson, *Old Flag*, vol. 1, pp. 53; *O.R.*, Ser. 1 Vol. XLIII, pt. 2, p. 33, 21–22; Catton, *Stillness*, pp. 281–282.
13. Boudrye, *War Journal*, p. 163.
14. Boudrye, *Historic*, p. 227.
15. Boudrye, ibid., pp. 227–228, 214.
16. Boudrye, ibid., pp. 229–230; Boudrye, *War Journal*, p. 164.
17. Boudrye, *War Journal*, p. 164; Bush, *Articles from Wyoming County*, p. 59.
18. Boudrye, *War Journal*, p. 167.
19. Boudrye, ibid., p. 168; Norton, *Deeds of Daring*, p. 90.
20. Starr, *Union Cavalry*, vol. 2, p. 260.
21. Boudrye, *War Journal*, 168.
22. Jeffry D. Wert, *From Winchester to Cedar Creek: The Shenandoah Valley Campaign of 1864* (Carlisle: South Mountain Press, 1987), pp. 47–56; Wilson, *Old Flag*, vol. 1, p. 551.
23. Boudrye, *War Journal*, p. 170.
24. Starr, ibid., p. 272.
25. Boudrye, *War Journal*, 170.
26. Starr, ibid., p. 277; Boudrye, *Historic*, pp. 178, 214; Wilson, *Old Flag*, vol. 1, pp. 555–557.
27. Starr, ibid., pp. 277–287.
28. Boudrye, *War Journal*, p. 171.
29. Boudrye, *Historic*, p. 173.
30. Starr, ibid., p. 287; Boudrye, *Historic*, pp. 173–174.
31. Boudrye, ibid., p. 174.
32. Quoted in Starr, ibid., pp. 278–288.
33. Starr, ibid., p. 289.
34. Boudrye, *War Journal*, p. 172.
35. Boudrye, ibid., p. 173.
36. Boudrye, *Historic*, p. 175; Starr, ibid., p. 293.
37. Boudrye, *War Journal*, pp. 173–175; Boudrye, *Historic*, p. 176.
38. Starr, ibid., pp. 293–294; Norton, *Deeds of Daring*, pp. 93–94; Charles A. Dana, *Recollections of the Civil War* (New York: D. Appleton, 1899), pp. 62, 73.
39. Boudrye, *War Journal*, p. 175.
40. Sheridan, *Memoirs*, p. 281.
41. Boudrye, *Historic*, p. 176.
42. Boudrye, *War Journal*, p. 175.
43. Sheridan, ibid., p. 284.
44. Boudrye, *Historic*, p. 177.
45. Boudrye, *War Journal*, p.175.
46. Boudrye, *Historic*, pp. 177–178, 214.
47. Sheridan, ibid., pp. 284–285.
48. Boudrye, *Historic*, p. 187.
49. Benedict, *Vermont in the Civil War*, vol. 2, pp. 663–664.
50. Eric J. Wittenberg, "The Battle of Tom's Brook, October, 9, 1864," *North and South* X, No. 1, p. 37; quoted in "Tom's Brook," p. 38; Starr, *Union Cavalry*, vol. 2, p. 298.
51. Quoted in Starr, ibid., p. 299.
52. Boudrye, *War Journal*, 176.
53. Starr, ibid., p. 299; William N. Pickerill, *History of the Third Indiana* (Indianapolis: privately issued, 1906), p. 167.
54. Wittenberg, "Tom's Brook," p. 39.
55. Boudrye, *War Journal*, p. 176; Phisterer, *New York in the War of the Rebellion*, vol. 2, p. 822ff.
56. Boudrye, *War Journal*, pp. 177, 178–179.

Chapter 11

1. Boudrye, *War Journal*, p. 179.
2. Starr, *Union Cavalry*, vol. 2, pp. 305–306.
3. Boudrye, *War Journal*, p. 178.
4. Kidd, *Personal Recollections*, p. 406; Starr, ibid., p. 308.
5. Kidd, ibid., p. 411; Boudrye, *War Journal*, p. 179.
6. Starr, ibid., p. 308–309.
7. Quoted in Starr, ibid., p.310.
8. Starr, ibid., p. 311–312.
9. Boudrye, *Historic*, p. 179.
10. Boudrye, ibid., p. 180; *O.R.*, Ser.1, Vol. XLIII, pt. 1, p. 523
11. Quoted in Starr, ibid., p. 317.
12. Boudrye, *Historic*, p. 181.
13. *O.R.*, ibid., p. 525.

14. Starr, ibid., p. 317.
15. *O.R.*, ibid., pp. 525–526.
16. Starr, ibid., p. 318.
17. Quote in Starr, ibid., p. 318, note 86; Catton, *Stillness*, p. 316.
18. Benjamin A. Crowninshield, *The Battle of Cedar Creek, October 19, 1864* (Cambridge, MA: privately issued, 1879), p. 28–29.
19. Boudrye, *Historic*, p. 181.
20. Boudrye, *War Journal*, pp. 179–180, 294–295, 306; www.History.Army.mil.
21. Boudrye, *Historic*, p. 204.
22. Boudrye, *War Journal*, p. 184; Bush, *Articles from Wyoming County*, pp. 120, 159; Starr, *Union Cavalry*, vol. 2, p. 328; Tenney, *War Diary*, p. 134.
23. Allen Nevins, *The Ordeal of the Union*, vol. 4: *The Organized War to Victory, 1864–1865* (New York: McMillan, 1971), p. 135; 5th Regiment Cavalry, Newspaper Clippings.

Chapter 12

1. Bush, *Articles from Wyoming County*, pp. 166–167.
2. Boudrye, *War Journal*, pp. 185–187.
3. Boudrye, ibid., p. 187.
4. Boudrye, *Historic*, p. 204; Starr, *Union Cavalry*, vol. 2, pp. 329–340.
5. Boudrye, ibid., pp. 191–192, 194, 198–199.
6. Chauncy Norton, *The Red Neck Ties*, p. 65; Boudrye, *Historic*, pp. 190, 205; Boudrye, *War Journal*, p. 205.
7. Boudrye, *Historic*, pp. 191, 191–192; Pickerill, *History of the Third Indiana*, pp. 171–172; Starr, *Union Cavalry*, vol. 2, pp. 372–373.
8. Boudrye, *Historic*, p. 192.
9. Starr, *Union Cavalry*, vol. 2, pp. 374–375; Boudrye, *Historic*, pp. 215, 218; *O.R.*, Ser. 1, Vol. XLVI, pt. 1, pp. 528–529.
10. Boudrye, *Historic*, p. 193.
11. Boudrye, ibid., p. 194.
12. Boudrye, ibid., pp. 193–194.
13. Boudrye, *War Journal*, p. 216.
14. Boudrye, ibid., pp. 220–221; Starr, *Union Cavalry*, Vol. 2, pp. 496–497.
15. Boudrye, ibid., p. 222.
16. Boudrye, ibid., p. 224.
17. Boudrye, *Historic*, p. 196.
18. Boudrye, *War Journal*, p. 229.
19. Boudrye, ibid., p. 222.
20. Boudrye, ibid., p. 228.
21. Boudrye, ibid., pp. 231–232.
22. Boudrye, ibid., p. 232.
23. Boudrye, *Historic*, pp. 197–198.
24. Boudrye, ibid., pp. 195–199.

Epilogue

1. *In Memoriam: John Hammond*, p. 76; Boudrye, *War Journal*, p. 232.
2. *New York Times*, July 21, 1865.
3. Boudrye, *Historic*, pp. 200–201.
4. Prisoner of War Record, National Archives, Washington, D.C.
5. Prisoner of War Records. Corporal Lamb began receiving a veteran's pension as an invalid in July 1881, according to the General Pension Index in the National Archives. The amount is not recorded.
6. Boudrye, *Historic*, p. 206; Bush, *Articles from Wyoming County*, p. 168; Boudrye, *Historic*, p. 272–275; Phisterer, *New York in the War of Rebellion*, vol. 2, p. 882ff.
7. Eliza Frances Andrews, *The War-Journal of a Georgia Girl, 1864–1865* (New York: D. Appleton, 1908), pp. 64, 79.
8. Robert Manson Myers, *The Children of Pride: A True Story of Georgia and the Civil War*, Abridged Edition (New Haven: Yale University Press, 1984), pp. 490–491. Dr. Jones's report to the Confederate Surgeon General is in *O.R.*, Series 2, Vol. VII, pp. 1012–1013.
9. www.bufordsboys.com/5thNYMon.hmt; Phisterer, *New York in the War of the Rebellion*, vol. 2, p. 822ff; Boudrye, *Historic*, pp. 272–275.
10. *In Memoriam: John* Hammond, p. 54; Boudrye, *Historic*, 205.
11. Boudrye, *Historic*, p. 34; *Annual Report of the Adjutant-General for the Year 1894* (Albany: J.B. Lyon, 1895), vol. 2, p. 3, 14, www.dmna.state.ny.us/ historic.
12. *Annual Report*, ibid., p. 6, 26, 32, 38, 112, 196, 226.
13. *In Memoriam: John Hammond*, p. 89.
14. U.S. Congress, Biographical Dictionary, www.bioguide.congress.gov, *New York Times*, December 5, 1886; *New York Times*, July 1, 1888; *In Memoriam: John Hammond*, pp. 9–13.
15. Boudrye, *War Journal*, p. 235.
16. Boudrye, ibid., pp. 235–236.

Bibliography

Agassiz, George R. *Meade's Headquarters, 1863–1865: Letters of Colonel Theodore Lyman.* Boston: Massachusetts Historical Society, 1922.

Andrews, Eliza Frances. *The War-Time Journal of a Georgia Girl, 1864–1865.* New York: D Appleton, 1908.

Annual Report of the Adjutant-General for the Year 1894. Vol. 2. Albany: J.B. Lyon, State Printer, 1895.

Basler, Roy P., ed. *The Collected Works of Abraham Lincoln.* 9 vols. New Brunswick, NJ: Rutgers University Press, 1953–1955.

Beaudrye, Richard E., ed. *War Journal of Louis N. Beaudrye, Fifth New York Cavalry: The Diary of a Union Chaplain, Commencing February 16, 1863.* Jefferson, NC: McFarland, 1996.

Benedict, George G. *Vermont in the Civil War, 1861–1865,* 2 vols. Burlington: Free Press Association, 1888.

Bigelow, John A. "Flashing Sabers." *National Tribune,* November 10, 1887.

Billington, Ray Allen. *The Far Western Frontier, 1830–1860.* New York: Harper and Row, 1956.

Boatner, Mark M. *The Civil War Dictionary.* New York: David McKay, 1959.

Boudrye, Louis N. *Historic Records of the 5th New York Cavalry in the Civil War.* Albany: J. Munsell, 1868.

Bush, B. Conrad, comp. *Articles from Wyoming County Newspapers and Letters from Soldiers of the 5th New York Cavalry.* West Falls, NY: Bush Research, 2000.

Capehart, Henry. "Fighting His Way." *National Tribune,* January 3, 1895.

Carter, Samuel. *The Last Cavaliers: Confederate and Union Cavalry in the Civil War.* New York: St. Martin's Press, 1979.

Catton, Bruce. *The Army of the Potomac.* Vol. 3: *A Stillness at Appomattox.* New York: Doubleday, 1962.

Clark, Stephen A. "Farnsworth's Death," *The National Tribune,* December 3, 1891.

———. "Hanover, Pa." *National Tribune,* February 23, 1888.

Crowninshield, Benjamin A. *The Battle of Cedar Creek, October 19, 1864.* Cambridge, MA: privately issued, 1879.

Dana, Charles A. *Recollections of the Civil War.* New York: D. Appleton, 1899.

Davis, William C. *Death in the Trenches: Grant at Petersburg.* New York: Time-Life, 1986.

Forbes, George S. *Leaves from a Trooper's Diary.* Philadelphia: privately issued, 1869.

Freeman, Douglas S. *Lee's Lieutenants: A Study in Command.* Edited by Stephen W. Sears. Old Saybrook, CT: Konecky and Konecky, 1998.

Freemantle, Arthur J.L. *The Freemantle Diary.* Walter Lord, ed. Boston: Little, Brown, 1954.

Gause, Isaac. *Four Years with Five Armies.* New York: Neale, 1908.

Glazier, Willard. *Battles for the Union.* Hartford: Dustin, Gilman & Co., 1875.

———. *Three Years in the Federal Cavalry.* New York: R.H. Ferguson, 1874.

Grant, Ulysses S. *Memoirs and Selected Letters.* Reprint. New York: Literary Classics of the United States, 1990.

Hall, Hillman A. *History of the Sixth New York Cavalry (Second Ira Harris Guard).* Worcester, MA: Blanchard, 1908.

Humphreys, Andrew A. *The Virginia Campaign of '64 and '65.* New York: Charles Scribner, 1903.

Imboden, John D. "The Confederate Retreat

from Gettysburg." In *Battles and Leaders of the Civil War*, vol. 3. Comp. Robert Underwood and Clarence Clough Buell. New York: Century, 1887–1888.

In Memoriam: John Hammond. Chicago: P.F. Pettibone, 1890.

Jacobs, M. *Notes on the Rebel Invasion of Maryland and Pennsylvania....* Philadelphia: J.B. Lippincott, 1864.

Kidd, James H. *Personal Recollections of a Cavalryman with Custer's Michigan Cavalry Brigade in the Civil War*. Ionia, MI: Sentinel, 1908.

Law, Evander M. "The Struggle for Round Top." In *Battles and Leaders of the Civil War*, vol. 3. Comp. Robert Underwood Johnson and Clarence Clough Buell. New York: Century, 1887–1888.

Lee, Robert E. *Recollections and Letters*. New York: Barnes & Noble, 2004.

Lichtenberg, L.J. "The Wilderness: How the 5th N.Y. Cav. Had a Hand in Opening the Fight." *National Tribune*, September 30, 1886.

Longacre, Edward G. *The Cavalry at Gettysburg: A Tactical Study of Mounted Operations during the Civil War's Pivotal Campaign, 9 June–14 July, 1863*. Lincoln: University of Nebraska Press, 1986.

_____. *From Union Stars to Top Hat: A Biography of the Extraordinary Career of General James Harrison Wilson*. Harrisburg, PA: Stackpole, 1972.

_____. *Lincoln's Cavalrymen: A History of the Mounted Forces of the Army of the Potomac, 1861–1865*. Harrisburg, PA: Stackpole, 2000.

Longstreet, James. *From Manassas to Appomattox: Memoirs of the Civil War in America*. Bloomington: Indiana University Press, 1960.

Lord, Walter, ed. *The Fremantle Diary*. Boston: Little, Brown, 1954.

McPherson, James M. *The Battle Cry of Freedom: The Civil War Era*. New York: Oxford University Press, 1988.

_____. *This Mighty Scourge: Perspectives on the Civil War*. New York: Oxford University Press, 2007.

Merington, Marguerite, ed. *The Custer Story: The Life and Intimate Letters of George A. Custer and His Wife Elizabeth*. New York: Devin-Adair, 1950.

Moore, James. *Kilpatrick and Our Cavalry*. New York: W.J. Middleton, 1865.

Morrison, Samuel E. et al. *The Growth of the American Republic*. New York: Oxford University Press, 1969.

Mosby, John S. "A Bit of Partisan Service." In *Battles and Leaders of the Civil War*, vol. 3. Comp. Robert Underwood Johnson and Clarence Clough Buell. New York: Century, 1887–1888.

_____. *The Memoirs of Colonel John Singleton Mosby*. Bloomington: Indiana University Press, 1959.

Myers, Robert Manson. *The Children of Pride: A True Story of Georgia and the Civil War*. Abridged Edition. New Haven, CT: Yale University Press, 1984.

Nevins, Allen. *The Ordeal of the Union*, Vol. 4: *The Organized War to Victory, 1964–1865*. New York: McMillan, 1971.

New York Monuments Commission for the Battlefields of Gettysburg and Chattanooga. *Final Report on the Battlefield of Gettysburg (New York at Gettysburg)*. Albany: J.B. Lyon, 1902.

Norton, Chauncey. *"The Red Neck Ties" or History of the Fifteenth New York Volunteer Cavalry*. Ithaca, NY: Journal Book and Job Printing House, 1891.

Norton, Henry. *Deeds of Daring, or, History of the Eighth N.Y. Volunteer Cavalry*. Norwich, NY: Chenango Telegraph Printing House, 1889.

Parsons, C.H. "Farnsworth's Charge and Death." *Battles and Leaders of the Civil War*, vol. 3. Comp. Robert Underwood Johnson and Clarence Clough Buell. New York: Century, 1887–1888.

_____. "Gettysburg: The Campaign was a Chapter of Accidents." *National Tribune*, August 7, 1890.

Penfield, James. *The 1863–1864 Civil War Diary of Captain James Penfield*. Penfield Foundation, 1999.

Phisterer, Frederick. *New York in the War of the Rebellion*. 6 Vols. 3rd ed. Albany: J.B. Lyon, 1912.

Pickerill, William N. *History of the Third Indiana*. Indianapolis, privately issued, 1906.

Pleasonton, Alfred. "The Campaign of Gettysburg." In *The Annals of War: Written by the Leading Participants, North and South, Originally Published in the Philadelphia Weekly Times*. Philadelphia: Weekly Times Publishing Co., 1879.

Publication Committee of the Regimental Association. *History of the Eighteenth Regiment of Cavalry, Pennsylvania Volunteers*,

1862–1865. New York: Wynkoop, Hallenbeck, Crawford, Co., 1909.

Rhea, Gordon C. "Union Cavalry in the Wilderness: The Education of Phillip H. Sheridan and James H. Wilson." In *The Wilderness Campaign.* Edited by Gary W. Gallagher. Chapel Hill: University of North Carolina Press, 1997.

Rhodes, Charles D. *History of the Cavalry of the Army of the Potomac,* Kansas City: Hudson-Kimberley, 1900.

Robbins, D.H. "Who Opened the Fight in the Wilderness." *National Tribune,* May 13, 1909.

Schaff, Morris. *The Battle of the Wilderness.* Boston: Houghton, Mifflin, 1910.

Sears, Stephen W. *Gettysburg.* Boston: Houghton, Mifflin, 2003.

Sheridan, Phillip H. *Personal Memoirs of P.H. Sheridan.* New York: Barnes & Noble, 2006.

Starr, Stephen Z. *The Union Cavalry in the Civil War: From Fort Sumter to Gettysburg, 1861–1863.* Baton Rouge: Louisiana State University Press, 1979.

———. *The Union Cavalry in the Civil War,* Vol. 2: *The War in the East from Gettysburg to Appomattox, 1863–1865.* Baton Rouge: Louisiana State University Press, 1981.

Swinton, William. *Campaigns of the Army of the Potomac, 1861–1865.* New York: Charles B. Richardson, 1866.

Tenney, Luman Harris. *War Diary, 1861–1865.* Oberlin, OH: privately issued, 1914.

Trudeau, Noah Andre. *Gettysburg: A Testing of Courage.* New York: Harper-Collins, 2002.

———. *The Last Citadel: Petersburg, Virginia, June 1864–April 1865.* Boston: Little, Brown, 1991.

U.S. Congress. *Biographical Directory of the American Congress, 1774–1949.* Washington: Government Printing Office, 1950.

———. *Report of the Joint Committee on the Conduct of the War.* Washington: Government Printing Office, 1865.

U.S. War Department. *War of Rebellion ... Official Records of the Union and Confederate Armies.* 128 vols. Washington: Government Printing Office, 1880–1901.

Wert, Jeffry D. *From Winchester to Cedar Creek: The Shenandoah Valley Campaign of 1864.* Carlisle, PA: South Mountain Press, 1987.

———. *Mosby's Rangers.* New York: Simon and Schuster, 1990.

Wiley, Bell I. *The Life of Billy Yank.* Indianapolis: Bobbs-Merrill, 1951.

Williamson, James J. *Mosby's Rangers.* New York: Ralph B. Kenyon, 1896.

Wilson, James Harrison. *Under the Old Flag.* 2 vols. New York: D. Appleton, 1912.

Wittenberg, Eric J. "The Battle of Tom's Brook, October 9, 1864." *North and South* 10, no. 1.

———. *Gettysburg's Forgotten Cavalry Actions: Farnsworth's Charge, South Cavalry Field, and the Battle of Fairfield, July 3, 1863.* New York: Savas Beatie, 2011.

Wittenberg, Eric J., and Karla Jean Husby, eds. *Under Custer's Command: The Journal of James H. Avery.* Dulles, VA: Brassey's, 2000.

Wittenberg, Eric J., and J. David Petruzzi. *Plenty of Blame to Go Around: Jeb Stuart's Controversial Ride to Gettysburg.* New York: Savas Beatie, 2006.

Wittenberg, Eric J., J. David Petruzzi, and Michael F. Nugent. *One Continuous Fight: The Retreat from Gettysburg and the Pursuit of Lee's Army of Northern Virginia, July 4–14, 1863.* New York: Savas Beatie, 2008.

Wright, Edmund. *The Desk Encyclopedia of World History.* New York: Oxford University Press, 2006.

Internet Sites

Biographical Directory of the United States Congress, 1774 to Present: bioguide.congress.gov

New York State Military Museum: www.dnma.state.ny.us/historic

U.S. Army Center of Military History: www.history.Army.mil

Vermont in the Civil War: www.vermontcivilwar.org

Buford's Boys: www.bufordsboys.com

Newspapers and Periodicals

National Tribune
New York Times
North and South

Index

Abbottstown, PA 74, 76, 84
Albany, NY 14, 23
Aldie, VA 49, 52, 53, 63, 64, 144
Alexander, Bradley 126
Alexandria, VA 136, 166
Allegany County, NY 14, 125, 126
Ames, Sergeant J.F. "Big Yankee" 49–52, 226
Andersonville Prison Camp 1, 16, 163, 177, 217, 264, 265, 266, 267
Annapolis, MD 17, 19, 20, 148, 264
Antietam Campaign 42, 43, 45, 65, 168, 224
Appleby, Henry 34
Appomattox 67, 177, 236, 257, 269
Arlington House 41
Armstrong, Doctor 189, 231, 260
Army of Northern Virginia 1, 41, 44, 45, 59, 65, 66, 72, 82, 86, 108, 125, 174
Army of the James 195
Army of the Potomac 19, 27, 36, 39, 40, 45, 47, 54, 59, 60, 62, 65, 66, 67, 72, 89, 91, 101, 104, 108, 118, 119, 125, 131, 146, 155, 156, 164, 169, 171, 176, 179, 184, 185, 186, 188, 189, 190, 191, 193, 195, 206, 209, 210, 211, 213, 217, 250
Ashby's Cavalry 31, 39
Ashby's Gap 128, 223
Ashland, VA 189
Ashland Station, VA 189
Atlanta, GA 168, 249
Avery, James 110, 112

Bacon, Lt. Col. William P. 93, 226, 227, 228
Baltimore and Ohio Railroad 29
Baltimore Pike 89
Banks, Major General Nathaniel 29–36, 41, 132, 133, 134
Barber, Edmund 165
Barber, William 268
Barker, Capt. Augustus 137
Barker, Capt. Elmer 47, 49, 50, 55, 56, 134, 137, 238, 249, 260
Bartly, Lt. Ruben 161
Battle Mountain 128
Bealeton Station 50, 141

Beatty, General John 4, 102
Beaumont, Pvt. John 30
Beaver Creek 120
Belle Island, Richmond 148
Benedict, Lt. Jonas 19
Berlin, PA, (East Berlin) 80, 82, 83, 84, 85
Berryville, VA 219, 222, 223, 224, 227, 231, 257
Berryville Canyon 219, 222, 223, 224, 227, 230, 231, 257
Berryville Pike 230, 231
Bigelow, John A., Fifth Michigan Cavalry 111
Blackwater River 207
Blenker, General 131
Bliss, Col. W.S. 14
Blue Ridge Mountains 29, 61, 219
Bogardus, Jeremiah 269
Boice, Lt. Theodore 114, 228, 244, 254, 256; "special duty" 225–226
Boonsboro, MD 114, 117, 119, 120, 121, 122, 130, 131
Boudrye, Charles 26, 46
Boudrye, Chaplin Louis N. 4, 5, 31, 36–40, 42, 46, 53, 60, 64–65, 70, 119, 121, 182, 136, 137, 140–142, 144–148, 150, 152–155, 157–159, 164–167, 171, 175–177, 181, 184, 186–188, 190, 193, 196, 198–200, 204, 280, 212, 215, 217–218, 221–224, 227–229, 231, 233–235, 237–243, 245–246, 248, 250, 252–255, 257–260, 263–265, 271; background 25; becomes chaplain 2, 25–26; and De Forest 130–135; on Hammond 61; at Hanover 73–74, 76–77, 81, 84, on July 3, 1863 90, 106; on July 4, 1863 109–110, 112; on Mosby 47, 49, 50, 51, 52, 54, 55; on Rev. Bowman 259–260; seeks transfer 221–222; and temperance 53, 150, 175
Bowman, Rev. Mr. 259–260
Bowman's Ford 244
Boylston, Edgar 269
Bragg, General Braxton 136
Brandy Station 62, 63, 140, 153, 272
Bridgewater, VA 235
Broad Run 142, 143

289

290 Index

Brookin's Ford 138
Brown, John 224
Brown, John, Co. B. 269
Brown's Store 139
Bryan, Col. Timothy H. 173, 175, 182
Bryan, Lt. 118, 124
Buckland Mills, VA 64, 141, 142, 143
Buckland Races 142, 144
Buckley, Pvt. John 92
Buford, Brigadier General John 7, 38, 67, 96, 115–123, 126, 128, 138; at Gettysburg 85–86
Bull Run 10, 11, 14, 19, 27, 34, 41, 42, 43, 61, 63, 64, 130, 141
Bull Run, Second Battle of 67
Bunker Hill 78, 81
Burke, Pvt. Thomas 77, 78
Burkeville (Jct.), VA 199, 200
The Burning 237–238
Burnside, Major General Ambrose 45
Bushman Hill 94
Butler, General Benjamin 158, 161, 162, 163, 166
Buttstown 73, 75, 77, 78

Cameron, Secretary of War Simon 9, 10
Camp Hammond 260
Camp Harris 20, 22, 26, 29
Camp Scott 14, 15, 17, 18, 19, 20, 30, 268
Capehart, Major Charles E. 101
Capehart, Surgeon Henry 105, 111
Carlisle, PA 82
Cary, Captain William B. 179
Cashtown, PA 83
Catharpin Road 179, 182
Catton, Bruce 160, 169, 177
Cavalry Bureau 172
Cavalry Regiments: Eighth Illinois 51; Eighth New York 62, 197, 200, 205, 228, 236; Eighteenth Pennsylvania 46, 49, 50, 72, 73, 74, 75, 76, 77, 85, 91, 93, 95, 99, 105, 111, 227, 230, 240; in Farnsworth's charge 94–100; Fifteenth New York 22, 254; Fifth Michigan 111, 159; First Connecticut 135, 168, 171, 206, 243, 252; First Maine 159; First Massachusetts 187; First Michigan 37, 136; First New Hampshire 256; First New York 266; First Vermont 6, 30, 51, 55, 57, 69, 72, 74, 76, 77, 78, 79, 80, 89, 109, 110, 115, 116, 117, 123, 126, 136, 159, 175, 182, 183, 189, 190, 201, 204, 214, 240, 247, 248; First West Virginia 46, 53, 72, 74, 76, 77, 78, 79, 80, 94, 97, 99, 101, 112, 116, 122, 130, 140; Second New York 24, 38, 139, 140, 143, 159, 162, 206, 230; Second North Carolina 77, 78, 81; Second Ohio 168, 185, 190, 196, 202, 203, 204, 205, 206, 207, 229, 240, 251, 252; Sixth Michigan 62, 71, 165, 166; Sixth New York 19, 20; Third Indiana 184, 198, 200, 241, 255; Third New Jersey 229, 240; Thirteenth Virginia 78; Twelfth Pennsylvania 260; Twenty-fifth New York 185; Twenty-second New York 175, 185

Cedar Creek 223, 228, 241, 252, 258; Battle of 228, 242–251
Cedar Mountain 40
Cemetery Hill 87
Cemetery Ridge 87, 89, 90, 105
Centerville, VA 50, 51, 64, 139, 141
Chambersburg, PA 70, 83, 85, 86, 108
Chambliss, Col. Robert 77, 82
Chancellorsville, VA 59, 60, 65, 66, 67, 104, 182, 185, 186; Battle of 65
Chantilly, VA 44, 46, 50, 52
Chapman, Farquin 23, 148
Chapman, Col. George 175, 182, 196, 199, 201, 204
Charlestown, VA 224
Chattanooga, TN 136, 139, 172
Chester Gap 128
Chickahominy River 161, 166, 192
Chillson, Sergeant 209
City Point, VA 197, 208, 221
Clark, Fred J. 126
Clark, Stephen 79
Claus, John H. 41
Clough, Sergeant 39
Cold Harbor, VA 190, 191
Colt .44, Model 1860 21, 29, 55
Columbia County, NY 14
Columbia Furnace 240
Columbia Mills, VA 160
Comer, Pvt. William 24
Conroy, Francis 16, 17, 23
Cook, Major 162
Copperheads 63, 156
Cornwall, NY 16, 264, 265
Cotoctan Mountains 70
Coyle, Captain Thomas 24
Craig's Meeting House 179, 182, 183
Crampton's Gap 64
Crater, Battle of 217
Crawford, General Samuel 38, 39
Criddle, William 259
Crowley, Pvt. John 175–176
Crown Point, NY 14, 18, 56, 58, 61, 129, 227, 268, 270–271
Crown Point Iron Works 270
Crum, Pvt. Henry 187
Culpeper Court House, VA 37, 136, 137, 138, 140
Curtis, Lt. Levi 27
Custer, Brigadier General George A. 65, 69, 71, 87, 88, 89, 91, 108, 110, 123, 124, 130, 131, 138, 140, 141, 142, 152, 156, 159, 174, 175, 213–214, 234, 235, 236, 239, 240, 241, 253, 254, 255, 257; at Cedar Creek 246–249; at Hanover 74, 75, 81

Dahlgren, Ulrich 116, 152, 165, 166, 214, 272; raid on Richmond 155–164
Dana, Charles A. 212, 214, 216, 235
Davenport, Corporal Keyes 205
Davies, Colonel Henry E. 134, 138, 139, 140, 141, 142, 143, 144, 145, 156, 167, 174, 175

Index

Davis, Colonel 115
Davis, Jefferson 60, 66, 163, 261
Davis, William 187
Dayton, VA 237
De Forest, Benjamin 132
De Forest, Colonel Othneil 10, 14, 15, 18, 32, 39, 45, 54, 62, 69, 122, 130; relieved and charged 130–134; and wagon train 34–35, 135
desertion 268–270
Devil's Den 97, 98
Dinwiddie Court House, VA 198, 199
Double Bridges 202, 215
Dover, PA 82, 87
Dover Mills, VA 160
Drainsville, VA 63, 222
Drake, Corporal Orlando 56
Dry Tortugas 176
D'Uasey, Colonel 131
Dye, Second Lt. Elem S. 126
Dye, Captain William P. 125, 126

Eagle, NY 57
Earl, Hiram H. 44
Early, General Jubal 220, 223, 229, 242, 245, 249, 255
Edinburg, VA 241, 253, 254
Edwards Ferry 64
Ehman, Fred J. 126
Elder's Battery 78, 79, 80, 81, 83, 88, 91, 92, 93, 94, 95, 96, 97, 98, 100, 114, 116, 117, 118, 120, 135, 138, 139, 140, 268
Eleventh Corps 120
Ellis' Ford 155
Ely's Ford 155, 159, 185
Emmitsburg, PA 71, 89, 94, 95, 108, 109
Emmitsburg Road 91, 94, 95, 98, 102, 103
Essex County, NY 14, 129, 227
Essex County Republican 227
Ewell, General Richard 70, 72, 73, 82, 83, 87, 108, 110, 111, 113

Fairfax, VA 26, 44, 47, 49, 50, 53, 54, 62, 63, 64, 134, 141, 154
Fairfax Station 46
Fairfield, PA 103, 108
Fairfield Pass 108
Falmouth, VA 46, 49, 59
Farnsworth, Brigadier General Elon 65, 69, 70, 71, 92, 93, 94, 95, 96, 102, 103, 104, 105, 106, 107, 112, 122, 130, 131, 133, 143, 272; background 70; charge July 3, 1863 96–97, 98, 99, 100, 102; at Hanover 72, 74, 76, 77, 78
Fifth Corps 66, 103, 178, 179, 180, 181
Fifth New York Veteran Volunteer Cavalry Association 271
First Cavalry Division 67, 69, 85, 91, 213
Fish, Colonel William 135
Fisher's Hill 232, 233, 234, 239, 242, 248
Fishersville, VA 235
Fishkill, NY 228

Folger, Pvt. Abram 77
Foote, Shelby 273
Ford's Station 198, 199
Forrest, General Nathan Bedford 237
Fort McHenry 225
Fort Milroy 223
Fourth Delaware Volunteers 154
Fowler, Halstead Hickson 23
Frank Leslie's Illustrated Newspaper 151
Frazer, Quarter Master Sergeant Archibald 39
Frederick Hall Station 159
Frederick, MD 64, 69, 70, 111, 130, 220
Fredericksburg, VA 45, 59, 60, 104
Freeman, Harris 137
Fremantle, Lt. Col. Arthur 91
Frenyer, Thomas 269
Front Royal, VA 32, 33, 34, 233
Funkstown, MD 122

Gaines' Cross-Roads 129
Gainesville, VA 64, 142, 143
Gause, Isaac 190, 202, 229
Gear, Lieutenant 39
Geisboro Point 217, 221, 222
Germanna Ford 184, 185
Germanna Plank Road 185
Germantown, VA 16, 26, 44, 46
Gettysburg, PA 70, 71, 72, 80, 82, 83, 84, 85, 87, 88, 89, 90, 91, 92, 93, 94, 96, 97, 101, 102, 104, 106, 107, 108, 109, 110, 123, 125, 126, 128, 129, 130, 138, 141, 158, 166, 168, 219, 226, 270, 272; Battle of 85–86, 87, 91, 94; Campaign 1, 2, 51, 62, 64, 65, 78, 119, 124
Gilpin, Samuel 184, 198, 200
Glazier, Willard 139
Gloucester Point 161
Goat Hill 114
Gooney Run 233
Gordonsville, VA 36, 37, 38, 138, 253
Graham, Captain William 96, 100
Grant, General U. S. 1, 65, 167, 168, 169, 171, 172, 173, 174, 175, 177, 184, 185, 186, 188, 189, 190, 191, 193, 194, 209, 210, 211, 212, 213, 220, 221, 223, 224, 225, 230, 235, 248, 253, 256, 257, 266, 272
Graves, Mrs. 252
Graves, Pvt. Hiram 252, 257
Green County, NY 14
Greenleaf, Charles H. 22, 24, 33, 34, 193, 201, 224
Greenwich, VA 54, 56
Greenwood 83
Gregg, Brigadier General David 89, 91, 109, 183
Groveton, VA 41, 141, 142
Guiney Station 187

Hagerstown, MD 64, 110, 114, 115, 116, 118, 119, 120, 121, 122, 123, 124, 126, 129
Halleck, Major General Henry W. 66, 122
Halltown, VA 223

Index

Hammond, C. F. 14
Hammond, John 1, 3, 4, 5, 14, 15, 18, 19, 21, 23, 24, 29, 35, 38, 39, 43, 45, 46, 48, 51, 52, 54, 55, 56, 58, 59, 60, 61, 62, 63, 92, 93, 94, 95, 96, 97, 107, 112, 113, 114, 116, 117, 118, 120, 129, 132, 134, 135, 137, 138, 141, 143, 145, 153, 155, 157, 165, 167, 173, 175, 176, 184, 185, 186, 187, 189, 190, 192, 195, 208, 209, 216, 217, 221, 226, 228, 254, 263, 267, 268; after the war 270–271; Camp Hammond 260; early life 61; at Hanover 74, 76–83; leaves the Fifth New York 226–227; at Parker's Store 178–182
Hampton, General Wade 81, 82, 87, 88, 144, 166, 195, 199, 202, 203, 204, 205, 213, 216
Hancock, Major General Winfield Scott 103, 185, 257
Hannaford, Quarter Master Sergeant Roger 196, 197, 200, 201, 206, 207, 213, 215
Hanover, PA 70, 71, 83, 84, 85, 87, 90, 93, 105, 109, 115, 121, 126, 167, 179, 226, 269; Battle at 72–82
Hanover Court House, VA 189
Hardy, Sergeant John 163
Harpers Ferry, VA 29, 64, 66, 124, 125, 253, 261
Harper's Weekly Magazine 151
Harris, Captain 109
Harris, Senator Ira 14, 17, 263
Harrisburg, PA 66, 67, 70, 72, 113
Harrisonburg, PA 30, 31, 234, 237, 258
Hart, Lieutenant 163
Hart Island, NY 261, 263, 265, 272
Hartwood Church 84, 137
Hatch, General John P. 30, 31, 35, 36, 37, 38
Hay Market, VA 443
Heintzelman, General Samuel P. 41
Herr Ridge 86
Highgate, VT 25
Hill, Major General A. P. 124, 179
Historic Records of the 5th New York Cavalry 2, 5, 25, 26, 27
Hoffman, General 265
Hogan, Scout 159
Hood, General John B. 95, 102, 182, 245
Hood's Texans 92
Hooker, Mr. F.J. 66
Hooker, Major General Joseph 59, 60, 62, 63, 64, 65, 66, 67, 69, 124, 178, 185, 186, 187
Hopkins, Pvt. Merlin 219
Hoskins, Captain Bradford 56
Huey, Colonel Pennock 109, 110
Humphreys, General Andrew A. 195
Hungry Station, VA 161
Hunterstown, PA 85, 87, 88, 89, 115
Hurley, Daniel 92

Ira Harris Guard 11, 14, 133

Jackson, John W. 55, 57, 83, 88, 124, 128, 129, 135, 145, 149, 154, 164, 228, 250

Jackson, General Thomas "Stonewall" 40, 41, 187; Chancellorsville 59–60; Valley Campaign of 1862 29, 30, 31, 32, 34, 35, 36
Jackson, Mount 253, 256
Jacksonville, FL 264
James City, VA 37, 139
James River 40, 41, 158, 160, 186, 190, 191, 192, 193, 208
James River Canal 253
Jenkins, Pvt. George H. 55
Jenkins' Cavalry 113
Johndro, Elijah 164–165
Johnson, General Joseph E. 39
Johnstone, Lt. Col. Robert 42, 51, 60; returns to the Fifth New York 134–135
Joint Committee on the Conduct of the War 101, 103, 104
Jones, Dr. Joseph 266, 267

Kautz, Brigadier General August V. 195, 196, 197, 198, 199, 200, 201, 202, 204, 205, 206, 207, 210, 212, 217
Kearneysville, VA 223
Kelly's Ford 136, 144
Kenly, Colonel 32, 33
Kenwell, Pvt. Richard 131
Kernstown, VA 29, 250, 252, 253, 254
Kettle Run, VA 54, 62
Keyes, Orson S. 126
Keysville, VA 200, 201
Kidd, James H. 57, 165, 166
Kilpatrick, Brigadier General Hugh Judson 7, 65, 69, 70, 84, 85, 89, 91, 100, 105, 107, 107, 110, 111, 113, 114, 123, 121, 123, 126, 128, 129, 130, 135, 136, 138, 139, 140, 141, 142, 143, 145, 146, 147, 151, 152, 167, 171, 172, 173, 174, 175, 184, 206, 214, 272; Farnsworth's charge 91–99; at Hagerstown 115–117, 118, 119; at Hanover 71–83; at Hunterstown 87–88; Kill-Cavalry nickname 68; raid on Richmond 115–166; takes command of Third Cavalry Division 67–68
Kinderhook, NY 46, 148, 271
Kings and Queens Court House 162
Kossuth, Lajos 53
Krom, Abram H. 24, 45, 52, 53, 79, 228, 237, 249

Labounty, Louis 119
Lacey Spring, VA 256
Lamb, Corporal George 1, 2, 16, 217, 265
Lamb, Susan 265
Law, Brigadier General Evander M. 95, 99, 102, 104
Lawrence, Sergeant G. D. 251
Lebanon Church 241
Lee, Captain Provost Marshall 237
Lee, General Fitzhugh 51, 54, 82, 140, 142, 143, 147, 233
Lee, General Robert E. 1, 45, 51, 129, 136, 137, 138, 139, 140, 141, 142, 143, 144, 146, 147, 148,

Index

158, 159, 163, 166, 167, 190, 191, 193, 194, 195, 199, 202, 204, 208, 209, 212, 213, 218, 219, 220, 238, 257; Chancellorsville 59, 60; commanding Army of Northern Virginia 39–44; Gettysburg Campaign 57–58, 60–67, 69, 70, 71, 72, 74, 82, 83, 84, 85, 86, 87, 89, 90, 91, 92, 94, 101, 102, 103, 104; retreat from Gettysburg 107–108, 110, 115, 120, 121, 122, 123, 125, 126; in the Wilderness 174, 178, 185–186, 188
Lee, General Rooney 199
Leesburg, VA 63, 64, 222
Letcher, Governor 259
Libby Prison, Richmond, VA 2, 84, 113, 126, 129, 137, 144, 148, 158, 160, 167, 259
Liberty Mills, VA 138
Lincoln, President Abraham 9, 11, 13, 27, 29, 36, 45, 50, 52, 66, 125, 129, 157, 158, 169, 176, 250, 251, 258, 259
Lincoln's Amnesty Proclamation 158, 166
Little Bighorn 236
Little Round Top 89, 103, 109
Littlestown, PA 70, 71, 73, 74, 80, 82, 106
Logan Mountain 257
Longstreet, General James 103, 136
Longstreet's Corps 92
Loudon County, VA 124, 125
Lucas, Captain 115, 118, 119, 124, 129
Luray Valley 32, 34, 37, 232, 233, 234
Lyman, Theodore 168

Madison Court House, VA 138, 139
Major, Benjamin, 269
Manassas, VA 10, 40, 141
Manassas Gap Railroad 51, 233
Manassas Junction 63, 143
Marcy, Major 244
Marshall, William 34
Martinsburg. VA 33, 34, 35, 36
Massanutten Mountain 32, 232, 233, 234
Massaponax Court House, VA 186
McClellan, Major General George B. 27, 28, 29, 32, 36, 39, 40, 41, 42, 45, 250, 251
McIntosh, Colonel John 167, 175, 181, 182, 196, 200, 201, 203, 204, 206, 209, 229, 230, 231
McNair, Captain 20
McPherson, James M. 13, 60
McPherson's Ridge 86
Meade, Major General George 108, 119, 122, 123, 124, 125, 126, 129, 130, 136, 138, 139, 141, 142, 144, 146, 148, 157, 163, 164, 165, 166; allows Pleasonton's command changes 69; Gettysburg Campaign 70, 80, 82, 83, 85, 91, 100, 103, 104, 105, Overland Campaign 171, 181, 182, 183, 184, 186, 187, 195, 207, 209, 210; takes command of the Army of the Potomac 66–67
Meadow Bridge 166
Mechanicstown, VA 113
Medal of Honor 4, 40, 147, 229, 249
Meems, David 160

Meherrin, Va 201
Meherrin Station 200
Meigs, Lieutenant 237
Meigs, Major General 237
Merriman, Lieutenant 118, 124, 126
Merritt, Lieutenant Henry A.D. 159, 160, 161, 162, 163, 260
Merritt, Brigadier General Wesley 69, 89, 94, 96, 98, 99, 100, 102, 103, 174, 175, 232, 233, 234, 239, 241, 246, 247, 248, 249, 260
Middleburg, MD 64
Middleburg, VA 52, 53, 61, 62, 63
Middletown, VA 245, 246, 250
Milford, VA 234
Milford Creek 233, 234
Milford Station 187
Mills, William 31
Millwood, VA 223
Mine Run 146, 147, 149, 178
Monocacy Creek 220
Monroe, Henry W. 126
Monterey Pass 108–112
Moore, Henry 85
Moore, John 269
Moras, Dick 54
Morse, John 21, 265–266
Morton, Captain George 143
Mosby, Captain John 47, 51, 52, 53, 54, 55, 56, 62, 222, 224, 225, 226, 269; raid of March 9, 1863 47–49, 50, 51
Mount Holly Church 137
Mount Jackson, VA 256
Mount Sidney, VA 256
Mountain Road 238
Mudtown 73

New Baltimore, VA 64
New Bethel Church 187
New Hope Church 178
New Market, VA 27, 31, 232, 233, 234, 248, 256, 258
New York Adjutant General's Report 268
New York in the War of Rebellion 134
New York State Military Museum 131, 135
New York Times 31, 112, 114, 132, 133, 135, 152, 156, 169, 263
Newburgh, NY 16
North Anna River 188
North Fork of the Shenandoah River 244, 256
Norton, Henry 205, 228, 236
Nottoway Court House, VA 199, 200
Nottoway River 202, 215
Nouse, Sergeant 129
Ny River 187

Olcott, Colonel 131
Olmstead, Frank 126
Opequon Creek 224, 229, 230, 231
Orange and Alexandria Railroad 136
Orange County, NY 14, 16, 265
Orange Court House, VA 36, 38, 39, 178

294　　　　　　　　　　Index

Orange Plank Road 178, 179, 181
Orange Turnpike 178, 181
Osawatomie, Old 224
Overland Campaign 169, 191, 196, 226, 249, 254, 269, 272

Packard, Pvt. Loren F. 147
Parker's Store 178, 179, 181, 182
Parson, Henry C. 57, 95, 96, 97, 98, 100, 101
Patrick, General 187
Paul Edward A. 112
Payne, Lt. Col. William 77, 78, 81, 82
Pemberton, General 65
Penfield, James 19*, 45, 52, 58, 59, 117, 118, 119, 124, 129
Pennington, Col. A.C.M. 249
Pennington's Battery 78, 79, 81, 88, 110, 117
Petersburg, VA 1, 190, 191, 192, 193, 195, 198, 211, 212, 218, 220, 221, 223, 249, 256, 257
Petersburg and Lynchburg Railroad 208
Petticoat Gap 223
Phisterer, Frederick 134
Pickett, General George 90, 91, 94, 95, 96, 100, 101, 102, 103, 105, 123
Pierce, Charles T. S. 14
Pink Monument 270
Plainfield, NJ 14
Pleasonton, General Alfred 57, 62, 63, 64, 65, 67, 69, 70, 80, 81, 82, 83, 108, 130, 157, 171; on July 3, 1863 83, 89, 94, 100, 101, 102, 103, 104
Plum Run 97
Po River 187
Pope, Major Edmund 200, 205
Pope, General John 38, 40, 41, 42
Port Conway, VA 135
Port Republic, VA 30, 32
Portier, Emile 85, 167
Potter, Lt. Henry C. 74, 75
Powell's Creek 217
Preston, Lt. Col. Addison 79, 96, 98, 110, 189, 190
Prince George Court House 195, 203
Purcellville, VA 1

Quinn, Pvt. 39

Raccoon Ford 39
Rapidan Ford 36, 37
Rapidan River 137, 144, 149, 164, 169
Rappahannock River 44, 45, 47, 54, 59, 60, 61, 62, 65, 128, 135, 136, 137, 139, 141, 144, 149, 155
Rawlins, General John 175
Reams Station 198, 204, 205, 206, 208, 210, 211, 212, 213, 214, 229, 241
Rensselaer Polytechnic Institute 61
Reserve Brigade 89, 91, 94
Reynolds, Major General John 64, 67, 86
Richmond, Colonel Nathaniel 112, 115, 116, 117, 118, 122, 130

Roanoke Bridge 202
Roanoke Station 201
Robbins, Corporal D.H. 74, 180, 181
Robinson, Colonel 39
Rockville, MD 72
Roebling, Washington 180
Rosser, General Thomas 238, 239, 240, 241, 242, 244, 245, 246, 247, 256, 257, 258
Round Top Mountain 239
Row, Newton C. 236
Rowand, Charles L. 132
Royce, George 21
Rude's Hill 256, 257
Russell's Ford 139

St. Albans Academy 61
Salem Church, VA 190
Salisbury, NC 228
Sawyer, Adjutant F. M. 76, 84
Sayles, Captain James A. 200
Scofield, Sergeant David S. 249
Scott, General Winfield 9, 10, 21
Seddon, James 161, 163
Sedgwick, General John 184
Seminary Ridge 86, 90, 92, 100, 108
Seward, William H. 258
Shady Grove, VA 191
Sharps Carbine 21
Sheridan, General Philip 171, 172, 173, 174, 175, 182, 183, 188, 191, 195, 199, 202, 219, 220, 221, 222, 232, 224, 225, 226, 227, 229, 234, 235, 251, 253, 254, 255, 256, 257; Battle of Winchester 230, 231, 232; the burning 239, 241; Cedar Creek 242, 244, 246, 248; meeting with Meade 186; Tom's Brook 239, 241; on Wilson's Raid 209, 210, 211
Sherman, General William T. 168, 171, 175, 235, 249, 266
Shoney, Corporal James 252
Shriver, Herbert 73
Slyder, J. 97
Smith Charles Don 176
Smithburg, MD 93, 107
South Anna River 189
South Mountain 107, 108, 109, 113, 114, 120
Southside Railroad 1, 194, 198, 199
Spencer, Asabel A. 31
Spencer Carbine 21, 22, 88, 152, 172, 179, 180, 181, 190, 196, 204, 223, 230, 255
Spotsylvania Court House, VA 159, 186, 187
Spring Hill, VA 235
Stahl, General Julius 45, 54, 64, 69
Stahl's Cavalry Division 53, 63, 66, 67, 69
Stanton, Edwin 133, 157, 212, 214, 216, 242
Starr, Stephen Z. 6, 17, 42, 101, 104, 142, 166, 196, 167
Staunton, VA 38, 234, 235, 253, 255, 256, 258, 259, 260
Staunton River 201
Stevensburg, VA 136, 145, 148, 149, 152, 156, 166, 167

Index

Stevenson's Station 261
Stony Creek 205, 208
Stony Creek, VA 202, 203, 204, 208, 212, 213, 217, 264
Stony Creek Station 202, 203, 204, 205
Stoughton, Brigadier General Edward 47, 49, 50, 51
Strasburg, VA 30, 31, 32, 33, 34, 35, 133, 232, 241, 248, 269
Stuart, General J.E.B. 23, 54, 62, 63, 64, 67, 68, 73, 80, 81, 82, 83, 84, 85, 87, 88, 89, 90, 110, 113, 114, 115, 116, 118, 119, 120, 121, 122, 123; in the fall 1863 128, 129, 136, 137, 138, 142, 143, 152; at Hanover 72, 73, 75, 77, 78, 79; Overland Campaign 185, 188, 195, 269
Summit Point VA 223
Susquehanna River 66, 72

Taneytown, PA 80
Taylor, Chaplain O. 113
Thompson, Col. John L. 256, 257
Thoroughfare Gap 141, 143, 144
Timball's Crossroads 119
Tioga County, NY 14, 40, 228
Tolles, Edward 31, 129
Tolles, James 27
Tolles, Ralph 20, 24, 27, 31
Tom's Brook 239, 240, 241
Torbert, General A.T.A 226, 232, 233, 234, 235, 239, 246, 253
Trevilian Station, VA 191, 239
Tribe, Quarter Master Sergeant John 40
Trobridge, Sergeant John S. 126
Turner's Gap 64
Two Taverns 89, 94

The Union Cavalry in the Civil War 4
Union Mills, MD 73, 75, 77, 78, 81
University of Michigan 70
Upperville, VA 63, 83, 124

Valley Pike 29, 31, 34, 35, 219, 223, 232, 238, 2139, 241, 245, 246, 249, 256, 258, 260
Vandermark, John 187
Vermont Morgan Horses 15
Vidette (picket posts) 46, 47, 52, 185
Virginia Central Railroad 188, 253
Vought, Major Philip 32, 33

Wadesville, VA 223
Wales, Sergeant Seldon 23, 76
Warrenton, VA 40, 54, 55, 64, 81, 128, 135
Washburn, B.F. 188
Waterloo Bridge 40, 128
Watson, William 34
Waugh, Lieutenant 52, 153
Waynesboro, VA 235

Waynesboro, Battle of 255
Welch, Corporal John 249
Weldon Railroad 1, 194, 198, 201, 202
Wells, George 115
Wells, Gideon 157
Wells, Major William 95
West Point 13, 16, 27, 66, 68, 172, 213, 239
Western New Yorker Newspaper 30, 37, 42, 251
Westminster, MD 72, 75
Wheeler, Captain Washington 27, 30, 37, 41, 42
Whitaker, Captain 203
Whitcomb, William H. 31
White, Amos H. 34, 52, 137, 140, 153, 189, 228, 254, 256, 261, 263
White Oak Swamp 191
Whitehall and Plattsburg Railroad 270
Whittlesey, L. H. 266
Wilderness Tavern 178, 179, 181, 182, 185
Williamson, James 50, 51, 52
Williamson, Lieutenant 114
Williamsport, MD 33, 35, 108, 114, 115, 116, 117, 118, 119, 122, 123, 124, 126
Wilson, Brigadier General James H. 6, 167, 173, 174, 175, 190, 191, 192, 221, 228, 233, 235, 241, 265, 272; background 172; on Hammond 226-227; leaves Third Cavalry Division 235-236, 237; result of raid 209-213, 214, 215, 216; Scouts 225-226; takes command of Third Cavalry Division 171; in the wilderness 178-179, 182, 183, 184; at Winchester 230, 231, 232; Wilson's Raid 194-218
Winchester, VA 29, 30, 33, 34, 35, 36, 219, 222, 223, 224, 229, 242, 246, 252, 253, 256, 257, 258, 260, 261, 263, 269; Battle of 230, 231, 232
Wolf's Tavern 113
Wolftown 37, 40
Woodbury. Lieutenant 51
Woods, Dr. Lucius P. 136
Woodstock, VA 30, 253
Woodstock Races 241
Woodville, VA 37, 140
Wooster, Corporal Joseph 209
Wright, Daniel 23
Wyanoke Landing 191
Wyliesville, VA 202
Wyndham, Colonel Percy 50, 51
Wyoming County, NY 30, 31, 57, 115, 228
Wyoming County Mirror 57, 83, 128, 228

Yellow Tavern 188, 239, 272
York, PA 70, 72, 80, 82, 87
York River 28
Youngs Island Ford 64